SLAVERY AND THE SLAVE TRADE WERE AND ARE CRIMES AGAINST HUMANITY!

A MODEL FREEDOM OF INFORMATION GUIDE: WHO, WHERE, WHAT, WHEN & WHY

BOB BROWN
PAN-AFRICAN ROOTS

D1294764

AFRICAN DIASPORA PUBLISHING CORPORATION
COLUMBUS, OHIO

Pan-African Roots
1247 E Street SE
Washington, DC 20003
paroots02@yahoo.com

African Diaspora Publishing Corporation
P.O. Box 091036
Columbus, Ohio 43209-9998

Printed in the United States of America

Dedicated

To Alice Brown, my mother, her children, grand-children and great-grand children;
To Thokozille, Malaika and Zion, my daughters and grandson;
To Fannie Carter, my father's aunt;
To Earl Mosley, my mother's cousin, who recruited me to the Movement, 41 years ago; and
To Mabel Carmichael, Nagib Malik and the family of Kwame Ture!

To Barney Jones

for Mother Africa and Her
billion children who are scattered,
suffering and struggling in over 122
countries in the world.

Victory is inevitable!

Bob Brown
11/29/2004
B. More

PREFACE

The history of Africa, as presented by European scholars, has been encumbered with malicious myths. It was even denied that we were a historical people. It s said that whereas other continents had shaped history, and determined its course, Africa had stood still, held down by inertia; that Africa was only propelled into history by the European contact. African history was therefore presented as an extension of European history... [S]uch disparaging accounts had been given of African society and culture as to appear to justify slavery, and slavery, posed against these accounts, seemed a positive deliverance of our ancestors. When the slave trade and slavery became illegal, the experts on Africa yielded to the new wind of change, and now began to present African culture and society as being so rudimentary and primitive that colonialism was a duty of Christianity and civilization.

Osagefyo Kwame Nkrumah
Consciencism: Philosophy and the Ideology for De-colonization. Page 63.

In 2001, I was enabled and empowered by my family, co-workers and friends, especially the Pan-Africanist Congress of Azania (PAC), to participate in the Non-Governmental Forum of the 3rd United Nations World Conference Against Racism, Racial Discrimination, Xenophobia and Related Intolerance which was held in Durban, Azania (South Africa). I refused to attend the Governmental Session that followed, because PAC, despite the undeniable fact that it shed rivers of blood in the Azanian (South African) Liberation Movement, was not permitted to participate; and because I was and remain appalled at the blatant corruption of the "diplomatic" process and the filthy disregard for the truth. I decided to spend the week instead, with the PAC cadre, my adopted family, and African youth on the ground. I also decided, to research and publish this book, in order to directly, militantly and uncompromisingly confront at least two of these malicious myths:

- The malicious myth that man-stealing, woman-stealing, child-stealing and kidnapping, that piracy and privateering, that slavery and the slave trade, especially the Trans-Atlantic Slave Trade, were legal and acceptable, as practiced against African People; that they are crimes against humanity today and should have always been so; and that there is nothing that one billion African People scattered, suffering and struggling in over 122 countries in the world can do about it.

- The malicious myth that time and the elements have destroyed all records, all evidence, all proof of who committed or aided in the commission of these crimes against humanity; and of who was and continues to be unjustly enriched by this unprecedented theft of lives, labor, and land.

Three years and 10,000 hours of Internet research later, I pass this information on, in the hopes that African youth will seize it, correct its errors, improve it, educate and organize themselves world-wide, and help liberate African History, the African Continent, African People, and World Humanity.

Bob Brown
Durban, Pretoria, Johannesburg, Chicago, Harare, Washington, DC, Port of Spain and Baltimore
September 3, 2001 to October 25, 2004

ACKNOWLEDGEMENTS

No one comes into or leaves this world alone, and no one can negotiate its commanding heights or treacherous depths or alone. We owe whatever we are, and whatever we achieve to the People, especially those who blessed our lives with their presence and support, intellectual, moral, personal, organizational and financial. Kwame Ture (aka Stokely Carmichael) never tired of saying that the greatest crime that anyone could commit is the crime of being ungrateful.

Permit me to express my eternal gratitude to the following and countless other People, Movements and Organizations whom I have had the honor and privilege to work, study and struggle with over the past 41 years:

- Jerry Holloman, Dolores Mentor, Kinsel Peyton, Kemba Nzinga, and the African Diaspora Publishing Corporation, for their assistance and support in publishing this book.

- Kamau Benjamin for providing the cover art; Michelle Wright for the cover design; Sara Powell and Kwaku Leak for providing editorial assistance; BCP Digital Printing, our printer in Baltimore; Clarence McClain, our computer guru; Andy Thompson and Conrad Worrill, my sparing partners; Alice Hammond, the African expert on slavery, cotton, textiles and banks; Banbose Shango and Susan Ribero for keeping me focused.

- The members, staff and supporters of the Congress of Racial Equality, the Student Nonviolent Coordinating Committee, the Black Panther Party, the Movement To Take Nkrumah Back To Ghana, and the Democratic Party of Guinea.

- David Brothers, and the current and former organizers of the All-African People's Revolutionary Party.

- Dr. Motsoko Pheko, and the members of the Pan-Africanist Congress of Azania.

- Vernon Bellecourt, Bill Means, Andrea Carmen, Tony Gonzales, Chief Billy Tyac, and the members of the American Indian Movement, the International Indian Treaty Council and LISTEN.

- Dr. Laxmi Berwa, and the members of the Dalit Movement.

- Peter Urban, Dawn Gould, and the members of the Irish Republican Socialist Party.

- Yasser Arafat, and the members of Palestinian Liberation Organization.

- My extremely large and extended Movement Family, especially:

- A.J., Ramon Acevedo, Jamil al-Amin, Imani Alexander X, Hodari Ali, Kamano Ali, Jamila Allston, Ona Alston Dosunmu, Amafujo, Mesfin & Thando Aman, Thomas Amonoo, Raymond Archer, Prince Ntum ba Azah (Lester Lewis), Jan Bailey, Lyman Baker, Thomas Baker, Jabriel Ballatine, Babatunji Balogun, Morenga Bambatta, Folashade Bandele, Stuart & Eva Barbee, Marion Barry, Senghor Jawara Baye El, Asha Bediako, Kamou Benjamin, Lydia Bennett, Chip Berlet, Brother Bey, Djabi Billo, Justice Blackquest, Ed Boston, Starr Bowie, Folasade Brawner, Gary Brown, Bobbi & Wesley Brown, David & Sissy Brown, Richard Brown, Roy Brown, Martin Burrows, Mike Burson, Dr. Cliff Bush, George Caffentzis, Hasinatu Camara, Karen Camm, Kenneth Carstens, Tommy Carter, Al Changa, Yero Chango, David Clarke, Javier Clavelo, Charlie Cobb, Mustapha Dahleb, Tumika Daima, Ron Daniels, Maxine Davis, Alpha & Shirley Diallo, Rema Diallo, Mohammed Dione, Donna Dixon, Ivanhoe Donaldson, Najiyyah Duncan, Chipo Dunduza, Ibrahim Ebeid, Dr. Ramona

Edelin, Stuart Edwards, Obi Egbuna, Henry English, Englishman, Deborah Evans and "Tuethi" Evans.

- Al Malik Farrakhan, Koko Farrow, Steve Farrow, Jameelah Fernandez, Darwin Fishman, Bill Fletcher, Liz Foster, Akosua Freeman, Tuba & Harriet Frost, Joanne Gavin, Nozipho Glenn, Eugene Godfried, Dr. Ralph Gomes, Kevin Gray, Addie Green, Dick Gregory, Arturo Griffin, Ann Guise, Morgan Guyton, Rev. Graylan Scott Hagler, Craig Hall, Sherona Hall, Paul Hamilton, Ayo Handy, Gwen & Jamette Hargreaves, Mousa Hawamdeh, Nellie Hester-Bailey, Dr. Cynthia Hewitt, Brandon Hewitt, Asari & Tracy Hill, R. Akua Holt, Marilyn Hoosen, Dr. Mary Hoover, Matt Horton, Moreme Hunt, Abayomi Huria, Nefta Huria, Jonathan Hutto, Brien Hyman, Dorothy Hyman, Brother Innuni, Aminata Ipiana, Chawki Irving, Jafar Jafari, Lori Johns-Jallo, David Johnson, Dr. Charles Jones, Will Jones, Tendai Jordan, John Judge, Nubia Kai, Khafra and Asha Kambon, Minister Eric Kareem, Chuck Kaufman, Damani & Ifateyo Keane, Lucani Keita, Mwalimu Keita, Dedan Kimathi, Yvonne King, Rev. Keith Kitchen, Djeniba Kouyatte, Mwongozo Kudjoe, Akili Kumasi, Nia Kuumba, Oluremi Ladeji, Dolores Landry, Zozo & Robert Laird, Kwakou Leak, Ahmadu Leigh, Dr. & Mary Lewis, Bob Lucas, Jama & Moriba Lumumba and Munyiga Lumumba.

- Matsimela Mapfumo (Mark Thompson), Lorenzo Martin, Von Martin, Dr. Thad Mathis, Seku Mbacke, Ousanie Mbenga, Roberta McCloud, Akilah & Mary McFall, Rev. John Mendez, Matt & Meg Meyer, Ethel Minor, Kwaku Mitchell, Maurice Mitchell, Kathleen & Al Mosely, Daleb Moussa, Dr. Zizwe Mtafuta-Ukweli, Curtis Muhammad, Jendayi Mukamtagara, Odinga Muktar, Explo Nani-Kofi, Seku Neblett, Howard Newell, Atiba Nkrumah, Kwazi Nkrumah, Seku & JuJu Nkrumah, Felipe Noguera, Sylvia Oldham, Daniel Osuna, Dr. Lucius Outlaw, Jorja Palmer, Herb Parker, Dr. Harold Pates, Annie & Lamarr Patrick, Dr. Ron Patterson, Kokoyou Patterson, Gerald Perreira, Dino Pollock, Tom Porter, Sara Powell, Dr. Marilyn Preston-Killingham, Paul Pumphrey, Spartacus R, Rene Rabouin, Nicholas Reese. Dr. Bob Rhodes, Mukassa Ricks, Lee Robinson, Mike Rollins and Dennis Rogers.

- Fulani Saji, Bill Sales, Koro Sallah, Kofi Sanders, Carlotta Scott, Akili Seck, Dr. Malik Seku, Dr. Cleve & Gwen Sellers, Dr. Nana & Jerry Seshebe, Macheo Shabaka, Assata Shakur, Asante Shakuur, Mark & Mrs. Shinners, Sibongile Shoba, Randy Short, Reggie Shucks, Myodi Shuta, Kwame Simmons, Sarah Sloan, Karen Spellman, Alphonso Sonii, Dr. Bob Starks, John Steinbach, Kokaiya Summoner, John Claude T., Ziad Taqdomeyeh, Carolyn "Tiambe" Taylor, Juanita Taylor, Phillip Taylor, Zizwe Tchiguka, Fredy Tehdaj, Dera Thompkins, Senfo Tonkam, Dr. John Trimble, Connie Tucker, Seku Ture, Dr. Bill Turner, Dr. James Turner, Antonio Valle, Jose Vargas, Devin Walker, Roy & Grace Walker, Hannah Walsh, Jerry Washington, Gregg Watson, Jaote Wawatu, Rasheida & Maurice Weaver, Dr. Tom Whitney, Ellis & Belinda Wicks, Louis Wiley, Anthony Williams, Michael Williams, Dr. Roosevelt Williams, Warren Wills, Louis Wolf, Paul Wolf, Brian Wood, Helen Woodruff, Nancy Wright, Vivene Younger and Lou Zapata.

- The true believers of the Reparations Movement, especially:

- Baba Hannibal Afrik, Mrs. Dorothy Lewis-Benton, Queen Mother Erline Arikpo, Kalonji Tor Olusegun, Atty. Adjoa A. Aiyetoro, Atty. Nkechi Taifa, Wautella ibn Yusuf, Kibibi Tyehimba, Fahima Seck, Julius Jefferson, and the members of N'COBRA.

- Dr. Conrad Worrill, Jetu Weusi, Bill Grace, Atty. Mickey Dean, and the members of the National Black United Front.

- Minister Louis Farrakhan, Akbar Muhammad, Minister Abdul Aim Muhammad, Minister Khadir Muhammad, Minister Robert Muhammad, Askia Muhammad, Brenda Muhammad, Donald Muhammad, Marvin Muhammad, and the laborers of the Nation of Islam.

- Atty. Malik Zulu Shabazz, Kedar Muhammad, Zayid Muhammad, and the soldiers of the New Black Panther Party.

- Dr. Maulana Karenga, and the members of US.

- Senghor Jawara Baye-El, Babatunji Balogun, Mwariama Dhoruba Kamau, and the members of the Universal Negro Improvement Association.

- Rev. Al Sharpton, and the members of the National Action Network.

- Sam Anderson, Bill Fletcher, Danny Glover, Dr. Manning Marable, Cameron Barron, Jane English, the Black Radical Congress and Trans-Africa.

- Dr. Imari Obadele, Kwame Afoh, and the citizens of the Provisional Government of the Republic of New Africa.

- Viola Plummer, Atty. Roger Wareham, Coltrane Lumumba, Collette Penn, and the members of the December 12th Movement.

- Herman Ferguson, Efia Mwangaza, and the members of the Jericho Movement.

- Atty. Chokwe Lumumba, Achmed Obafemi, Nubia Kai, Dr. Akinyele Umoja, and the members of the New Afrikan Peoples Organization and Malcolm X Grassroots Movement.

- Congressman John Conyers, Councilpersons Dorothy Tillman, Charles Barron and Joan Watson, Deadria Farmer-Paellmann, Dr. Ron Walters, and Dr. Ray Winbush.

- All Political Prisoners, Prisoners of War, and Prisoners of Conscience, their families, co-workers, supporters, especially:

  - The Cuban Five.

  - The PAC Political Prisoners in Azania.

  - The Irish Republican Socialist Political Prisoners.

  - The Palestinian, Iraqi, Arab and Muslim Political Prisoners.

  - All Native American, Puerto Rican, Vieques, New Afrikan/African, Anarchist prisoners, including: Khalid Abdullah, Haki Malik Abdullah (s/n Michael Green), Mumia Abu-Jamal, Sundiata Acoli (s/n Clark Squire), Charles Sims Africa, Debbie Sims Africa, Delbert Orr Africa, Edward Goodman Africa, Janet Holloway Africa, Janine Phillips Africa, Michael Davis Africa, William Phillips Africa, Jamil Al-Amin (s/n H. Rap Brown), William Allen, Kalima Aswad (s/n Robert Duren), Zolo Azania, Abdul Aziz (s/n Warren Ballentine), Herman Bell, Hanif Shabazz Bey (s/n B Gereau), Kathy Boudin, Veronza Bowers Jr., Marilyn Buck, Judy Clark, Conor Claxton, Josh Raisler Cohn, Marshal Eddie Conway, Bill Dunne, Romaine 'Chip' Fitzgerald, Ana Lucia Gelabert, Larry Giddings, David Gilbert, Bashir Hameed (s/n James York), William Taylor (Bill) Harris, Eddie Hatcher, Robert Seth Hayes, Alvaro Luna Hernandez, James "Doc" Holiday, Kalonji Jihad, Jeremy John, Rebecca Johnson, Sekou Cinque T.M. Kambui (s/n William Turk), Khalfani X. Khaldun (s/n Leonard McQuay), James Kilgore, Yu Kikumura, Mohamman Geuka Koti, Jaan Laaman, Richard Mafundi Lake, Wopashitwe Mondo Eyen we Langa (s/n David Rice), Maliki Shakur Latine, Raymond Luc Levasseur, Oscar Lopez-Rivera, Sundiata Lumumba, Ojore Lutalo, Ruchell Cinque Magee, Abdul Majid (s/n Anthony Laborde), Thomas Manning, Masai Mugmuk,

Martin Mullan, Ramiro "Ramsey" R. Muñiz, Jalil Muntaqim (aka Anthony Jalil Bottom), Antonio Camacho Negrón, Prince Imari Obadele, Sekou Odinga, Leonard Peltier, Hugo "Dahariki" Pinell, Ed Poindexter, Luis V. Rodríguez, Charity Ryerson, Kojo Bomani Sababu (s/n Grailing Brown), Kamau Sadiki a/k/a Freddie Hilton, Juan Segarra Palmer, Abdul Shakur, Dr. Muntulu Shakur, Shaka Shakur, Tsutomo Shirosaki, Russel Maroon Shoats, Anthony Smyth, Kathleen Soliah (Sara Jane Olson), James "Ashante" Sullivan, Carlos Alberto Torres, Daud Obida Tulam, Gary Tyler, Tayari Uhuru (s/n Ronald Payne), Herman "Hooks" Wallace, Hugh Williams, Richard Williams, Albert Woodfox and Paul Wright.

- The Movement Attorneys, especially Adjoa A. Aiyetoro, Carol Ann Anderson, Bernetta Bush, Mawuli Davis, Mickey Dean, Jill Soffiyah Elijah, Doris Green, Lionel Jean-Baptiste, Aminata Ipiana, Omadare Jupiter, Chokwe Lumumba, Louis Meyers, Arif Muhammad, Efia Mwanzaa, Charles Ogletree, Ajamu Sankofa, Malik Zulu Shabazz, Gilda Sherrod-Ali, Jonathan Smith, Nkechi Taifa, Roger Wareham, Michael Warren, Stan Willis, Malik Zulu Shabazz, and the members of the National Conference of Black Lawyers, the National Lawyers Guild and the Center for Constitutional Rights.

Like Kwame Ture, (aka Stokely Carmichael), I will never be ungrateful to them, and I will never betray Mother Africa or Her Children, or the Nkrumahist-Toureist principles and Pan-African objective in which we believe. Permit me to hasten to add that the responsibility for all errors of commission or omission in this book, in my life, or in my life's work, is mine alone.

Contents

INTRODUCTION

The enslavement of Africans and African Descendants was a crime against humanity and a unique tragedy in the history of humanity ... because of its abhorrent barbarism, its magnitude, long duration, numbers of people brutalized and murdered, and because of negation of the very essence of humanity of its victims ... The brutal removal and the largest forced migration in history, caused the death of millions of Africans, destroyed African civilizations, impoverished African economies and formed the basis for Africa's under-development and marginalization which continues to date ... [Slavery and the slave trade were] based on economic exploitation, doctrines of racial supremacy and racial hatred and have subjected Africans and African descendants, Indigenous Peoples and many others to the most horrific denigration of their being including classification as sub-humans and chattel, subjugation to rape, forced labor, branding, lashings, murder, maiming, destruction of their languages, cultures, psychological and spiritual well-being resulting in structural subordination which continues to the present ... There is an unbroken chain from the slave trade, slavery, colonialism, foreign occupation, apartheid, racial discrimination and the contemporary forms of racism that maintain barriers to the full and equal participation of the victims of racism and discrimination in all spheres of public life.

Final Declaration and Programme of Action.
Non-Governmental Forum of the World Congress Against Racism, Racial Discrimination, Xenophobia and Related Intolerance.
Durban, Azania (South Africa)
September 3, 2000[1]

Joe R. Feagin, suggests that "the rationale for group compensation, [for reparations], lies in the stolen labor and lives of the millions enslaved, the stolen labor and lives of those legally segregated, and the continuing theft of the labor and lives of those who face contemporary discrimination. This theft of labor and lives,"[1] according to Feagin, "was carried out not only by whites acting as individuals, but also, for at least its first 350 years, by various local, state, and federal governments. Whites have been involved individually and collectively in the exploitation and oppression of [Africans in America]," he declared, "for nearly four centuries."[2] His paper speaks eloquently about the concept of unjust enrichment, and its conjoint twin, unjust impoverishment.

Permit us here, to Pan-Africanize Feagin's suggestion by including the massive and unparalleled theft of land and resources, in Africa and the Americas. Second, permit us to suggest that this theft has occurred for at least 569-years, since the first Africans were kidnapped in the Canary Islands by Spain in 1435, the initial crime that launched the Trans-Atlantic Slave Trade. This theft of the lives, labor and land continues and intensifies today.

---

[1] Joe R. Feagin. *"Documenting the Costs of Slavery, Segregation, and Contemporary Discrimination: Are Reparations in Order for African Americans?"* This paper was commissioned for the Inclusion in Asset Building: Research and Policy Symposium, Center for Social Development, Washington University in St. Louis, September 21-23, 2000. The symposium was sponsored by the Ford Foundation and the George Warren Brown School of Social Work at Washington University. Available from http://www.millionsforreparations.com/feagin.html.

[2] Ibid.

Most importantly, permit us to suggest that we not forget or minimize the role of the Vatican and the Catholic Church, and the countries in Europe and the Americas who participated in, continue to participate in, and were and continue to be unjustly enriched by and through these thefts, the "greatest "thefts the world has ever seen, these crimes against African and world humanity. Disorganization, disempowerment, dispersion and dehumanization are the causes and consequences of unjust enrichment and unjust impoverishment.

Stolen Lives

Thomas Cooper in the *Supplement to Mr. Cooper's Letter on the Slave Trade*, Dr. W.E.B. DuBois in *The Suppression of the Slave Trade*, Toni Morrison in *Beloved*, Joseph Miller in *The Way of Death: Merchant Capitalism and the Angolan Slave Trade 1730-1830*, and Piers Larsen, in T*he Museum of Slavery in the Americas* website, suggests that a minimum of 28 million, and perhaps as many as 180 million Africans were murdered or enslaved in the Trans-Atlantic Slave Trade, between 1435 and 1888.

Cooper suggests that for every 100 Africans who were kidnapped and enslaved, 1,000 were murdered in European inspired or exacerbated warfare in Africa, 20 were murdered on the "way of death "in Africa and the Middle Passage, and 70 were murdered during seasoning, for a total of 170 million deaths. Miller suggests that for each 100 Africans seized in Angola, 75 reached the marketplaces in the interior, 64 arrived at the slave forts and the holding pens on the coast, 57 stepped onto Brazilian soil, 48 lived to behold their first slave master or mistress, and only 28 or 30 of the original 100 Africans seized in Angola, were alive 3 to 4 years later.

Larsen suggests that one-half of all captured Africans, an estimated 15 to 20 million African People, two women for every man, were held in slavery in Africa. Philip D. Curtin, in *The African Slave Trade, A Census,* and Joseph E. Inikori, in *Forced Migration,* suggest that 10 to 15 million kidnapped Africans were landed alive and in chains in the Western Hemisphere, two men for every woman.

We are reminded, in The Ideology of Racial Hierarchy and the Construction of the European Slave Trade, that:

> No African slaves were removed from Africa, only African People were removed. They were blacksmiths, farmers, fishers, priests, members of royal families, musicians, soldiers, and traders. They were captured against their wills and then enslaved in the Caribbean and Americas."[3]

David Eltis, in the *Trans-Atlantic Slave Trade: A Database on CD-ROM,*[4] suggests that the Trans-Atlantic Slave Trade consisted of a minimum of 34,482 and perhaps a maximum of 35,561 slave voyages, 27,233 of which are documented in the database. According to Eltis:

- Portugal and Brazil were and are responsible for at least 7,300 of these voyages (26.8%), and at least 5,074,900 (45.9%) of the Africans who were forcibly, illegally and immorally transported from Africa. Using Cooper's order of magnitude, Portugal and Brazil were and are responsible for the murder, kidnapping, and enslavement of more than 73 million Africans.

- Britain was and is responsible for at least 11,632 of these voyages (42.7%), and at least 3,112,300 (28.1%) of the Africans who were forcibly, illegally and immorally transported from Africa. Britain was and is responsible for the murder, kidnapping, and enslavement of 52.2 million Africans.

---

[3] Quoted from a Paper delivered at *"The Route Of The Slaves"* Conference, which was sponsored by UNESCO and held in Lisbon, Portugal, from 9-12 December 1998.

[4] David Eltis, Stephen D. Behrendt, David Richardson, and Herbert S. Klein. *The Trans-Atlantic Slave Trade: A Database on CD-RO*M. Cambridge and New York. Cambridge University Press. 1999.

- France was and is responsible for at least 4,038 of these voyages (14.8%), and at least 1,456,000 (13.2%) of the Africans who were forcibly, illegally and immorally transported from Africa. Using Cooper's order of magnitude, France was and is responsible for the murder, kidnapping, and enslavement of 21.6 million Africans.

- Spain was and is responsible for at least 1,116 of these voyages (4.1%), and at least 517,000 (4.7%) of the Africans who were forcibly, illegally and immorally transported from Africa. Using Cooper's order of magnitude, Spain was and is responsible for the murder, kidnapping, and enslavement of 8.5 million Africans.

Eltis documents the impact of the Trans-Atlantic Slave Trade and slavery on eight regions in Africa: Senegambia, which accounted for 4.5 percent of the Trans-Atlantic Slave Trade; Sierra Leone (3.7 percent), the Windward Coast (1.7 percent), the Gold Coast (9.4 percent), the Bight of Benin (8.4 percent), the Bight of Biafra (13.7 percent), West Central Africa (44.2 percent) and South East Africa. The present day countries of Nigeria, Angola, Ghana, Senegambia, Sierra Leone and all of the other African regions combined, accounted for 24 percent, 24 percent, 16 percent, 11 percent, 6 percent and 6 percent of the 10 to 15 million Africans forcibly, illegally and immorally transported from Africa, respectively, and of the more than 180 million Africans who were murdered, kidnapped and enslaved.[5] Untold numbers of families, clans, tribes, societies, villages, nations, and civilizations in Africa were invaded, disrupted, disorganized, pillaged, raped, and destroyed during the slave trade and colonialism. These crimes continue and intensify today.

Eltis further documents the participation, to some degree or another in the Trans-Atlantic Slave Trade and slavery, of almost every country in the Western Hemisphere, especially fifteen regions in the America's: the British Mainland of North America, the British Leewards, the British Windwards and Trinidad, Jamaica, Barbados, Guyana, the Spanish American Mainland, the Spanish Caribbean, Northeast Brazil, Bahia, Southeast Brazil and other areas.[6] According to Eltis, 40.6 per cent of all kidnapped Africans were shipped to Brazil, 29 percent to the British colonies in the Caribbean and North America, 14.3 percent to the Spanish colonies in the Americas, 12 percent to the French colonies, and 2.7 percent to the Dutch Americas.[7]

Dr. Walter Rodney proves, in *How Europe Underdeveloped Africa*, that the 569-year old and continuing Maafa was and is a war of unprecedented scope and scale, and any characterization of it as trade, is another malicious myth. The Maafa's enormity, repercussion, and impact can be better understood if we compare it to the cost of the U.S. Civil War, which was waged for only five years.

Keith T. Poole teaches, in his *American Economic History Class* at the University of Houston, that the Civil War had the largest land armies in history, with 1,650,000 men under arms in 1863, and battles involving 100,000 and 200,000 men commonplace. It caused a record number of casualties, with 5,000 men killed and 20,000 wounded in one day at Antietam, and 618,000 dead and 500,000 wounded during five years of war. The total cost, all war spending by the Union and Confederate Governments, plus destroyed physical capital, plus destroyed human capital, was $10 billion: $3.4 billion in spending for the North and $3.3 billion in spending for the South, plus $.03 billion to draft and maintain 462,000 men, plus $1.5 billion in physical capital destruction in the South, plus $2.3 billion in human capital destruction ($1.6 billion for the 618,000 dead and $.63 billion for the 500,000 wounded), minus $.434 billion in risk premium. Ten billion dollars in 1865 money equals $180 billion to $210 billion today.[8]

United States Secretary of War Cameron claimed, in the Original Draft of his Report on the Confiscation Act of 1861, that, "the principal wealth and power of the rebel States is a peculiar species of

[5] David Eltis." *The Volume and Structure of the Transatlantic Slave Trade: A Reassessment."*
[6] Ibid.
[7] Ibid.
[8] K.T, Poole. *American Economic History Class.* University of Houston.

property, consisting of the service or labor of African slaves, or the descendants of Africans. This property has been variously estimated at the value of from seven hundred million to one thousand million dollars,"[9] $175 to $250 per slave. This estimate was extremely low. In 1839, a prime male slave could be purchased in Cuba for $400 and then sold into slavery for life in Richmond for $1,000, in Charleston for $1,150, in Savannah for $1,200, or in New Orleans for $1,250.

The $10 billion spent and lost during the Civil War could have provided $5 billion in compensation to the 393,000 families in the United States who owned 4 million slaves in 1860, $1,250 per slave or $12,722.65 per slave-holding family, saved their plantations and infrastructure from destruction, and avoided the death and wounding of 1.1 million men. This money could have also could have also provided $5 billion in compensation to 4 million slaves, $1,250 per slave. Only a very small percentage of Europeans in the United States made, or was worth, $1,000 in 1865. The average wage for white workers was $1 per day.

The cost to Africa and the African Diaspora, of the 569-year historical and continuing Maafa, which was and is an unprecedented war, is staggering, perhaps in the thousands of trillions of dollars. This cost continues to be paid by Africa and the African Diaspora today, directly and indirectly. The facts speak for themselves.

Stolen Labor

For more than 6 centuries and 30 generations, the theft of African labor, in Africa and the African Diaspora, and of the untold wealth that it produced, has, paraphrasing Feagin, "redistributed income and wealth earned by black labor to generations of [Europeans], leaving the former relatively impoverished as a group and the latter relatively privileged as a group."[10] According to Feagin:

- The "value of the slave labor expropriated by whites [in the United States] from 1620 to 1865 ranges from about $1 trillion to as much as $97 trillion, depending on the rate of interest chosen."[11]

- "The cost of labor market discrimination for 1929-1969 (in 1983 dollars) [was] $1.6 trillion.. The cost of anti-black discrimination from the end of slavery in 1865 to the year 1965, the end of legal segregation.. would likely increase that wage-loss estimate to several trillion dollars."[12]

- "The estimate of the cost of continuing racial discrimination in employment has been put in the range of $94-123 billion.. Estimating a dollar figure for the period since the end of segregation to the present day would doubtless bring this figure of lost income and purchasing power from continuing discrimination to another several trillion dollars."[13]

- "The sum total of the worth of all the black labor stolen by whites [in the United States] through the means of slavery, segregation, and contemporary discrimination, taking into account lost interest over time and putting it in today's dollars, is in the range perhaps of $5 to $24 trillion."[14]

There are more than one billion People of African descent, scattered, suffering and struggling in over 122 countries in the world today. All Africans have suffered, and continue to suffer, the theft of their labor, and of their ancestor's labor. The 40 million Africans in the United States represent less than 4% of

---

[9] *Original Draft of Secretary of War Cameron's Report.* Available from http://www.history.umd.edu/Freedmen/cameron.htm.
[10] Joe R. Feagin. *"Documenting the Costs of Slavery, Segregation, and Contemporary Discrimination: Are Reparations in Order for African Americans?"*
[11] Ibid.
[12] Ibid.
[13] Ibid.
[14] Ibid.

all Africans in the world today. If the value of the stolen labor of Africans in the United States is in the range of $5 to $24 trillion, then we suggest that the value of the stolen labor of more than 1 billion Africans is more than $125 to $600 trillion dollars. Here, we have not included the value of the stolen wealth that this stolen labor created.

Stolen Land and Resources

The massive, unprecedented, and continuing theft and colonization of land in the Americas and Africa, and the resultant and continuing theft of their mineral, agricultural, animal, water and air resources, is a root cause of the Maafa, and of its continuation today, albeit in more sophisticated forms-- neo-colonialism and globalization.

The Kingdom of Spain

Spain "was the center of the first global empire."[15] Columbus' "discovery" of the Americas, inaugurated its Golden Age. Spain lost her colonies in the Americas with the sale of Florida in 1803, the Independence Movements in Central and South America, and the loss of Cuba, Puerto Rico, and the Philippines during the Spanish American War. She colonized the Western Sahara and Equatorial Guinea to substitute for these losses. Western Sahara remains a colony today.

Through her participation in the 569-year historical and continuing Maafa, the Kingdom of Spain was and is responsible for the condition and fate of more than 50.6 million African People, 40.6% of all Africans in the world today, including, but not limited to the following:

Countries	Estimated Number of Africans in 2000
Europe	
Spain	977,698
Sub-Total	977,698
Africa	
Equatorial Guinea	442,516
Western Sahara	223,000
Sub-Total	665,516
Western Hemisphere	
Argentina	894,950
Bolivia	76,699
Chile	362,704
Colombia	5,238,561
Costa Rica	88,354
Cuba	6,819,405
Dominican Republic	6,609,734
Ecuador	1,210,512

[15] Spain. *Wikipedia, the free encyclopedia.*

El Salvador	141,546
Guatemala	292,142
Mexico	2,439,084
Nicaragua	438,640
Panama	2,262,470
Paraguay	141,291
Peru	767,218
Puerto Rico	3,828,506
Uruguay	130,828
Venezuela	17,245,233
Sub-Total	48,987,877
GRAND TOTAL	50,631,091

The French Republic

France's first colonial empire began with the foundation of the colony of Acadia in what is now Nova Scotia in 1605, New France in what is now Quebec in 1608, Senegal and French Guiana in 1624, Saint-Domingue (today's Haiti) in 1694 and Louisiana in 1699. Bokman's slave revolt in Haiti in 1791, France's richest colony; the liberation of all slaves in France and the French Colonies by the French National Assembly in 1794; the defeat of Napoleon and General Leclerc by Toussaint L'Ouverture and the loss of 30,000 French soldiers; the illegal sale of Louisiana in 1803; and the Haitian Revolution of 1804 destroyed the first French colonial empire. The second French colonial empire dates from the invasion and colonization of Algeria in 1830.

Through its participation in the 569-year historical and continuing Maafa, especially its historical and continuing theft and colonization of land, the French Republic was and is responsible for the condition and fate of more than 181 million African People, 18% of all African People in the world today, including, but not limited to the following:

Countries	Estimated Number of Africans in 2000
Europe	
France	1,465,232
Sub-Total	1,465,232
Africa	
Algeria	29,830,370
Benin	5,902,178
Burkina Faso	10,891,159
Central African Republic	3,342,051
Chad	7,166,023
Comoros	528,893
Congo, Republic	2,583,198
Cote d'Ivoire	14,986,218

8

Djibouti	434,116
Gabon	1,190,159
Guinea-Conakry	7,405,375
Madagascar	14,061,627
Mali	9,788,904
Mauritania	2,411,317
Morocco	30,619,561
Niger	9,388,859
Senegal	9,403,546
Tunisia	9,245,284
Sub-Total	169,178,838
Western Hemisphere	
French Guiana	156,946
Guadeloupe	411,823
Haiti	6,611,407
Martinique	402,984
St. Martin	
Sub-Total	10,606,526
GRAND TOTAL	181,250,596

France still controls the Caribbean islands of Guadeloupe and Martinique, Rion in the Indian Ocean, French Guiana in South America, French Polynesia, French Southern and Antarctic Lands, New Caledonia, Mayotte in the Indian Ocean, and St. Pierre and Miquelon near Newfoundland.

The United Kingdom of Great Britain and Northern Ireland

The British Empire "came together over 300 years through a succession of phases of expansion by trade, [including the Trans-Atlantic Slave Trade], settlement or conquest, interspersed with intervals of pacific commercial and diplomatic activity, or imperial contraction. Its territories were scattered across every continent and ocean, and it was described as "the empire on which the sun never sets."[16]

Between 1885 and 1914, after more than 300 years of participation in the Trans-Atlantic Slave Trade, "Britain took nearly 30% of Africa's population under her control, compared to 15% for France, 9% for Germany, 7% for Belgium and only 1% for Italy: Nigeria alone contributed 15 million subjects, more than in the whole of French West Africa or the entire German colonial empire ... In 1899, Britain set out to complete her takeover of South Africa, begun with the annexation (1795) of the Cape ... The British South Africa Company had already seized the land to the north, renamed Rhodesia."[17] At its height in 1897, the British Empire controlled "400-500 million people (roughly a quarter of the world's population), and covered nearly 30 million square kilometres, (roughly two-fifths of the world's land)."[18]

Through its participation in the 569-year historical and continuing Maafa, the United Kingdom of Great Britain and Ireland was and is responsible for the condition and fate of more than 409 million African People, 41% of all African People in the world today, including, but not limited to:

---

[16] Britain. *Wikipedia, the free encyclopedia.*

[17] Ibid.

[18] Ibid.

Countries	Estimated Number of Africans in 2000
Europe	
United Kingdom	1,439,792
Sub-Total	1,439,792
Africa	
Azania	42,327,458
Botswana	1,500,765
Egypt	64,824,466
Gambia	1,248,085
Ghana	18,100,703
Kenya	28,803,085
Lesotho	2,007,814
Liberia	2,602,068
Malawi	9,609,081
Mauritius	1,154,272
Nigeria	107,129,469
Seychelles	78,107
Sierra Leone	4,891,546
Somalia	6,590,325
Sudan	32,594,128
Swaziland	1,031,600
Uganda	20,604,874
Zambia	9,349,975
Zimbabwe	11,423,175
Sub-Total	365,870,996
Western Hemisphere	
Anguilla	10,785
Antigua and Barbuda	63,739
Australia	460,971
Bahamas	234,550
Barbados	207,005
Belize	83,125
Bermuda	62,569
Canada	758,433
Cayman Islands	36,153
Dominica	66,633
Grenada	95,537
Guyana	706,116
Honduras	230,055
Jamaica	2,615,582
Montserrat	12,800

New Zealand	61
Saint Kitts and Nevis	41,803
Saint Lucia	150,630
Saint Vincent & the Grenadines	119,092
Trinidad and Tobago	644,292
Turks and Caicos Islands	14,631
United States	34,834,119
Virgin Islands	108,603
Sub-Total	41,557,285
GRAND TOTAL	408,868,073

The remaining British colonies include: Anguilla, Bermuda, British Virgin Islands, Cayman Islands, Gibraltar, Montserrat, Turks and Caicos Islands, British Antarctic Territory, British Indian Ocean Territory, Falkland Islands, Pitcairn Island, Saint Helena, South Georgia & South Sandwich Islands, Isle of Man, Channel Islands, Guernsey and Jersey. The struggle to reclaim and return to the land, which is at the core of the Pan-African Reparations Movement today, continues and intensifies, especially in Zimbabwe and Azania (South Africa).

Conclusion

At its founding conference in 1993, the UNESCO Slave Route Archives Project declared, that "the holdings of national and departmental archives and the archives of religious orders relating to the slave trade and the Black Diaspora, constitute indispensable sources of documentation for the scientific study of the subject."[19] UNESCO was and is a driving force in past and continuing efforts to rewrite the history of Africa, the African Diaspora and the Maafa from an African-centered perspective; to reinterpret the history of slavery and the slave trade, and slave-like practices and conditions including colonialism, segregation and apartheid; and to have them declared crimes against humanity, both currently and historically.

With this UNESCO declaration in mind, and building upon its sterling contributions and achievements, Pan-African Roots filed, on 24 August 2004, the first round in a series of historic and precedent setting Freedom of Information Act, Open and Public Records Act, and Information Requests in an uncompromising and unyielding effort to compel the archives of the world to open their files and give them to us with a waiver of all associated costs. We are firmly and irrevocably convinced that these records, in the hands of the People, especially the Reparations Movement, once properly interpreted will:

- Bear witness to and prove, once and for all, that piracy, slavery and the slave trade, including the Trans-Atlantic Slave Trade, and slave-like conditions and practices, including colonialism, segregation and apartheid, were illegal and prohibited, and were recognized as crimes against humanity when and where they were committed.

- Help define and mark the successive stages in the development of the 569-year historical and continuing Maafa, and of the unyielding and continuing struggle against it.

- Document who the victims of the Maafa were, and who their descendants are today; who committed these crimes, which were and are the greatest theft of land, lives and labor in human

---

[19] *The UNESCO Slave Route Project* Available from http://portal.unesco.org/culture/en/ev.php-URL_ID=5322&URL_DO=DO_TOPIC&URL_SECTION=201.html

11

history; how this unjust and illegal wealth was converted, consolidated, preserved and transferred across generations and centuries; and who owns and benefits from this unjust enrichment today.

Since our filing, we have amended and re-filed our Requests, published them as a model and educational tool, and now provide them to the Reparations Movement in the hope that hundreds, perhaps thousands of similar requests will be filed in every corner of Europe, Africa, and the Americas.

The table of contents reveals the outline of our research-political-legal strategy, and the plan of this book. The first part publishes twelve requests for Public Commitment and Information from the major candidates in the 2004 U.S. Presidential Campaign and the political parties that they represent. The second part publishes seven federal FOIA Requests. The third part publishes fourteen Requests for Public Commitment, State Open Records, and International Freedom of Information. The conclusion is a call for more study and work, and more militant and mass education, organization and struggle.

These Requests also call for the disclosure of governmental records on a number of companies within the shipping, arms and munitions, sugar-molasses-rum, cotton-textile-apparel, agricultural equipment, railroad, mining and energy, finance and insurance industries, colleges and universities, and non-governmental organizations. Several of these companies and non-governmental entities are listed in Appendix A. By including this information, we seek to arm the Reparations Movement with an expanded arsenal of weapons and strategies as it goes over to a new and more exciting phase. Biographical information about Bob Brown is included in Appendix B.

We are confident that the Reparations Movement will grow and develop in its intensity, scope and scale, world-wide, and become increasingly more Pan-African and more radical. We hope that this initial and incomplete research effort contributes, in some small way, to its inevitable victory. We are honored to be afforded the privilege of making this humble contribution!

PART I: REQUESTS FOR PUBLIC COMMITMENT AND INFORMATION

Resolved by the Senate and House of Representatives, that Slavery is a crime against humanity, and a sore evil in the body politic that was excused by the framers of the Federal Constitution as a crime entailed upon the country by their predecessors, and tolerated solely as a thing of inexorable necessity.

Joint Resolution No. 42.--Resolutions Relating To The Subject of Slavery
Vermont State Legislature
November 12, 1849

7. That the new dogma that the Constitution of its own force carries slavery into any or all of the territories of the United States, is a dangerous political heresy, at variance with the explicit provisions of that instrument itself, with contemporaneous exposition, and with legislative and judicial precedent, is revolutionary in its tendency and subversive of the peace and harmony of the country.

8. That the formal condition of all the territory of the United States is that of freedom; that as our republican fathers, when they had abolished slavery in all our national territory, ordained that no "person should be deprived of life, liberty or property, without due process of law," it becomes our duty, by legislation, whenever such legislation is necessary, to maintain this provision of the constitution against all attempts to violate it; and we deny the authority of congress, of a territorial legislature, or of any individuals, to give legal existence to slavery in any territory of the United States.

9. That we brand the recent re-opening of the African Slave Trade, under the cover of our national flag, aided by perversions of judicial power, as a crime against humanity, and a burning shame to our country and age, and we call upon congress to take prompt and efficient measures for the total and final suppression of the execrable traffic.

National Republican Platform
Adopted at the 2nd National Republican Convention
Chicago, Illinois
May 17, 1860

Pan-African Roots

1247 E Street SE
Washington, DC 20003
Tel: (202) 544-9355 - Fax: (202) 544-9359
Email: paroots02@yahoo.com

25 October 2004

Mr. Ed Gillespie, Chairman
Republican National Committee
310 First Street SE
Washington, DC 20003

AMENDED REQUEST FOR PUBLIC COMMITMENT AND INFORMATION.

Dear Mr. Gillespie:

As you are aware, on May 17, 1860, the second National Republican Convention adopted its 1860 National Republican Platform, which declared it resolved:

> 7. That the new dogma that the Constitution of its own force carries slavery into any or all of the territories of the United States, is a dangerous political heresy, at variance with the explicit provisions of that instrument itself, with contemporaneous exposition, and with legislative and judicial precedent, is revolutionary in its tendency and subversive of the peace and harmony of the country.

> 8. That the formal condition of all the territory of the United States is that of freedom; that as our republican fathers, when they had **abolished slavery in all our national territory**, ordained that no "person should be deprived of life, liberty or property, without due process of law," it becomes our duty, by legislation, whenever such legislation is necessary, to maintain this provision of the constitution against all attempts to violate it; and we deny the authority of congress, of a territorial legislature, or of any individuals, **to give legal existence to slavery in any territory of the United States. [Emphasis added.]**

> 9. That we brand the recent re-opening of the African Slave Trade, under the cover of our national flag, aided by perversions of judicial power, as a **crime against humanity, and a burning shame to our country and age,** and we call upon congress to take prompt and efficient measures for the total and final suppression of the execrable traffic.[20] **[Emphasis added.]**

In 1808, the United States Government prohibited its citizens from participating in the international slave trade declaring it piracy in 1820, and participation in it punishable by death. Despite this prohibition, a minimum of 250,000 and perhaps as many as 1,000,000 Africans were kidnapped, enslaved, and illegally imported into the United States via Cuba between 1809 and 1861. In 1839, a prime male slave could be purchased in Cuba for $400 and then sold into slavery for life in Richmond for $1,000 or Charleston for $1,150 or Savannah for $1,200 or New Orleans for $1,250. The average daily wage for a white worker was $1. President James Madison reported to Congress in 1810 that:

> It appears that American citizens are instrumental in carrying on a traffic in enslaved Africans, equally in violation of the laws of humanity, and in defiance of those of their own country. The

---

[20] Central Pacific Railroad Photographic History Museum. *Republican Party National Platform, 1860.*
http://cprr.org/Museum/Ephemera/Republican_Platform_1860.html.

same just and benevolent motives, which produced the interdiction in force against this criminal conduct, will doubtless be felt in Congress, in devising further means of suppressing the evil.[21]

The 1860 Republican National Convention selected Abraham Lincoln as its presidential nominee. He campaigned on this platform, and "won the presidency with almost half a million votes more than [Stephen] Douglas, his closest rival. [Lincoln] won the election garnering 39.8 percent of the popular vote. This election firmly established the Republican hold on the presidency for 60 of the next 100 years."[22] Within five years of the 1860 Republican National Convention, slavery had been abolished, 4 million slaves were liberated, and the 13th Amendment was passed banning slavery and the slave trade forever from U.S. soil.

Upon information and belief, members of the Republican Party, especially its Abolitionist and Reconstruction wing, played an important role in these victories. William Lloyd Garrison was the first person to declare slavery a crime against humanity in the inaugural edition (1831) of his Liberator newspaper. On November 12, 1849, the Vermont Legislature passed "*Joint Resolution No. 42.-- Resolutions Relating To The Subject of Slavery*," declaring it:

> Resolved by the Senate and House of Representatives, That Slavery is a **crime against humanity**, and a sore evil in the body politic that was **excused** by the framers of the Federal Constitution as **a crime entailed** upon the country by their predecessors, and **tolerated** solely as a thing of inexorable necessity.[23] **[Emphasis added.]**

On the eve of the Republican National Convention held from 30 August to 2 September 2004 in New York City, we formally and publicly request that you, the Republican National Convention, especially its Platform Committee, and Mr. George W. Bush, your Presidential nominee, publicly reaffirm your commitment to the 1860 Republican National Platform, especially the above quoted paragraphs, and your continued resolve that slavery and the slave trade were crimes against humanity in 1860, and are crimes against humanity today.

We formally and publicly request that you, the Republican Party, and President Bush publicly and immediately commit to give us access to or copies of all records created or obtained by, or under the authority and control of the Republican Party (national, state and local), and of all Republican office-holders (federal, state, county and local), that pertain to, or reference:

- The Republican Party's and the United States Government's role, operations and activities, historically and currently, in facilitating, prohibiting or combating piracy and privateering, slavery and the slave trade, especially the Trans-Atlantic Slave-Trade; and on their role in the struggle to declare them crimes against humanity, and repair the damages and injuries that were and continue to be inflicted upon untold generations of African People.

- The Republican Party's and the United States Government's role, operations and activities, historically and currently, in facilitating, prohibiting or combating slave-like conditions and practices, including, but not limited to certain practices under colonialism, segregation and apartheid; racism and racial discrimination, xenophobia and related intolerance.

- Slave, urban and racial disturbances, riots, rebellions, and revolts; runaway slaves, fugitives beyond borders, and related claims or extradition requests; and all demands and proposals for compensation, restitution, reparations or repatriation (emigration). All governments, agencies

---

[21] Lawrence R. Tenzer. *The Forgotten Cause of the Civil War: A New Look at the Slavery Issue. Chapter 4: The Illicit Slave Trade*. October/November 2001. http://www.multiracial.com/readers/tenzer4.html.

[22] Central Pacific Railroad Photographic History Museum. *Republican Party National Platform, 1860*. http://cprr.org/Museum/Ephemera/Republican_Platform_1860.html.

[23] *The Acts and Resolves Passed By The Legislature Of The State of Vermont At The October Session, 1849*. Published By authority. Montpelier: E. P. Walton & Son. 1849.

(federal, state, county or local), corporations, non-governmental organizations, institutions, churches, families, individuals, or entities, domestic or foreign, who participated or invested in, or made profits from the above referenced crimes against humanity; and who owns or benefits from these historical and continuing crimes today, including but not limited to those listed in Appendix A.

We also formally and publicly request that you comply in an expedited manner with this Request for Commitment and Information, and that you waive all associated costs.

Please be advised that we have sent a copy of this Information Request to President George W. Bush, Senator John Kerry and the Democratic Party, Mr. David Cobb and the Green Party, Mr. Ralph Nader and the Reform Party/Nader Campaign, Mr. Bill Van Auken and the Socialist Equality Party, Mr. Walt Brown and the Socialist Party USA, Mr. Roger Calero and the Socialist Workers Party, Mr. John Parker and the Workers World Party, and other Presidential candidates requesting that they publicly and immediately commit, if elected President and Commander-in-Chief of the United States Government, that they will order all departments and agencies under their authority and control to comply in full and in an expedited manner with our FOIA Request, and that they will waive all associated fees. We have also released this Request to the media.

Please also be advised that we have filed the first round of a series of historic and precedent setting FOIA, State Open Records, Public Records, and Information Requests with:

- Mr. Ed Gillespie, Chairman of the Republican National Committee; President George W. Bush; Mr. Terry McAuliffe, Chairman of the Democratic National Committee; Senator John Kerry, Mr. Ralph Nader, and other Presidential candidates; Secretary of State Colin Powell; Defense Secretary Donald Rumsfeld; Treasury Secretary John Snow; Attorney General John Ashcroft; Interior Secretary Gale Norton and Mr. John Carlin of the National Archives and Records Administration.

- His Holiness John Paul II, the Spiritual Leader of the Roman Catholic Church and the Head of the Vatican; Brother Carlos Azpiroz Costa, OP of the Dominicans; Father General Peter-Hans Kolvenbach SJ, the Superior General of the Society of Jesus; Reverend Monsignor William P. Fay, General Secretary of the U.S. Conference of Catholic Bishops and Father Bradley M. Schaeffer, President of the U.S. Jesuit Conference.

- King Juan Carlos V of the Kingdom of Spain; Governor Jeb Bush of Florida; President Vicente Fox of Mexico; Governor Rick Perry of Texas; President Jacques Chirac of the French Republic; Governor Kathleen Blanco of Louisiana; Queen Elizabeth II of the United Kingdom of Great Britain; Prime Minister Paul Martin of Canada; Governor Mark Warner of Virginia; Governor James H. Douglas of Vermont and Governor Rod Blagojevich of Illinois.

We expect your positive response to this historic and precedent setting Information Request within 20 working days. Please be assured that we will exhaust administrative, political, and legal remedies. Thank you for your consideration.

Sincerely,
Bob Brown, co-director
Pan-African Roots

Pan-African Roots
1247 E Street SE
Washington, DC 20003
Tel: (202) 544-9355 - Fax: (202) 544-9359
Email: paroots02@yahoo.com

25 October 2004

President George W. Bush
The White House
1600 Pennsylvania Ave NW
Washington, DC 20500

AMENDED REQUEST FOR PUBLIC COMMITMENT AND INFORMATION.

Dear President Bush:

This is to officially and publicly inform you that we have sent the enclosed letter to Mr. Ed Gillespie Chairperson of the Republican National Committee formally and publicly requesting that he, the Republican National Convention, especially its Platform Committee, and you, their Presidential nominee, publicly reaffirm their commitment to the 1860 Republican National Platform, especially the paragraphs quoted in our letter, and their continued resolve that slavery and the slave trade were crimes against humanity in 1860, and are crimes against humanity today.

We further requested that the Republican Party publicly and immediately commit to give us access to or copies of all records created or obtained by, or under the authority and control of the Republican Party and all Republican office-holders that pertain to, or reference the subjects listed therein. We also formally and publicly requested that he comply in an expedited manner with this Information Request, and that he waive all associated costs.

We advised Mr. Gillespie that we have sent a copy of our Request to you (Republican Party); Mr. Terry McAuliffe and Senator John Kerry (Democratic Party); David Cobb (Green Party); Mr. Shawn O'Hara and Mr. Ralph Nader (Reform Party/Independent); Mr. Bill Van Auken (Socialist Equality Party); Mr. Walt Brown (Socialist Party USA); Mr. Roger Calero (Socialist Workers Party) and Mr. John Parker (Workers World Party) requesting them to publicly and immediately commit that if they or their candidates are elected President and Commander-in-Chief of the United States Government, they will order all departments and agencies under their authority and control to comply in full and in an expedited manner with our FOIA Request, and that they will waive all associated fees. We have also released this Request to the media.

We also advised Mr. Gillespie that we have filed the first round of a series of historic and precedent setting FOIA, State Open Records, Public Records, and Information Requests with you and all of the federal departments and agencies under your authority and control, including, but not limited to the Departments of State, Defense, Treasury, Justice and Interior; and the National Archives and Records Administration; and other State Open Records and Freedom of Information Requests.

We expect your positive response to this historic and precedent setting Request within 20 working days. Please be assured that we will exhaust all political remedies. Thank you for your consideration.

Sincerely,
Bob Brown, co-director
Pan-African Roots

Pan-African Roots
1247 E Street SE
Washington, DC 20003
Tel: (202) 544-9355 - Fax: (202) 544-9359
Email: paroots02@yahoo.com

25 October 2004

Senator John Kerry
Democratic National Committee
499 S Capitol St SW
Washington, DC 20003

AMENDED REQUEST FOR PUBLIC COMMITMENT AND INFORMATION.

Dear Senator Kerry:

This is to officially and publicly inform you that we have sent the enclosed letter to Mr. Ed Gillespie, Chairperson of the Republican National Committee formally and publicly requesting that he, the Republican National Convention, especially its Platform Committee, and George W. Bush, their Presidential nominee, publicly reaffirm their commitment to the 1860 Republican National Platform, especially the paragraphs quoted in our letter, and their continued resolve that slavery and the slave trade were crimes against humanity in 1860, and are crimes against humanity today.

We further requested that the Republican Party publicly and immediately commit to give us access to or copies of all records created or obtained by, or under the authority and control of the Republican Party and all Republican office-holders that pertain to, or reference the subjects listed therein. We also formally and publicly requested that he comply in an expedited manner with this Information Request, and that he waive all associated costs.

We advised Mr. Gillespie that we have sent a copy of our Request to President Bush (Republican Party); Mr. Terry McAuliffe and you (Democratic Party); David Cobb (Green Party); Mr. Shawn O'Hara and Mr. Ralph Nader (Reform Party/Independent); Mr. Bill Van Auken (Socialist Equality Party); Mr. Walt Brown (Socialist Party USA); Mr. Roger Calero (Socialist Workers Party) and Mr. John Parker (Workers World Party) requesting them to publicly and immediately commit that if they or their candidates are elected President and Commander-in-Chief of the United States Government, they will order all departments and agencies under their authority and control to comply in full and in an expedited manner with our FOIA Request, and that they will waive all associated fees. We have also released this Request to the media.

We also advised Mr. Gillespie that we have filed the first round of a series of historic and precedent setting FOIA, State Open Records, Public Records, and Information Requests with President Bush, and all of the federal departments and agencies under his authority and control, including, but not limited to the Departments of State, Defense, Treasury, Justice and Interior; and the National Archives and Records Administration.

We expect your positive response to this historic and precedent setting Request within 20 working days. Please be assured that we will exhaust all political remedies. Thank you for your consideration.

Sincerely,
Bob Brown, co-director
Pan-African Roots

Pan-African Roots
1247 E Street SE
Washington, DC 20003
Tel: (202) 544-9355 - Fax: (202) 544-9359
Email: paroots02@yahoo.com

25 October 2004

Mr. Terry McAuliffe, Chairman
Democratic National Committee
499 S Capitol St SW
Washington, DC 20003

AMENDED REQUEST FOR PUBLIC COMMITMENT AND INFORMATION.

Dear Mr. McAuliffe:

This is to officially and publicly inform you that we have sent the enclosed letter to Mr. Ed Gillespie Chairperson of the Republican National Committee formally and publicly requesting that he, the Republican National Convention, especially its Platform Committee, and George W. Bush, their Presidential nominee, publicly reaffirm their commitment to the 1860 Republican National Platform, especially the paragraphs quoted in our letter, and their continued resolve that slavery and the slave trade were crimes against humanity in 1860, and are crimes against humanity today.

We further requested that the Republican Party publicly and immediately commit to give us access to or copies of all records created or obtained by, or under the authority and control of the Republican Party and all Republican office-holders that pertain to, or reference the subjects listed therein. We also formally and publicly requested that he comply in an expedited manner with this Information Request, and that he waive all associated costs.

We advised Mr. Gillespie that we have sent a copy of our Request to President George W. Bush (Republican Party); you and Senator John Kerry (Democratic Party); Mr. David Cobb (Green Party); Mr. Shawn O'Hara and Mr. Ralph Nader (Reform Party/Independent); Mr. Bill Van Auken (Socialist Equality Party); Mr. Walt Brown (Socialist Party USA); Mr. Roger Calero (Socialist Workers Party) and Mr. John Parker (Workers World Party) requesting you and them to publicly and immediately commit that if you or they are elected President and Commander-in-Chief of the United States Government, you or they will order all departments and agencies under your or their authority and control to comply in full and in an expedited manner with our FOIA Request, and waive all associated fees. We have also released this Request to the media.

We also advised Mr. Gillespie that we have filed the first round of a series of historic and precedent setting FOIA, State Open Records, Public Records, and Information Requests with President Bush, and all of the federal departments and agencies under his authority and control, including, but not limited to the Departments of State, Defense, Treasury, Justice and Interior; and the National Archives and Records Administration.

We expect your positive response to this historic and precedent setting Request within 20 working days. Please be assured that we will exhaust all political remedies. Thank you for your consideration.

Sincerely,
Bob Brown, co-director
Pan-African Roots

Pan-African Roots
1247 E Street SE
Washington, DC 20003
Tel: (202) 544-9355 - Fax: (202) 544-9359
Email: paroots02@yahoo.com

25 October 2004

Mr. David Cobb
Green Party
33 West 19th Street, Suite 309
New York, New York 1001

AMENDED REQUEST FOR PUBLIC COMMITMENT AND INFORMATION.

Dear Mr. Cobb:

This is to officially and publicly inform you that we have sent the enclosed letter to Mr. Ed Gillespie, Chairperson of the Republican National Committee formally and publicly requesting that he, the Republican National Convention, especially its Platform Committee, and George W. Bush, their Presidential nominee, publicly reaffirm their commitment to the 1860 Republican National Platform, especially the paragraphs quoted in our letter, and their continued resolve that slavery and the slave trade were crimes against humanity in 1860, and are crimes against humanity today.

We further requested that the Republican Party publicly and immediately commit to give us access to or copies of all records created or obtained by, or under the authority and control of the Republican Party and all Republican office-holders that pertain to, or reference the subjects listed therein. We also formally and publicly requested that he comply in an expedited manner with this Information Request, and that he waive all associated costs.

We advised Mr. Gillespie that we have sent a copy of our Request to President George W. Bush (Republican Party); Mr. Terry McAuliffe and Senator John Kerry (Democratic Party); you (Green Party); Mr. Shawn O'Hara and Mr. Ralph Nader (Reform Party/Independent); Mr. Bill Van Auken (Socialist Equality Party); Mr. Walt Brown (Socialist Party USA); Mr. Roger Calero (Socialist Workers Party) and Mr. John Parker (Workers World Party) requesting you and them to publicly and immediately commit that if you or they are elected President and Commander-in-Chief of the United States Government, you or they will order all departments and agencies under your or their authority and control to comply in full and in an expedited manner with our FOIA Request, and waive all associated fees. We have also released this Request to the media.

We also advised Mr. Gillespie that we have filed the first round of a series of historic and precedent setting FOIA, State Open Records, Public Records, and Information Requests with President Bush, and all of the federal departments and agencies under his authority and control, including, but not limited to the Departments of State, Defense, Treasury, Justice and Interior; and the National Archives and Records Administration.

We expect your positive response to this historic and precedent setting Request within 20 working days. Please be assured that we will exhaust all political remedies. Thank you for your consideration.

Sincerely,
Bob Brown, co-director
Pan-African Roots

Pan-African Roots

1247 E Street SE
Washington, DC 20003
Tel: (202) 544-9355 - Fax: (202) 544-9359
Email: paroots02@yahoo.com

25 October 2004

Mr. Ralph Nader
Reform Party/Independent
P.O. Box 18002
Washington, DC 20036

AMENDED REQUEST FOR PUBLIC COMMITMENT AND INFORMATION.

Dear Mr. Nader:

This is to officially and publicly inform you that we have sent the enclosed letter to Mr. Ed Gillespie, Chairperson of the Republican National Committee formally and publicly requesting that he, the Republican National Convention, especially its Platform Committee, and George W. Bush, their Presidential nominee, publicly reaffirm their commitment to the 1860 Republican National Platform, especially the paragraphs quoted in our letter, and their continued resolve that slavery and the slave trade were crimes against humanity in 1860, and are crimes against humanity today.

We further requested that the Republican Party publicly and immediately commit to give us access to or copies of all records created or obtained by, or under the authority and control of the Republican Party and all Republican office-holders that pertain to, or reference the subjects listed therein. We also formally and publicly requested that he comply in an expedited manner with this Information Request, and that he waive all associated costs.

We advised Mr. Gillespie that we have sent a copy of our Request to President George W. Bush (Republican Party); Mr. Terry McAuliffe and Senator John Kerry (Democratic Party); Mr. David Cobb (Green Party); Mr. Shawn O'Hara and you (Reform Party/Independent); Mr. Walt Brown (Socialist Party USA); Mr. Roger Calero (Socialist Workers Party); Mr. Bill Van Auken (Socialist Equality Party) and Mr. John Parker (Workers World Party) requesting you and them to publicly and immediately commit that if you or they are elected President and Commander-in-Chief of the United States Government, you or they will order all departments and agencies under your or their authority and control to comply in full and in an expedited manner with our FOIA Request, and waive all associated fees. We have also released this Request to the media.

We also advised Mr. Gillespie that we have filed the first round of a series of historic and precedent setting FOIA, State Open Records, Public Records, and Information Requests with President Bush, and all of the federal departments and agencies under his authority and control, including, but not limited to the Departments of State, Defense, Treasury, Justice and Interior; and the National Archives and Records Administration.

We expect your positive response to this historic and precedent setting Request within 20 working days. Please be assured that we will exhaust all political remedies. Thank you for your consideration.

Sincerely,
Bob Brown, co-director
Pan-African Roots

Pan-African Roots

1247 E Street SE
Washington, DC 20003
Tel: (202) 544-9355 - Fax: (202) 544-9359
Email: paroots02@yahoo.com

25 October 2004

Mr. Shawn O'Hara
Reform Party/Independent
P.O. Box 18002
Washington, DC 20036

AMENDED REQUEST FOR PUBLIC COMMITMENT AND INFORMATION.

Dear Mr. O'Hara:

This is to officially and publicly inform you that we have sent the enclosed letter to Mr. Ed Gillespie, Chairperson of the Republican National Committee formally and publicly requesting that he, the Republican National Convention, especially its Platform Committee, and you, their Presidential nominee, publicly reaffirm their commitment to the 1860 Republican National Platform, especially the paragraphs quoted in our letter, and their continued resolve that slavery and the slave trade were crimes against humanity in 1860, and are crimes against humanity today.

We further requested that the Republican Party publicly and immediately commit to give us access to or copies of all records created or obtained by, or under the authority and control of the Republican Party and all Republican office-holders that pertain to, or reference the subjects listed therein. We also formally and publicly requested that he comply in an expedited manner with this Information Request, and that he waive all associated costs.

We advised Mr. Gillespie that we have sent a copy of our Request to President George W. Bush (Republican Party); Mr. Terry McAuliffe and Senator John Kerry (Democratic Party); Mr. David Cobb (Green Party); you and Mr. Ralph Nader (Reform Party/Independent); Mr. Walt Brown (Socialist Party USA); Mr. Roger Calero (Socialist Workers Party); Mr. Bill Van Auken (Socialist Equality Party) and Mr. John Parker (Workers World Party) requesting you and them to publicly and immediately commit that if you or they are elected President and Commander-in-Chief of the United States Government, you or they will order all departments and agencies under your or their authority and control to comply in full and in an expedited manner with our FOIA Request, and waive all associated fees. We have also released this Request to the media.

We also advised Mr. Gillespie that we have filed the first round of a series of historic and precedent setting FOIA, State Open Records, Public Records, and Information Requests with President Bush, and all of the federal departments and agencies under his authority and control, including, but not limited to the Departments of State, Defense, Treasury, Justice and Interior; and the National Archives and Records Administration.

We expect your positive response to this historic and precedent setting Request within 20 working days. Please be assured that we will exhaust all political remedies. Thank you for your consideration.

Sincerely,
Bob Brown, co-director
Pan-African Roots

Pan-African Roots

1247 E Street SE
Washington, DC 20003
Tel: (202) 544-9355 - Fax: (202) 544-9359
Email: paroots02@yahoo.com

25 October 2004

Mr. Bill Van Auken
Socialist Equality Party
P.O. Box 48377
Oak Park, Michigan 48237

AMENDED REQUEST FOR PUBLIC COMMITMENT AND INFORMATION.

Dear Mr. Van Auken:

This is to officially and publicly inform you that we have sent the enclosed letter to Mr. Ed Gillespie, Chairperson of the Republican National Committee formally and publicly requesting that he, the Republican National Convention, especially its Platform Committee, and George W. Bush, their Presidential nominee, publicly reaffirm their commitment to the 1860 Republican National Platform, especially the paragraphs quoted in our letter, and their continued resolve that slavery and the slave trade were crimes against humanity in 1860, and are crimes against humanity today.

We further requested that the Republican Party publicly and immediately commit to give us access to or copies of all records created or obtained by, or under the authority and control of the Republican Party and all Republican office-holders that pertain to, or reference the subjects listed therein. We also formally and publicly requested that he comply in an expedited manner with this Information Request, and that he waive all associated costs.

We advised Mr. Gillespie that we have sent a copy of our Request to President George W. Bush (Republican Party); Mr. Terry McAuliffe and Senator John Kerry (Democratic Party); Mr. David Cobb (Green Party); Mr. Shawn O'Hara and Mr. Ralph Nader (Reform Party/Independent); you (Socialist Equality Party); Mr. Walt Brown (Socialist Party USA); Mr. Roger Calero (Socialist Workers Party) and Mr. John Parker (Workers World Party) requesting you and them to publicly and immediately commit that if you or they are elected President and Commander-in-Chief of the United States Government, you or they will order all departments and agencies under your or their authority and control to comply in full and in an expedited manner with our FOIA Request, and waive all associated fees. We have also released this Request to the media.

We also advised Mr. Gillespie that we have filed the first round of a series of historic and precedent setting FOIA, State Open Records, Public Records, and Information Requests with President Bush, and all of the federal departments and agencies under his authority and control, including, but not limited to the Departments of State, Defense, Treasury, Justice and Interior; and the National Archives and Records Administration.

We expect your positive response to this historic and precedent setting Request within 20 working days. Please be assured that we will exhaust all political remedies. Thank you for your consideration.

Sincerely,
Bob Brown, co-director
Pan-African Roots

Pan-African Roots
1247 E Street SE
Washington, DC 20003
Tel: (202) 544-9355 - Fax: (202) 544-9359
Email: paroots02@yahoo.com

25 October 2004

Mr. Walt Brown
Socialist Party
339 Lafayette Street #303
New York, NY 10012

AMENDED REQUEST FOR PUBLIC COMMITMENT AND INFORMATION.

Dear Mr. Brown:

This is to officially and publicly inform you that we have sent the enclosed letter to Mr. Ed Gillespie, Chairperson of the Republican National Committee formally and publicly requesting that he, the Republican National Convention, especially its Platform Committee, and George W. Bush, their Presidential nominee, publicly reaffirm their commitment to the 1860 Republican National Platform, especially the paragraphs quoted in our letter, and their continued resolve that slavery and the slave trade were crimes against humanity in 1860, and are crimes against humanity today.

We further requested that the Republican Party publicly and immediately commit to give us access to or copies of all records created or obtained by, or under the authority and control of the Republican Party and all Republican office-holders that pertain to, or reference the subjects listed therein. We also formally and publicly requested that he comply in an expedited manner with this Information Request, and that he waive all associated costs.

We advised Mr. Gillespie that we have sent a copy of our Request to President George W. Bush (Republican Party); Mr. Terry McAuliffe and Senator John Kerry (Democratic Party); Mr. David Cobb (Green Party); Mr. Shawn O'Hara and Mr. Ralph Nader (Reform Party/Independent); Mr. Bill Van Auken (Socialist Equality Party); you (Socialist Party USA); Mr. Roger Calero (Socialist Workers Party) and Mr. John Parker (Workers World Party) requesting you and them to publicly and immediately commit that if you or they are elected President and Commander-in-Chief of the United States Government, you or they will order all departments and agencies under your or their authority and control to comply in full and in an expedited manner with our FOIA Request, and waive all associated fees. We have also released this Request to the media.

We also advised Mr. Gillespie that we have filed the first round of a series of historic and precedent setting FOIA, State Open Records, Public Records, and Information Requests with President Bush, and all of the federal departments and agencies under his authority and control, including, but not limited to the Departments of State, Defense, Treasury, Justice and Interior; and the National Archives and Records Administration.

We expect your positive response to this historic and precedent setting Request within 20 working days. Please be assured that we will exhaust all political remedies. Thank you for your consideration.

Sincerely,
Bob Brown, co-director
Pan-African Roots

Pan-African Roots

1247 E Street SE
Washington, DC 20003
Tel: (202) 544-9355 - Fax: (202) 544-9359
Email: paroots02@yahoo.com

25 October 2004

Mr. Roger Calero
Socialist Workers Party
152 West 36th Street #401
New York City, NY 10018

AMENDED REQUEST FOR PUBLIC COMMITMENT AND INFORMATION.

Dear Mr. Calero:

This is to officially and publicly inform you that we have sent the enclosed letter to Mr. Ed Gillespie Chairperson of the Republican National Committee formally and publicly requesting that he, the Republican National Convention, especially its Platform Committee, and George W. Bush, their Presidential nominee, publicly reaffirm their commitment to the 1860 Republican National Platform, especially the paragraphs quoted in our letter, and their continued resolve that slavery and the slave trade were crimes against humanity in 1860, and are crimes against humanity today.

We further requested that the Republican Party publicly and immediately commit to give us access to or copies of all records created or obtained by, or under the authority and control of the Republican Party and all Republican office-holders that pertain to, or reference the subjects listed therein. We also formally and publicly requested that he comply in an expedited manner with this Information Request, and that he waive all associated costs.

We advised Mr. Gillespie that we have sent a copy of our Request to President George W. Bush (Republican Party); Mr. Terry McAuliffe and Senator John Kerry (Democratic Party); Mr. David Cobb (Green Party); Mr. Shawn O'Hara and Mr. Ralph Nader (Reform Party/Independent); Mr. Bill Van Auken (Socialist Equality Party); Mr. Walt Brown (Socialist Party USA); you (Socialist Workers Party) and Mr. John Parker (Workers World Party) requesting you and them to publicly and immediately commit that if you or they are elected President and Commander-in-Chief of the United States Government, you or they will order all departments and agencies under your or their authority and control to comply in full and in an expedited manner with our FOIA Request, and waive all associated fees. We have also released this Request to the media.

We also advised Mr. Gillespie that we have filed the first round of a series of historic and precedent setting FOIA, State Open Records, Public Records, and Information Requests with President Bush, and all of the federal departments and agencies under his authority and control, including, but not limited to the Departments of State, Defense, Treasury, Justice and Interior; and the National Archives and Records Administration.

We expect your positive response to this historic and precedent setting Request within 20 working days. Please be assured that we will exhaust all political remedies. Thank you for your consideration.

Sincerely,
Bob Brown, co-director
Pan-African Roots

Pan-African Roots

1247 E Street SE
Washington, DC 20003
Tel: (202) 544-9355 - Fax: (202) 544-9359
Email: paroots02@yahoo.com

25 October 2004

Mr. John Parker
Workers World Party
55 West 17th Street
New York, NY 10011

AMENDED REQUEST FOR PUBLIC COMMITMENT AND INFORMATION.

Dear Mr. Parker:

This is to officially and publicly inform you that we have sent the enclosed letter to Mr. Ed Gillespie, Chairperson of the Republican National Committee formally and publicly requesting that he, the Republican National Convention, especially its Platform Committee, and George W. Bush, their Presidential nominee, publicly reaffirm their commitment to the 1860 Republican National Platform, especially the paragraphs quoted in our letter, and their continued resolve that slavery and the slave trade were crimes against humanity in 1860, and are crimes against humanity today.

We further requested that the Republican Party publicly and immediately commit to give us access to or copies of all records created or obtained by, or under the authority and control of the Republican Party and all Republican office-holders that pertain to, or reference the subjects listed therein. We also formally and publicly requested that he comply in an expedited manner with this Information Request, and that he waive all associated costs.

We advised Mr. Gillespie that we have sent a copy of our Request to President George W. Bush (Republican Party); Mr. Terry McAuliffe and Senator John Kerry (Democratic Party); Mr. David Cobb (Green Party); Mr. Shawn O'Hara and Mr. Ralph Nader (Reform Party/Independent); Mr. Bill Van Auken (Socialist Equality Party); Mr. Walt Brown (Socialist Party USA); Mr. Roger Calero (Socialist Workers Party) and you (Workers World Party) requesting you and them to publicly and immediately commit that if you or they are elected President and Commander-in-Chief of the United States Government, you or they will order all departments and agencies under your or their authority and control to comply in full and in an expedited manner with our FOIA Request, and waive all associated fees. We have also released this Request to the media.

We also advised Mr. Gillespie that we have filed the first round of a series of historic and precedent setting FOIA, State Open Records, Public Records, and Information Requests with President Bush, and all of the federal departments and agencies under his authority and control, including, but not limited to the Departments of State, Defense, Treasury, Justice and Interior; and the National Archives and Records Administration.

We expect your positive response to this historic and precedent setting Request within 20 working days. Please be assured that we will exhaust all political remedies. Thank you for your consideration.

Sincerely,
Bob Brown, co-director
Pan-African Roots

PART II: FREEDOM OF INFORMATION ACT REQUESTS

The state of slavery is of such a nature, that it is incapable of being introduced on any reasons, moral or political, but only by positive law, which preserves its force long after the reasons, occasion, and time itself from whence it was created, is erased from memory. It is so odious that nothing can be suffered to support it, but positive law. Whatever inconveniences, therefore, may follow from the decision, I cannot say this case is allowed or approved by the law of England; and therefore the black must be discharged.

Somerset vs. Stewart
Lord Mansfield
June, 1772

The King of Britain has waged cruel war against human nature itself, violating it's most sacred rights of life and liberty in the persons of a distant people who never offended him, captivating and carrying them into slavery in another hemisphere, or to incure miserable death in their transportation hither. This piratical warfare, the opprobrium of infidel powers, is the warfare of the Christian king of Great Britain. Determined to keep open a market where MEN should be bought and sold, he has prostituted his negative for suppressing every legislative attempt to prohibit or to restrain this execrable commerce determining to keep open a market where MEN should be bought and sold: and that this assemblage of horrors might want no fact of distinguished die, he is now exciting those very people to rise in arms among us, and to purchase that liberty of which he had deprived them, by murdering the people upon whom he also obtruded them: thus paying off former crimes committed against the liberties of one people, with crimes which he urges them to commit against the lives of another.

Original Draft of the Declaration of Independence
Thomas Jefferson
1776

It appears that American citizens are instrumental in carrying on a traffic in enslaved Africans, equally in violation of the laws of humanity, and in defiance of those of their own country. The same just and benevolent motives which produced the interdiction in force against this criminal conduct, will doubtless be felt in Congress, in devising further means of suppressing the evil.

President James Madison's Report to Congress
1810

Pan-African Roots

1247 E Street SE
Washington, DC 20003
Tel: (202-) 544-9355 - Fax: (202) 544-9359
Email: paroots02@yahoo.com

25 October 2004

Mr. John Carlin and Mr. Walter B. Hill
National Archives and Records Administration
NWCTF - Room 6350
8601 Adelphi Road
College Park, MD 20740

AMENDED FREEDOM OF INFORMATION ACT REQUEST.
Fee Waiver and Expedited Review Request.

Dear Mr. Carlin and Mr. Hill:

Pursuant to the federal Freedom of Information Act (5 U.S.C. Sec. 552) and the Electronic FOIA Amendments of 1996 and 1997 ("EFOIA Amendments" and 5 U.S.C. Sec. 552 (f)(2) (effective March 31, 1997), we request access to and copies of all records created or obtained by, or under the control of the National Archives that relate to, or contain information about:

- The role, operations, and activities of the Continental and Confederation Congresses, the Constitutional Convention, the Senate, the House of Representatives and Joint Committees of Congress in facilitating, prohibiting and combating privateering, slavery and the slave trade, especially the Trans-Atlantic Slave Trade; and slave-like conditions and practices, including colonialism, segregation and apartheid, forced and compulsory labor, racism and racial discrimination, xenophobia and related intolerance.

- Slave, urban and racial disturbances, riots, rebellions and revolts, runaway slaves, fugitives beyond borders, related claims or requests, and demands for restitution and reparations.

- All treaties or agreements, bilateral or multilateral, or diplomatic communications, correspondence, discussions between the United States Government and its Officials (all levels, branches and agencies) and the British, Canadian, French, Spanish, Mexican, or any other government with respect to the above or related subjects.

- All efforts by African People (People of African descent) in the United States, the African Diaspora, or Africa to lodge complaints against the U.S. with the League of Nations, the United Nations, and all other international or regional bodies.

- All governments, agencies (federal, state, county or local), corporations, non-governmental organizations, institutions, churches, families, individuals, or entities, domestic or foreign who participated or invested in, or made profits from the above referenced crimes against humanity; and who owns or benefits from these historical and continuing crimes today, including but not limited to those listed in Appendix A.

We request that you search the Records of the Continental and Confederation Congresses and the Constitutional Convention (Record Group 360); the Records of the United States Senate (Record Group 46); the Records of the United States House of Representatives (Record Group 233); the Records of Joint Committees of Congress (Record Group 128); the Publications of the U.S. Government (Record Group 287); and all other record groups that are relevant or related to this FOIA Request. Additional FOIA Requests will specifically address other branches, departments, and agencies.

We request that you give us access to or copies of the 168 documents that refer to Negroes, the 104 documents that refer to Slaves, the 12 documents that refer to the Slave Trade, the 29 documents that refer to Slavery and the 2 documents that refer to Slave Ships that can be found in the Records of the First and Second Continental Congress which met from 1774 to 1782; and all other documents relevant or related to our Request within all record groups, including but not limited to those that pertain to Foreign Affairs, Fiscal Affairs, Military Affairs, Naval Affairs, Judicial, Justice or Interior Affairs, Commercial or Trade Affair, Treaty or Diplomatic Affairs, and the Postal System.

We also request that you give us access to or copies of the following and all other records that are listed in "American Slavery and the International Slave Trade,"[24] and all other records responsive to our request, including but not limited to:

The Sessional Indexes to the Annals of the Congress, 1789-1813, Volume 1:

- 1st Congress, March 3, 1789 - March 3, 1791, House 1st Session: Importation of certain persons to the United States, p366; Bill deferred, p903; James Madison, slave trade p1185, p1189, p1203.

- House 2nd Session: Page of Virginia, slave trade, p1190, p1203; Parker of Virginia, slave trade, p1184; Philadelphia Quakers petition opposing slave trade, p1182, p1197; Scott of Pennsylvania, slave trade, p1199; Sedgwick of Mass, slave trade, p1187; Petition form Philadelphia/New York Society of Friends, p1182; Debate on motion to refer to petition, p1184; Laid on table, p1191; Benjamin Franklin, petition from Pennsylvania Abolition Society, p1197; Debate concerning petition, p1198; Referred, p1205; Report on the petitions, p1413; Taken up and discussed, p1414; Discussion resumed, p1450, p1466, p1472; Entered into journal, p1472, p1473; Smith of Maryland, slave trade, pp1184, 1188, 1201,1204, 1416, 1453; Stone of Maryland, slave trade, p1185, p1190; Sylvester, New York, slave trade, p1201; Tucker, South Carolina, p1190, p1198; White, Virginia, slave trade, p1189, p1451.

- 2nd Congress, October 24, 1791 - March 2, 1793, House 1st Session: Petition from Warner Mifflin, p728; Debate on petition, p730; Clerk ordered to return petition, p731.

- 3rd Congress, Dec. 2, 1793 - March 3, 1795, Senate 1st Session: Quakers, memorial to abolish slave trade, p36; Quaker petition to suppress trade laid on table, p36; Petition from abolition societies presented, p38; Bill to prohibit trade form from the U.S. to foreign countries, p64; Motion to postpone the bill to next session, p70; Ordered to a third reading, p71; Read third time and passed, p72.

- House 1st Session: Memorial from Abolition Societies, p319; Reported on, ordered to be committed to the Committee of the Whole, p448; Resolution reported and agreed to, p455; French Emigrants from St. Domingo, debate on the subject of relief, p169, p349; committee to bring bill for the support, p352; bill reported, p411; passed, p422; Remarks of Mr. Madison on proposed relief to French emigrants from St. Domingo, p170; Quakers, memorial relative to slave trade, p249; slave trade, petition to abolish, referred to committee, p349; Report of the committee read and committed to Committee of the Whole, p448; committee appointed to bring in a bill for suppression of trade, 455; bill presented, read twice and committed, p469; bill passed, p483.

- 4th Congress, December 7, 1795 - March 3, 1797, House 1st Session: Madison, Mr., On the resolution for caring the Treaty with Great Britain into effect, p975; Negroes, resolution respecting the kidnapping of, resented and agreed to, p1025; Northwestern Territory, petitions relative to certain lots and praying permission to import slaves into the Territory, read and referred, p1171; Slaves, adverse report on slave importation petition, p1349.

---

[24] United States National Archives & Records Administration. Records that pertain to American Slavery and the International Slave Trade: II. Civil Records. General Records of the Department of State (Record Group 59). http://www.archives.gov/research_room/research_topics/slavery_records_civil.html.

- Senate 2nd Session: Fugitives, a committee appointed to report on the measures necessary respecting fugitives from justice and persons escaping from service, p1528;

- House 2nd Session: Kidnapping negroes, consideration of a report made last session on a memorial from Delaware, on the subject of, p1730; Committee of the Whole discharged from the further consideration of he report and a motion made to recommit it, p1735; further consideration of the report postponed, p1737; report recommitted, p1767; another report made, p1895; Manumitted slaves, petition of certain, praying a redress of grievances, p2015; debate on the question of receiving the petition, p2018; petition rejected, p2024; Refugees, report concerning certain, received and referred to Committee of the Whole, p1601; motion to go into consideration of subject, lost consideration of subject, p1683, p1727; committee appointed to bring in a bill, p1730; the bill reported, read twice and committed, p1943; Slaves, debate on the resolution for laying a tax on, p1933; resolution agreed to, p1941; a petition from sundry manumitted slaves, p2015; debate on the question of resolving the petition, p2018; House refuse to receive it, p2024.

- 5th Congress May 15, 1791 - March 3, 1799, Senate, 2nd Session: Quakers, memorial and address from Society of Friends, requesting the attention of the Congress to the oppressed condition of the African race, p475; Withdrawn, p475; Lands and dwelling houses, a bill to provide for the valuation of and for the Numeration of slaves in the United States, received p579; committed, p580; reported, p585; recommended, p587; reported, p588; considered, p594; ordered to third reading, p595; further considered, p596; passed with amendments, p597; the amendment concurred in, p598.

- House 2nd Session: Quakers, a memorial on the condition of the African brethren p656; debate on second reading p658; referred to a select committee p670; report of the committee made p945; committed p946; debated p1032; concurred in p1033; Slaves, a bill to provide for the enumeration of, reported p1869; Taxes, a report recommending a direct tax upon houses, lands and slaves p1569; recommitted p1566; reported p1567; a bill for the assessment p1683; debated p1837; third reading p2061; passed p2066; amended by the Senate p2139; amendment laid on table p2171; taken up and debated p2172; Appendix-Public Acts, 2nd Session, act to enumerate slaves, p37.

- 6th Congress, December 2, 1799 - March 3, 1801, Senate 1st Session: slave trade, motion to revise law prohibiting trade p15; bill for that purpose reported p159; passed p164; amendments received p173; amended p175.

- House 1st Session: Free Blacks, petition of, presented p229; part of it referred p238; other action in reference thereto pp240, 245; Randolph, Mr., remarks of, on the petition of free blacks p221; Slaves, a bill to permit the bringing of, into the Mississippi territory, p700; reported and passed p709; slave trade, a bill to amend the act prohibiting, reported p668; a bill from the Senate for that purpose, received p676; considered pp686,688; amended p697; passed p699; Thatcher, Mr., remarks of, on the petition of the free blacks pp232, 240, 244; Appendix-Public Documents and Acts. Slave Trade bill p1511.

- 7th Congress, December 1801 - March 3, 1803, House 1st Session: Fugitives, a bill respecting, reported p336; debated p423; rejected p425.

- Senate, 2nd Session: Importation of certain persons, a bill to prevent the, received and reported p100; referred and reported p101; passes p207.

- 8th Congress, October 17, 1803 - March 3, 1805, Senate 1st Session: Abolition of slavery. A petition of the American Convention presented and read p 238.

- House 1st Session: Mr. Bedinger, of Kentucky, remarks of, on a resolution in regards to slaves p993, p997; Mr. Elmer, of New Jersey, on slaves p1034; Mr. Eppes, of Virginia, on slaves p1028;

Mr. Findley, of Pennsylvania, on slaves p999; Mr. Holland, of North Carolina, on slaves p1007; Mr. Huger, of South Carolina, on slaves pp1004, 1016; Importation of slaves, resolution respecting the, Offered p820; Debated pp991, 1012; Adopted p1020; Bill in pursuance presented p1021; Postponed p1036; Mr. Jackson, of Virginia, on slaves p1031; Mr. Lowndes, of South Carolina, on a resolution respecting slaves, pp991,1024; Mr. Lucas, of Pennsylvania, remarks of, on a resolution in relation to slaves p1008; Messages, one respecting slaves imported into New Orleans p1123; Mr. Moore, of Tennessee, remarks of, on a resolution respecting slaves p1003; Mr. Rodney, of Delaware, remarks on the importation of slaves, p1132; Mr. Stanton, of Rhode Island, on a resolution respecting slaves, p1026; Yeas and Nays, on the bill respecting slaves, p1036.

- Senate, 2nd Session: Quakers, a petition from the people called, relating to the African race, received and read by the yeas and nays, p39.

- House 2nd Session: Slaves, resolution offered to impose a tax on the importation of, p1189; Letter presented from the Government of Massachusetts relative to the importation of, p1222; a memorial on the subject of importation of, p1596.

- 9th Congress, December 2, 1805 - March 3, 1807, Senate 1st Session: Mr. Adams, objections of, to the proposition to suspend commercial intercourse with St. Domingo, p29; Bonaparte, proclamation of, to the inhabitants of St. Domingo; Craft, Gershom, petition of, praying the abolition of slavery, read, p92; Mr. Hillhouse, speech of, suspending trade with St. Domingo, p35; Le Clerc, Captain General, proclamation of, to the inhabitants of St. Domingo, p122; Mr. Logan, remarks of, on asking leave to bring in a bill to suspend commercial intercourse with St. Domingo, p26; Mr. Mitchell, speech of, on the St. Domingo bill, p31; St. Domingo, notice of a bill to suspend commercial intercourse with, p20; Slavery, a memorial respecting the abolition of, read, p92; Slaves, leave ask for a bill to prohibit the importation of, after January 1, 1808, p20; Question of the leave ask, taken by yeas and nays and granted, p21; Bill in pursuance thereof, presented and read, p21; Read a second time and indefinitely postponed, p21; A resolution, to amend the Constitution on the same subject, postponed to the next session, p232; Mr. White, speech of, on the St. Domingo bill, p117; Yeas and Nays, on the amendments to the bill suspending commercial intercourse with St. Domingo, p83; On amendments to the bill suspending trade with St. Domingo, p114.

- House 1st Session: Abolition Convention, memorial of the American, read and referred to a select committee p445; Alston, Mr., remarks of, on the taxing the importation of slaves pp349, 360; Bidwell, Mr., remarks on the bill to tax the importation of slaves p435; Bedinger, Mr., on the resolution to tax the importation of slaves p371; Broom, Mr., speech of, on the taxing of the importation of slaves pp365, 373; Clark, Mr., remarks on the resolution to tax the importation of slaves pp347, 358; Clay, Joseph, remarks on the bill imposing a tax on the importation of slaves p438; Crownshield, Mr., remarks of, on the bill to prohibit intercourse with St. Domingo p510; Dana, Mr., remarks of, on the resolution to tax the importation of slaves pp349, 359, 363, 373; on the bill imposing a tax on the importation of slaves p439; on the bill to prohibit intercourse with St. Domingo p512; Dawson, Mr., remarks on the resolution to tax the importation of slaves(with a motion to postpone) p372; Early, Mr., on the St. Domingo bill p514; Elmer, Mr., on the St. Domingo bill p514; Ely, Mr., on the St. Domingo bill p515; Eppes, Mr., remarks on the St. Domingo bill p515; Fisk, Mr., remarks of, on the resolution to tax the importation of slaves p351; France, documents showing the complaints made by, against our commerce with St. Domingo p1216; Jackson, Mr., remarks on the bill to tax the importation of slaves p443.

- Macon, Mr., on the resolution to tax the importation of slaves p360; Marion, Mr., on the resolution to lay a tax on the importation of slaves p347; Moore, Mr., T., remarks of, on the resolution to tax the importation of slaves p374; Nelson, Roger, Mr., remarks of, on the resolution

remarks of, on the bill to prohibit the importation of slaves p240; Elliot, Mr., remarks of, on the bill to suspend the non-importation act p120; Early, Mr., introductory of a motion to amend the bill to prohibit the importation of slaves p477; Elmer, Mr., remarks of, on the bill to prohibit the importation of slaves p235; Ely, Mr., remarks of, on the bill to prohibit the importation of slaves pp179, 232, 239; Fisk, Mr., remarks of, on Mr. Bidwell's amendment to the bill to prohibit the importation of slaves p224; Goldsborough, Mr., remarks of, on the modifications reported by the conferees on the slave bill p626; Hastings, Mr., remarks of, on the bill to prohibit the importation of slaves p227; Holland, Mr., remarks of, on the bill to prohibit the importation of slaves p239; Kelly, Mr., remarks of, on the bill to prohibit the importation of slaves p184; Lloyd, Edward, remarks of, on the bill to prohibit the importation of slaves p236.

- Macon, Mr., remarks on, on the bill to prohibit the importation of slaves pp172, 176,178, 225; Marion, Mr., remarks of, on the bill to prohibit the importation of slaves 478; Mosely, Mr., remarks of, on the bill to prevent the importation of slaves p233; Olin, Mr., remarks of, on the bill to prohibit the importation of slaves p237; Pitkin, Mr., remarks of, on the bill to prohibit the importation of slaves p185; Quiney, Mr., remarks of, on the bill to prevent the importation of slaves pp176, 183, 297; Randolph, John, against receding from the ninth amendment to the bill to prohibit the importation of slaves p528; Slaves, a bill presented to prohibit the importation of, read twice and committed p151; debate on the bill p167, 180; recommitted to a select committee p189; said committee reported an amendatory bill which was read twice and committed p190; debate on the same p200, 220; the question taken on Mr. Bidwell's amendment and lost p228; several amendments were made and reported to the House p228; debate on the amendments p 231; several amendments agreed to p244; Mr. Sloan moves another amendment, which is lost p254; Mr. Early moved an amendment, which was agreed to p264; Mr. Bidwell offered a proviso, which was negatived p266; Mr. Pitkin's amendment adopted and the bill ordered to a third reading p267; read a third time and a motion to recommit to a select committee p270; the bill recommitted, as moved p273; said committee reported another amendatory bill, which was twice read and committed to the Committee of the Whole p373; Mr. Early moved an amendment p477.

- A bill from the Senate on the same subject, read and committed p427; All the bills considered and the Senate bill reported with amendments p481; the amendments agreed to and the bill further amended p484; ordered to a third reading p485; read a third time and passed as amended p486; returned from the Senate with disagreement to the ninth amendment p502; the House insist and the conference agreed upon p528; the Senate agreed to the modifications reported by the committee of conference p621; those modifications debated p626; and agreed to p627; Mr. Randolph presented an explanatory bill on the subject, which was twice read and committed to the Committee of the Whole p637; Slave Trade, a memorial on the subject of the p992; Sloan, Mr., on the bill to prohibit the importation of slaves pp169, 175, 184, 226, 231, 478; Smilie, Mr., on the Senate's amendment to the bill to prevent the importation of slaves pp232, 634; Southard, Mr., remarks of, on the bill to prohibit the importation of slaves p226; Stanton, Mr., remarks of, on the bill to prohibit the importation of slaves p240; Tallmadge, Mr., remarks of, on the bill to prohibit the slave trade p232; Varnum, Mr., remarks of, on the bill to prohibit the importation of slaves p243; Yeas and Nays - on Mr. Bidwell's amendment to the slave importation bill p264; Public Act - An Act to prohibit the importation of slaves into any port or place within the jurisdiction of the United States, from and after the first day of January, in the year of our Lord one thousand eight hundred and eight p1266.

- 10th Congress, October 26, 1807 - March 3, 1809, House 1st Session: District of Columbia, a petition relating to the removal of slaves from one country to another in the, was referred to the same committee p1840; Public Act - An Act making an appropriation to supply a deficiency in an appropriation for the support of the Government during the present, year and making an appropriation for defraying the expenses incident to the valuation of homes, lands and the enumeration of slaves within the United States.

- House 2nd Session: Clarkson's History of Slavery, presented for deposit in the Library of Congress p 1451; Indiana Territory, a letter from the President of the Legislative Council of, protesting against the admission of slavery in and other papers, read p 501.

- 11th Congress, May 22, 1809 - March 3, 1811, Senate 1st and 2nd Sessions: District of Columbia, a bill to authorize the removal of slaves from one part to another of the, read first and second time and referred to a select committee p531; Free Negroes, Mr. Brent gave notice of a bill to prevent the future emigration of, to the District of Columbia p595; Penalties and forfeitures, a bill to remit certain, read, etc. p36; Read a second time, amended and ordered to a third reading p37; Read a third time and postponed p38; Referred to a select committee p39; Reported with amendments p41; Agreed to, read a third time and passes as amended p43; Returned from the House of Representatives with amendments p48; Which were concurred in p49; Mr. Lloyd gave notice of a bill to authorize the Secretary of the Treasury in certain cases to remit the, on vessels arriving from France, etc. p43; Slaves, the importation of, on motion of Mr. Giles a committee was appointed to inquire into the expediency of providing for the remission of penalties, etc., for violation of the act to prohibit p34; Yeas and Nays, on amending the bill to authorize the removal of slaves from one part of the District of Columbia to another part p585.

- House 1st and 2nd Session: District of Columbia, a bill to authorize the removal of slaves from one part to another of the, read twice and committed p783; Reported without amendment and ordered to a third reading p1215; Read a third time and passed p1218; Lindsey, Thomas, the petition of, praying restitution of his vessel, condemned for bringing a French family with their slaves from the island of Cuba, etc. p322; Penalties and Forfeitures, a bill from the Senate for the remission of certain p380; Read twice, discussed, read a third time and passed p465; So much of the Message as relates to, involuntarily incurred by infractions of the non-intercourse act, referred to the Committee of Commerce and Manufactures p688; On motion of Mr. Montgomery, the said committee was instructed to inquire into the expediency of extending the benefits of the act for the remission of, to cases of expulsion from the Island of Cuba p706; A report from said committee on several individual cases, by name p2209.

- Senate 3rd Session.

- House 3rd Session: Importation, Mr. Cheves laid before the House two letters suggesting amendments to the act to prohibit the, of slaves, referred to the Committee on Commerce and Manufactures p431; Slave Trade, so much of the President's Message as relates to the laws interdicting the, was referred to the Committee of Commerce and Manufactures p387.

- 12th Congress November 4, 1811 - March 3, 1813, Senate 1st Session.

- Senate 2nd Session: Abolition of Slavery, Mr. Bradley presented the memorial of the Pennsylvania Society for the, read p87.

- House 2nd Session: Abolition of Slavery, Mr. Milnor presented a memorial of the Pennsylvania Society for the, etc., referred to a select committee p1074; Report of said committee p1090.

The Sessional Indexes to the Annals of the Congress, 1813-1844; Vol. 2:

- 13th Congress May 24, 1813 – March 3, 1815, Senate 1st Session, House 1st Session.

- Senate 2nd Session: Cuffee, Paul, Mr. Gore presented the petition of, referred p569; A bill allowing, to depart with vessel and cargo for Sierra Leone, read p570; Read a second time p572; Ordered to a third reading p601; Read a third time and passed p602; Yeas and nays, on the bill to permit the final departure of Paul Cuffee, etc. p601; House 2nd Session: Cuffee, Paul (a colored man,) Mr. Wheaton presented the petition of, which was read and referred to the Committee of Commerce and Manufactures p861; A bill from the Senate to provide for the departure of, with vessel, etc., to; Sierra Leone p1150; Read twice and referred p1195; Report of the committee thereon ordered to be printed p1265; The third reading of the bill negatived p1881; Property captured or destroyed, etc., a bill authorizing payment for, read twice, etc. p806; Reported without amendment and recommitted p2008; Ordered to lie on the table p2025; Taken up and amended p2028; Laid over by general consent p2029; Property Impressed, etc., the Committee of Claims were instructed to inquire into the expediency of allowing full value to the owners of p806; A bill to provide for paying for, read twice p1696; Ordered to a third reading p1933; Read a third time and passed p1934.

- Senate 3rd Session: Ghent, the President transmitted communications from the Commissioners at p118; Negroes, traffic in, by the enemy, on motion of Mr. Goldsborough, the President of the United States was requested to lay before the Senate the proof, if any, of a, alluded to in the instructions to the Plenipotentiaries p31; Negroes Captured, A Message from the President, in relation to the sale of, by the enemy, read and ordered to be printed p288; Documents accompanying the said Message p289; Property Lost or Destroyed, a bill from the House of Representatives to authorize payment for, read p202; Read a second time p207; Referred to a committee p214; Reported with amendments p281; Read a third time and passed as amended p292; The House of Representatives agree and disagree p298; Bill indefinitely postponed p299.

- House 3rd Session: Ghent Commissioners, the President transmitted the last communication received from the, ordered to be printed and referred p701; The President also transmitted copies of the instructions given to the, as to the basis of a Treaty of Peace p1285; Instructions to Plenipotentiaries, the President communicated copies of the, which were ordered, with certain exceptions, to be printed p393; Payment for Property lost, etc., a bill authorizing, twice read p1111; Private Property lost, etc., on motion of Mr. Hall, the Committee of Claims was instructed to inquire into the expediency of providing for payment of p326; Treaty of Peace, copy of the, as finally agreed upon and signed p1409.

- 14th Congress December 4, 1815 - March 3, 1817, Senate 1st Session: Abolition of Slavery, Mr. Roberts presented the memorial of the American Convention for promoting the, read and referred to a select committee p147; The committee discharged from consideration of the subject p326 Property lost, etc., a bill from the House of Representatives, to authorize payment for, read p32; Read a third time and referred p34; Reported with amendments p95; Amendments read and recommitted p103; Reported, with other amendments p124; Discussed and further amended p205; Ordered to a third reading p207; Read a third time and passed as amended p210; The House of Representatives agreed with amendments, which were concurred in p257.

- House 1st Session: Abolition of Slavery, Mr. Sergeant presented the American Convention for the, referred p1068; Kentucky Abolition Society, Mr. Clark presented the petition of the, referred p451; Adverse report concurred in p691; Loss of property during the War, on motion of Mr. Johnson, of Kentucky, the Committee of Claims were instructed to inquire into the expediency of liquidating the claims of citizens for the p382; Property lost, captured, or destroyed by the enemy, a bill to authorize payment for, twice read and committed p389; Reported with amendments p401; Ordered to a third reading p407; Read a third time and passed p409; Returned from the Senate with amendments p1224; Referred to the Committee of Claims p1238; Reported with amendments p1289; Considered and concurred in p1300; Removal of Slaves into the District of Columbia, on motion of Mr. Lewis, the Committee on the District of Columbia were instructed to inquire into the expediency of equalizing the laws respecting the, from Virginia and Maryland p736; Traffic in Slaves, in the District of Columbia, on motion of Mr. Randolph a committee was appointed to inquire into the existence of a p1117; Mr. Randolph asked and obtained leave for the committee to send for persons and papers p1127; Report of said committee laid on the table

on the motion to suspend the act concerning property lost, etc. p293; Hopkinson, Mr., remarks of, on the motion to suspend the act concerning property, etc. p290; Hulbert, Mr., remarks of, on the motion to suspend the act concerning property, etc. pp286, 291; On the bill to amend the act for payment for property, etc. p440; Johnson, Richard M., speech of, on the motion to suspend the act paying for property, etc. pp283, 294; On the bill to amend the said act pp372, 375, 425, 438; Manumission Society of Tennessee, the Speaker presented the petition of the, referred p769; Persons of Color, a bill from the Senate concerning the transportation of p996; Read twice and referred p1019; Reported without amendment p1021; Pitkin, Timothy, of Connecticut, remarks of, on the motion to suspend the act for payment for property, etc. p285; Property Lost, etc., a Message from the President, recommending a revision of the act authorizing payment for, referred p245; Report, together with a bill to amend the act referred to, twice read, etc. p299; Read a third time and passed p462; Returned from the Senate with amendments p1028; Referred to the Committee of Claims p1035; Said committee recommended agreement p1040; To which the House consented p1051.

- Papers communicated in relation to p1211; Randolph, John, of Virginia, speech of, on the motion to suspend the act concerning lost property pp289, 292; On the bill to amend the act paying for property lost, etc. p386; Robertson, Mr., of Louisiana, remarks of on the motion to suspend the act paying for property lost, etc. p282; Ross, John, of Pennsylvania, remarks of, on the motion to suspend the property act p288; On the bill to amend the property act; Sheffey, Daniel, of Virginia, speech of, on the bill to amend the property act p381; Taul, Mr., of Kentucky, remarks of, on the motion to suspend the property act p282; Traffic in Negro Slaves, Mr. Pickering presented the petition of the Society of Friends on the subject of, referred p312; Mr. Hopkinson also presented similar petitions from several societies p442; Wilde, Mr., remarks of, on the bill to amend the property act p439; Wright, Mr., speech of, on the motion to suspend the property act p286; Yancey, Mr., remarks of, on the provisions of the act paying for property lost, etc. p278; On the motion to suspend the said act p280; Yeas and Nays, on amending the bill to amend the property act p441, 445; Public Acts and Resolutions; Property lost, etc., an act to amend the act authorizing payment for 1345.

- 15th Congress December 1, 1817 - March 3, 1819, Senate 1st Session: African slave trade, Mr. Burrill submitted a resolution on the subject of p71; Agreed to and resolution referred p108; Burrill, Mr., remarks of, on his resolution concerning the African slave trade pp74, 76; Speech of, in support of the same p95; Campbell, George W., of Tennessee, remarks of, on the resolution respecting the African slave trade p76; Introduction of Slaves, a bill in addition to the act to prohibit the, read p307; Read a second time p312; Ordered to a third reading p351; Read a third time and passed p358; Returned from the House of Representatives with amendments p378; Read and concurred in p379; King, Mr. Speech of, on the resolution respecting the African slave trade p75, 87; On the motion to strike out the latter clause of the same p105; Lacock, Mr., speech of, on the resolution respecting the African slave trade p107; Morril, Mr., speech of, on the resolution concerning the African slave trade p102; On the fugitive slave bill p242; Slaves, Mr. Roberts submitted a resolution respecting the introduction of, into the United States p266; Agreed to and referred to a select committee p267; Smith, Mr., speech of, on the Fugitive Slave bill p231; Traffic in Negroes, Mr. Goldsborough presented a memorial of the Society of Friends on the subject of, referred p61; Transportation of Persons of Color, a bill respecting the, read p172; Read a second time p174; Ordered to a third reading p261; Read a third time and passed p263; Troup, George M., of Georgia, remarks of, on Mr. Burrill's resolution relating to the African slave trade pp74, 75; Yeas and Nays, on striking out part of the resolution on the African slave trade p108; Yeas and Nays on amending the Fugitive Slave bill pp225, 259; Yeas and Nays, on indefinite postponement of the Fugitive Slave bill p258; On the final passage of the same p262.

- House 1st Session: Abolition Society of Kentucky, Mr. Trimble presented the petition of the, referred p517; Mr. Sergeant presented a similar petition from Pennsylvania, also referred p829; Adams, Mr., of Massachusetts, remarks of, on the Fugitive Slave bill p837; African Colonization, Mr. Mercer's report on the subject of p1771; American Colonization Society, on motion of Mr. Mercer, the committee on the memorial of the, were instructed to inquire into the expediency of more effectual provision for prohibiting the African slave trade p528; Baldwin, Henry, of Pennsylvania, remarks of, on the Fugitive Slave bill p828; Clagett, Mr., of New Hampshire, speech of, on the Fugitive Slave bill p825; Clay, Henry, remarks of, on the Fugitive Slave bill p828; Cobb, Mr., of Georgia, speech of, on the Fugitive Slave bill p828; Fugitive Slaves, on motion of Mr. Pindall, a committee was appointed to inquire into the expediency of making further provision on the subject of p446; A bill to amend the act for the recovery of read twice and referred p513; Reported, with amendments p829; Ordered to a third reading p831.

- Read a third time and passed p840; Returned from the Senate, with amendments p1339; Read and ordered to lie on the table p1393; Holmes, Mr., remarks of, on the Fugitive Slave bill pp828, 838; Livermore, Mr., remarks of, on the fugitive Slave bill pp830, 837; Maclay, William P., remarks of, on the Fugitive Slave bill p830; Manumission and Colonization Society of North Carolina, Mr. Settle presented the petition of the, referred p533; Mr. Blount presented the petition of a similar society of Tennessee, referred p799; Mason, Mr., of Massachusetts, remarks of, on the Fugitive Slave bill p838; Mercer, Chas. F., of Virginia, remarks of, on his resolution respecting African slave trade p518; Persons of Color, Mr. Mercer presented the petition of a Society of Friends, concerning p488; Pindall, Mr., speech of, on the Fugitive Slave bill pp827, 834; Rhea, Mr., remarks of, on the Fugitive Slave bill pp834, 838; Sergeant, John, of Pennsylvania, speech of, on the Fugitive Slave bill p830; Slavery, Mr. Livermore submitted an amendment to the Constitution on the subject of p1675; Read and the question of consideration negatived p1676; Slaves, a bill from the Senate to prohibit the importation of p1715; Read twice p1718; Ordered to a third reading p1749; Amended, read the third time and passed p1744; A bill prohibiting the introduction of, into the United States, twice read p650; Mr. Middleton offered a substitute, which was agreed to and ordered to be printed and referred p1662; Reported with amendments p1720; Smith, Samuel, of Maryland, remarks of, on the Fugitive Slave bill p830; Storrs, Mr., of New York remarks of, on the Fugitive Slave bill pp828, 839; Whitman, Mr., remarks of, on the Fugitive Slave bill p839; Williams, Mr., of Connecticut, remarks of, on the Fugitive Slave bill p839; Yeas and Nays, on the third reading of the Fugitive Slave bill p831; Yeas and Nays, on considering the Senate's amendments to the Fugitive Slave bill p1716.

- Senate 2nd Session: Abolition of Slavery, Mr. Roberts presented the memorial of the American Convention for the promotion of the, referred p85; Columbian United Abolition Society, Mr. Noble presented the petition of the p161; Importation of Slaves, Mr. Eaton submitted a resolution concerning the p68; Agreed to and a committee appointed p69; Mr. Lacock presented a petition of a number of citizens on New York and Pennsylvania, praying a revision of the act relating to the, referred p77; Mr. Lacock also presented a similar petition from Carlisle, referred p88; Mr. Lacock presented another petition on the same subject, referred p90; Mr. Hunter, the same from inhabitants of Newport, referred p97; Mr. Daggett, the same from Connecticut, referred pp113, 197; Mr. Burrill, the same from Massachusetts, referred p162; Mr. Dickerson, the same from New Jersey, referred p167; Mr. Roberts also presented a similar petition, referred pp173, 189; Mr. Wilson, the same from New Jersey, referred p176.

- A bill supplemental to the act to prohibit the, read p213; Read a second time p224; The bill amended p269; Manumission of Slaves, Mr. Sanford presented the memorial of New York Society for the, referred p83; Restitution of Slaves, Mr. Fromentin submitted a resolution requesting information of President of the United States, touching the execution of the first article of the treaty with Great Britain, in relation to the p21; Agreed to and committee appointed to wait on the President p23; A Message from the President in reply p36; Runaways, on motion of Mr. Forsyth, the Committee on the District of Columbia were instructed to inquire into the expediency of annulling the laws regulating the seizure of persons of color suspected to be p208; Said committee discharged p278; slave trade, a bill from the House of Representatives in addition to the act to prohibit the, read p279; Read a second time and referred p280; Reported without amendment; read the third time and passed p280; Slaves impressed into the public Service, Mr. Macon submitted a resolution concerning p174; Agreed to and referred to a committee p177; The committee discharged p278; Transportation of persons of color, etc., a bill respecting the, read p58; Wilson, James J., of New Jersey, attended remarks of, on a resolution to instruct the committee on the slave trade p75; Yeas and Nays, on indefinite postponement of the bill respecting the transportation of persons of color p252.

- House 2nd Session: Abolition of Slavery, Mr. Sergeant presented the memorial of the American convention for the, referred p430; American Colonization Society, the Speaker presented a letter from a committee of the, referred p721; Colston, Edward, of Virginia, remarks of, on Mr. Linn's resolutions concerning the migration of slaves p337; Fugitive Slaves, on motion of Mr. Pindall, a committee was appointed to inquire into the expediency of providing, by law, for the delivering up of, etc. p546; A bill to that effect read twice p551; Importation of Slaves, on motion of Mr. Middleton, the bill of last session supplementary to the act to prohibit the, was referred p320; Mr. Hostetter, of Pennsylvania, presented a petition, on the subject of the, was referred p320; Linn, John, remarks of, on his resolution concerning the migration of slaves p336; Manumission of Slaves, Mr. Irving presented the memorial of the New York Society for promoting the, referred p430; Referred to the Committee of Foreign Affairs p540.

- That committee discharged and subject referred to Committee of the Whole p551; Mercer, Charles F., of Virginia, attended remarks of, on his resolution relative to the slave trade p442; Poindexter, George, of Mississippi, remarks of, on the resolution concerning the migration of slaves p336; Slaves, appointment of a select committee, on the unlawful introduction of p293; slave trade, two resolutions by Mr. Mercer relative to the, agreed to p442; A letter from the Secretary of the Navy transmitting copies of all instructions to commanders, on the subject of the p515; Ditto from the Secretary of the Treasury, with a statement of vessels seized and condemned under the laws prohibiting the p662; A bill in addition to the act to prohibit the, read twice p540; Ordered to a third reading p1431; Read the third time and passed p1433; Returned from the Senate with amendments and concurred in p1435; Transportation of Persons of Color, a bill from the Senate respecting the p1393; Read twice and referred p1402; Reported without amendment p1415; Transportation of Slaves, Mr. Linn, of New Jersey, submitted a resolution relative to p336; Considered and negatived p337; Public Acts and Resolutions; slave trade, an act in addition to the acts prohibiting the p2544.

- 16th Congress December 6, 1819 - March 3, 1821, Senate 1st Session: Abolition of Slavery, Mr. Roberts presented the memorial of the American Convention for promoting the, read p24; American Colonization Society, Mr. Pinckney presented the memorial of thep360; Referred to a select committee p460; Barbour, James, President pro tem., on the amendment restricting slavery p314; Burrill, James, of Rhode Island, on the resolutions respecting the slave trade p697; Edwards, Ninian, of Illinois, speech of, on the motion of Mr. Roberts to exclude slavery, etc. p187; Elliot, John, of Georgia, speech of, on Mr. Roberts' slavery resolution p129; Lowrie, Walter, of Pennsylvania, speech of, on the restriction of slavery in Missouri p201; Maine and Missouri, Mr. Thomas offered an amendment to the Missouri branch of the bill, prohibiting slavery north of latitude 36' 30" excepting within the limits of said proposed State p424.

- Mr. T. withdrew said amendment and moved a new section, to the bill p427; Which new section was adopted p428; The bill thus amended and further amended in its title, was read the third time and passed p430; The House of Representatives refused to receive the amendment of the Senate

Proceedings and memorial of the people of Newport p2452; Proceedings and memorial of the people of Hartford p2457; slave trade, a Message from the President of the United States in relation to the, referred p741; Mr. Cuthbert submitted a resolution concerning the p925; Agreed to and referred to a committee p926; A joint resolution authorizing the President to negotiate with foreign Powers on the means of abolishing the African, read twice p2216; Read the third time and passed p2236; Suppression of the slave trade, appointment of a select committee on the p707; Paylor, John W., of New York, remarks of, on his second resolution restricting slavery p802; Yeas and Nays, on laying on the table the resolution respecting the slave trade p2236.

- Senate 2nd Session: African slave trade, a list of vessels that imported slaves into Charleston from 1804 to 1807, inclusive p73; Introduction of Slaves, a resolution was adopted requesting the President of the United States to communicate what proceedings have been had in relation to officers of Government, charged with being concerned in the p380; Restriction of Slavery, Mr. Sanford presented a resolution of the Legislature of New York concerning the, read p23; Mr. Tichenor presented a similar resolution of the Legislature of Vermont, read p78.

- House 2nd Session: African slave trade, Mr. Mercer submitted a resolution on the subject of the p476; Agreed to and a committee appointed to present it to the President p476; A Message, transmitting the report of the Secretary of State, in reply p743; Another Message, with documents omitted in the first pp865, 1469; Report of the select committee on the p1164; The resolution reported by that committee p1071; Mr. Meigs submitted a resolution on the subject of the p1170; Fugitive Slaves, Mr. Brown presented a resolution of the legislature of Kentucky on the subject of, which, being decided by the Speaker to be informal, was withdrawn p941; slave trade, appointment of a select committee on the p441; Suppression of the slave trade, documents relating to the negotiations of the Government for the pp1313, 1469.

- 17th Congress December 3, 1821 - March 3, 1823, Senate 1st Session: Abolition of Slavery and the slave trade, Mr. Lowrie presented the memorial of the Pennsylvania Society for promoting the, read and referred p137; American Colonization Society, Mr. Pinckney presented the memorial of the, read p178.

- House 1st Session: Abolition of Slavery, Mr. Rhea presented a petition for the, in the District of Columbia, referred p709; American Colonization Society, memorial of the, presented by Mr. Colden and referred p922; Colden, C., remarks of, on the bill for the rendition of fugitive slaves pp1379, 1380; Fairfax and Loudon Counties, Virginia, Mr. Mercer presented a memorial from, on the suppression of the slave trade, referred p824; La Pensee, French slave ship, Mr. Gorham submitted a resolution calling on the President for a copy of proceedings in the case of the p1612; Adopted p1617; Message, etc., in reply p1743; slave trade, so much of the President's annual Message as relates to the, referred to a select committee p527.

- Mr. Sergeant presented the memorial of the Pennsylvania Society for suppression of the, referred p747; Mr. Colden presented a similar petition from New York, referred p1150 A report from the committee on the p1535; Slaves, Mr. Wright presented a resolution of the General Assembly of Maryland, complaining of the protection afforded by citizens of Pennsylvania to absconding p553; Mr. Wright submitted a resolution for appointing a committee to inquire into the expediency of making provisions for the reclamation of, agreed to p557; A bill to provide for the reclamation of, reported, read twice and committed p710; Debate on the bill p1379; Bill recommitted to a select committee p1415; Reported with amendments and laid on the table p1444.

- Senate 2nd Session.

- House 2nd Session: Manumission Society of Tennessee, Mr. Rhea presented the memorial of the eighth convention of the, respecting the situation of colored persons in the United States, referred p642; Mercer, Charles F., of Virginia, speech of, on his resolution relative to the slave trade p1147; slave trade, Mr. Taylor moved to refer so much of the President's Message as relates to the suppression of the, to a select committee p331; Debate thereon p332; Agreed to p333; Appointment of the committee p333; Mr. Mercer submitted a resolution requesting the President to enter into negotiations with the several maritime Powers for the abolition of the African p928; Called up and debated p1147; Agreed to p1155; Wright, Robert, of Maryland, speech of, on the suppression of the slave trade p1153; Public Documents, Acts, etc; American Vessels, a memorial of the masters of certain, respecting colored seamen p1305.

- 18th Congress 1st Session December 1, 1823 - May 27, 1824, Senate 1st Session: Rawle, W., Mr. Lowrie presented the petition of, praying the abolition of slavery in the District of Columbia, read and laid on the table p375.

- House 1st Session: Amendment to the Constitution, Mr. Abbot submitted a resolution for, in relation to persons of color, read twice p1399; Florida, Mr. Call presented a petition from the inhabitants of East, in relation to a right claimed by Indians to certain Negroes, referred p1756; The committee discharged and the petition referred to the Secretary of War p1792; Slavery, Mr. Breck presented a petition from the "Pennsylvania Society "praying the abolition of, referred p1756; The committee discharged p1792; The petition laid on the table p1792; slave trade, so much of the President's Message as relates to the African, referred to a select committee p800; Mr. Mercer submitted a resolution calling for information respecting negotiations with foreign governments in relation to the p1204; A message in reply, received p1870; Referred p2090; A resolution from the Legislature of Ohio respecting the abolition of the, referred p1428; The committee discharged and the resolution laid on the table p1460; The committee on the suppression of the, instructed to inquire into the expediency of amending the existing laws for the abolition of the trade p1808; A bill respecting the, reported and read twice p2397; A copy of the bill p2397; Public Documents, Acts, etc; Slave Trade sundry documents in relation to the African p3001; Articles of a convention for the suppression of the African p3022.

- Sessional Indexes to the Register of Debates in the U.S. Congress, 1824 - 1837; Vol. 3:

- 18th Congress 2nd Session December 6, 1824 - March 4, 1825, Senate 2nd Session: Public Lands, resolution appropriating them as a fund for the emancipation of slaves; laid on the table, p625; Counter Resolution pp696, 697; slave trade, resolution for printing the report of the committee on the, p625; Debate thereon, pp625-628; Adopted p628; Resolution recommending negotiations for the abolition of the, p697; Rejected p736; On the same subject, deprecating the exposure of our vessels to be searched p739; Index to the Appendix; Act, (British,) for the Suppression of the Slave Trade pp18, 19; Convention for the Suppression of the slave trade. See slave trade. Message of the President of the United States transmitting additional documents on the Slave Trade p18; Reports of committee of the H. of R. on the slave trade, pp20-21, 73-75; slave trade, convention between the United States and Great Britain for the suppression of the, pp12-14; British counter project pp14-16; Proceedings of the Senate thereon pp17, 19, 21, 22; Messages relative to the p18, 19, 20; British act for the suppression of the pp18-19; Reports of committees of the H. of R. on the, pp20-21, 73-75; Yeas and Nays in the Senate on the convention for suppressing the Slave Trade pp21-22.

- 19th Congress December 5, 1825-March 4, 1827, Senate 1st Session: Negro Slavery in South America, call for information on p113; Motion to postpone p115; Debate thereon, pp115-132; Resolution laid on the table p132.

- House 1st Session: Appropriation, debate on agency for captured Africans, pp1346-1348; Amendment and debate thereon, pp1347, 1348, 1352-1354; Adopted p1354; Slaves in Florida, debate on call for information on Spanish claims to certain, pp2008, 2009; slave trade, debate on authorizing committee to send for persons and papers pp1491, 1492; Committee reports p2688;

Debate on resolution, pp2689, 2690; Amendment p2689; Negatived p2690; Resolution adopted p2690; Index to the Appendix; Message (annual) of the President U.S. on the suppression of the slave trade p38; Report on suppressing the slave trade p38; slave trade, message and documents relative to the convention for suppressing the, pp38, 39.

- Senate 2nd Session: Colonization Society, debate on presenting memorial of the, pp289-296; Papers withdrawn p296; Debate on referring memorial pp318-334; Laid on the table p334.

- House 2nd Session: Deported slaves, bill reported for adjusting claims for p836; Preamble and resolution p878; Debate thereon, pp878-881; Amendments pp879, 881; Debate continued pp894, 895; Resolution laid on the table p895; Free people of color, resolution concerning an appropriation for the transportation of p635; House refuses to consider it p636; Slave Convention. See Deported Slaves; Slavery in the District of Columbia, debate on printing a memorial concerning, pp1099-1101; Negatived p1101.

- 20th Congress December 3, 1827-March 4, 1829, Senate 1st Session: Claims of South Carolina for slaves, the bill supplementary to an act of 1827, for the adjustment of claims of persons entitled to indemnification under the Treaty of Ghent, was taken up p406; Ordered to be engrossed p411; Bill returned from the house with an amendment, which was concurred with p787; Debate commences p406; slave trade, the bill making appropriations for the suppression of the slave trade, taken up and laid on the table p806; Again taken up p808; A motion to strike out the first section, providing $30, 000 to restore Negroes to the coast of Africa, negatived and the bill ordered to a third reading p809 Debate commences p806; Slaves, deported, a supplementary bill introduced for the adjustment of claims to indemnification, under the Treaty of Ghent, 406; Ordered to be engrossed p411; The bill returned from the house with an amendment, laid on the table p728; Amendment of the House concurred with p787; Debate commences p406; Slaves, captured, a bill passed, cancelling a bond in relation to them p30; Yeas and Nays on engrossing the bill for adjusting claims for slaves under the Treaty of Ghent p411.

- House 1st Session: Captured Africans, a bill from the Senate to authorize the cancelling of a bond therein mentioned, was twice read p915; Ordered to lie on the table p916; Bill again taken up p955; Recommitted, with instructions that the facts of the case be reported p968; The Judiciary Committee make their Report p998; The bill from the Senate on the same subject referred to the same Committee of the Whole, with the bill of this House p1005; Debate commences p955; D'Auterive Marigny, amendment proposed providing a compensation for the lost time of the petitioner's slave and the expenses of medical treatment p900; After discussion of this amendment for several days in committee of the whole, on the committee's rising, the House refused leave to sit again p1029; A motion was made to discharge the committee of the whole from the further consideration of the bill, a division of the question being called for and the question for discharging the committee passed in the affirmative p1029.

- A motion was then made to recommit the bill and report to the Committee of Claims p1029; An amendment proposing an additional section allowing $234 for the injury done to the slave p1048; Adopted and the bill ordered to be engrossed p1122; On its third reading, a motion to recommit the bill carried p1486; Debate commences p899; Slaves, a resolution introduced, instructing the Committee of Ways and Means to enquire into the expediency of repealing so much of the 16th section of an act to prohibit the importation of slaves, etc. as requires that the owner or captain intending to transport a slave coastwise, shall previously deliver to the collector a manifest, etc. p897; Adopted p898; Deported, a resolution instructing the committee to whom the bill from the Senate on this subject is or may be referred p1811; Agreed to p1835.

- A bill to extend the time of the sitting of the Ghent commissioners on this subject - a motion to discharge the committee from the further consideration of it p2314; The Committee of the Whole discharged form the further consideration of the bill and the bill passed p2576; slave trade, a bill to abolish the U. States agency on the Coast of Africa and to provide otherwise for suppressing the slave trade, taken up p2744; Bill passed p2576; Index to Speakers' Names in the Senate; Berrien, Mr. on a supplementary bill for adjusting claims for deported Slaves pp406, 407; Chambers, Mr. on the suppression of the Slave Trade pp806, 809; Chandler, Mr. on suppression of the slave trade p808; Hayne, Mr. on adjusting claims for deported slaves p410; On South Carolina Claims pp418, 419, 421; On suppression of the slave trade pp806, 808; Johnston, Mr. Louisiana on adjusting claims for deported slaves pp408, 786; King, Mr. on the suppression of the Slave Trade pp806, 808; Macon, Mr. on the suppression of the slave trade pp806, 809; M'lane, Mr. on the suppression of the slave trade p806; Smith, Mr. of Maryland on the claims of South Carolina p420; Tazewell, Mr. on adjusting claims for deported slaves pp407, 408, 786.

- Webster, Mr. on the suppression of the slave trade p806; White, Mr. on adjusting claims for deported slaves p410; Index to the Speakers' Names in the House; Archer, Mr. on deported slaves p2332; Barbour, Mr. P.P. on the case of captured Africans pp915, 955, 956; On deported slaves p2315; Bartlett, Mr. on the bill in relation to captured Africans pp955, 963; Carson, Mr. on deported slaves p1834; Everett, Mr. on deported slaves p1812; Floyd, Mr. on deported slaves p2314; Gilmer, Mr. on deported slaves pp1832, 1835, 2316, 2352, 2356; Haynes, Mr. on deported slaves p1834; Marvin, Mr. on deported slaves p1834; Mercer, Mr. on captured Africans p958; Miner, Mr. on captured Africans pp962, 963, 966; Mitchell, Mr. S.C. on transporting slaves coastwise p897; Moore, Mr. of Alabama, on deported slaves pp1832, 1834, 1835; Owen, Mr. on deported slaves pp1812, 1831; Rives, Mr. on deported Slaves p2475; Taylor, Mr. on the bill in relation to captured Africans p956; Ward, Mr. on deported slaves p1832; Weems, Mr. on the bill in relation to captured slaves p1832; Wickliffe, Mr. on the bill in relation to captured Africans p959; On deported slaves pp2314, 2333; Wilde, Mr. on deported slaves pp1832, 2333.

- Senate 2nd Session.

- House 2nd Session: Slavery in the District of Columbia, preamble and resolutions submitted to take into consideration the laws in relation to and to provide for the gradual abolition of p167; Question of consideration moved p167; Agreed to p167; Motion to strike out the preamble pp168, 175; To lay the preamble and resolutions on the table, negatived p191; Motion to suspend the rule limiting the consideration of resolutions to an hour, negatived p191; Preamble modified p191; Previous question moved and sustained p191; Divided and taken first on the preamble p192; Preamble rejected and the resolutions agreed to p192; Yeas and Nays on laying on the table preamble and resolutions in relation to slavery in the District of Columbia p191; On agreeing to same p192; Index to the Speakers' Names in the Senate; Index to the Speakers' Names in the House: Bartlett, Mr. on resolutions relative to slavery in the District of Columbia p191; Culpeper, Mr. on resolutions relative to slavery in the District of Columbia p168; Miner, Mr. on resolutions relating to slavery in the District of Columbia pp168, 175; Weems, Mr. on resolutions relating to slavery in the District of Columbia pp168, 181, 191; Wickliffe, Mr. on resolutions relating to slavery in the District of Columbia pp168, 191; Wright, Mr. of Ohio on resolutions relative to slavery in the District of Columbia p191.

- 21st Congress December 7, 1829-March 4, 1831, Senate 1st Session: Index to the Speakers' Names in the Senate.

- House 1st Session: Index to the Speakers' Names in the House.

- Senate 2nd Session: Africans, resolution to inquire into the expediency of making further provision for the support of captured, introduced and agreed to p40; Index to the Speakers' Names in the Senate; Livingston, Mr. on making further provision for the support of captured Africans p40.

- House 2nd Session: Colonization Society, memorial of inhabitants of Virginia, praying aid from Congress for the, presented pp619, 626; Hall of the House, use of granted to a member of the Society of Friends and to the Colonization Society p519; slave trade, motion to suspend rule of the House, to introduce resolution in relation to, negative p725; Again moved and agreed to p850; Resolution requesting the President of the United States to prosecute negotiations with maritime Powers of Europe and America, for the effectual abolition of the, introduced and agreed to p850; Yeas and Nays on adopting resolution in relation to the abolition of the African slave trade by the maritime Powers of Europe and America p850; Index to the Speakers' Names in the House: Bouldin, Mr. on petition praying aid to Colonization Society pp619, 626; Mercer, Mr. on granting Hall to Colonization Society p519; On suppression of slave trade p850.

- 22nd Congress December 5, 1831-March 4, 1833, Senate 1st Session: Colonization Society. A memorial from citizens of Kentucky was presented, inviting the attention of Congress to the subject, which, after some discussion, was laid on the table p641; Index to the Names in the Senate: Clay, Mr. on Colonization Society p641; Hayne, Mr. on Colonization Society pp642, 646.

- House 1st Session: Census, aggregate amount of each description of persons p1422; Colonization of free negroes, a resolution proposing a committee to inquire into the expediency of making an appropriation for the purpose of removing them to Africa p1537; Postponed p1538; Referred to the committee to whom was referred the New Jersey memorial p1676; A memorial from the New Jersey Society praying for an appropriation in favor of colonization p1673; Memorials from Kentucky and one from persons in England, in favor of colonization p2332; Copy of the English memorial p2350; Slavery in the District of Columbia, a petition presented, praying for the abolition of p1425; Report on the petition, in which the committee ask to be discharged from its further consideration p1442; Index to Speakers' Names in the House; Archer, Mr. on colonizing free negroes pp1538, 1663, 1664, 1676; Coke, Mr. on colonizing the free negroes p1628; Craig, Mr. on colonizing free persons of color p1674; Jenifer, Mr. on colonizing free Negroes pp1537, 1538, 1626; Mason, Mr. on colonizing free persons of color p1675; Mercer, Mr. on colonization of free Negroes p1663; Speight, Mr. on colonizing free Negroes p1537; Thompson, Mr. on colonizing free Negroes p1662; Ward, Mr. on claims of South Carolina p1457; Wayne, Mr. on South Carolina claims p1465; Index to the Appendix.

- Senate 2nd Session: Index to the Speakers' Names in the Senate.

- House 2nd Session: Slavery in the District of Columbia, a memorial from Pennsylvania for its abolishment therein p1584; Referred 1585; Index to the Speakers' Names in the House; Adams, Mr., from Massachusetts, on abolishing slavery in the District of Columbia p1585; Craig, Mr. from Kentucky, on abolishing slavery in the District of Columbia p1585; Heister, Mr., from Pennsylvania, on abolishing slavery in the District of Columbia p1584; Jenifer, Mr., from Maryland, on abolishing slavery in the District of Columbia p1535; Mason, Mr., from Virginia, on abolishing slavery in the District of Columbia p1585; Index to the Appendix.

- 23rd Congress December 2, 1833-March 4, 1835, Senate 1st Session: Muskingum county (Ohio) memorial, praying for the abolition of slavery in the District of Columbia p1260; Slavery in the District of Columbia, petitions presented against it pp198, 1260; Index to the Speakers' Names in the Senate; Chambers, Mr., on slavery in the District p198; Preston, Mr., on slavery in the District of Columbia pp198, 199; Shepley, Mr., on slavery in the District of Columbia p198; Sprague, Mr., on slavery in District of Columbia p198.

- House 1st Session: Slavery in the District of Columbia, memorials from Connecticut on this subject p2539; Index to the Speakers' Names in the House; Ellsworth, Mr., (Connecticut) on slavery in the District p2539; Index to the Appendix.

- Senate 2nd Session: Index to the Speakers' Names in the Senate.

- House 2nd Session: Slavery in the District of Columbia, on the reference of sundry petitions on the subject of p1131; Yeas and nays on reference of petitions for the abolition of slavery in the District of Columbia p1141; Index to the Speakers' Names in the House; Boon, Mr., Indiana, printing a petition in favor of abolition p1394; Bouldin, Mr., Virginia, on printing an abolition petition pp1394, 1400; Chinn, Mr., Virginia, on slavery in the District of Columbia pp1140, 1394; Denny, Mr., Pennsylvania, on slavery in the District of Columbia p1141; Dickson, Mr., New York, on slavery in the District of Columbia p1131; Abolition of slavery in the District of Columbia pp1393, 1394; Evans, Mr. Maine on the memorial for the abolition of slavery p1392; Fillmore, Mr., New York, on printing an abolition petition p1395; Gholson, Mr., New York, on printing an abolition petition p1398; Jackson, Mr., Massachusetts, petition praying for the abolition of slavery in the District of Columbia p1464; McKinley, Mr., Massachusetts, on memorial for abolition of slavery p1392; Slade, Mr., Vermont on petition from Addison county for the abolition of slavery in the District of Columbia p1463; White, Mr. New York, on printing an abolition petition p1398; Wise, Mr., Virginia, on printing an abolition petition pp1398, 1400.

- All other records relevant or related to our FOIA Request from all Congresses and all Sessions of the Senate and House from 1835 to the present.

- Records of the United States House of Representatives (Record Group 233):

- Committee Papers and Reports:

- 9th Congress, 1805-07: select committee: Northwest Ordinance of 1787 introduction of slaves - 9A-C5.

- 14th Congress, 1815-17: select committee: slave trade in District of Columbia - 14A-C17.4; 17th Congress, 1821-23; select com.: suppression of the slave trade -17A- C27.4.

- 19th Congress, 1825-27: select com.: suppression of the slave trade -19A- D23.11; com. on the District of Columbia: sale of free blacks into slavery- 19A-D5.3.

- 20th Congress, 1827-29: select committee: colonization and related subjects - 20A-D25.3; 32nd Congress, 1851-53; com. on Ways and Means: colonization of free Negroes in Liberia - 32A-G24.6.

- 36th Congress, 1859-61: com. on the Judiciary: slavery in the Territory of New Mexico - 36A-D13.9.

- 37th Congress, 1861-63: com. on Military Affairs: former slaves employed as servants in the Army of Kentucky - 37A-E10.4; com. on Ways and Means: suppression of the African Slave Trade - 37A-E20.17.

- 38th Congress, 1863-65: com. on Ways and Means: Emancipation - 38A-E23.2; 39th Congress, 1865-67; Committee on Freedmen Affairs: funds received by the Bureau of Freedmen, Refugees and Abandoned Lands - 39A-F10-2.

- All other Committee Papers and Reports that are relevant or related to our Request from all Congresses and all Session of the Senate and House from 1776 to the present.

- Petitions and Memorials:

- 6th Congress, 1799-1801: select committee: fugitive slave laws-impact on freedmen - 6A-F4.2.

- 8th Congress, 1803-05: select com.: slavery in territories - 8A-F5.5.

- 11th Congress, 1809-11: com. on Commerce and Manufactures: violation of act prohibiting slaves in the United States - 11A-F2.2.

- 14th Congress, 1815-17: select com.: slave trade - 14A-F16.6.

- 15th Congress, 1817-19: select com.: protection and colonization for free people;15A-G17.1; com. of the Whole House: slave trade -15A-G18.1.

- 16th Congress, 1819-21: select com.: slavery - 16A-G21.1.

- 17th Congress, 1821-23: select com.: suppression of the slave trade -17A- F18.3.

- 19th Congress, 1825-27: protection and colonization of free people -19A- G22.2; com. on the District of Columbia: slavery in the District -19A-G4.2.

- 20th Congress, 1827-29: com. on the District of Columbia: slavery in the District - 20A-G5.1; select com.: colonization of free people - 20A-G22.1; com. on the Whole House: slavery in the District of Columbia - 20A-G23-3.

- 22nd Congress, 1831-33: com. on the District of Columbia: slavery -22A-G5.2.

- 23rd Congress, 1833-35: select com.: abolition of slavery in the District of Columbia - 23A-G21.6; com. on the District of Columbia: slavery - 23A- G4.3.

- 24th Congress, 1835-37: select com.: slavery in the District of Columbia - 24A- G22.4.

- 28th Congress, 1843-45: com. on the Judiciary: abolition of slavery - 28A- G10.2; repeal of the fugitive slave law - 28A-G10.12.

- 29th Congress, 1845-47: com. on the District of Columbia: slavery and the slave trade in the District - 29A-G3.3; com. on the Judiciary: slavery and the slave trade - 29A-G8.9; com on the Whole House: abolition of slavery - 29A-G24.1.

- 30th Congress, 1847-49: com. on the District of Columbia: slavery - 30A-G5.1; com. on the Judiciary: slavery - 30A-G9.2; com on the Territories: slavery - 30A-G23.1.

- 31st Congress, 1849-51: com. on the District of Columbia: slavery - 31A-G4.1; com. on the Judiciary: slavery - 31A-G9.5.

- 32nd Congress, 1851-53: com. on the Judiciary: abolition of slavery -32A- G10.3; repeal of the fugitive slave law -32A-G10.6; com. on Ways and Means: colonization of free Negroes in Liberia - 32A-G24.6.

- 33rd Congress, 1853-55: com. on the District of Columbia: abolition of slavery in the District of Columbia - 33A-G5.1; com. on the Judiciary: abolition of the interstate slave trade - 33A-G10.1, protection of free colored citizens within the jurisdiction of the several slave states - 33A-G10.8, repeal of the Fugitive Slave Act of 1850 - 33A-G10.10, sale of a slave for debts due to the United States - 33A-G10.11; com. on the Territories: exclusion of slavery and slave trade from the territories and the District of Columbia - 33A-G24.1;com. of the Whole House: exclusion of the slave trade and slavery from the territories - 33A-G26.1, advocacy for the repeal of the fugitive slave law - 331-G26.4.

- 34th Congress, 1855-57: com. on the District of Columbia: slavery in the District - 34A-G4.5; com. on the Judiciary: slavery - 34A-G9.8, com. on the Territories: slavery in the territories - 34A-G21.2.

- 36th Congress, 1859-61: com. on Foreign Affairs: slave trade - 36A-G7.2, com on the Judiciary: Crittenden Compromise - 36A-G10.3, fugitive slave law - 36A- G10.4, abolition of slavery - 36A-G10.5; slavery in the District of Columbia - 36A-G10.6, slaves, freeing by purchase - 36A-G10.7, slave trade - 36A-G10.8.

- 37th Congress, 1861-63: com. on the Judiciary: abolition of slavery in the District of Columbia 37A-G7.1, abolition of slavery in the United States - 37A-G7.2, advise to the Congress to drop the Negro question and attend to the business of the country 37A-G7.3; repeal of the Fugitive Slave Act - 37A-G7.4, 37A- G7.11; confiscation of property and liberation of the slaves of persons supporting the rebellion - 37A-G7.13; colonization of ex-slaves in territories from the states of Georgia, South Carolina and Florida - 37A-G7.15; com. on Military Affairs: enactment of a law calling upon all persons bond and free to aid the Government in suppressing the rebellion - 37A-G8.12, abolition of slavery - 37A-G8.13; com on Ways and Means: Drop the Negro Question - 37A-G20.1; Select com.: Emancipation - 37A-G21.4.

- 38th Congress, 1863-65: com. on the Judiciary: amendment to abolish slavery - 38A-G10.1, slavery - 38A-G10.4; com on Military Affairs: colored troops 38A- G12.6; select com.: Emancipation - 38A-G25.1.

- 39th Congress, 1865-67: com. on Freedmen Affairs; 39A-H11.1.

We further request that you provide us access to or copies of any and all records that are relevant or related to our Request from all Congresses and all Sessions of the Senate and House from 1865 to the present, especially those that reference slave-like conditions and practices, including peonage, share-cropping, convict-lease, prison labor, colonialism, segregation (Jim Crow), apartheid, etc.

In order to help you determine our status and make your decision on our fee waiver request, you should know that Bob Brown is an organizer and researcher, who has worked, studied and struggled for 41 years, within and for the Student, Civil and Human Rights, Black Power, National Liberation, Pan-African, and Peace Movements. See Attachment B.

Disclosure of the requested information is in the public interest because it will be meaningfully informative in relation to the subject matter of this FOIA Request; because most of the requested records are not in the public domain and those that are in the public domain are not accessible to the public that we serve; because their release will contribute significanticantly to greater public understanding of the United States Government's, especially Congresses' role, operations and activities, positive and negative, historically and currently, in the struggle to criminalize, prohibit and abolish these crimes against humanity; because this FOIA Request is not primarily in our commercial interest; and because we are highly qualified to understand, extract, convey and disseminate the information to the public at large, especially the African community worldwide.

Please provide expedited provide an expedited review of this FOIA Request, which concerns a matter of urgency. As scholars, organizers and activists, we have been primarily engaged in disseminating information and education for more than 40-years. The public has an urgent need for the requested information because:

- The need involves an ongoing discussion about slavery and the slave trade, crimes against humanity and reparations to which informed members of the public might contribute through further research and publication, mass education, organization and mobilization, lobbying or other contacts with public officials, and any delay would further rob the public of detailed information about the role, activities and operations of the United States Government, positive and negative, historically and currently, in the struggle to facilitate, prohibit, or abolish these crimes against humanity. Further delay would also rob the public of its ability to discuss and debate these concerns, make known its views, and contribute to the resolution of issues involved in a timely manner.

- The public, especially the African community, wants and needs to address serious allegations of governmental wrongdoing and cover-up, historically and currently, with respect to these issues in a timely manner.

- Moreover, these crimes against African and world humanity have been committed for over 569-years, and continue to be committed through denial, cover-up, lies, and fraud, governmental and non-governmental; and over 100 million African People have suffered, and their descendants continue to suffer, as a result of these crimes and the continuing denial and cover-up. It is time to redress these issues and resolve them, one way, or the other.

We expect your positive response to this historic and precedent setting FOIA Request within 20 working days as the statute provides. If our request is denied in whole or part, we ask that you justify the denial or all deletions by reference to specific exemptions of the act. We also expect you to release all segregable portions of otherwise exempt material.

Please be assured that we will exhaust all administrative, legal, and political remedies to successfully conclude this FOIA Request. Thank you for your consideration.

Sincerely,
Bob Brown, co-director
Pan-African Roots

Pan-African Roots
1247 E Street SE
Washington, DC 20003
Tel: (202-) 544-9355 - Fax: (202) 544-9359
Email: paroots02@yahoo.com

25 October 2004

President George W. Bush
The White House
1600 Pennsylvania Ave NW
Washington, DC 20500

AMENDED FREEDOM OF INFORMATION ACT REQUEST.
Fee Waiver and Expedited Review Request.
c/o FOIA Officer and FOIA Appeals Officer.

Dear President Bush:

Pursuant to the federal Freedom of Information Act (5 U.S.C. Sec. 552) and the Electronic FOIA Amendments of 1996 and 1997 ("EFOIA Amendments" and 5 U.S.C. Sec. 552 (f)(2) (effective March 31, 1997), we request access to and copies of all records created or obtained by the United States Government, or under your authority and, that relate to, or contain information about:

- The role, operations, and activities of the United States Government, its legislative, executive and judicial branches, all departments and agencies, in facilitating, prohibiting and combating privateering, slavery and the slave trade, especially the Trans-Atlantic slave Trade; and slave-like conditions and practices, including colonialism, segregation and apartheid, forced and compulsory labor, racism and racial discrimination, xenophobia and related intolerance.

- Slave, urban and racial disturbances, riots, rebellions and revolts, runaway slaves, fugitives beyond borders, related claims or requests, and demands for restitution and reparations.

- All treaties or agreements, bilateral or multilateral, or diplomatic communications, correspondence, discussions, public and secret, between the United States Government and its Officials (all levels, branches and agencies) and the British, Canadian, French, Haitian, Spanish, Mexican, or any other government with respect to the above or related subjects, including their proclamations, edicts and laws liberating slaves in their countries and colonies, and granting them citizenship; their encouragement of and assistance to slaves to revolt and runaway; their evacuation or harboring of slaves; their refusal to return fugitive slaves or pay compensation; and related claims or requests.

- All efforts by African People (People of African descent) in the United States, the African Diaspora, or Africa to lodge complaints against the U.S. with the League of Nations, the United Nations, and all other international or regional bodies.

- The United Nations World Conference Against Racism, Racial Discrimination, Xenophobia and Related Intolerance (WCAR), including its preparatory, regional and expert meetings and seminars, the White House Interagency Task Force on the U.N. World Conference Against Racism, the U.S. Governmental Delegation, the U.S. Non-Governmental Delegation, the UN Intergovernmental Working Group on the effective implementation of the Durban Declaration and Programme of Action, and the UNESCO Slave Route Project.

- Your, Mr. Colin Powell's and Ms. Condoleeza Rice's trips to Africa, especially Senegal, and all trips, visits, delegations, discussions, communications, agreements, etc., by United States

Government Officials to Africa, the Caribbean, Central and South America or Europe relating to or referencing WCAR.

- All governments, agencies (federal, state, county or local), corporations, non-governmental organizations, institutions, churches, families, individuals, or entities, domestic or foreign who participated or invested in, or made profits from the above referenced crimes against humanity; and who owns or benefits from these historical and continuing crimes today, including but not limited to those listed in Appendix A.

We have also filed the first round of a series of historic and precedent setting FOIA, State Open Records, Public Records, and Information Requests with you and all of the departments and agencies under your authority and control, including, but not limited to the Departments of State, Defense, Treasury, Justice and Interior; and the National Archives and Records Administration. As the President and Commander-in-Chief of the United States Government, we ask that you order all departments and agencies under your authority and control to comply in an expedited manner with this FOIA Request, and waive all associated fees. We have released this Request to the public and the media.

As you are aware, the world Conference Against Racism, Racial Discrimination, Xenophobia and Related Intolerance (WCAR) met from 31 August to 3 September 2001, in Durban, South Africa.. Reports reveal that 18,810 delegates from 170 countries participated in WCAR, including 16 heads of state, 58 foreign ministers, 44 ministers, 7,000 non-governmental representatives, and 1,300 journalists. The WCAR Final Declaration and Programme of Action:

> Acknowledge[s] that slavery and the slave trade, including the Trans-Atlantic Slave Trade, were appalling tragedies in the history of humanity not only because of their abhorrent barbarism but also in terms of their magnitude, organized nature, [and] especially their negation of the essence of the victims, … acknowledge[s] that slavery and the slave trade are a crime against humanity **and should have always been so**, especially the transatlantic slave trade and are among the major sources and manifestations of racism, racial discrimination, xenophobia and related intolerance,… and invite[s] the international community members to honour the memory of the victims of these tragedies …[**Emphasis added.**]
>
> Further note[s] that some [countries} have taken the initiative of regretting or expressing remorse or presenting apologies, and call[s] on all those who have yet contributed to restoring the dignity of all the victims to find appropriate ways to do so… [25]

On July 8, 2003 in Senegal, you said that slavery was "one of the greatest crimes in history," noted that we can "fairly judge the past by the standard of John Adams who called slavery an evil of 'colossal magnitude,' [and] acknowledged that "many of the issues that still trouble America have their roots "in slavery."[26]

It is well-settled, as the WCAR Final Declaration and your speech confirm, that prohibitions against piracy and privateering, slavery and the slave trade, including the Trans-Atlantic Slave Trade, and against slave-like conditions and practices, including colonialism, segregation and apartheid, forced and compulsory labor, racism and racial discrimination, xenophobia and related intolerance have achieved the level of customary international law, have attained the status of jus cogens, and are obligato erga omnes. Unfortunately, the overwhelming majority of the WCAR Delegates and the public, especially African People worldwide, wrongly believe that this status has only recently been acquired.[27]

---

[25] World Conference Secretariat. Office of the United Nations High Commissioner for Human Rights. http://www.unhchr.ch/html/racism/02-documents-cnt.html.

[26] Ibid.

[27] People incorrectly believe that "the term was first used in the preamble of the Hague Convention of 1907. " Wikipedia. Crime against humanity. Available from http://en.wikipedia.org/wiki/Crime_against_humanity.

Permit us to suggest, as Ethan A. Nadelman suggests, that "most global prohibition regimes, including those targeted against piracy, slavery, and drug trafficking, evidence a common evolutionary pattern consisting of four or five stages."[28] At different stages in their development: (1) the activity is legal and some states participate in it; (2) national and international forces, non-governmental and governmental, attempt to redefine the activity as evil and illegal; (3) these forces agitate for its suppression and criminalization; (4) the activity becomes the subject of national and international criminal laws, conventions and treaties, police and military action; and (5) finally, the activity is prohibited globally. It is axiomatic that this development is extremely uneven, unequal, and costly in time, space and human lives, in justice and equity.

Permit us also to suggest that Judge Fouad Ammoun of the International Court of Justice (ICJ) "has [accurately] described the development of Africa ... [and] eloquently remarked on the evolution of mankind's struggle with the issues of slavery and colonization."[29] He informs us that "before there fell upon it the two greatest plagues in the recorded history of mankind: the slave trade, which ravaged Africa for centuries on an unprecedented scale; and colonialism, which exploited humanity and natural wealth to a relentless extreme, ... Africa boasted thriving states and empires dating back to Roman times."[30]

Judge Ammoun also informs us that "historians have outlined the upward march of mankind from the time when homo sapiens appeared on the face of the globe, first of all in the Near East in what was the land of Canaan[31], up to the age of the greatest thinkers and more particularly, throughout the whole of history of social progress, from the slavery of Antiquity to man's [and woman's] inevitable, irreversible drive towards equality and freedom. This march is like time itself. It never stops. Nothing can stand in its way for long. The texts, whether they be laws, constitutions, declarations, covenants or charters, do but define it and mark its successive phases. They are a mere record of it. In other words, the progressive rights which men, [women] and peoples enjoy are the result much less of those texts than of human progress to which they bear witness."[32]

We are confident that the records requested by and through this historic and precedent setting series of FOIA Request will:

- Bear witness to and prove, once and for all, that piracy, slavery and the slave trade, including the Trans-Atlantic Slave Trade, and slave-like conditions and practices, including colonialism, segregation and apartheid, were illegal and prohibited, and were recognized as crimes against humanity when and where they were committed.

- Help define and mark the successive stages in the development of the 569-year historical and continuing Maafa,[33] and of the unyielding and continuing struggle against it.

- Document who the victims were, and who their descendants are today; who committed these crimes, which were and are the greatest theft of land, lives and labor in human history; how this unjust and illegal wealth was converted, consolidated, preserved and transferred across generations and centuries; and who owns and benefits from this unjust enrichment today.

---

[28] Ethan A. Nadelman. *Global prohibition regimes: the evolution of norms in international society. Printed in Transnational Crime* / edited by Nikos Passas.

[29] *Legal Consequences For States of the Continued Presence of South Africa in Namibia (South West Africa) Notwithstanding Security Council Resolution 276, 1971 I.C.J. 16, 86 (1971) (separate opinion of Judge Ammoun).*

[30] Ibid. Recent evidence documents that African civilizations predate Roman times.

[31] Recent evidence documents that homo sapiens first emerged in East Africa.

[32] Ethan A. Nadelman. *Global prohibition regimes.*

[33] Dr. Marimba Ani. *Let The Circle Be Unbroken.* Maafa is a Kiswahili word for the 563-year historical and continuing enslavement and colonization of Africa and African People.

Upon information and belief, piracy and privateering, slavery and the slave trade, including the Trans-Atlantic slave trade, were illegal, and were a crime against humanity when and where they were committed:

- "Because God makes no slaves in the womb;"[34] because the prohibition of the slave trade is well-settled in the Bible in Timothy 1:10, Exodus 21:16, Deuteronomy 24:7, 1 Corinthians 5:11, 1 Corinthians 6:10 and Timothy 1:10-1; and because the Catholic Church was in the forefront of the struggle from 441 AD to prohibit and abolish the trafficking in and enslavement of Christians, Europeans, the Indigenous Peoples of the Western Hemisphere, and African People.

- Because in 1494, Queen Isabella freed 500 Indigenous Slaves were illegally kidnapped by Christopher Columbus and sent them home; because in 1500, Queen Isabella freed all slaves in the Western Hemisphere; because King Charles V of Spain prohibited slavery in 1530; because Emperor Charles II ordered all slaves, including African slaves, be set free in 1540; because King Charles II of Spain issued Royal Edicts in 1693 and on November 7, 1695 giving sanctuary to all runaway slaves in Florida and "liberty to … all men as well as all women ... so that by their example and by [his] liberality others will do the same;"[35] because slavery and the slave trade was again declared illegal and prohibited in Spain and all of its colonies, including Florida, Mexico and Texas in 1811; because they refused to return runaway slaves; and because the liberty and property of all Spanish citizens, including former slaves, was and is protected by treaties between Spain, Mexico and the United States.

- Because King Louis X of France issued an edict in 1315 abolishing slavery in France and the French Kingdom, and declaring that," as all men are by nature free born, and as this kingdom is called the Kingdom of the Franks [freemen], it shall be so in reality;"[36] because slavery and the slave trade was contrary to the common law of France, and "no slave could touch French soil without instantly becoming a freeman;"[37] because the Code Noir and its offshoots, including the Louisiana Code, were repugnant and inferior to cannon law and customary international law, were never approved by the French Parliament, and were therefore null and void; because Champagny was the first village in France to demand once again in 1789, that slavery be abolished in France; because the French National Assembly abolished slavery once again, on February 4, 1794, in France and all French colonies, including Louisiana, and made more than 40,000 illegally enslaved Africans in Louisiana citizens of France; because the liberty and property of all French citizens, including the former slaves, was protected by treaties between France and the United States.

- Because in 1102, a national ecclesiastical council, held at Westminster, under the leadership of Saint Anselm, the Archbishop of Canterbury, declared that "it was forbidden to sell men like cattle, which had been too generally practised in England;"[38] because by 1350, slavery as a custom and practice had disappeared in England; because the Charter of English liberties, which was regarded as the law of the land guaranteed justice and right to every man and woman, and prepared the way for the total abolition of slavery in the kingdom; and because:

    Ireland has the honor of the first general emancipation act known in history, when the great Synod of Ireland, under the leadership of St. Lawrence O'Toole denounced the slave trade in which the Irish had made bond slaves of the English, contrary to the right

---

[34] Rev. John G. Fee. *An Anti-Slavery Manual, or, The Wrongs of American Slavery Exposed By the Light of the Bible and of Facts, with A Remedy for the Evil (1851)*. Available from http://members.tripod.com/medicolegal/feeasm1851.htm

[35] Quoted *at Fort Mose's People*. http://www.millennium.scps.k12.fl.us/fortmose3.html.

[36] Edward C. Rogers. *Slavery Illegality in All Ages and Nations*. http://medicolegal.tripod.com/rogersuos.htm

[37] Ibid.

[38] Ibid.

53

of Christian freedom, [and declaring also, that] they had purchased of robbers and pirates, as well as of merchants—a crime for which God took vengeance upon the nation by delivering them into like bondage," and therefore unanimously decreed and ordained, that all the English throughout Ireland in a state of slavery, should be restored to their natural freedom.[39]

- Because in 1562, when Queen Elizabeth first heard that John Hawkins had committed an act of piracy, kidnapped and traded in slaves, and thereby launched England's involvement in the slave trade, she reportedly detested the slave trading voyages as "detestable ventures" and "commented that he would have to pay a very high price for dealing in human lives;"[40] because in 1569, the Courts decided that "England was too pure an air for slaves to breathe in;"[41] because in 1645, the English Parliament passed an Ordinance prohibiting kidnapping; because in 1662, it was declared that "any of His Majesty's subjects of England, Ireland and His Plantations are to be accounted English and no other;"[42] because Lord Mansfield declared in Rev vs. Cowle that the "supremacy of English courts extends itself over its Dependencies;"[43] because in 1706, English "common law [took] no notice of the Negroes for being different from others as, by the common law no man can have property in another except in special instances."[44]

- Because in 1772, in the landmark Somerset vs. Stewart decision, Lord Mansfield declared that the common law of England was incompatible with slavery and neither recognized it nor permitted its existence in England. Lord Mansfield also declared that:

  > The state of slavery is of such a nature, that it is incapable of being [legally] introduced [established] on [for] any reasons, moral or political, but only by positive [written] law, which preserves its force long after the reasons, occasion, and time itself from whence it was created, is erased from memory. It [slavery] is so odious that nothing can be suffered to support it, but positive law. Whatever inconveniences, therefore, may follow from the decision, I cannot say this case is allowed or approved by the law of England; and therefore the black must be discharged.[45] [This decision freed 15,000 African slaves in London.]

- Because this decision "guarantee[ing] to every man his freedom as soon as he set foot on British soil, extended beyond the limits of the empire;"[46] because these "ideas were disseminated by the military authorities defending the [British] Crown in America [d]uring the Revolutionary War [and] many of the British commanders issued proclamations of freedom to the Negro slaves;"[47] because "the status of the Negro during this 'emergency' as regarded by Great Britain was that of a freeman;"[48] because British troops freed and evacuated more than 100,000 freed slaves;[49] and

[39] Ibid.

[40] *Spain vs. England: The Early History of the Slave Trade.* http://beatl.barnard.columbia.edu/students/his3487/lembrich/seminar51.html

[41] William Goodell. *Slavery and Anti-Slavery.* http://members.tripod.com/medicolegal/goodellsaas.htm

[42] W. J. Ashley. *"The Commercial Legislation of England and the American Colonies, 1660-1760."* Quarterly Journal of Economics 14 (November 1899): 1-29. Reprinted at Dinsmore Documentation. http://www.dinsdoc.com/ashley-1.htm.

[43] Goodell. *Slavery and Anti-Slavery.*

[44] Ibid.

[45] *Somerset v. Stewart. Lofft 1-18; 20 Howell's State Trials 1, 79-82; Eng Rep 499-510 (King's Bench, 22 June 1772).*

[46] Arnett G. Lindsay. *"Diplomatic Relations between the United States and Great Britain Bearing on the Return of Negro Slaves, 1783-1828."* Journal of Negro History 5 (October 1920): 391-419. Republished by Dinsmore Documentation presents Classics on American Slavery.

[47] Ibid.

[48] Ibid.

[49] Ibid.

because the British Government refused to return them to slavery or compensate the U.S. government for them.

- Because the Slave Codes, including but not limited to the Barbados Code, Virginia Code, Black Codes and Jim Crow Laws, like the Nazi and Apartheid Laws, were inferior and repugnant to cannon law, customary international law, and to the municipal, imperial and colonial laws of European, Christian, and other Nations, then and now, and therefore were and are null and void.

- Because the Governments in the 13 British Colonies made several efforts to abolish slavery and the slave trade before their Declaration of Independence in 1776; and because Thomas Jefferson, in the original draft of the Declaration of Independence, declared that:

    [The King of Britain] has **waged cruel war against human nature itself**, violating it's most sacred rights of life and liberty in the persons of a distant people who never offended him, captivating and carrying them into slavery in another hemisphere, or to incure miserable death in their transportation hither. This **piratical warfare**, the opprobrium of infidel powers, is the warfare of the Christian king of Great Britain. [Determined to keep open a market where MEN should be bought and sold,] he has prostituted his negative for suppressing every legislative attempt to prohibit or to restrain this execrable commerce [determining to keep open a market where MEN should be bought and sold]: and that this assemblage of horrors might want no fact of distinguished die, he is now exciting those very people to rise in arms among us, and to purchase that liberty of which he had deprived them, by murdering the people upon whom he also obtruded them: **thus paying off former crimes committed against the liberties of one people, with crimes which he urges them to commit against the lives of another**.[50] [**Emphasis added.**]

- Because Vermont prohibited the slave trade and slavery in 1777, followed by Massachusetts and Pennsylvania in 1780, and Connecticut in 1784.

- Because Article VI of the Northwest Ordinance of 1787 prohibited slavery and involuntary servitude in Ohio, Indiana, Illinois, Michigan, Wisconsin and Minnesota; and because in 1845, the Illinois Supreme Court upheld the constitutionality of the Northwest Ordinance in Jarrot v. Jarrot (2 Gilm. 1), and liberated more than 1,000 Africans in Illinois "from the bondage which for fifty-eight years had illegally deprived them and their ancestors of their freedom."[51] The Court also ordered the defendant to pay the $5 which was owed him for five years of withheld slave wages, setting a precedent for the payment of reparations for stolen slave labor.

- Because the U.S. Congress passed legislation on March 22, 1794 and May 10, 1800, prohibiting U.S citizens and residents from engaging in the transportation of slaves from the U.S. to another country or place, or from one country to another; because the U.S. Congress passed legislation prohibiting the importation of slaves into the U.S. as of January 1, 1808; and Because President James Madison reported to Congress in 1810 that:

    It appears that American citizens are instrumental in carrying on a traffic in enslaved Africans [through Cuba], equally **in violation of the laws of humanity**, and in defiance of those of their own country. The same just and benevolent motives, which produced the

---

[50] Ibid.

[51] Honorable Judge P. Hand. Negro Slavery in Illinois. Illinois Trails and History Genealogy. Available from http://www.iltrails.org.

interdiction in force against this **criminal conduct**, will doubtless be felt by Congress, in devising further means of suppressing the evil.[52] [**Emphasis added.**]

- Because Canada prohibited slavery and the slavery trade in 1803; and because Canada offered sanctuary and citizenship to, and refused to return runaway slaves.

- Because the Legislature of the State of Vermont passed "*Joint Resolution No. 42-- Resolutions Relating To The Subject of Slavery*," in 1849, declaring it:

  Resolved, by the [Vermont] Senate and House of Representatives, That Slavery is a crime against humanity, and a sore evil in the body politic, that was excused by the framers of the Federal Constitution as **a crime entailed upon the country** by their predecessors, and tolerated solely as a thing of inexorable necessity.[53] [**Emphasis added.**]

- Because the 1860 National Republican Platform adopted by the National Republican Convention held in Chicago on May 17, 1860, declared:

  7. That the new dogma that the Constitution of its own force carries slavery into any or all of the territories of the United States, is a dangerous political heresy, at variance with the explicit provisions of that instrument itself, with contemporaneous exposition, and with legislative and judicial precedent, is revolutionary in its tendency and subversive of the peace and harmony of the country.

  8. That the normal condition of all the territory of the United States is that of freedom. That as our Republican fathers, **when they had abolished slavery in all our national territory,** ordained that "no person should be deprived of life, liberty or property, without due process of law," it becomes our duty by legislation, whenever such legislation is necessary, to maintain this provision of the Constitution against all attempts to violate it; and **we deny the authority** of Congress, of a territorial legislature, or of any individuals, **to give legal existence to slave**ry in any territory of the United States." [**Emphasis added.**]

  9. That we [the Republican Party] brand the recent re-opening of the African Slave Trade [from Cuba], under the cover of our national flag, aided by perversions of judicial power, as **a crime against humanity,** and a burning shame to our country and age, and we call upon congress to take prompt and efficient measures for the total and final suppression of that execrable traffic.[54] [**Emphasis added.**]

In 1808, the United States Government prohibited its citizens from participating in the international slave trade, declaring it piracy in 1820, and participation in it punishable by death. Despite this prohibition, a minimum of 250,000 and perhaps as many as 1,000,000 Africans were kidnapped, enslaved, and illegally imported into the United States via Cuba between 1809 and 1861. In 1839, a prime male slave could be purchased in Cuba for $400 and then sold into slavery for life in Richmond for $1,000, or Charleston for $1,150, or Savannah for $1,200 or New Orleans for $1,250. The average daily wage was $1. President James Madison reported to Congress in 1810 that:

It appears that American citizens are instrumental in carrying on a traffic in enslaved Africans, equally in violation of the laws of humanity, and in defiance of those of their own country. The

---

[52] Lawrence R. Tenzer. *The Illicit Slave Trade. The Multiracial Activist.* Available from http://www.multiracial.com/readers/tenzer4.html.

[53] *The Acts and Resolves Passed By The Legislature Of The State of Vermont At The October Session, 1849.* Published By authority. Montpelier: E.P. Walton & Son. 1849.

[54] Central Pacific Railroad Photographic History Museum. *Republican Party National Platform, 1860.* http://cprr.org/Museum/Ephemera/Republican_Platform_1860.html.

same just and benevolent motives, which produced the interdiction in force against this criminal conduct, will doubtless be felt in Congress, in devising further means of suppressing the evil.

The 1860 Republican National Convention selected Abraham Lincoln as its Presidential nominee. He campaigned on this platform, and "won the presidency with almost half a million votes more than [Stephen] Douglas, his closest rival. [Lincoln] won the election garnering 39.8 percent of the popular vote. This election firmly established the Republican hold on the presidency for 60 of the next 100 years." Within five years of the 1860 Convention, slavery had been abolished, 4 million slaves were liberated, and the 13th Amendment was passed banning slavery and the slave trade forever from U.S. soil.

The requested records will prove that despite the above and countless other undeniable legal and historical facts, more than:

- 694,000 Africans were illegally held in slavery in the 13 British Colonies from 1619 to 1776; 3,208,393 Africans were still being illegally held in slavery in these states in 1865; and their descendants were and are forced to suffer slave-like conditions and practices, segregation, racism and racial discrimination until today.

- 1,500 Africans were illegally held in slavery in the Northwest Territories from at least 1787 to the 1840s, especially, but not limited to, the more than 1,000 Africans were still being illegally held in slavery in Illinois until the 1845 Illinois Supreme Court Decision of Jarrot v. Jarrot (2. Gilm. 1); and their descendants were and are forced to suffer slave-like conditions and practices, segregation, racism and racial discrimination, xenophobia and related intolerance until today.

- 40,000 Africans were illegally held in slavery in Louisiana on the eve of its Purchase in 1803; 557,772 Africans were still being illegally held in slavery in Louisiana, Missouri and Arkansas in 1865; and their descendants were and are forced to suffer slave-like conditions and practices, segregation, racism and racial discrimination, xenophobia and related intolerance until today.

- 15,000 Africans slaves were illegally held in slavery in Florida on the eve of its Purchase in 1819; 61,000 Africans were illegally held in slavery in Florida until 1865; and their descendants were and are forced to suffer slave-like conditions and practices, segregation, racism and racial discrimination, xenophobia and related intolerance until today.

- 10,000 Africans were illegally removed from Florida to Indian Territory during the "Trail of Tears "in the 1820s and 1830s; 14,000 Africans were still being illegally held in slavery in Oklahoma in 1866; and their descendants were and are forced to suffer slave-like conditions and practices, segregation, racism and racial discrimination, xenophobia and related intolerance until today.

- 3,000 Africans were illegally held in slavery in Texas on the eve its Independence in 1835; 200,000 Africans were still being illegally held in slavery in the Spanish colony of Mexico, and its provinces in Texas and the Southwestern portion of the United States in 1865; and their descendants were and are forced to suffer slave-like conditions and practices, segregation, racism and racial discrimination, xenophobia and related intolerance until today.

- 250,000 Africans were illegally trafficked into the United States through Cuba after the United States ban on the slave trade in 1808.

It is an uncontested fact that from the passage of the 14th Amendment to the U.S. Constitution in 1865, which officially abolished and prohibited slavery, to the Passage of the Civil and Voting Rights Acts of 1964 and 1965, more than 4,000,00 freed slaves, and their descendants, were forced to endure slave-like conditions and practices, forced and compulsory labor, peonage and sharecropping, convict lease, chain-gang or prison labor, lynchings and terror, and de jure segregation (Jim Crow), and more than 40,000,000 Africans continue to suffer from de facto segregation, slave-like conditions and practices, racism and racial discrimination, xenophobia and related intolerance today.

Joe R. Feagin suggests that "the rationale for group compensation, [for reparations], lies in the stolen labor and lives of the millions, enslaved, the stolen labor and lives of those legally segregated, and the continuing theft of labor and lives of those who face contemporary discrimination."[55] Permit us to add here, the unparalleled and continuing theft of black land and resources, in Africa and the Americas.

James Marketti has suggests, according to Feagin," the dollar value of the labor taken from enslaved African Americans from 1790 to 1860 at, depending on the historical assumptions, from $7 billion to as much as $40 billion."[56] Marketti further estimates that," if that stolen income is multiplied by taking into account lost interest from then to the present, the 1983 economic loss (income diverted) for [Africans in America] ranges from $2.1 to $4.7 trillion. Updating these 1983 estimates places the current value of the diverted labor income in the trillions of U.S. dollars."[57]

"Under legal segregation," according to Feagin," the economic losses for [Africans in America] were again high. One research study suggests the cost of labor market discrimination for 1929-1969 (in 1983 dollars) at $1.6 trillion. ... Calculating the cost of anti-black discrimination from the end of slavery in 1865 to the year 1969, the end of legal segregation, and putting that calculation into year-2000 dollars would likely increase that wage-loss estimate to several trillion dollars."[58]

"Since the end of official segregation," according to Feagin, Africans in America "have suffered additional economic losses. A number of economic studies have suggested how much [black] workers annually lose from continuing discrimination and informal segregation in employment. For one year in the 1970s, the estimate of the cost of continuing racial discrimination in employment has been put in the range of $94-123 billion. Estimating a dollar figure for the period since the end of segregation to the present day would doubtless bring this figure of lost income and purchasing power from continuing discrimination to another several trillion dollars."

We request once again, that you order all departments and agencies under your authority and control to comply in full and in an expedited manner with this historic and precedent setting FOIA Request, and to waive all applicable fees.

In order to help you determine our status and make your decision on our fee waiver request, you should know that Bob Brown is an organizer and researcher, who has worked, studied and struggled for 41 years, within and for the Student, Civil and Human Rights, Black Power, National Liberation, Pan-African, and Peace Movements. See Attachment B.

Disclosure of the requested information is in the public interest because it will be meaningfully informative in relation to the subject matter of this FOIA Request; because most of the requested records are not in the public domain, and those that are in the public domain are not accessible to the public that we serve; because their release will likely to contribute to greater public understanding of the United States Government's role, operations and activities, positive and negative, historically and currently, in the struggle to criminalize, prohibit and abolish these crimes; because this FOIA Request is not primarily in our commercial interest; and because we, and the professionals whom we will recruit to assist and advise us, are highly qualified to understand, extract, convey and disseminate the information to the public at large.

Please provide an expedited review of this FOIA Request, which concerns a matter of urgency. As scholars, organizers and activists, we have been primarily engaged in disseminating information and education for more than 40-years. The public has an urgent need for the requested information because:

---

[55] Joe R. Feagin. *Documenting the Costs of Slavery, Segregation, and Contemporary Discrimination: Are Reparations in Order for African Americans.*

[56] Ibid.

[57] Ibid.

[58] Ibid.

- The need involves an ongoing discussion about slavery and the slave trade, crimes against humanity and reparations to which informed members of the public might contribute through further research and publication, mass education, organization and mobilization, lobbying or other contacts with public officials, and any delay would further rob the public of detailed information about the role, activities and operations of the United States Government, positive and negative, historically and currently, in the struggle to facilitate, prohibit, or abolish these crimes against humanity. Further delay would also rob the public of its ability to discuss and debate these concerns, make known its views, and contribute to the resolution of issues involved in a timely manner.

- The public, especially the African community, wants and needs to address serious allegations of governmental wrongdoing and cover-up, historically and currently, with respect to these issues in a timely manner.

- Moreover, these crimes against African and world humanity have been committed for over 569-years, and continue to be committed through denial, cover-up, lies, and fraud, governmental and non-governmental; and over 100 million African People have suffered, and their descendants continue to suffer, as a result of these crimes and the continuing denial and cover-up. It is time to redress these issues and resolve them, one way, or the other.

We expect your positive response to this historic and precedent setting FOIA Request within 20 working days as the statute provides. If our request is denied in whole or part, we ask that you justify the denial or all deletions by reference to specific exemptions of the act. We also expect you to release all segregable portions of otherwise exempt material.

Please be assured that we will exhaust all administrative, legal, and political remedies to successfully conclude this FOIA Request. Thank you for your consideration.

Sincerely,
Bob Brown, co-director
Pan-African Roots

cc: Dr. Condoleeza Rice, National Security Advisor
        National Security Council
        The White House
        1600 Pennsylvania Ave NW
        Washington, DC 20500

Pan-African Roots

1247 E Street SE
Washington, DC 20003
Tel: (202-) 544-9355 - Fax: (202) 544-9359
Email: paroots02@yahoo.com

25 October 2004

Mr. Colin Powell, Secretary of State
Department of State
2201 C Street NW
Washington DC 20520

AMENDED FREEDOM OF INFORMATION ACT REQUEST.
Fee Waiver and Expedited Review Request.
cc: FOIA Officer and FOIA Appeals Officer.

Dear Mr. Powell:

Pursuant to the federal Freedom of Information Act (5 U.S.C. Sec. 552) and the Electronic FOIA Amendments of 1996 and 1997 ("EFOIA Amendments" and 5 U.S.C. Sec. 552 (f)(2) (effective March 31, 1997), we request access to and copies of all records created or obtained by, or under the control of the United States Government that relate to, or contain information about:

- The role, operations, and activities of the United States Government, especially the Department of State, in facilitating, prohibiting and combating privateering, slavery and the slave trade, especially the Trans-Atlantic Slave Trade and slave-like conditions and practices, including colonialism, segregation and apartheid, forced and compulsory labor, racism and racial discrimination, xenophobia and related intolerance.

- Slave, urban and racial disturbances, riots, rebellions and revolts, runaway slaves, fugitives beyond borders, related claims or requests, and demands for restitution and reparations.

- All treaties or agreements, bilateral or multilateral, or diplomatic communications, correspondence, discussions between the United States Government and its Officials (all levels, branches and agencies) and the British, Canadian, French, Spanish, Mexican or any other government with respect to the above or related subjects.

- All efforts by African People (People of African descent) in the United States, the African Diaspora, or Africa to lodge complaints against the U.S. with the League of Nations, the United Nations, and all other international or regional bodies.

- The world Conference Against Racism, including its preparatory, regional and expert meetings and seminars, the White House Interagency Task Force on the U.N. World Conference Against Racism, the UN Intergovernmental Working Group on the effective implementation of the Durban Declaration and Programme of Action, the UNESCO Slave Route Project.

- All governments, agencies (federal, state, county or local), corporations, non-governmental organizations, institutions, churches, families, individuals, or entities, domestic or foreign who participated or invested in, or made profits from the above referenced crimes against humanity; and who owns or benefits from these historical and continuing crimes today, including but not limited to those listed in Appendix A.

We have also filed the first round of a series of historic and precedent setting FOIA, State Open Records, Public Records, and Information Requests with you and all of the departments and agencies under your authority and control, including, but not limited to the Departments of State, Defense,

60

Treasury, Justice and Interior; and the National Archives and Records Administration. As the President and Commander-in-Chief of the United States Government, we ask that you order all departments and agencies under your authority and control to comply in an expedited manner with this FOIA Request, and waive all associated fees. We have released this Request to the public and the media.

As you are aware, the world Conference Against Racism, Racial Discrimination, Xenophobia and Related Intolerance (WCAR) met from 31 August to 3 September 2001, in Durban, South Africa. Reports reveal that 18,810 delegates from 170 countries participated in WCAR, including 16 heads of state, 58 foreign ministers, 44 ministers, 7,000 non-governmental representatives, and 1,300 journalists. The WCAR Final Declaration and Programme of Action:

> Acknowledge[s] that slavery and the slave trade, including the Trans-Atlantic Slave Trade, were appalling tragedies in the history of humanity not only because of their abhorrent barbarism but also in terms of their magnitude, organized nature, and especially their negation of the essence of the victims, … **acknowledge[s] that slavery and the slave trade are a crime against humanity and should have always been so**, especially the transatlantic slave trade and are among the major sources and manifestations of racism, racial discrimination, xenophobia and related intolerance,… and invite[s] the international community members to honour the memory of the victims of these tragedies …[**Emphasis added.**]

> Further note[s] that some [countries} have taken the initiative of regretting or expressing remorse or presenting apologies, and call on all those who have yet contributed to restoring the dignity of all the victims to find appropriate ways to do so…[59]

On July 8, 2003 in Senegal, President Bush said that slavery was "one of the greatest crimes in history," and noted that we can "fairly judge the past by the standard of John Adams who called slavery an evil of 'colossal magnitude,' [and] acknowledged that "many of the issues that still trouble America have their roots "in slavery.[60]

It is well-settled, as the WCAR Final Declaration and President Bush's speech confirm, that prohibitions against piracy and privateering, slavery and the slave trade, including the Trans-Atlantic Slave Trade, and against slave-like conditions and practices, including colonialism, segregation and apartheid, forced and compulsory labor, racism and racial discrimination, xenophobia and related intolerance have achieved the level of customary international law, have attained the status of jus cogens, and are obligato erga omnes. Unfortunately, the overwhelming majority of the WCAR Delegates and the public, especially African People worldwide, wrongly believe that this status has only recently been acquired.[61]

Permit us to suggest, as Ethan A. Nadelman suggests, that "most global prohibition regimes, including those targeted against piracy, slavery, and drug trafficking, evidence a common evolutionary pattern consisting of four or five stages."[62] At different stages in their development: (1) the activity is legal and some states participate in it; (2) national and international forces, non-governmental and governmental, attempt to redefine the activity as evil and illegal; (3) these forces agitate for its suppression and criminalization; (4) the activity becomes the subject of national and international criminal laws, conventions and treaties, police and military action; and (5) finally, the activity is

---

[59] World Conference Secretariat. Office of the United Nations High Commissioner for Human Rights. Available from http://www.unhchr.ch/html/racism/02-documents-cnt.html.

[60] Ibid.

[61] People incorrectly believe that "the term was first used in the preamble of the Hague Convention of 1907." Wikipedia. Available from http://en.wikipedia.org/wiki/Crime_against_humanity.

[62] Ethan A. Nadelman. Global prohibition regimes: the evolution of norms in international society. Printed in Transnational Crime / edited by Nikos Passas.

prohibited globally.[63] It is axiomatic that this development is extremely uneven, unequal, and costly in time, space and human lives, in justice and equity.

Permit us also to suggest that Judge Fouad Ammoun of the International Court of Justice (ICJ) "has [accurately] described the development of Africa … [and] eloquently remarked on the evolution of mankind's struggle with the issues of slavery and colonization."[64] He informs us that "before there fell upon it the two greatest plagues in the recorded history of mankind: the slave trade, which ravaged Africa for centuries on an unprecedented scale; and colonialism, which exploited humanity and natural wealth to a relentless extreme," … Africa boasted thriving states and empires dating back to Roman times."[65]

Judge Ammoun also informs us that "historians have outlined the upward march of mankind from the time when homo sapiens appeared on the face of the globe, first of all in the Near East in what was the land of Canaan[66], up to the age of the greatest thinkers and more particularly, throughout the whole of history of social progress, from the slavery of Antiquity to man's [and woman's] inevitable, irreversible drive towards equality and freedom. This march is like time itself. It never stops. Nothing can stand in its way for long. The texts, whether they be laws, constitutions, declarations, covenants or charters, do but define it and mark its successive phases. They are a mere record of it. In other words, the progressive rights which men, [women] and peoples enjoy are the result much less of those texts than of human progress to which they bear witness."[67]

We are confident that the records requested by and through this historic and precedent setting series of FOIA Request will:

- Bear witness to and prove, once and for all, that piracy, slavery and the slave trade, including the Trans-Atlantic Slave Trade, and slave-like conditions and practices, including colonialism, segregation and apartheid, were illegal and prohibited, and were recognized as crimes against humanity when and where they were committed.

- Help define and mark the successive stages in the development of the 569-year historical and continuing Maafa,[68] and of the unyielding and continuing struggle against it.

- Document who the victims were, and who their descendants are today; who committed these crimes, which were and are the greatest theft of land, lives and labor in human history; how this unjust and illegal wealth was converted, consolidated, preserved and transferred across generations and centuries; and who owns and benefits from this unjust enrichment today.

Upon information and belief, piracy and privateering, slavery and the slave trade, including the Trans-Atlantic slave trade, were illegal, and were a crime against humanity when and where they were committed:

- "Because God makes no slaves in the womb;"[69] because the prohibition of the slave trade is well-settled in the Bible in Timothy 1:10, Exodus 21:16, Deuteronomy 24:7, 1 Corinthians 5:11, 1 Corinthians 6:10 and Timothy 1:10-1; and because the Catholic Church was in the forefront of

---

[63] Ibid.

[64] *Legal Consequences For States of the Continued Presence of South Africa in Namibia (South West Africa) Notwithstanding Security Council Resolution 276, 1971 I.C.J. 16, 86 (1971) (separate opinion of Judge Ammoun).*

[65] Ibid. Recent evidence documents that African civilizations predate Roman times.

[66] Recent evidence documents that homo sapiens first emerged in East Africa.

[67] Ethan A. Nadelman. *Global prohibition regimes.*

[68] Dr. Marimba Ani. *Let The Circle Be Unbroken.* Maafa is a Kiswahili word for the 563-year historical and continuing enslavement and colonization of Africa and African People.

[69] Rev. John G. Fee. *An Anti-Slavery Manual, or, The Wrongs of American Slavery Exposed By the Light of the Bible and of Facts, with A Remedy for the Evil (1851).* Available from http://members.tripod.com/medicolegal/feeasm1851.htm

the struggle from 441 AD to prohibit and abolish the trafficking in and enslavement of Christians, Europeans, the Indigenous Peoples of the Western Hemisphere, and African People.

- Because King Charles V of Spain prohibited slavery in 1530; because Emperor Charles II ordered all slaves, including African slaves, be set free in 1540; because King Charles II of Spain issued Royal Edicts in 1693 and on November 7, 1695 giving sanctuary to all runaway slaves in Florida and "liberty to … all men as well as all women ... so that by their example and by [his] liberality others will do the same;"[70] because slavery and the slave trade was again declared illegal and prohibited in Spain and all of its colonies, including Florida, Mexico and Texas in 181; because they refused to return runaway slaves; and because the liberty and property of all Spanish citizens, including former slaves, was and is protected by treaties between Spain, Mexico and the United States.

- Because King Louis X of France issued an edict in 1315 abolishing slavery in France and the French Kingdom, and declaring that," as all men are by nature free born, and as this kingdom is called the Kingdom of the Franks [freemen], it shall be so in reality;"[71] because slavery and the slave trade was contrary to the common law of France, and "no slave could touch French soil without instantly becoming a freeman;"[72] because the Code Noir and its offshoots, including the Louisiana Code, were repugnant and inferior to cannon law and customary international law, were never approved by the French Parliament, and were therefore null and void; because Champagny was the first village in France to demand once again in 1789, that slavery be abolished in France; because the French National Assembly abolished slavery once again, on February 4, 1794, in France and all French colonies, including Louisiana, and made more than 40,000 enslaved Africans in Louisiana citizens of France; because the liberty and property of all French citizens, including the former slaves, was protected by treaties between France and the United States.

- Because in 1102, a national ecclesiastical council, held at Westminster, under the leadership of Saint Anselm, the Archbishop of Canterbury, declared that "it was forbidden to sell men like cattle, which had been too generally practised in England;"[73] because by 1350, slavery as a custom and practice had disappeared in England; because the Charter of English liberties, which was regarded as the law of the land guaranteed justice and right to every man and woman, and prepared the way for the total abolition of slavery in the kingdom; and because:

    > Ireland has the honor of the first general emancipation act known in history, when the great Synod of Ireland, under the leadership of St. Lawrence O'Toole denounced the slave trade in which the Irish had made bond slaves of the English, contrary to the right of Christian freedom, and declaring also, that "they had purchased of robbers and pirates, as well as of merchants—a crime for which God took vengeance upon the nation by delivering them into like bondage," and therefore unanimously decreed and ordained, that all the English throughout Ireland in a state of slavery, should be restored to their natural freedom.[74]

- Because in 1562, when Queen Elizabeth first heard that John Hawkins had committed an act of piracy, kidnapped and traded in slaves, and thereby launched England's involvement in the slave trade, she reportedly detested the slave trading voyages as "detestable ventures" and "commented

---

[70] Quoted at *Fort Mose's People*. Available from http://www.millennium.scps.k12.fl.us/fortmose3.html.

[71] Edward C. Rogers. *Slavery Illegality in All Ages and Nations.* Available from http://medicolegal.tripod.com/rogersuos.htm

[72] Ibid.

[73] Ibid.

[74] Ibid.

that he would have to pay a very high price for dealing in human lives;"[75] because in 1569, the Courts decided that "England was to pure an air for slaves to breathe in;"[76] because in 1645, the English Parliament passed an Ordinance prohibiting kidnapping; because in 1662, it was declared that "any of His Majesty's subjects of England, Ireland and His Plantations are to be accounted English and no other;"[77] because Lord Mansfield declared in Rev vs. Cowle that the "supremacy of English courts extends itself over its Dependencies;"[78] because in 1706, English "common law [took] no notice of the Negroes for being different from others as, by the common law no man can have property in another except in special instances;"[79] and because in 1772, in the landmark Somerset vs. Stewart decision, Lord Mansfield declared that the common law of England was incompatible with slavery and neither recognized it nor permitted its existence in England. Lord Mansfield also declared that:

> The state of slavery is of such a nature, that it is incapable of being [legally] introduced [established] on [for] any reasons, moral or political, but only by positive [written] law, which preserves its force long after the reasons, occasion, and time itself from whence it was created, is erased from memory. It [slavery] is so odious that nothing can be suffered to support it, but positive law. Whatever inconveniences, therefore, may follow from the decision, I cannot say this case is allowed or approved by the law of England; and therefore the black must be discharged.[80] [This decision freed 15,000 slaves in London.]

- Because this decision "guarantee[ing] to every man his freedom as soon as he set foot on British soil, extended beyond the limits of the empire;"[81] because these "ideas were disseminated by the military authorities defending the [British] Crown in America [d]uring the Revolutionary War [and] many of the British commanders issued proclamations of freedom to the Negro slaves;"[82] because "the status of the Negro during this 'emergency' as regarded by Great Britain was that of a freeman;"[83] because British troops freed and evacuated more than 100,000 freed slaves;[84] and because the British Government refused to return them to slavery or compensate the U.S. government for them.

- Because the Slave Codes, including but not limited to the Barbados Code, Virginia Code, Black Codes and Jim Crow Laws, like the Nazi and Apartheid Laws, were inferior and repugnant to cannon law, customary international law, and to the municipal, imperial and colonial laws of European, Christian, and other Nations, then and now, and therefore were and are null and void.

- Because the Governments in the 13 British Colonies made several efforts to abolish slavery and the slave trade before their Declaration of Independence in 1776; and because Thomas Jefferson, in the original draft of the Declaration of Independence, declared that:

---

[75] Quoted from *Spain vs. England: The Early History of the Slave Trade.* Available from http://beatl.barnard.columbia.edu/students/his3487/lembrich/seminar51.html

[76] William Goodell. *Slavery and Anti-Slavery.* Available from http://members.tripod.com/medicolegal/goodellsaas.htm

[77] W. J. Ashley. *"The Commercial Legislation of England and the American Colonies, 1660-1760."* Quarterly Journal of Economics 14 (November 1899): 1-29. Available from Dinsmore Documentation. http://www.dinsdoc.com/ashley-1.htm.

[78] Goodell. *Slavery and Anti-Slavery.*

[79] Ibid.

[80] *Somerset v. Stewart. Lofft 1-18; 20 Howell's State Trials 1, 79-82; Eng Rep 499-510 (King's Bench, 22 June 1772).*

[81] Arnett G. Lindsay. *"Diplomatic Relations between the United States and Great Britain Bearing on the Return of Negro Slaves, 1783-1828."* Journal of Negro History 5 (October 1920): 391-419. Available from Dinsmore Documentation presents Classics on American Slavery.

[82] Ibid.

[83] Ibid.

[84] Ibid.

[The King of Britain] has waged cruel war against human nature itself, violating it's most sacred rights of life and liberty in the persons of a distant people who never offended him, captivating and carrying them into slavery in another hemisphere, or to incure miserable death in their transportation hither. This piratical warfare, the opprobrium of infidel powers, is the warfare of the Christian king of Great Britain. [Determined to keep open a market where MEN should be bought and sold,] he has prostituted his negative for suppressing every legislative attempt to prohibit or to restrain this execrable commerce [determining to keep open a market where MEN should be bought and sold]: and that this assemblage of horrors might want no fact of distinguished die, he is now exciting those very people to rise in arms among us, and to purchase that liberty of which he had deprived them, by murdering the people upon whom he also obtruded them: thus paying off former crimes committed against the liberties of one people, with crimes which he urges them to commit against the lives of another.[85] [**Emphasis added.**]

- Because Vermont prohibited the slave trade and slavery in 1777, followed by Massachusetts and Pennsylvania in 1780, and Connecticut in 1784.

- Because Article VI of the Northwest Ordinance of 1787 prohibited slavery and involuntary servitude in Ohio, Indiana, Illinois, Michigan, Wisconsin and Minnesota; and because in 1845, the Illinois Supreme Court upheld the constitutionality of the Northwest Ordinance in Jarrot v. Jarrot (2 Gilm. 1) and liberated more than 1,000 Africans in Illinois "from the bondage which for fifty-eight years had illegally deprived them and their ancestors of their freedom."[86] The Court also ordered the defendant to pay the plaintiff $5 which was owed him for five years of withheld slave wages, setting a precedent for the payment of reparations for stolen slave labor.

- Because the U.S. Congress passed legislation on March 22, 1794 and May 10, 1800, prohibiting U.S citizens and residents from engaging in the transportation of slaves from the U.S. to another country or place, or from one country to another; because the U.S. Congress passed legislation prohibiting the importation of slaves into the U.S. as of January 1, 1808; and Because President James Madison reported to Congress in 1810 that:

    It appears that American citizens are instrumental in carrying on a traffic in enslaved Africans [through Cuba], equally **in violation of the laws of humanity, and in defiance of those of their own country**. The same just and benevolent motives, which produced the interdiction in force against this criminal conduct, will doubtless be felt by Congress, in devising further means of suppressing the evil.[87] [**Emphasis added.**]

- Because Canada prohibited slavery and the slavery trade in 1803; and because Canada offered sanctuary and citizenship to, and refused to return runaway slaves.

- Because the Legislature of the State of Vermont passed "*Joint Resolution No. 42.-- Resolutions Relating To The Subject of Slavery*" in 1849, declaring it:

    Resolved, by the [Vermont] Senate and House of Representatives, That **Slavery is a crime against humanity**, and a sore evil in the body politic, that was excused by the

[85] Ibid.

[86] Honorable Judge P. Hand. *Negro Slavery in Illinois. Illinois Trails and History Genealogy*. The complete article can be found at http://www.iltrails.org.

[87] Lawrence R. Tenzer. *The Illicit Slave Trade*. The Multiracial Activist. Available from http://www.multiracial.com/readers/tenzer4.html.

framers of the Federal Constitution as a crime entailed upon the country by their predecessors, and tolerated solely as a thing of inexorable necessity.[88] [**Emphasis added.**]

- Because the 1860 National Republican Platform adopted by the National Republican Convention held in Chicago on May 17, 1860, declared:

  7. That the new dogma that the Constitution of its own force carries slavery into any or all of the territories of the United States, is a dangerous political heresy, at variance with the explicit provisions of that instrument itself, with contemporaneous exposition, and with legislative and judicial precedent, is revolutionary in its tendency and subversive of the peace and harmony of the country.

  8. That the normal condition of all the territory of the United States is that of freedom. That as our Republican fathers, when they had abolished slavery in all our national territory, ordained that "no person should be deprived of life, liberty or property, without due process of law," it becomes our duty by legislation, whenever such legislation is necessary, to maintain this provision of the Constitution against all attempts to violate it; and we deny the authority of Congress, of a territorial legislature, or of any individuals, to **give legal existence to slavery in any territory of the United Sta**tes." [**Emphasis added.**]

  9. That we [the Republican Party] brand the recent re-opening of the African Slave Trade [from Cuba], under the cover of our national flag, aided by perversions of judicial power, as a **crime against humanity**, and a burning shame to our country and age, and we call upon congress to take prompt and efficient measures for the total and final suppression of that execrable traffic."[89] [**Emphasis added.**]

In 1808, the United States Government prohibited its citizens from participating in the international slave trade, declaring it piracy in 1820, and participation in it punishable by death. Despite this prohibition, a minimum of 250,000 and perhaps as many as 1,000,000 Africans were kidnapped, enslaved, and illegally imported into the United States via Cuba between 1809 and 1861. In 1839, a prime male slave could be purchased in Cuba for $400 and then sold into slavery for life in Richmond for $1,000, or Charleston for $1,150, or Savannah for $1,200 or New Orleans for $1,250. The average daily wage was $1. President James Madison reported to Congress in 1810 that:

  It appears that American citizens are instrumental in carrying on a traffic in enslaved Africans, equally in violation of the laws of humanity, and in defiance of those of their own country. The same just and benevolent motives, which produced the interdiction in force against this criminal conduct, will doubtless be felt in Congress, in devising further means of suppressing the evil.

The 1860 Republican National Convention selected Abraham Lincoln as its Presidential nominee. He campaigned on this platform, and "won the presidency with almost half a million votes more than [Stephen] Douglas, his closest rival. [Lincoln] won the election garnering 39.8 percent of the popular vote. This election firmly established the Republican hold on the presidency for 60 of the next 100 years.

The requested records will prove that despite the above and countless other undeniable legal and historical facts, more than:

- 694,000 Africans were illegally held in slavery in the 13 British Colonies from 1619 to 1776; 3,208,393 Africans were still being illegally held in slavery in these states in 1865; and their

---

[88] *The Acts and Resolves Passed By The Legislature Of The State of Vermont At The October Session, 1849.* Published By authority. Montpelier: E.P. Walton & Son. 1849.

[89] Central Pacific Railroad Photographic History Museum. *Republican Party National Platform, 1860.* Available from http://cprr.org/Museum/Ephemera/Republican_Platform_1860.html

descendants were and are forced to suffer slave-like conditions and practices, segregation, racism and racial discrimination until today.

- 1,500 Africans were illegally held in slavery in the Northwest Territories from at least 1787 to the 1840s, especially, but not limited to, the more than 1,000 Africans were still being illegally held in slavery in Illinois until the 1845 Illinois Supreme Court Decision of Jarrot v. Jarrot (2. Gilm. 1); and their descendants were and are forced to suffer slave-like conditions and practices, segregation, racism and racial discrimination, xenophobia and related intolerance until today.

- 40,000 Africans were illegally held in slavery in Louisiana on the eve of its Purchase in 1803; 557,772 Africans were still being illegally held in slavery in Louisiana, Missouri and Arkansas in 1865; and their descendants were and are forced to suffer slave-like conditions and practices, segregation, racism and racial discrimination, xenophobia and related intolerance until today.

- 15,000 Africans slaves were illegally held in slavery in Florida from 15xx to its Purchase in 1819; 61,000 Africans were illegally held in slavery in Florida until 1865; and their descendants were and are forced to suffer slave-like conditions and practices, segregation, racism and racial discrimination, xenophobia and related intolerance until today.

- 10,000 Africans were illegally removed from Florida to Indian Territory during the "Trail of Tears "in the 1820s and 1830s; 14,000 Africans were still being illegally held in slavery in Oklahoma in 1866; and their descendants were and are forced to suffer slave-like conditions and practices, segregation, racism and racial discrimination, xenophobia and related intolerance until today.

- 3,000 Africans were illegally held in slavery in Texas on the eve its Independence in 1835; 200,000 Africans were still being illegally held in slavery in the Spanish colony of Mexico, and its provinces in Texas and the Southwestern portion of the United States in 1865; and their descendants were and are forced to suffer slave-like conditions and practices, segregation, racism and racial discrimination, xenophobia and related intolerance until today.

- 250,000 Africans were illegally trafficked into the United States through Cuba after the United States ban on the slave trade in 1808.

We request that you search in the following and all other Record Groups, General Records of the United States State Department (Record Group 59); General Records of the U.S. Government (Record Group 11); Records of International Conferences, Commissions, and Expositions (Record Group 43); Records of Boundary and Claims Commissions and Arbitration's (Record Group 76); Records of the Foreign Service Posts of the Department of State (Record Group 84); Records of Interdepartmental and Intradepartmental Committees (State Department) (Record Group 353); Records of the American Commission to Negotiate Peace (Record Group 256); Records of the Agency for International Development (Record Group 286); Record copies of publications of the Department of State in Publications of the U.S. Government (Record Group) 287); Records of the U.S. Information Agency (Record Group 306); Records of the U.S. Arms Control and Disarmament Agency (Record Group 383); Records of the U.S. High Commissioner for Germany (Record Group 466); Records of U.S. Foreign Assistance Agencies, 1948-1961 (Record Group 469) and Security-Classified Records.

We also request that you give us access to or copies of the following that are referenced in "*American Slavery and the International Slave Trade*,"[90] and all other records responsive to our request, that are referenced in:

---

[90] United States National Archives & Records Administration. Records that pertain to *American Slavery and the International Slave Trade: II. Civil Records. General Records of the Department of State (Record Group 59)*. Available from http://www.archives.gov/research_room/research_topics/slavery_records_civil.html.

- Records Relating to the Territories: Kansas Territory, 1854-1861; Conflict between pro-slavery and anti-slavery factions; Orleans Territory, 1764-1823, the importation of slaves from the West Indies; fugitive slaves seeking refuge in Texas; Special Series of Domestic and Miscellaneous Letters; Correspondence With the President and Congress Miscellaneous Letters from Congressional Committees. 1830-186; Censuses of slaves. entry 144; Miscellaneous Petitions and Memorials Proclamations Addressed to President Lincoln by Antislavery Societies. 1862- 1864. entry 160; Index to United States Documents Relating to Foreign Affairs 1828-1861.

Part I:

- Abbot Devereux, Slaver (Myers), p7; Aberdeen, Lord (George Hamilton Gordon), p9; Abreo (Antonio Rodrigo), Slave Dealer, p9; Adams (John Quincy), of Mass., pp11-14; Adams Gray, Amer. Slaver Brigantine, p15; Addington (Henry Unwin), p16; Advance, Amer. Slaver Schr., p17; Albert, Amer. Slaver Brig (Woodberry), p21; Alecto, H.B.M. Sloop (Hunt), p23; Alicia, Slaver, p24; Alienage, Citizenship, Naturalization, p31; Amistad, Spanish Schr., pp49-51; Anaconda, Amer. Slaver Schr. (Knight), p52; Anderson (John), Fugitive Slave, p53; Anderson (W.E.), Witness Against Slave Dealers, p54; Andover (Mass.) Citizens, p54; Appleton (John), of Me., p58; Archer (William S.) of Va., p62; Ardennes, Amer. Slaver Bank (Marsh), p64; Argaiz (Pedro Alcantara), p65; Armstrong (Mass.) Citizens, p71; Arteta (Domingo), Master Amer. Slaver Schr. Rebecca; see Rebecca; Asp, Amer. Schr. (Weems), pp73-74; Augusta Religious Anti-Slavery Conv., p76; Bacon (J.), Master Amer. Slaver Schr. Mary Anne Cassard; see Mary Anne Cassard; Bacon (John F.) of N.Y., p80; Bagley (Arthur P.), of Ala., p81; Baptiste (Manuel), Deponent in Case of Slaver Bark Fame; see Fame; Barclay (Anthony), of Nova Scotia, p90; Barksdale (William), Repr. From Miss., p90; Bayard (James A. Jr.), Sen. From Del., p99; Beaver Co. (Pa.) Citizens, p102; Bedinger (Daniel), p102; Bell (Charles H.), of N.Y., p104; Bell (John), p105; Benjamin (Judah Peter), p107; Bentinotti (Miguel), Slave Dealer, p108; Benton (Thomas H.), pp108-109; Berrien (John McPherson), p110; Berry (James), Master Slaver Bark Pons; see Pons; Beverly (Mass.) Citizens, p112.

- Birch (Thomas F.), Comdr. H.B.M. Brig Wizard, p116; Black (Jeremiah S.), of Penn., p117; Blythe (Andrew K.), of Miss., p122; Bonham (Milledge L.), Repr. From S.C., p126; Boxer, U.S. Brig, p132; Bradford (Mass.) Citizens, p133; Bradford Co. (Penn.) Citizens, p134; Branch (John), Secy. Navy, U.S.A., p135; Branch (Lawrence O'B.), Repr. From N.C., p135; Brand, Mater Amer. Slaver Brig Peerless; see Peerless; Braxton Co. (Va.) Citizens, p136; Brazil, Slaver Brig (Bevans, Faulkner), p143; Bremen, Amer. Slaver Brigantine (Forest), p144; Bright (Jesse D.), Sen. From Ind., p147; Brookfield (Ut.) Citizens, p150; Brown (Albert Gallatin), p152; Brown (James), of La., p152; Bruce (Henry W.), Rear-Admiral, H.B.M. Navy, p155; Buchanan (James), of Penn., ppP161-163; Buckingham Co. (Va.) Citizens, p163; Bucks Co. (Pa.) Citizens, p164; Bulwer (Sir Henry Lytton), p166; Burbank, Master Slaver Brig Chatsworth; see Chatsworth; Burges (Tristam), Repr. From R.I., p167; Burnett (Henry C.), Repr. From Ky., p168; Butler (Andrew Pickens), Sen. From S.C., p170; Byfield (Mass.) Citizens, p175; Caballero, Amer. Slaver Brig (Huffington), p175; Cabarga (Antonio), Slave Dealer, p175; Cabo Verde, Port. Schr., p175; Cacique, Amer. Slaver Str., p176; Caire (F.C. Paul), p176; Calderon de la Barca (Angel), pp176-178; Calhoun (John Caldwell), of S.C., pp179-180, 182; Calhoun, Amer. Slaver (Gordon), p187; Calhoun, Amer. Ship (Fales), p182; Camargo, Amer. Slaver (Gordon), p187; Camden (N.Y.) Citizens, p188; Camilla, Amer. Slaver Schr., p188; Campbell (A.), H.B.M. Consul at Lagos, p188; Camperdown, Slaver, p191; Canal (Francisco), Master Amer. Slaver Schr. Delores; see Delores; Canning (Stratford), p202; Capture, etc., of Property: Cases, pp204-205; Carlos Sp. Slaver, p208; Carmen, Braz. Schr., Slaver, p208; Carnahan (A.M.), et al., p208; Case (Charles), Repr. From Indiana, p212; Cass (Lewis), of Mich., pp216-218, 220-224; Castlereagh (Viscount), Robert Henry Stewart, Afterwards 2nd Marquess of Loudonderry, p227-228; Catherine, Amer.

68

U.S. Brig, p544; Erie, Amer. Slaver (Gordon), p544; Erie Co. (O.) Citizens, p545; Erving (George W.), of Mass., p546; Esperanza, Amer. Slaver Schr., Formerly The Mary Reed; see Chauncey (M.) and Winn (W.); Espiegle, H.B.M. Sloop (Hancock), p547; Essex Co. Anti-Slavery Society, Mass., p548; Euphrates, Amer. Slaver Schr. (Molan), p548; Evans (George R.), of Me., p550; Evansville (Ind.) Citizens, p550; Everett (Alexander Hill), of Mass, pp551-552, 555-556; Ewing (Andrew), Representative From Tenn., p559; Excellent, Brigantine Slaver, p559.

- "Expedition for Africa", p560; Extradition, pp569-566; Fairy, Amer. Slaver Sloop, p571; Falcon, H.B.M. Ship (Fitz Roy), p571; Falmouth (Mass.) Citizens, p572; Fame, Amer. Slaver Bark (Marks), p573; Fenix, Span. Slaver Schr., p578; Fernandez, Slave Dealer, p579; Ferroz Africano, Port. Slaver; see Diligente; Fessenden (William Pitt), p580; Figaniere E Morao (Joaquinn Cesar de), p581; Fish (Samuel), p586; Fitzgerald (Charles), Comdg. H.B.M. Brigantine Buzzard, p587; Flournoy (J.J.), p529; Flying Eagle, Slaver, p592; Fonseca (Manuel Pinto) de, Slave Dealer, p593; Foote (Henry Stuart), pp594-595; Foote (John), Comdr. H.B.M. Sqdn. West Coast of Africa, p595; Ford (Richard), Master Amer. Slaver Brig William D. Miller; see William D. Miller; Forest (Tom), Master Amer. Slaver Bremen; see Bremen; Forester, H.B.M. Brig (Norcock), p597; Formosa, Slaver Schr., p598; Forsythe (John), of Ga., pp599-601, 605, 608; Fox (Henry Stephen), pp610-611; Framingham (Mass.) Citizens, p612; Frances Ann, Amer. Slaver Schr., p640; Fraser (Daniel), Colored Br. Subject, p642; Freedmen; see Negroes, Colonization of; Liberia; Freeman, Master Slaver Ship Chancellor; see Chancellor; Friends, Society of, p646; Fronte (Raimond), Master Amer. Slaver Schr. Sarah Anne; see Sarah Anne; Gabriel (Edmund), H.B.M. Comr. Mixed Commission for Suppression of Slave Trade, Loanda; see Slave Trade, Loanda; see Slave Trade. African Coast; Gabriel, Slaver Brig; see Two Friends; Gallatin (Albert), of Penn, p651; Gantois and Pailhet, p652; Garcia (Carlos), p652; Geeren (John H.), Settler of Key Biscayne, Fla., p657; General de Kalb, Amer. Slave Vessel, p662; General Pickney, Slaver (Pierce), p663; Genesee Co. (N.Y.) Citizens, p664; George William Jones, Amer. Slaver Brig, p665; Georgetown (DC) Mayor, Aldermen, and Council, p665; Georgetown (Mass.) Citizens, p665; Georgia, p665; Germantown, U.S. Sloop, p666; Gertrudes, Sp. Slaver, p666; Gettysburg (Pa.) Citizens, p666; Gibbs (Howard), Amer. Cons. Agt. Nuevitas, p667; Giddings (Joshua R.) of Ohio, p669; Gillmer (John S.), of Md., p670; Gilpin (H. D.), Atty. Gen. U.S.A., p671.

- Glamorgan, Amer. Slaver Brig, p671; Gloucester (Mass.) Citizens, p672; Gooch (Daniel W.) Repr. From Mass., p675; Goodrich, Master Amer. Slaver Brig Yankee; see Yankee; Goodrich (Edmund) [sic], H.B.M. Comr. Brit. and Portuguese Mixed Commission for Suppression of Slave Trade Under Treaty of 1842; see Slave Trade. African; Gordon (Nathaniel), Master Amer. Slaver Camargo; see Camargo; Gordon (Nathaniel), Master Amer. Slaver Erie; see Erie; Graham (John), Master Barque Pons; see Pons; Graham (William A.), of N.C., p680; Grampus, U.S. Schr., p681; Great Britain, pp684, 687-689; Green (James S.), of Missouri, p693; Greene Co. (O.) Citizens, p693; Gregory XVI, p694; Grey (Frederick W.), p695; Grey Eagle, Amer. Slaver Brig, p695; Groesbeck (William S.), of Ohio, p697; Grundy (Felix), of Tenn., p698; Guadaloupe, Slaver, p698; Guerediaga (Ramon De), Slave Dealer, p713; Guerrero, Span. Slaver Brig, p713; Guimaraes (Isidoro Francisco), Gov. of Macao, p714; Guimaraes (Manuel Antonio); Involved in Case of Slaver Herald; see Herald; Gurley (R.R.), Secy. Amer. Colonization Society, p714; Gwin (W.M.), Sen. From Calif., p717; Hackley (William R.), U.S. Atty. So. Distr. Fla., p718; Hagan (John), et al., p718; Haidee, Slaver, p718; Haiti, p720; Hale (John Parker), pp722-723; Hale (Matthew), Master Amer. Slaver Brig Sophia; see Sophia; Hall (Christopher J.), Master Amer. Brig Kremlin. Deposition; see Fenix, Span. Slaver; Hall (James), p724; Hallett (Benjamin F.), U.S. Distr. Atty., Mass., p725; Hamilton (Hamilton), H.B.M.E.E. and M.P., p726; Hamilton Co. (O.) Citizens, p727; Hamlin (Edward S.), Repr. From O., p727; Hamlin (Hannibal), of Me., pp727-728; Hammond (James H.), Sen. From S.C., p729; Hanna, Master Amer. Slaver Bark Orion; see Orion; Hantsman (Henry), Master Span. Slaver Schr. Laura; see Laura; Hardesty

(Samuel), p734; Harlan (James), Sen. From Iowa, p735; Harlequin, H.B.M. Sloop Russell), p735; Harriet, Amer. Slaver, p736; Harris (Isham G.), Repr. From M.D., p736; Hastings (George F.), Senior Officer So. Div. H.B.M. Forces S.West Coast of Africa, p741; Haverhill (Mass.) Citizens, p743; Hayne (Robert Y.), Sen. From S.C., p747; Hecate, H.B.M. Ship (Burgess), p749; Helm (Charles J.), of Ky., p750; Hemphill (John), Sen. From Texas, p751; Henley (John D.), of Md., p751.

- Henry Co. (Ind.) Citizens, p752; Herald, Amer. Slaver (Barker), pp752-753; Hermosa, Amer. Schr. (Chattin); Claim vs. Gr. Br., p753; Hero, Amer. Schr. (O'Connell), p735; Hesketh (Robert), British Consul at Rio de Janeiro, p755; Highland Co. (O.) Citizens, p758; Hill, Master Amer. Slaver Brig Pilgrim; see Pilgrim; Hill (Joshua), of Ga., p758; Hill (Stephen J.), Gov. of Sierra Leone, p758; Hillsborough (Ind.) Citizens, p759; Hillyer (Junius), p759; Himmaleh, Amer. Slaver Brig, p760; Hodges (Benjamin), Claimant, p762; Holabird (W.S.), U.S. Atty. Dist. Conn., P765; Holland (Wm. T.), Clerk to Amer. Cons. at Rio de Janeiro, p766; Honore, Slave, p770; Hook (L.), p770; Hooker (Samuel B.), Master Amer. Slaver Clara; see Clara; Hoover (Frederick), p770; Hope, Amer. Slaver Brig (Driscoll), p770; Horatio, Slaver Brig, pp771-772; Hound, Amer. Slaver Schr., p772; Hubbard (Henry), Repr. From N.H., p778; Hudson, Amer. Slaver Brig, p779; Huffington, Master Amer. Slaver Brig Caballero; see Caballero; Hunt (James), Comdr. H.B.M. Sloop Alecto, p786; Hunt (Thomas W.), Master Amer. Slaver Schr. Shakespeare; see Shakespeare; Hunter (Robert M.T.), pp787-788; Hunter (William), of R.I., p789; Hunter (William, Jr.) of R.I., p789; Huntington (E.), Master Amer. Slaver Schr. Ontario; see Ontario; Huron Co. (O.) Citizens, p791and Hyde de Neuville (Jean Guillaume), p793.

Part II:

- Iago, Amer. Schr. (Dupony), p795; Illinois, p795; Illinois, Amer. Slaver Schr. (Swift), p796; Imogene, Amer. Bark, p796; Indiana, pp799-800; Ingersoll (Charles J.), pp800-801; Ingersoll (Ralph I.), of Conn., p803; Inman (William), of N.J., pp804-805; Intervention and Mediation, p809; Iowa, p809; Iris, H.B.M. Ship (Tucker); see Illinois, Amer. Slaver Schr.; Isturiz (Franciso Javier), p811; Iverson, p812; J. Harris, Slaver, p813; J.J. Cobb, Amer. Bark (Vent), p813; Jackson (George) and Gabriel (Edmund), p815; Jackson Co. (O.) Citizens, p816; James Buchanan, Slaver Schr., p817; Jamestown, Slaver Brig, p818; Janet, Slaver, p819; Jasper, Amer. Slaver Bark (Young), pp820-821; Jefferson, Master Slaver schr. H.N. Gambril; see H.N. Gambril; Jefferson (Thomas), of Va., p822; Jenifer (Daniel), of Md., p823; Jiro (Manuel Francisco), Deponent; see Senator, Amer. Slaver Brig; John Adams, Slaver Brigantine, p829; John Adams U.S. Sloop, p829; Johnson (Reverdy), p831; Johnson (William), Judge Supreme Court of S.C., p833; Johnstown (N.Y.) Citizens, p833; Jones (George W.), Repr. From Tenn., p835; Jones (John J.), Repr. From Ga., p836; Jones (Hohn W.), p836; Jones (William), Sr. Officer Br. Forces West Coast of Africa, p838; Joseph H. Record, Slaver, p840; Josephine, Slaver Brig, p840; Julia Dean, Amer. Bark, p840; Juliana, Amer. Slaver Brig, p840; Juliet, Amer. Slaver Brig, p840; Jupiter, Amer. Slaver Schr., p841; Keitt (Lawrence M.), Repr. From S.C., p846; Kellett (Arthur), Lieut. Comdg. H.B.M Brig Brisk, p846; Kelly (John), Master Slaver Brig Senator; see Senator; Kendall (Amos), Fourth Auditor U.S. Treasury Dept., p847; Kennedy (J.), Br. Comr. at Havana Under Mixed Commission for Suppression of slave trade; see slave trade. Cuban Waters.; Kennedy (John P.) of Md., p848; Kent (Edward), p849; Kentucky, p849; Kentucky, Amer. Slaver Brig (Douglass), p850; Kerr (John L.) Repr. From Md., p851; King (William), Master Slaver Schr. Anaconda, p859; Koeler (George C.), Deponent in Case of Slaver Senator; see Senator; Kremlin, Amer. Brig; see Fenix, Span. Slaver; Kroomen, p866; Lafayette (Ind.) Citizens, p869; Lake (John, Jr.), Master Slaver Bark Louisa; see Louisa; Laporte Co. (Ind.) Citizens, p873; Lara (Jose), p873; Lark, Span. Slaver Schr. (Solomon), p873; Larkin, Master Slaver Schr. Merchant; see Merchant; Lasher (Nicholas), Master Amer. Slaver Brig Solon; see Solon; Latrobe (John H. B.), p875; Laura, Span. Slaver Schr. (Hantsman), p875.

- Pizarro, Span. Man-of-War, p1290; Pleasants (B.F.), Actg. Solicitor Treasury, U.S., p1291; Pluto, H.B.M. Str. (Simpson); see Amer. Bark Orion; Polk (James Knox), of Tenn., pp1297-1298; Polk (Trusten), p1299; Pons, Amer. Slaver Bark (Graham; Berry), p1301; Pontifical States, p1302; Porpoise, Amer. Brig (Libby), p1303; Porpoise, U.S. Schr., p1304; Porter (Augustus S.), Sen. From Mich., p1306; Porter (Edward), H.B.M. Consul at Bahia, p1307; Porter (James M.), p1307; Porter (John), Lieut. Comdg. U.S. Brig Boxer, p1307; Powell (Lazarus W.), Sen. From Ky., p1313; Powell (Levin M.), of Va., p1313; Pratt, Master Amer. Slaver Brig Pamelia; see Pamelia; Pratt (Thomas G.), of Md., p1314; Preston (William Campbell), of S.C., p1320; Privateering, p1323; Prometheus, H.B.M. Sloop (Hope), p1326; Prometheus, U.S. Brig, p1326; Prova, Port. Slaver Schr. (Dias), p1326; Providence (R.I.) Citizens, p1326; Pryor (Roger A.), Repr. From Va., p1327; Pugh (George E.), Sen. From O., p1328; Purvis (J.B.), Comdr. H.B.M. Ship Alfred, p1328; Putnam (Ind.) Citizens, p1329; Pylades, H.B.M. Schr. (Castle), p1329 and Quintuple Treaty, p1331.

Part III:

- Racer, H.B.M. Brig (Reed), p1333; Rachel P. Brown, Amer. Slaver Schr., p1333; Ramos (Jose Peres), and Costales (I. Manuel), Deponents in Case of Jasper; see Jasper; Ramsay (William W.), of Va., p1336; Randolph Co. (Ill.) Citizens, p1337; Randolph Co. (Ind.) Citizens, p1338; Ranger (Francis), Master Amer. Slaver William Clarke; see William Clarke; Raritan, U.S. Frigate, p1338; Rauch (Charles), Master Amer. Slaver Brig Uncas; see Uncas, p1338; Reagan (John H.), Repr. From Texas, p1339; Rebecca, Amer. Slaver Schr. (Watson, Arteta), p1340; Rebecca, Amer. Ship (Carter), p1340; Recognition, p1383; Redfield (Hemon J.), Collector of Customs, New York City, p1384; Reed (Archibald), Comdr. H.B.M. Ship Racer, p1384; Reeve (John), Comdr. H.B.M. Sloop Lily, p1388; Reform Convention, Annapolis, p1389; Rego (Jose Ricardo de Sa), p1389; Rendall (John), H.B.M. Consul at Boa Vista, Cape Verde, p1391; Reynolds (John H.), Repr. From N.Y., p1394; Rezende (Manoel Jose de), Slave Dealer, p1394; Rhode Island, p1395; Rhoderick Dhu, Amer. Bark (Sims), p1396; Richard Cobden, Amer. Ship (Black), p1399; Rives (William Cabell), of Va., p1408; Roach, Master Slaver Uncas; see Uncas; Roarer, Amer. Slaver, p1409; Robert McClelland, U.S. Revenue Cutter (Morrison), p1410; Robert Wilson, Slaver Schr., p1410; Roberts (J.J.), p1411; Robertson (Joseph W.), p1413;

- Robertson (William H.), of La., pp1413-1415; Robinson (Ann), Claimant, p1416; Robinson (C.W.), Master Amer. Slaver Schr. Enterprise; see Enterprise; Roderick, Master Slaver Brig Nancy; see Nancy; Rodeur, Fr. Slaver, p1419; Rosa, Slaver, p1423; Ross, Co. (O.) Citizens, p1424; Rudd (Edward), Claimant, pp1425-1426; Rufus Soule, Amer. Brigantine (Anderson; Davis), pp1426-1427; Rush (Richard), of Penn, p1428; Rush Co. (Ind.) Citizens, p1428; Rusk (Thomas Jefferson), of Texas, p1429; Russell (John) Lord, p1431; Russwurm (John B.), Agt. Md. State Colonization Society, p1433; Ruverosa Y Urgellis (Francisco), p1434; Ryan (Albert F.), Master Amer. Slaver Schr. Swift; see Swift; Sa (Bernardino da), Slave Dealer, p1434; St. Andrews, Amer. Slaver Brigantine, p1435; St. Joseph's Co. (Ind.) Citizens, p1436; Salisbury (Mass.) Citizens, p1440; San Antonio, Port. Slaver Brig, p1442; San Joseph, Spanish Slaver, p1443; Sandy Bay (Mass.) Citizens, p1447; Sappho, H.B.M. Sloop (Moresby); see Moresby (F.); see also Panchita, Amer. Bark; Charles Slaver; Sarah Anne, Amer. Slaver Schr. (Fronte), p1450; Sartiges (Etienne Gilbert Eugene), p1453; Saucy Jack, Amer. Privateer, Slaver, p1453; Savage (Thomas), pp1455-1456; Sawyer (William), Repr. From O., p1457; Schenck (Robert C.), of O., p1458; Schrnley (Edward W.H.), p1459; Sea Eagle, Amer. Brig (Smith), p1464; Seddon (James A.), Repr. From Va., p1466; Sedgwick (Thomas), Counsel for Africans On Board Amistad; see Amistad; Semmes (Benedict I.), Repr. From Md., p1467; Senator, Amer. Slaver Brig (Kelly), p1468; Seneca Co. (N.Y.) Citizens, p1468; Serrano (Francisco), Capt. Gen. of Cuba, p1469; Sete de Avril, Port. Schr. Martinho), p1469.

74

- Sevier (Ambrose H.), of Ark., P1471; Seward (James L.), Repr. From Ga., pp1471, 1473-1474; Seys (John), U.S. Agt. For Liberated Africans, p1475; Shakespeare, Amer. Slaver Schr. (Hunt), p1476; Sharkey (W.L.), of Miss., p1477; Sharpshooter, H.B.M. Str., p1477; Shelby Co. (Ind.) Citizens, p1478; Sheldon (Daniel, Jr.), of Conn., p1478; Sherman (John) of O., p1480; Sierra de Pillar, Por. Brig of War (Rodoralho), p1486; Silenus, Amer. Slaver Brig, p1487; Silva, Don, Slave Dealer, p1487; Silva Paranhos (Jose Maria da), Visconde do Rio Branco, p1487; Simmons (James F.), Sen. From R.I., p1488; Simonds (Lewis E.), of Mass., p1488; Singleton (Otho R.), of Miss., p1490; Skene (John D.), Comdr. H.B.M. Ship Philomel, p1490; Slacum (George W.), of DC, p1490; Slave Dealers, p1493; slave trade, pp1493-1519; Slidell (John), of La., pp1519, 1521; Smith (Benjamin Everett), of Md., p1524; Smith (William), of Va., p1531; Soares (Joao), Slave Dealer, p1533; Solomon (T.M.), Master Span. Slaver Schr. Lark; see Lark; Solon, Amer. Slaver Brig (Lasher), p1534; Sooy, Amer. Slaver Brig (Leeds), p1535; Sophia, Amer. Slaver Brig (Hale), p1535; Soule (Pierre), of La., pp1536-1537; South Carolina, p1541; Southern (Henry), H.B.M.E.E. and M.P. in Brazil, p1542; Sovereignty, p1543; Spain, pp1554-1556; Spaulding (Eldridge G.), of N.Y., p1558; Speight (Jesse), p1559; Spencer (William A.), of N.Y., p1559; Spitfire, Slaver Schr., p1560; Splendid (Or, Velha Annita), Slaver Bark (Rich), p1561; Spy, H.B.M. Brigantine (Raymond), p1526; Stanly (Edward), of N.C., p1565; Stanton (Frederick P.), of Tenn., p1567; Staples (S.P.), Counsel for Africans On Board Amistad; see Amistad, p1567; Star, H.B.M. Brig, p1567; Stevens (A.H.), p1570; Stevens (Lucius), Deponent in Case of Brig Creole; see Creole; Stevenson (Andrew), of Va., pp1571-1572; Stevenson (Michael) Master Slaver Schr. N. Hand; see N. Hand; Stewart (James A.), Repr. From Md., p1574; Storm King, Amer. Slaver Brigantine, p1577.

- Stowe (Vt.) Citizens, p1578; Strange (Robert), Sen. From N.C., p1578; Suiters (Joseph), p1581; Sumner (G.W.); see Sophia, Amer. Brig, p1582; Susan, Amer. Brig (Wilford), pp1583-1584; Susquehannah Co. (Penn.) Citizens, p1585; Swift (Benjamin), Sen. From Vt., p1587; Swift (J.), Master Amer. Slaver Schr. Illinois; see Illinois; Swift, Amer. Slaver Schr., Late Conchita (Ryan), p1587; Taney (Roger Brooke), p1590; Taylor (Miles), p1593; Taylor (Zachary), p1594; Tazewell (Littleton Walker), of Va., p1594; Teazer, H.B.M. Str. (Grubbe), p1595; Tejedor (Gregorio), Slave Dealer, p1595; Temerario, Brazilian Slaver Brig, p1595; Temple (William), Deponent in Case of Slaver Brig Senator; see Senator; Termagant, H.B.M. Brig (Seagram), p1597; Texas (Republic), pp1603-1606, 1608-1609, 1611, 1621, 1625; Texas (State), p1633; Thomas (John Addison), of N.Y., p1637; Thompson (J.), p1639; Thompson (Jacob), p1640; Tigris, Amer. Brig (Frye), p1644; Tilden (Daniel R.), Repr. From O., p1645; Timas (Antonio Soares), p1645; Titi, Amer. Brig, p1646; Tod (David), of O., pp1650-1651; Toombs (Robert), of Ga., p1653; Topham (George W.), Deponent in Case of Sooy; see Sooy; Toreado (Peter), Slave Dealer, p1654; Totten (Benjamin J.), of N.Y., p1656; Toucey (Isaac), of Conn., pp1657-1658; Treaty, Amer. Slaver, p1659; [Trenchard (Edward)], of N.J., p1659; Trescot (William H.), of S.C., p1660; Trist (Nicholas P.), of Va., pp1661-1664; Triton, H.B.M. Ship (Burton), p1664; Triton, Slaver, p1664; Triuphante, Slaver, p1664; Trousdale (William), of Tenn., p1665; Trumbull (Lyman), Sen. From Ill., p1665; Truxton, U.S. Brig, p1666; Tuck (Amos), Repr. From N.H., p1666; Tucker (William), Senior Officer, H.B.M. Navy, West Coast of Africa, p1667.

- Tudor (John), Comdr. H.B.M. Str. Firefly, p1667; Tudor (William, Jr.), of Mass., p1669; Turner (Daniel), of R.I., p1675; Turney (Hopkins L.), Sen. From Tenn., p1676; Two Friends, Late The Gabriel, Amer. Slaver Brig (Durkee), p1677; Tyler (Alexander H.), of Md., p1679; Tyler (John), of Va., pp1680-1681; Tyler (William J.), Master Slaver Brig Sooy; see Sooy; Uncas, Slaver Brig (Roach), p1682; Underwood (Joseph R.), of Ky., pp1682-1683; United States of America, pp1766, 1770; Upshur (Abel P.), of Va., pp1857-1859; Usher (George M.), Owner of Slaver Magoun p1861; Vail (Aaron, Jr.) of N.Y., pp1861-1862; Valedes (Jose Antonio), Secy. Mixed Court Justice, Havana, p1863; Van Buren (Martin), pp1865, 1867; Van Dyke (James C.), U.S. Distr. Atty., Eastern Distr. Penn., p1869; Vandalia, U.S. Sloop, p1877; Vaughan (Charles

Richard), p1879; Velha Aunto, Slave Str; see Splendid; Venable (Abraham W.), Repr. From N.C., p1880; Venganza, Slaver, p1881; Venus, Late Duquesa de Braganza, Amer. Slaver Corvette (Wallace; Phillips), p1882; Venus, Amer. Slaver Bark, p1882; Venus Havannera, Sp. Slaver, p1882.

- Vermont, pp1883-1884; Vernon (Conn.) Citizens, p1884; Vernon (N.Y.) Citizens, p1884; Vesey (Charles), Comdr. H.B.M. Str. Styx, p1884; Vessels, p1886; Vesta, Amer. Slaver, p1886; Victoria, Port. Slaver Brig (Alfonso), p1887; Vintage, Amer. Slaver Brig, p1889; Violante, Port. Slaver Schr. (Marcolino), p1889; Viper, Amer. Slaver Schr., p1889; Viper, H.B.M. Ship (Hodgkinson; Hewett), p1889; Visit and Search, pp1890-1898; Vixen, U.S. Str., p1898; Volador, Spanish Slaver Brig, p1898; Volusia, Amer. Brigantine; Claim vs. Gr. Br., p1898; W.D. Miller, Amer. Slaver Brig; see William D. Miller; Walker (Isaac P.), Sen. From Wisc., p1902; Walker (Robert J.), p1903; Wallace (William), Master Amer. Slaver Venus; see Venus; Walton (N.Y.) Citizens, p1906; Wanderer, Slaver Yacht, p1906; Warren, U.S. Sloop, p1911; Washington (DC), p1911; Washington (Penn.) Citizens, p1911; Washington Amer. Slaver Bark (Neill); see Senhora da Boa Viagem, Port. Schr.; Washington's Barge, Amer. Slaver Brig (Matson), p1915; Watson (Artate), Master Amer. Slaver Schr. Rebecca; see Rebecca; Webster (Daniel), of Mass., pp1919-1922, 1925; Webster (Daniel Fletcher), of Mass., p1929.

- Weems (Wilson L.), Master Slaver Asp; see Asp; Weetman, Br. Subject, p1930; Whig, Amer. Slaver Brig, p1943; Whitcomb (James), p1943; Whitley Co. (Ind.) Citizens, p1945; Wigfall (Louis T.), Sen. From Tex., p1947; Wildfire, Slaver, pp1947-1948; William, Amer. Slaver Bark (Weston, Alias Symmes), p1949; William Clarke, Amer. Slaver (Ranger), p1950; William D. Miller, Amer. Slaver Brig (Ford, Abarroa), p1950; William Ridgway, Amer. Slaver Schr. (Chase), p1950; Williams (Mary L.), p1952; Williams (Nathaniel), U.S. Atty. For Distr. of Md., p1952; Willis (John G.), Amer. Coml. Agt. St. Paul de Loanda, p1954; Wilmot (Arthur P.E.), Comdr. H.B.M. Sloop Harlequin, p1955; Wilmot (David), Repr. From Penn., p1955; Wilson (Edmund), Comdr. H.B.M. Brig Cygnet, p1955; Wilson (Henry), Sen. From Mass., pp1955-1956; Wilson (James P.), of Md., p1956; Windward, Amer. Slaver Schr., p1957; Winthrop (Robert C.), pp1958-1959; Wise (Charles A.), Comdr. H.B.M. Naval Forces, African Station, p1960; Wise (Henry A.), pp1960-1961; Wise (Henry A.), Legal Repr. of J.J. Wise, p1962; Wittich (William), Prof. at London University, p1962; Wizard, Slaver Brig (Miller), p1963; Wolverine, H.B.M. Sloop (Tucker), p1963; Wood (Edmond), Deponent in Case of St. Andrews, p1964; Woodbury (Charles Levi), Comr. Circ. Ct. U.S. Distr. Mass., p1965; Woodside (William), Deponent in Case of Creole; Creole; Wyoming, Amer. Slaver Brigantine (Christopher; Edwards), pp19711-1972; Yankee, Amer. Slaver Brig (Goodrich), p1972; York Springs (Penn.) Anti-Slavery Socy., p1975; Yorktown, U.S. Sloop, p1975; Young (James), Claim vs. Gr. Br., p1975; Young (Samuel), Master Amer. Slaver Bark Jasper; see Jasper; Young Men's Anti-Slavery Society of Philadelphia, p1976; Yulee (David Levy), p1978; Zenobia, Amer. Slaver Schr., p1980; Zephyr, Amer. Slaver, p1980.

- Records of the Mixed Claims Commission (established by convention of 1822); Minutes of the Mixed Commission. Aug. 25, 1823-Mar. 26, 1827, 1 vol., entry 181; Docket of 1822 Commission. Ca. 1825-26, 1 vol. entry 183; Index to Miscellaneous Records, N.d. 3 in., entry 184; Miscellaneous Records. Ca. 1814-28, 7 vols., entry 185; Records Relating to Detained American Vessels. Ca. 1812-19, 17 ft., entry 186; Records of the Domestic Claims Commission; Minutes of the Domestic Claims Commission. July 10, 1827-Aug. 31, 1828, 3 vols., entry 187; List (Docket) of Claims. 1826, 1 vol., entry 188; Index to Claimants. N.d. 16 in., entry 189; Case Files. Ca. 1814-28, 3.5 ft., entry 190; List of Awards. Ca. 1827-28, 1 vol., entry 191; Definitive List of Slaves and Property. N.d. 1 vol., entry 192; Slave Lists. N.d. 2 vols., entry 193; Records of the Mixed Claims Commission (established by convention of 1853); Minutes of the Commission. Sept. 15, 1853-Jan. 15, 1855, 1 vol., entry 195; Index to Case Files of American and British

Claims. N.d. 9 in., entry 196; Miscellaneous Claims; Index to Miscellaneous Claims; Miscellaneous Claims. Ca. 1797-1853,6 in., entry 201; The Case of the Vessel "Jehossee." Ca. 1860, 1 in., entry 203.[91]

We further request, as referenced above, that you provide us access to or copies of all records that are relevant or related to our Request from all Congresses and all Sessions of the Senate and House from 1865 to the present, especially those that reference slave-like conditions and practices, including peonage, share-cropping, convict-lease, prison labor, chain-gang labor, colonialism, segregation (Jim Crow), apartheid, etc. We request that you order all agencies under your authority to comply in full and in an expedited manner with this historic and precedent setting FOIA Request, and that you waive all applicable fees.

In order to help you determine our status and make your decision on our fee waiver request, you should know that Bob Brown is an organizer and researcher, who has worked, studied and struggled for 41 years, within and for the Student, Civil and Human Rights, Black Power, National Liberation, Pan-African, and Peace Movements. See Attachment B.

Disclosure of the requested information is in the public interest because it will be meaningfully informative in relation to the subject matter of this FOIA Request; because most of the requested records are not in the public domain, and those that are in the public domain are not accessible to the public that we serve; because their release will likely to contribute significantly to greater public understanding of the United States Government's role, operations and activities, positive and negative, historically and currently, in the struggle to criminalize, prohibit and abolish these crimes; because this FOIA Request is not primarily in our commercial interest; and because we are highly qualified to understand, extract, convey and disseminate the information to the public at large.

Please provide an expedited review of this FOIA Request, which concerns a matter of urgency. As scholars, organizers and activists, we have been primarily engaged in disseminating information and education for more than 40-years. The public has an urgent need for the requested information because:

- The need involves an ongoing discussion about slavery and the slave trade, crimes against humanity and reparations to which informed members of the public might contribute through further research and publication, mass education, organization and mobilization, lobbying or other contacts with public officials, and any delay would further rob the public of detailed information about the role, activities and operations of the United States Government, positive and negative, historically and currently, in the struggle to facilitate, prohibit, or abolish these crimes against humanity. Further delay would also rob the public of its ability to discuss and debate these concerns, make known its views, and contribute to the resolution of issues involved in a timely manner.

- The public, especially the African community, wants and needs to address serious allegations of governmental wrongdoing and cover-up, historically and currently, with respect to these issues in a timely manner.

- Moreover, these crimes against African and world humanity have been committed for over 569-years, and continue to be committed through denial, cover-up, lies, and fraud, governmental and non-governmental; and over 100 million African People have suffered, and their descendants continue to suffer, as a result of these crimes and the continuing denial and cover-up. It is time to redress these issues and resolve them, one way, or the other.

We expect your positive response to this historic and precedent setting FOIA Request within 20 working days as the statute provides. If our request is denied in whole or part, we ask that you justify the

---

[91] United States National Archives & Records Administration. Records that pertain to *American Slavery and the International Slave Trade II. Civil Records. Records of Boundary and Claims Commissions and Arbitration (Record Group 76).*

denial or all deletions by reference to specific exemptions of the act. We also expect you to release all segregable portions of otherwise exempt material.

Please be assured that we will exhaust all administrative, legal and political remedies to successfully conclude this FOIA Request. Thank you for your consideration.

Sincerely,
Bob Brown, co-director
Pan-African Roots

Pan-African Roots
1247 E Street SE
Washington, DC 20003
Tel: (202-) 544-9355 - Fax: (202) 544-9359
Email: paroots02@yahoo.com

25 October 2004

Mr. John Snow, Secretary of the Treasury
Department of Treasury
1500 Pennsylvania NW
Washington, DC 20220

AMENDED FREEDOM OF INFORMATION ACT REQUEST.
Fee Waiver and Expedited Review Request.
cc: FOIA Officer and FOIA Appeals Officer.

Dear Mr. Snow:

Pursuant to the federal Freedom of Information Act (5 U.S.C. Sec. 552) and the Electronic FOIA Amendments of 1996 and 1997 ("EFOIA Amendments" and 5 U.S.C. Sec. 552 (f)(2) (effective March 31, 1997), we request access to and copies of all records created or obtained by, or under the control of the United States Government that relate to, or contain information about:

- The role, operations, and activities of the United States Government, especially the Department of the Treasury, the United States Customs Service, the Bureau of the Census, the Office of Foreign Assets Control, in facilitating, prohibiting and combating privateering, slavery and the slave trade, especially the Trans-Atlantic Slave Trade and slave-like conditions and practices, including colonialism, segregation and apartheid.

- Slave, urban and racial disturbances, riots, rebellions and revolts, runaway slaves, fugitives beyond borders, related claims or requests, and demands for restitution and reparations.

- All treaties or agreements, bilateral or multilateral, or diplomatic communications, correspondence, discussions, public and secret, between the United States Government and its Officials (all levels, branches and agencies) and the British, Canadian, French, Spanish, Mexican or any other government with respect to the above or related subjects, including their proclamations, edicts and laws liberating slaves in their countries and colonies, and granting them citizenship; their encouragement of and assistance to slaves to revolt and runaway; their evacuation or harboring of slaves; their refusal to return fugitive slaves or pay compensation; and related claims or requests.

- All governments, agencies (federal, state, county or local), corporations, non-governmental organizations, institutions, churches, families, individuals, or entities, domestic or foreign who participated or invested in, or made profits from the above referenced crimes against humanity; and who owns or benefits from these historical and continuing crimes today, including but not limited to those listed in Appendix A.

Piracy and privateering, slavery and the slave trade, and the related Atlantic Trade, Colonial Trade, West Indies Trade, Coastal Trade, and the trade in slave-produced tobacco, cotton, sugar, molasses, rum, rice, indigo, hemp, etc. were and are at root economic. These economic activities were highly regulated and taxed at every level of the United States Government, especially the Treasury Department.

We therefore formally and publicly request that you search and provide us access to or copies of all relevant records in the following and other Record Groups:

- General Records of the Department of the Treasury (Record Group 56), Records of the United States Coast Guard (Record Group 26), Records of the U.S. Customs Service (Record Group 36), Records of the Bureau of Accounts (Treasury) (Record Group 39), Records of the Treasurer of the United States (Record Group 50), Records of the Bureau of the Public Debt (Record Group 53), Records of the Internal Revenue Service (Record Group 58), Records of the Solicitor of the Treasury (Record Group 206), Records of the Accounting Officers of the Department of the Treasury (Record Group 217), Record copies of publications of the Department of the Treasury in Publications of the U.S. Government (RG 287) and Security-Classified Records.

- Records of the Customs Division, the District of Columbia Division, the Division of Foreign Intercourse, the Division of Internal Revenue Accounts, the Division of Judiciary Accounts, the Public Debt Division, the Division of Public Lands, the Division of Territorial Accounts, the Indian Division, the Miscellaneous Claims Division and Office of the Commissioner of Customs.

- Records of the Bureau of the Census (Record Group 29) including, but not limited to decennial censuses of population and housing; quinquennial censuses of agriculture, state and local governments, manufactures, mineral industries, distributive trades, construction industries and transportation; statistics on foreign trade, imports, exports, and shipping; and Statistical Atlases of the United States showing political, social, and economic data such as population by race and nationality, vital statistics, wealth, employment, handicapped groups, agriculture, irrigation and drainage, Congressional districts, slaves, and non-population schedules of agriculture, industry, manufactures, mortality and social statistics.

- Records of Civil War Agencies of the Treasury Department (Record Group 366).

We request that you provide us access to or copies of all manifests and records that document the name, age and description of slaves; the name and residence of exporters, consignees and owners; name, tonnage and nationality of the vessels; date of arrival; name of master; the pledge that the slaves had not been imported after 1807; the trafficking and trade in slave-produced products such as tobacco, sugar, molasses, rum, cotton, rice, indigo and hemp at the following and other Ports and Customs Houses:

- Albany, NY; Albemarle (Elizabeth City), NC; Alexandria, VA; Annapolis, MD; Baltimore, MD; Bangor, ME; Barnstable, MA; Bath, ME; Beaufort, SC; Beaumont, TX; Belfast, ME; Bermuda Hundred (City Point), VA; Boston-Charlestown, MA; Brazos de Santiago, TX; Bridgeton, NJ; Bristol-Warren, RI; Brownsville, TX; Brunswick, GA; Buffalo Creek (Buffalo), NY; Buffalo, NY; Burlington, NJ; Burlington, VT; Camden, NC; Cedar Point, MD; Charleston, SC; Cherrystone, VA; Chester, PA; Chicago, IL; Corpus Christi, TX; Dallas, TX; Del Rio, TX; Dighton (Fall River), MA; Dumfries, VA; Eagle Pass, TX; Eastern District (Crisfield), MD; Edenton, NC; Edgartown, MA; Edinburgh, TX; Fairfield (Bridgeport), CT; Fernandina Beach, FL; Freeport, TX; Frenchmen's Bay, ME; Galveston, TX.

- Genesee (Rochester), NY; Georgetown (Washington), DC; Georgetown, SC; Gloucester, MA; Great Egg Harbor, NJ; Houston, TX; Jacksonville (St. Johns), FL; Kennebunk, ME; Key West, FL; Lake Charles, LA; Laredo, TX; Little Egg Harbor, NJ; Louisville, KY; Louisville, NY; Machias, ME; Marblehead, MA; Massena, NY; Memphis, TN; Memphremagogg, VT; Miami, FL; Middletown-Hartford, CT; Mobile, AL; Morgan City, LA; Morristown, NY; Nashville, TN; New Bedford, MA; New Bern, NC; New Haven, CT; New London, CT; New Orleans, LA; New York, NY; Newark, NJ; Newburyport, MA; Newport, OR; Newport, RI; Niagara, NY; Norfolk-Portsmouth, VA; Ocracoke, NC; Ogdensburg, NY; Oswegatchie, NY; Oswego, NY; Paducah, KY; Pamlico, NC; Passamaquoddy, ME; Pearl River, MS; Penobscot (Castine), ME; Pensacola, FL; Perth Amboy, NJ; Petersburg, VA.

- Philadelphia, PA; Pittsburgh, PA; Plymouth, MA; Plymouth, NC; Port Arthur, TX; Port Isabel, TX; Portland-Falmouth, ME; Portsmouth, NH; Presque Isle (Erie), PA; Providence, RI;

Providence, RI; Puerto Rico; Richmond, VA; Saco, ME; Sag Harbor, NY; Salem-Beverly, MA; Saluria, TX; San Antonio, TX; Savannah, GA; Savannah, GA; St. Augustine, FL; St. Louis, MO; St. Marks, FL; Stonington, CT; Tampa, FL; Teche, LA; Thousand Island State Park, NY; Tuckerton, NJ; Virgin Islands; Waddington, NY; Waldoboro, ME; Washington, NC; Wilmington, DE; Wilmington, NC; Wiscasset, ME; York, ME and Yorktown (Newport News), VA.

We also request that you give us access to or copies of the following that are listed in *"American Slavery and the International Slave Trade,"* [92] and in the records of the Solicitor of the Treasury (RG 206) including, but not limited to letters received by the Solicitor of the Treasury from U.S. district attorneys, marshals, and clerk of court; legal proceedings involving the collection of debts due the United States; letters relative to suits for the forfeiture of vessels involved in the slave trade; and the following:

- Index to Letters Received, September 1, 1865 - January 9, 1911: Volume 1, entry 2

- December 8, 1865 From the United States Attorney. New York, South District. Relative to proposition to compromise judgement against H.M. Bearnes and G.H. Blanchard on bond slaver barge "Weathergage."

- December 8, 1865 From the United States Attorney. New York, South District. Relative to proposition to compromise judgment against H.M. Bearnes and G.H. Blanchard on bond slaver barge "Weathergage."

- March 12, 1866 From the United States Attorney. New York, South District. Relative to proposition to settle case of barge "Weathergage."

- December 1, 1865 From the United States Attorney. New York, South District. Enclosing letter from Messrs. Beebe, Dean, and Donahue proposing compromise of liability of Henry M. Bearnes as surety on bond ship "Weathergage."

- December 8, 1865 From the United States Attorney. New York, South District. Relative to proposal to compromise judgment against H.M. Bearnes and G.H. Blanchard on bond slaver barge "Weathergage."

- December 8, 1865 From the United States Attorney. New York, South District. Relative to proposal to compromise judgment against H.M. Bearnes and G.H. Blanchard on bond slaver barge "Weathergage."

- March 12, 1866 From the United States Attorney. New York, South District. Relative to proposition to settle case of barge "Weathergage."

- April 23, 1866 From the Collector of Customs. Sandusky. Reporting Seizure of sloop "Jago."

- March 16, 1866 From Secretary of the Treasury. Washington, DC U.S. v. Sureties on Bond for Barge "Weathergage "accepts offer.

- Volume 2 entry 2

- July 9, 1866 From the United States Attorney. New York, South District. Relative to proposition made by Beebe, Dean, and Donahue in matter of "Weathergage."

- July 21, 1866 Waddell, West C. H. New York. Relative to the "Weathergage."

- Records of the United States General Accounting:

- Settled Accounts of Claimants and Disbursing Officers of the First Auditor.

---

[92] United States National Archives & Records Administration. *Records that pertain to American Slavery and the International Slave Trade: II. Civil Records.* Available from http://www.archives.gov/research_room/research_topics/slavery_records_civil.html.

- Claims case files, including: African shipping; bounties on Africans illegally imported; monies disbursed for the support of captured Africans were illegally entered into the United States; bounties for the capture of illegal slave ships; expenditures of the American Colonization Society and all other efforts or schemes to repatriate Africans to Africa.

- Abstract of Accounts for Bounty for the capture of ships in the Slave Trade.

- Records of the Board of Commissioners for the Emancipation of Slaves in the District of Columbia, and of all other proposals are schemes for compensated emancipation and repatriation.

We further request, as referenced above, that you provide us access to or copies of all records that are relevant or related to our Request from 1865 to the present, especially those that reference slave-like conditions and practices, including peonage, share-cropping, convict-lease, prison labor, chain-gang labor, colonialism, segregation (Jim Crow), apartheid, etc. We request that you order all agencies under your authority to comply in full and in an expedited manner with this historic and precedent setting FOIA Request, and that you waive all applicable fees.

In order to help you determine our status and make your decision on our fee waiver request, you should know that Bob Brown is an organizer and researcher, who has worked, studied and struggled for 41 years, within and for the Student, Civil and Human Rights, Black Power, National Liberation, Pan-African, and Peace Movements. See Attachment B.

Disclosure of the requested information is in the public interest because it will be meaningfully informative in relation to the subject matter of this FOIA Request; because most of the requested records are not in the public domain, and those that are in the public domain are not accessible to the public that we serve; because their release will likely to contribute to greater public understanding of the United States Government's role, operations and activities, positive and negative, historically and currently, in the struggle to criminalize, prohibit and abolish these crimes; because this FOIA Request is not primarily in our commercial interest; and because we are highly qualified to understand, extract, convey and disseminate the information to the public at large.

Please provide an expedited review of this FOIA Request, which concerns a matter of urgency. As scholars, organizers and activists, we have been primarily engaged in disseminating information and education for more than 40-years. The public has an urgent need for the requested information because:

- The need involves an ongoing discussion about slavery and the slave trade, crimes against humanity and reparations to which informed members of the public might contribute through further research and publication, mass education, organization and mobilization, lobbying or other contacts with public officials, and any delay would further rob the public of detailed information about the role, activities and operations of the United States Government, positive and negative, historically and currently, in the struggle to facilitate, prohibit, or abolish these crimes against humanity. Further delay would also rob the public of its ability to discuss and debate these concerns, make known its views, and contribute to the resolution of issues involved in a timely manner.

- The public, especially the African community, wants and needs to address serious allegations of governmental wrongdoing and cover-up, historically and currently, with respect to these issues in a timely manner.

- Moreover, these crimes against African and world humanity have been committed for over 569-years, and continue to be committed through denial, cover-up, lies, and fraud, governmental and non-governmental; and over 100 million African People have suffered, and their descendants continue to suffer, as a result of these crimes and the continuing denial and cover-up. It is time to redress these issues and resolve them, one way, or the other.

We expect your positive response to this historic and precedent setting FOIA Request within 20 working days as the statute provides. If our request is denied in whole or part, we ask that you justify the denial or all deletions by reference to specific exemptions of the act. We also expect you to release all segregable portions of otherwise exempt material.

Please be assured that we will exhaust all administrative, legal and political remedies to successfully conclude this FOIA Request. Thank you for your consideration.

Sincerely,
Bob Brown, co-director
Pan-African Roots

Pan-African Roots
1247 E Street SE
Washington, DC 20003
Tel: (202-) 544-9355 - Fax: (202) 544-9359
Email: paroots02@yahoo.com

25 October 2004

Mr. Donald Rumsfeld, Secretary of Defense
Department of Defense
The Pentagon
Washington, DC 20301-1155

AMENDED FREEDOM OF INFORMATION ACT REQUEST.
Fee Waiver and Expedited Review Request.
cc: FOIA Officer and FOIA Appeals Officer.

Dear Mr. Rumsfield:

Pursuant to the federal Freedom of Information Act (5 U.S.C. Sec. 552) and the Electronic FOIA Amendments of 1996 and 1997 ("EFOIA Amendments" and 5 U.S.C. Sec. 552 (f)(2) (effective March 31, 1997), we request access to and copies of all records created or obtained by, or under the control of the United States Government that relate to, or contain information about:

- The role, operations, and activities of the Department of Defense, and all agencies and structures under its authority and control, in facilitating, prohibiting or combating privateering, slavery and the slave trade, especially the Trans-Atlantic Slave Trade; and slave-like conditions and practices, including colonialism, segregation and apartheid, forced and compulsory labor, racism and racial discrimination, xenophobia and related intolerance.

- Slave, urban and racial disturbances, riots, rebellions and revolts, runaway slaves, fugitives beyond borders, related claims or requests, and demands for restitution and reparations.

- All treaties or agreements, bilateral or multilateral, or diplomatic communications, correspondence, discussions between the United States Government and its Officials (all levels, branches and agencies) and the British, Canadian, French, Spanish, Mexican or any other government with respect to the above or related subjects.

- Piracy and privateering, slavery and the slave trade, and the related Atlantic Trade, Colonial Trade, West Indies Trade, Coastal Trade, etc., could not have not occurred or be abolished without the participation or support of the military, especially the navy, the militias and the national guards of the slave-trading, slave-holding and colonizing nations of Europe and the Americas. From 1607, these military operations were highly regulated and controlled at every level of the United States Government, especially the Department of Defense.

- All governments, agencies (federal, state, county or local), corporations, non-governmental organizations, institutions, churches, families, individuals, or entities, domestic or foreign who participated or invested in, or made profits from the above referenced crimes against humanity; and who owns or benefits from these historical and continuing crimes today, including but not limited to those listed in Appendix A.

We formally and publicly request that you search and provides us access to or copies of all relevant records in the Records Collection of the Office of Naval Records and Library (Record Group 45), the Records of the Bureau of Indian Affairs (Record Group 75), the Records of the Adjutant General's Office (Record Group 94), the Records of the Bureau of Refugees, Freedmen, and Abandoned Lands (Record

Group 105), the Records of the Office of the Secretary of War (Record Group 107), the Records of the Office of the Inspector General (Record Group 159), the Records of U.S. Army Continental Commands (Record Group 393), the Record copies of publications of the Office of the Secretary of War in Publications of the U.S. Government (Record Group 287), the Records of the Office of the Secretary of the Army (Record Group 335) and all other relevant record groups.

We also request that you give us access to or copies of the following and all other records that pertain to "*American Slavery and the International Slave Trade,*"[93] which are referenced in the records.

Naval Records Collection of the Office of Naval Records and Library (Record Group 45).

- Miscellaneous Letters Received.

- Letters relating to the slave trade and the colonization of African Americans in Africa, letters from the American Colonization Society, and Navy agents.

- Letters to Officers, 1798 - 1886, 96 vols.

- Series of letters to officers, ships of war, containing letters and instructions from the Secretary of Navy to Officers of the African Squadron, 1863 - 61.

- Letters from Captains, 1805-61, 1866-85, 413 vols.

- Report by Capt. William M. Glendy," U.S.S. Saratoga", that the revival of the slave trade was occurring under the American flag.

- Letters from Federal Executive Agents, May 1837 - Dec 1886, 131 vols.

- Letters from Treasury and State Departments regarding the seizure of vessels suspected of engaging in the slave trade.

- Letters from the Attorney General, June 1807- Nov 1825, 1 vol.

- Replies to questions submitted by the Secy. of Navy on such subjects as the capture of slave vessels off the coast of Georgia, 1818; the authority given to the President by the Act of March 3, 1819, relating to the slave trade; and the application for money for the support of captured Africans in Savannah.

- Letters Sent Relating to Liberia, 1820-58, 1 vol.

- Communications to agents appointed under the act of March 3, 1819, prohibiting the slave trade; and to U.S. deputy marshals and district attorneys, relating mainly to the slave trade and recaptured Africans.

- Confidential Letters Sent, 1843 - 1879, 5 vols.

- Contain copies of letters sent by Secretary of Navy to officers of the African Squadron and to U.S. forces in the Mediterranean.

- African Squadron Letters, 1843 - 61, 13 vols.

- Letters from commanding officers of the Squadron, reports of officers of vessels in the Squadron, correspondence with British and other naval officers on the African coast, and with Liberian and other officials along the African coast.

---

[93] United States National Archives & Records Administration. *Records that pertain to American Slavery and the International Slave Trade: III. Military Records.* Available from http://www.archives.gov/research_room/research_topics/slavery_records_military.html.

- Logs, Journals, and Diaries of Officers of the U.S. Navy at Sea, March 1776 - June 1908, 234 vols.

- Personal accounts and records of activities, observations, and experiences of naval officers and personnel serving in the African Squadron.

Publications of the U.S. Government (Record Group 287).

Annual Reports of the Secretary of the Navy:

- 1828 pp.126-127, 1830 pp.42-43; 1834 p.315; 1836 pp.442-443, 450; 1837 pp.716, 725; 1848 pp.604, 605-606, 607; 1849 p.428.; 1850 pp.193, 194, 195.; 1851 pp.4-5.;1852 pp.291, 293, 299-301.; 1853 pp.298-299.; 1854 pp.386-387.;1855 pp.5-6.;1856 p.407.;1857 pp.576, 578.;1858 pp.5, 13-14.;1859 pp.1138-1139, 1144, 1149-1150.;1861 pp.20, 21.;1862 p.23 and 1865 p. XI.

We further request, as referenced above, that you provide us access to or copies of all records that are relevant or related to our Request from all Congresses and all Sessions of the Senate and House from 1865 to the present, especially those that reference slave-like conditions and practices, including peonage, share-cropping, convict-lease, prison labor, chain-gang labor, colonialism, segregation (Jim Crow), apartheid, etc. We request that you order all agencies under your authority to comply in full and in an expedited manner with this historic and precedent setting FOIA Request, and that you waive all applicable fees.

In order to help you determine our status and make your decision on our fee waiver request, you should know that Bob Brown is an organizer and researcher, who has worked, studied and struggled for 41 years, within and for the Student, Civil and Human Rights, Black Power, National Liberation, Pan-African, and Peace Movements. See Attachment B.

Disclosure of the requested information is in the public interest because it will be meaningfully informative in relation to the subject matter of this FOIA Request; because most of the requested records are not in the public domain, and those that are in the public domain are not accessible to the public that we serve; because their release will likely to contribute to greater public understanding of the United States Government's role, operations and activities, positive and negative, historically and currently, in the struggle to criminalize, prohibit and abolish these crimes; because this FOIA Request is not primarily in our commercial interest; and because we are highly qualified to understand, extract, convey and disseminate the information to the public at large.

Please provide an expedited review of this FOIA Request, which concerns a matter of urgency. As scholars, organizers and activists, we have been primarily engaged in disseminating information and education for more than 40-years. The public has an urgent need for the requested information because:

- The need involves an ongoing discussion about slavery and the slave trade, crimes against humanity and reparations to which informed members of the public might contribute through further research and publication, mass education, organization and mobilization, lobbying or other contacts with public officials, and any delay would further rob the public of detailed information about the role, activities and operations of the United States Government, positive and negative, historically and currently, in the struggle to facilitate, prohibit, or abolish these crimes against humanity. Further delay would also rob the public of its ability discuss ability to discuss and debate these concerns, make known its views, and contribute to the resolution of issues involved in a timely manner.

- The public, especially the African community, wants and needs to address serious allegations of governmental wrongdoing and cover-up, historically and currently, with respect to these issues in a timely manner.

- Moreover, these crimes against African and world humanity have been committed for over 569-years, and continue to be committed through denial, cover-up, lies, and fraud, governmental and non-governmental; and over 100 million African People have suffered, and their descendants continue to suffer, as a result of these crimes and the continuing denial and cover-up. It is time to redress these issues and resolve them, one way, or the other.

We expect your positive response to this historic and precedent setting FOIA Request within 20 working days as the statute provides. If our request is denied in whole or part, we ask that you justify the denial or all deletions by reference to specific exemptions of the act. We also expect you to release all segregable portions of otherwise exempt material.

Please be assured that we will exhaust all administrative, legal and political remedies to successfully conclude this FOIA Request. Thank you for your consideration.

Sincerely,
Bob Brown, co-director
Pan-African Roots

Pan-African Roots

1247 E Street SE
Washington, DC 20003
Tel: (202-) 544-9355 - Fax: (202) 544-9359
Email: paroots02@yahoo.com

25 October 2004

Mr. John Ashcroft, Attorney General
Department of Justice
10th Street and Constitution NW
Washington, DC 20530

AMENDED FREEDOM OF INFORMATION ACT REQUEST.
Fee Waiver and Expedited Review Request.
cc: FOIA Officer and FOIA Appeals Officer.

Dear Mr. Ashcroft:

Pursuant to the federal Freedom of Information Act (5 U.S.C. Sec. 552) and the Electronic FOIA Amendments of 1996 and 1997 ("EFOIA Amendments" and 5 U.S.C. Sec. 552 (f)(2) (effective March 31, 1997), we request access to and copies of all records created or obtained by, or under the control of the United States Government that relate to, or contain information about:

- The role, operations, and activities of the United States Government, especially the Department of the Treasury, the United States Customs Service and the Bureau of the Census, in facilitating, prohibiting and combating privateering, slavery and the slave trade, especially the Trans-Atlantic Slave Trade and slave-like conditions and practices,[94] including colonialism, segregation and apartheid, forced and compulsory labor, racism and racial discrimination, xenophobia and related intolerance.

- Slave, urban and racial disturbances, riots, rebellions and revolts, lynchings and race related violence and hate crimes, runaway slaves, fugitives beyond borders, related claims or requests, and demands for restitution and reparations.

- All governments, agencies (federal, state, county or local), corporations, non-governmental organizations, institutions, churches, families, individuals, or entities, domestic or foreign who participated or invested in, or made profits from the above referenced crimes against humanity; and who owns or benefits from these historical and continuing crimes today, including but not limited to those listed in Appendix A.

We formally and publicly request that you search and provides us access to or copies of all relevant records in the General Records of the Department of Justice [DOJ] (Record Group 60), the Records of District Courts of the United States (Record Group 21), the Records of the Federal Bureau of Investigation (Record Group 65), the Records of the Immigration and Naturalization Service (Record Group 85), the Records of United States Attorneys (Record Group 118 (formerly Records of United States Attorneys and Marshals (Record Group 118), the Records of the Bureau of Prisons (Record Group 129), the Records of the Office of the Pardon Attorney (Record Group 204), the Records of the Court of Claims Section (Justice) (Record Group 205), Publications of the US Government (Record Group 287), the Records of the Law Enforcement Assistance Administration (Record Group 423), the Records of the United States Marshals Service (Record Group 527) and all other relevant record groups.

---

[94] Including: peonage, share-cropping, debt-bondage, involuntary servitude, prison labor, convict lease, chain-gang, sweatshop labor, child labor, etc.

We request that you provide us access to or copies of the legal opinions and recommendations of the Attorney General and senior Department of Justice staff, and related case files on piracy and privateering, slavery and the slave trade, crimes against humanity, segregation, colonialism, apartheid, genocide, and other related issues and events.

We also request that you give us access to or copies of the following and all other records that are listed in "American Slavery and the International Slave Trade," [95] which are referenced in the General Records of the Department of Justice (Record Group 60):

Legal Opinions of the Attorney General, 1817-70.

- William Wirt, Attorney General, Nov. 13, 1817- Mar. 3, 1829. Volume 1

- No. 26 Negroes, Introduction of into the U.S.; seizure under the laws of the U.S. and Georgia, March 31, 1818.

- No. 29 When vessels having Negroes on board may be lawfully seized under act of 2nd March 1807, April 16,1819.

- No. 53 Run-away slaves, conveyance of, one State to another by captain of a vessel, August 29, 1819.

- No. 57 Introduction of Slaves into States in violation of act of 20 April 1818, Sept. 8, 1819.

- No. 64 Bond from foreign vessels clearing out of US for Africa under Act of 22 March 1794, Oct. 8, 1819.

- No. 68 Slave Laws of the U.S.A, King's Case.

- No. 70 Officer's share of a forfeiture under the Slave Laws of the U.S., Archibald Clark's case, Dec.16, 1819.

- No. 76 Manner of disposing of Negroes unlawfully brought into the United States prior to the act of March 3, 1819, Feb. 2, 1820.

- No. 77 Right of Officers to monies of forfeiture under the slave laws - Act 1807, Case of the "Carmelita," Feb. 5, 1820.

- No. 105 Seizure of a vessel suspected of being equipped for the slave trade, Case of the Chameleon, May 19, 1820.

- No. 146 Examination of the charges against General Mitchell of having unlawfully introduced Slaves into the U.S.A., Jan. 20, 1821.

- No. 166 Joseph F. Smith's application for pardon for breech of Slave-laws, Apr. 25, 1821.

Volume 2

- No. 183 Servants of Color introduced into U.S.A. by Passengers of Brig Cannon, August 16, 1821.

- No.192 Case of William J. Rogers. Transportation of Negroes Coastwise, October 11, 1821.

- No 198 Servants taken from U.S by Persons going to travel in foreign countries not within the Act 0f 1818, Nov. 5, 1821.

---

[95] United States National Archives & Records Administration. *Records that pertain to American Slavery and the International Slave Trade: II. Civil Records.* Available from http://www.archives.gov/research_room/research_topics/slavery_records_civil.html.

- No. 200 Case of the "La Jeune Eugenie "(captured slaver), Nov. 7, 1821.

- No. 201 Case of the Schooner "Farmer's Fancy "Nov. 7, 1821.

- No. 203 Case of Joseph F. Smith convicted of violations of the Slaves' Laws, Nov. 7, 1821.

- No. 204 Cases of the "St. Stephens" and the "Susan "(carrying slaves coastwise), November 7, 1821.

- No. 205 Are Free persons of Color in Virginia, citizens of the U.S. States within the meaning of the acts of Congress regulating the trade of the U.S.A., (can free blacks command vessels), Nov. 7, 1821.

- No. 218 Application by French Minister of France for restoration of a French vessel having Africans on board, Case of "La Pensee", Jan. 22, 1822.

- No. 234 Georgia claims, questions of Interest, June 11, 1822. (see also No.240.).

- No. 245 A slave, the property of a Danish subject, brought to the port of New York from St. Croix by Thomas Disney, Master of the American Ship, "Elias Burger." Have we the power or we under any obligation to restore said slave on the demand of the Danish Government? Sept.27, 1822.

- No. 265 Construction of several acts of Congress, as to the intention of Congress, to incorporate Negroes and people of colour within the army of the United States, March 27, 1823.

- No. 285 Claims of the Marshall of the state of Georgia for the support of Negroes constituting the cargo of the Spanish vessel, Ramirez, Dec.30, 1823.

- No. 299 Free Negroes and persons of colour - Construction of the Legislative Acts of South Carolina, December 20, 1820, -touching their seizure, and confinement when brought in said State, May 8,1824.

Volume 3

- P. 48 Georgia Claims, Creek Nation treaty with USA. Slave property involved, July 28, 1828.

- P. 86 Negroes claimed under Spanish Treaty, D. Nagles Case, March 31, 1829.

- P. 248 Free Negroes carried into South Carolina, March 25, 1829.

- Roger B. Taney, Attorney General, July 20, 1831- September 24, 1833.

- Benjamin F. Butler, Atty., General, Nov. 15, 1833 - Sept. 1, 1838.

- Felix Grundy, Atty. General, July 5, 1838 - Dec 1, 1839.

- Henry D. Gilpin, Atty. General, Jan. 11, 1840 - Mar. 4, 1841.

- John J. Crittenden, Atty. General, Mar. 5, 1841 - Sept. 13, 1841.

Volume 4

- P. 2 Pardon Petition for slave Donnelly, March 1, 1832.

- P. 165 Murder, Negroes slaves of white men, in Indian country, not triable be tried in an Indian court, but must be tried in United States court, December 26, 1834.

- P. 243 Ms. Thornton case, for pardon of her slave accused of attempted murder, February 25, 1836.

Volume 5

- P. 200 The President has no Constitutional authority to direct apprehension of slaves in the Indian Country, August 30, 1838.

- P. 280 Case of the "Amistad" and African Negroes, November, 1839.

- P. 296 Case of the "Amistad", April 11, 1840.

- P. 298 Transportation of slaves on the coastlines April 16, 1840.

- P. 297 Slaves killed by Indians, April 15, 1840.

- P. 347 Transportation of slaves on the coastline, July 29, 1840.

- P. 366 Case of the "Amistad", December 14, 1840.

- P. 491 Case of the "Amistad", April 6, 1842.

- Hugh S. Legare, Atty. General, Sept. 13, 1841 - June 20, 1843.

- John Nelson, Atty. General, July 1, 1843 - Mar. 3, 184.

- John Y. Mason, Atty. General, Mar. 6, 1845 - Sept. 9, 1846.

- Nathan Clifford, Atty. General, Oct. 17, 1846 - Mar. 17, 1848.

Volume 6

- P. 57 Colonization Society and reception of transported Africans, December 24, 1842.

- P. 62 Free people of colour entitled to benefit of preemption Act of 1841, March 15, 1843.

- P.121 Case of Jenkins, a Negro, distinction between slave and free, August 25,1843.

- P. 124 Slave Trade Acts: Exposition of terms, and of the rights and responsibilities of ship owners selling vessels deliverable on the Coast of Africa, August 29, 1843. 1) March 22, 1794; 2) May 10, 1800; 3) Feb.28, 1803; 4) May 2, 1807; 5) Apr. 20, 1818, ch 18; 6) Mar 3, 1819, ch 224; 7) May 15, 1820. (March 2, 1807, 2 Stat 426), Congress prohibited the importation of slaves into the U.S. of America after January 1, 1808).

- P. 144 Complaint of Portuguese Minister over the abduction of slave by American vessel from the Cape Verde islands, November 2, 1843.

- Isaac Toucey, Atty. General, June 21, 1848 - Mar.3, 1849.

Volume 7

- Volume lacked an index.

- Reverdy Johnson, Atty. General, Mar. 3, 1849 - July 20, 1850.

Volume 8

- Index indicated no citations.

- Caleb Cushing, Atty. General, Mar. 7, 1853 - Mar. 3, 1857.

Volume 9

- Index indicated no citations.

- Registers of Letters Received, 1809-1863, 3 volumes, see Letters Received, 1809-70, for documents (entry 9) LOC: 230/01/30/01, entry 6

Volume A: State Department Number

- 208 Oct 27, 1817 Slave from Barbados.

- 405 May 16, 1826 Slave Trade prosecution.

- 705 Nov. 23, 1831 African captives commandeered British slaver.

- 731 June 7, 1832 Execution of slave Donelly, Mobile, Alabama.

- 741 May 19, 1832 South Carolina laws regulating free blacks.

- 1568 July 22, 1833 Construction slave trade acts.

- 1594 Oct. 25, 1833 Slave taken from Verde Island.

- 2335 Nov. 22, 1850 Fugitives slaves: case of the Crafts.

- 2469 Nov. 1851 Questions re: slave trade.

War Department

- 393 July 22, 1825 Indian Spring Treaty and Negroes.

- 1002 Feb. 11, 1836 Slaves fleeing to Indian country.

- (There is a good chance that much of the correspondence discussing matters with Indian nations would have also concerned slaves).

Treasury Department

- 110 March 21, 1818 Negroes concerned w/ Mitchell case.

- 463 Dec. 6, 1827 Indemnification for slaves relative to the Treaty of Ghent.

- 1208 April 15, 1840 Manifest of slaves transported coastwise.

- 1263 July 28, 1840 Transportation of slaves between Mobile and New Orleans.

- 1303 Dec. 8, 1840 Opinion asked relative to purchase of Spanish schooner," Amistad."

- 1498 Dec. 14, 1842 Opinion asked relative to free colored person and the Pre-emption Act.

Navy Department

- 117 April 15, 1818 Orders to cruisers against the introduction of slaves.

- 172 March 24, 1819 Seizure of vessels with slaves trading under another flag.

- 204 Sept. 21, 1819 Case stated in a letter from President of colonization society.

- 418 Dec. 29, 1826 Negroes of the "Ramirez."

- 460 Nov. 9, 1827 Capture of the "Antelope" and "Ramerez"- claim of Capt. Jackson for bounty.

- 490 Apr. 10, 1828 Case of the "Antelope" and "Ramerez" slavers.

- 578 Sept. 19, 1829 Purchase of arms for defense of colony in Liberia.

- 617 May 21, 1830 Transporting Africans on the Washington barge.

- 634 Aug 16, 1830 Capture of slaver "Phoenix "by the "Grampus."

- 768 July 10, 1832 Case of Africans illegally introduced.

- 1202 March 27, 1840 Expenses of negroes taken on board "Amistad."

- 1207 April 11, 1840 Negro Evidence before a Court Martial.

- 1212 April 20, 1840 Court martial of Florida slave, G. Mason.

- 1358 Jan. 13, 1842 Salvage money of the "Amistad."

- 2100 April 14, 1849 American vessel suspected of being in the slave trade.

Interior Department

- 35 April 30, 1860 Sends copy of his paper containing evidence of the late fugitive slave case.

Attorney General

- 80 July 6, 1816 Opinion case hazard and half of the "Nancy."

- 193 Aug. 20, 1819 Affidavit relative to female slave brought from Savannah, Georgia.

- 125 Aug. 3, 1822 Case of James Barry a fugitive slave belonging to a Danish subject.

- 268 Jan. 22, 1822 Africans found aboard "La Pense."

- 353 June 12, 1824 Supreme Court mandate relative to the "Emily", and "Caroline "(slave ships).

- 2334 Nov. 18, 1850 Case of the fugitive slaves, West & E. Craft from Georgia against C. Devens, Jr. U.S. Atty., Mass.

President

- 205 Oct. 13, 1819 Colonization of African slaves.

- 2315 Sept. 18, 1850 Opinion asked relative to fugitive slave bill.

Alphabetical Listing of Sender: Correspondence Arranged by State

- 1306 Dec. 10, 1840 Asks an interview relative to the "Amistad."

- 1307 Dec. 10, 1840 Establishing meeting time for the "Amistad "interview.

- 6 Dec. 31, 1811 Cargoes of the "Penobscot" and the "Nancy."

- 2269 March 3, 1850 J.D. Lewis, of Virginia complaints of loss of slaves.

- 192 Aug. 21, 1819 Female slave arrived from Savannah on board the "General Jackson."

- 271 Feb 22, 1822 The "Caroline" and "Mite "slaving vessels.

- 307 Feb. 13, 1823 South Carolina law as to colored mariners, referred by Secy. of State.

- 119 Apr. 21, 1824 Constitutionality of slave law.

- 2333 Nov. 1, 1850 As to fugitive slaves William & Ellen Croft (Craft) case against C. Devens, Jr. U.S. Atty, Mass.

- 2393 Jan 24, 1851 Letter from A. Mathes, relative to arresting slaves in Indian territory (see 2391).

- 15 Mar. 3, 1813 Capture of the "Ariadne" and "S. Carolina."

- 68 Nov. 6, 1817 Case of the American brig," Nancy", Deposition of.

- 925 Sept. 7, 1834 A kidnapped slave brought from Jamaica.

- 1211 Apr 20, 1840 Liability of the U.S. for slaves killed in Florida.

- 730 Mar. 31, 1832 Case of Donelly slave condemned for murder of white man, applicant for pardon, Report of case enclosed.

- 270 Feb. 5, 1822 Case of C. Muloy and 150 Africans of the cargo of the "Ramerez."

- 390 June 28, 1825 Relative to the brig "Grampus "Enclosing decree in Circuit Court.

- 392 July 20, 1825 Galpin's claim for negroes, case falling under the Indian Spring Treaty referred Secy. of War.

- 1178 Feb. 3, 1840 Asks documents relative to slaves set free in Bermuda, case of the "Amistad."

- 1186 Feb. 20, 1840 Relative to proceedings against a fugitive from justice.

- 1193 Mar. 9, 1840 Relative to slaves on board the "Amistad "being Spanish property.

- 1310 Dec. 14, 1840 Case of the schooner," Amistad."

- 378 Feb. 3, 1825 Request for defer of the slave trade question.

- 1277 Aug. 31, 1840 Asks return of the argument, case of the "Amistad."

- 1294 Nov. 18, 1840 Record case of the U.S. vs the "Amistad."

- 304 Feb. 3, 1822 African slave case.

- 311 1830 Relative to imprisonment of D. Frazer, colored mariner. Referred by C.J. Steedman, Sheriff of Charleston.

- 987 1836 Asks copies of opinion of Attys. Genl Wirt and Berrien relative to colored people entering the United States.

- 2402 Feb. 22, 1851 As to scruples of jurors relative to fugitive slaves.

- 2392 Jan. 23, 1850 As to power to arrest fugitive slaves in Indian Territory (see 2393).

- 70 Nov. 18, 1817 Case of the brig, "Nancy." Ill treatment of negroes by the owner and mate, Hazzard and Haff.

- 309 Dec. 15, 1830 Imprisonment of D. Frazer, colored mariner.

- 10 Oct. 8, 1812 Merchants in Rhode Island engaged in the slave trade.

- 11 Oct. 13, 1812 Merchants in RI in the slave trade.

- 1202 March 27, 1840 Expenses of negroes taken on board the "Amistad."

- 1096 July 30, 1836 Opinion asked relative to hostile negroes in the Seminole Nation.

- 310 Dec. 16, 1830 Relative to the imprisonment of D. Frazer, colored mariner. Referred by British Consul, West Ogilby (see 309).

- 313 Feb. 27, 1823 Certain vessels and slaves captured on the coast of Florida.

- 1073 June 14, 1836 Relative to pardon of her servant boy, letter to Judge Taney within.

- 1292 Nov. 11, 1840 Asks copies of record in case of the "Amistad."

- 1315 Dec. 30, 1840 Asking when the case of the "Amistad "will be reached.

- 308 Dec. 26, 1830 Case of D. Frazer, a free colored man. Referred by Secy. of State Van Buren (see 309, 310).

- 658 Jan. 15, 1831 Release of D. Frazer, colored mariner. Letter from Consul at Charleston enclosed. Referred by Secy. of State (see 308, 309, 310).

Volume B

Attorney General

- 2788 Jul. 22, 1856 Relative to the "Amelia."

- 3103 Aug. 8, 1856 That the Sec. of State has determined to apply to Congress for appropriations to pay the expenses incurred in securing the cargo of the Bark," Amelia."

- 3194 Jan. 31, 1859 Relative to the African "slave trade."

- 3209 Mar. 31, 1859 Relating to the "Echo" case.

- 3224 Mar. 31, 1859 Relative to suppressing slave trade.

- 3237 Jun. 7, 1857 As to violation of "fugitive slave law "in case of "Add White."

- 3415 Jul. 24, 1857 Rel. to the Dep. Mar.'s account in the fugitive slave law, Boston.

- 4062 Jan. 10, 1859 Relative to t he case of the "Wanderer."

- 4077 Jan. 31, 1859 Rel. to the importation of African negroes by the "Wanderer."

- 4078 Feb. 1, 1859 Rel. to the importation of Africans by the "Wanderer."

- 4166 Apr. 13, 1859 Rel. to an account of $1500 in favor of J.West Mayne for services in the prosecution of the crew of the Brig, "Echo."

State Department

- 4228 Jun. 13, 1859 Foreign ships flying American flag (practice of slavers).

Treasury Department

- 3576 Dec. 22, 1857 As to violation of the Act of Congress for suppression of slave trade.

- 3479 Dec. 23, 1857 As to whether application has been received for pardon of Andie and of David, the slave one Brown.

- 4644 Sept. 26, 1860 Bargue "William" condemned as slaver.

- 4113 Mar. 5, 1859 Relative to "Wanderer" and two negroes.

- 3921 Aug. 27, 1858 As to whether under the Act of March 2, 1857, negroes slaves can be lawfully be paid for services in the War of 1812.

Interior Department

- 3477 Sept. 7, 1857 Can master of slave obtain patent invented by slave.

- 3583 Dec. 27, 1857 Is master entitled to patent invented by slave.

- 4115 Mar. 11, 1859 U.S. Marshal, South Carolina, seeks compensation for expenses incurred while detaining Africans from the brig "Echo."

- 4449 Jan. 4, 1860 Rel. to account for services of A.R. Allen in taking Capt. Farnham of the "Wanderer" to Savannah.

Alphabetical Listing of Sender: Correspondence Arranged by State

- 4056 Jan. 5, 1859 Rel. to suit of John F. Mason, (colored) v. Joseph C. and David Gamble.

- 4107 Feb 26, 1859 Prosecuting under Fugitive Slave Act.

- 3304 Apr. 3, 1857 Request for return of fugitive sl

- 3962 Nov. 13, 1858 Wants copies of the President's message and reports from State and Navy Depts. in reference to the "slave trade "which were transmitted to Senate April 21, 1858.

- 4466 Jan. 17, 1860 Ask that the military force at Ft. Leavenworth be placed at his disposal to aid in the arrest persons concerned in the violation of the Fugitive Slave Act.

- 4360 Sept. 18, 1859 About Mr. Swaynet's bill for service in Fugitive Slave case.

- 4456 Jan. 9, 1860 Wants to employ Mr. Arrington as "counsel "in a "fugitive slave "case with a fee of $1000.

- 4515 Apr. 5, 1860 Rel. to Mr. Arrington's bill for service in the Chicago "Fugitive slave rescue "case.

- 4579 Jul. 23, 1860 Reporting the arrival of the schooner "Clotilde" with African slaves on board.

- 4709 Apr 18, 1860 Ask about the bill of Mr. Arrington for legal services in the fugitive slave case in Chicago.

- 2886 Jul 8, 1854 Rel. to the fugitive slave law and revenue laws. Conflict of State and U.S. authorities.

- 3978 Dec. 3, 1858 Desires to know what compensation he is entitled to for custody of the captured African of the Brig "Echo."

- 3175 Apr. 20, 1859 With regards to the rescue of a runaway sl

- 3184 Apr. 25, 1859 Rel. to the violation of the fugitive slave law.

- 4606 Jul. 28, 1860 Writ of habeas corpus issued for the seizure of negroes imported into Alabama.

- 2901 Oct. 31, 1854 Rel. to one James Smith engaged in the "slave trade."

- 3590 May 30, 1857 As to resistance to the execution of the slave law in southern Ohio, in the case of Add White.

- 4529 Apr. 24, 1860 Rel. to slave rescue case. Wishes sanction Atty. General.

- 4094 Feb. 17, 1859 Relative to the Barque "Wanderer."

- 2706 May 25, 1853 Relative to the schooner Machet P. Brown captured on the West Coast of Africa.

- 2850 Jun. 9, 1854 States that an unusual number of criminal prosecutions, including several fugitive slave rescue cases are to be tried at the July term Dist. Court.

- 4593 Jul. 18, 1860 Rel. to recent importation of negroes into Alabama.

- 4600 Jul. 24, 1860 Rel. to the schooner "Clotilde" and Africans introduced by her.

- 4502 Mar. 20, 1860 Respecting the right of Congress to pass the slave trade laws.

- 4540 May 26, 1860 Reporting arrival of U.S. Steamer," Mohawk," at Key West with the Barque," Wildfire "with 350 Africans on board.

- 4542 May 15, 1860 Reporting the arrival of the U.S. Steamer, "Wyandott "at Key West with Barque," William "as a prize with 550 negroes.

- 4547 May 23, 1860 Sending an opinion of Judge Jonas on slave trade laws.

- 2687 Oct. 3, 1853 As to recapture of runaway negroes. Rel. to case of John B. Davis.

- 4512 Mar. 29, 1860 Is Captain Martin of the "Wanderer "to be demanded under the Extradition Treaty with England.

Volume C

Treasury

- 4726 Jan. 2, 1861 Rel. to D. H. Steward arresting and transporting Africans as marshal of Georgia.

- 6224 Sept. 24, 1862 Ask an opinion regarding colored free citizens.

Alphabetical Listing of Sender: Correspondence Arranged by State

- 6283 0ct. 25, 1862 Relative to action under the Confiscation Act of July 17, 1862.

- 6532 Mar. 9, 1863 Seizure of property under the Confiscation Act of July 1862.

- 5963 May 9, 1862 Maryland fugitives slaves entering District of Columbia - application of Law of 1850.

- 6181 Aug. 30, 1862 Complaints that his negroes have been taken away.

- 6182 Aug. 30, 1862 Wants a copy of the Confiscation Act sent.

- 5446 Sept. 19, 1861 Relative to Confiscation Act of Aug. 6, 1861.

- 6401 Dec. 31, 1862 Asks instructions as to proceedings under the Confiscation Act.

- 6412 Jan. 7, 1863 Relative to a question arising under the Confiscation Act.

- 6433 Jan. 16, 1863 Asks instruction under the Confiscation Act.

- 6467 Feb. 2, 1863 Asks as to proceedings under the Confiscation Act.

- 5651 Dec. 5, 1861 Cannot Negroes in Washington Jail be released.

- 5220 Jul. 11, 1861 Does the Govt. with the slave laws execute.

- 5429 Sept. 13, 1861 Does the Confiscation Act extends to stocks and money on deposit.

- 5742 Jan. 25, 1862 Encloses copy of an act to suppress the African Slave Trade and asks your opinion and suggestions.

- 5375 Sept. 5, 1861 Confiscation Act and proclamation prohibiting transportation of property to and from the revolted states.

- 5409 Sept. 10, 1861 Asks instruction as to Confiscation cases.

- 6542 Mar. 14, 1863 Ask for instructions under the Confiscation Act.

- 5332 Aug. 22, 1861 Rel. to seizure of goods declared forfeit by "force" and confiscation act.

- 5448 Sept. 19, 1861 Can real estate or the rents there of thereof be seized or confiscated under the acts of the 1st Session of the 37th Congress.

- 6289 Oct. 29, 1862 Has secured conviction of slaver Albert Horn.

- 6295 Oct. 2, 1862 Relative to an act to confiscate the property of Rebels.

- 5463 Sept. 21, 1861 Wants advice as to the construction of the Confiscation Act.

- 5395 Sept. 7, 1861 Construction of the Act of Aug. 6, 1861 - Confiscation Act.

- 5498 Oct. 9, 1861 Construction of the Confiscation Act.

- 5513 Oct. 14, 1861 Rel. to construction of the Confiscation Act, money of Rebels on deposit subject to draft.

- 6264 Oct. 14, 1861 An inquiry to the Confiscation Act.

Supreme Court Case Papers, 1809 - 1870

- Papers relating to cases before the U.S. Supreme Court of which the United States was a party or had an interest. LOC: 230/1/33/2.

Box 1

- United States v. Africans of the "Antelope".

- U.S. v. Brig "Mary Ann".

Box 2

- U.S. v. Brig "Emily", February, 1824.

- U.S. v. Brig "Caroline", February, 1824.

- U.S. v. Schooner "Catherine", December, 1839.

Box 3

- U.S. v. Schooner "Elmira Cornelius", December 1865.

- U.S. v. Schooners "Merino", Constitution, "Louisa", and African Slaves, 1818.

- U.S. v. Cornelius Coolidge, 1816.

- Lewis Cruger, Administrator of Charlles Murray, v. Wm. C. Daniel, Bill of Complaint.

- Bill of Complaint of Lewis Cruger, In Chancery.

- U.S. v. the cargo of the "Brig "Diana", 1814.

Box 4

- U.S. v. Schooner "Fenix", Sept. 1831.

Box 5

- U.S. v. Ship "Gavoune", 1836.

- U.S. v. John Gooding, 1826.

Box 6

- U.S. v. Antonio Huertas, 1834.

Box 7

- U.S. v. Bark. "Kate", 1864.

Box 8

- U.S. v. Schooner L'Epine, 1816.

- The Life and Fire Insurance Company of New York v. The Heirs of Nicholas Wilson, in the State of Louisiana, 1834.

- The Brig "Mary Anne" v. U.S, 1818.

Box 9

- U.S. v. Mulvey (Africans of the "Ramirez), 1825.

- U.S. v. brig, Nancy.

- U.S. v. The "Panther," 1845.

Box 11

- U.S. v. Schooner "St. Jago de Cuba", 1820.

- U.S. v. Brig "Josepa Segunde", 1807.

- U.S. v. Francis Sorrell ("Antelope" and "Ramirez"), 1822.

Box 13

- U.S. v. The Barque "Weathergage," 1860.

We further request, as referenced above, that you provide us access to or copies of all records that are relevant or related to our Request from all Congresses and all Sessions of the Senate and House from 1865 to the present, especially those that reference slave-like conditions and practices, including peonage, share-cropping, convict-lease, prison labor, chain-gang labor, colonialism, segregation (Jim Crow), apartheid, etc. We request that you order all agencies under your authority to comply in full and in an expedited manner with this historic and precedent setting FOIA Request, and that you waive all applicable fees.

In order to help you determine our status and make your decision on our fee waiver request, you should know that Bob Brown is an organizer and researcher, who has worked, studied and struggled for 41 years, within and for the Student, Civil and Human Rights, Black Power, National Liberation, Pan-African, and Peace Movements. See Attachment B.

Disclosure of the requested information is in the public interest because it will be meaningfully informative in relation to the subject matter of this FOIA Request; because most of the requested records are not in the public domain, and those that are in the public domain are not accessible to the public that we serve; because their release will likely to contribute to greater public understanding of the United States Government's role, operations and activities, positive and negative, historically and currently, in the struggle to criminalize, prohibit and abolish these crimes; because this FOIA Request is not primarily in our commercial interest; and because we are highly qualified to understand, extract, convey and disseminate the information to the public at large.

Please provide an expedited review of this FOIA Request, which concerns a matter of urgency. As scholars, organizers and activists, we have been primarily engaged in disseminating information and education for more than 40-years. The public has an urgent need for the requested information because:

- The need involves an ongoing discussion about slavery and the slave trade, crimes against humanity and reparations to which informed members of the public might contribute through further research and publication, mass education, organization and mobilization, lobbying or other contacts with public officials, and any delay would further rob the public of detailed information about the role, activities and operations of the United States Government, positive and negative, historically and currently, in the struggle to facilitate, prohibit, or abolish these crimes against humanity. Further delay would also rob the public of its ability to discuss and debate these concerns, make known its views, and contribute to the resolution of issues involved in a timely manner.

- The public, especially the African community, wants and needs to address serious allegations of governmental wrongdoing and cover-up, historically and currently, with respect to these issues in a timely manner.

- Moreover, these crimes against African and world humanity have been committed for over 569-years, and continue to be committed through denial, cover-up, lies, and fraud, governmental and non-governmental; and over 100 million African People have suffered, and their descendants continue to suffer, as a result of these crimes and the continuing denial and cover-up. It is time to redress these issues and resolve them, one way, or the other.

We expect your positive response to this historic and precedent setting FOIA Request within 20 working days as the statute provides. If our request is denied in whole or part, we ask that you justify the denial or all deletions by reference to specific exemptions of the act. We also expect you to release all segregable portions of otherwise exempt material.

Please be assured that we will exhaust all administrative, legal and political remedies to successfully conclude this FOIA Request. Thank you for your consideration.

Sincerely,
Bob Brown, co-director
Pan-African Roots

Pan-African Roots

1247 E Street SE
Washington, DC 20003
Tel: (202-) 544-9355 - Fax: (202) 544-9359
Email: paroots02@yahoo.com

25 October 2004

Mrs. Gale Ann Norton, Secretary of the Interior
Department of Interior
1849 C Street NW
Washington, DC 20240

AMENDED FREEDOM OF INFORMATION ACT REQUEST.
Fee Waiver and Expedited Review Request.
cc: FOIA Officer and FOIA Appeals Officer.

Dear Mrs. Norton:

Pursuant to the federal Freedom of Information Act (5 U.S.C. Sec. 552) and the Electronic FOIA Amendments of 1996 and 1997 ("EFOIA Amendments" and 5 U.S.C. Sec. 552 (f)(2) (effective March 31, 1997), we request access to and copies of all records created or obtained by, or under the control of the Department of the Interior, that relate to, or contain information about:

- The role, operations, and activities of he Department of the Interior, the Bureau of Indian Affairs, and all other relevant agencies in facilitating, prohibiting and combating privateering, slavery and the slave trade, especially the Trans-Atlantic Slave Trade; and slave-like conditions and practices, including colonialism, segregation and apartheid, forced and compulsory labor, racism and racial discrimination, xenophobia and related intolerance.

- Slave, urban and racial disturbances, riots, rebellions and revolts, lynchings and race related violence and hate crimes, runaway slaves, fugitives beyond borders, related claims or requests, and demands for restitution and reparations.

- All treaties or agreements, bilateral or multilateral, or diplomatic communications, correspondence, discussions between the United States Government and its Officials (all levels, branches and agencies) and the British, Canadian, French, Spanish, Mexican or any other government with respect to the above or related subjects.

- All governments, agencies (federal, state, county or local), corporations, non-governmental organizations, institutions, churches, families, individuals, or entities, domestic or foreign who participated or invested in, or made profits from the above referenced crimes against humanity; and who owns or benefits from these historical and continuing crimes today, including but not limited to those listed in Appendix A.

We also request that you give us access to or copies of the following and all other records that pertain to *American Slavery and the International Slave Trade,*[96] including, but not limited to:

- Records Relating to the Suppression of the African Slave Trade and to Negro Colonization in the Records of the Office of the Secretary of the Interior (Record Group 48):

- Register of Letters Received, 1858-1872. LOC: 150/7/16/05, 1 vol. ent 375.

---

[96] United States National Archives & Records Administration. Records that pertain *to American Slavery and the International Slave Trade: II. Civil Records.* Available from http://www.archives.gov/research_room/research_topics/slavery_records_civil.html.

- Letters Received and Other Records, 1854-1872. LOC: 150/7/16/06, boxes 1-5, ent. 376.

- Letters Sent, 1858-72.

- Records on the removal of Native Americans and Slaves from the South, especially Florida, to Indian Territory; and on the status and condition of slaves and other Africans living, historically and currently, on the Reservations of the Cherokee, Choctaw, Creek, Seminole and other Indigenous Nations.

- Records of the Government of the Virgin Islands (Record Group 55), including, but not limited to: Governor's orders, issued at St. Thomas, 1672- 1840, and St. Croix, 1733-1862; Daybook of Johan Lorentz, the Vice Commandant at St. Thomas, 1694-97; Governor Peter Clausen's letters to foreign officials, 1774-84; Governor Peter Carl Frederik von Scholten's letter books, 1834-53; Drafts of letters to Denmark, 1778-1831; Correspondence with consular officials in St. Thomas, 1839-1916; Protocols and other records of the sanitary, poor, health, quarantine, hospital, road, and other quasi-executive governmental commissions in St. Thomas and St. Croix, 1853-1917; General ledgers for St. Thomas, 1816-1908, and St. Croix, 1741-1850; Duplicate accounts of the St. Thomas colonial treasury, 1829-1916; Tax lists for St. Thomas, 1823-54, and St. Croix, 1743- 1850; Lists of the King's Negroes, 1820-33; Reports about slaves'' appraised value, 1846-52, and sugar exported from St. Croix, 1835-92; Record book of government-owned sugar plantations, 1835-88; Microfilm copies of records of the Danish West India and Guinea Company, 1672- 1740, and of the West Indian Local Archives, West Indian Government on St. Croix, 1755-1863 (19 rolls); Records relating to insurrections, 1848, 1878 and Miscellaneous administrative records, 1855-1917.

We further request, as referenced above, that you provide us access to or copies of all records that are relevant or related to our Request from all Congresses and all Sessions of the Senate and House from 1865 to the present, especially those that reference slave-like conditions and practices, including peonage, share-cropping, convict-lease, prison labor, chain-gang labor, colonialism, segregation (Jim Crow), apartheid, etc. We request that you order all agencies under your authority to comply in full and in an expedited manner with this historic and precedent setting FOIA Request, and that you waive all applicable fees.

In order to help you determine our status and make your decision on our fee waiver request, you should know that Bob Brown is an organizer and researcher, who has worked, studied and struggled for 41 years, within and for the Student, Civil and Human Rights, Black Power, National Liberation, Pan-African, and Peace Movements. See Attachment B.

Disclosure of the requested information is in the public interest because it will be meaningfully informative in relation to the subject matter of this FOIA Request; because most of the requested records are not in the public domain, and those that are in the public domain are not accessible to the public that we serve; because their release will likely to contribute to greater public understanding of the United States Government's role, operations and activities, positive and negative, historically and currently, in the struggle to criminalize, prohibit and abolish these crimes; because this FOIA Request is not primarily in our commercial interest; and because we are highly qualified to understand, extract, convey and disseminate the information to the public at large.

Please provide an expedited review of this FOIA Request, which concerns a matter of urgency. As scholars, organizers and activists, we have been primarily engaged in disseminating information and education for more than 40-years. The public has an urgent need for the requested information because:

- The need involves an ongoing discussion about slavery and the slave trade, crimes against humanity and reparations to which informed members of the public might contribute through further research and publication, mass education, organization and mobilization, lobbying or other contacts with public officials, and any delay would further rob the public of detailed information about the role, activities and operations of the United States Government, positive and negative, historically and currently, in the struggle to facilitate, prohibit, or abolish these crimes against humanity. Further delay would also rob the public of its ability to discuss and debate these concerns, make known its views, and contribute to the resolution of issues involved in a timely manner.

- The public, especially the African community, wants and needs to address serious allegations of governmental wrongdoing and cover-up, historically and currently, with respect to these issues in a timely manner.

- Moreover, these crimes against African and world humanity have been committed for over 569-years, and continue to be committed through denial, cover-up, lies, and fraud, governmental and non-governmental; and over 100 million African People have suffered, and their descendants continue to suffer, as a result of these crimes and the continuing denial and cover-up. It is time to redress these issues and resolve them, one way, or the other.

We expect your positive response to this historic and precedent setting FOIA Request within 20 working days as the statute provides. If our request is denied in whole or part, we ask that you justify the denial or all deletions by reference to specific exemptions of the act. We also expect you to release all segregable portions of otherwise exempt material.

Please be assured that we will exhaust all administrative, legal and political remedies to successfully conclude this FOIA Request. Thank you for your consideration.

Sincerely,
Bob Brown, co-director
Pan-African Roots

Pan-African Roots

1247 E Street SE
Washington, DC 20003
Tel: (202-) 544-9355 - Fax: (202) 544-9359
Email: paroots02@yahoo.com

25 October 2004

Mr. John Carlin and Mr. Walter B. Hill
National Archives and Records Administration
NWCTF - Room 6350
8601 Adelphi Road
College Park, MD 20740

AMENDED FREEDOM OF INFORMATION ACT REQUEST.
Fee Waiver and Expedited Review Request.
cc: FOIA Officer and FOIA Appeals Officer.

Dear Mr. Carlin and Mr. Hill:

Pursuant to the federal Freedom of Information Act (5 U.S.C. Sec. 552) and the Electronic FOIA Amendments of 1996 and 1997 ("EFOIA Amendments" and 5 U.S.C. Sec. 552 (f)(2) (effective March 31, 1997), we request access to and copies of all records created or obtained by, or under the control of the United States Government that relate to, or contain information about:

- The role, operations, and activities of the United States Supreme Court, all United States District Courts, and all judicial agencies in facilitating, prohibiting and combating privateering, slavery and the slave trade, especially the Trans-Atlantic Slave Trade and slave-like conditions and practices, including colonialism, segregation and apartheid, forced and compulsory labor, racism and racial discrimination, xenophobia and related intolerance.

- Slave, urban and racial disturbances, riots, rebellions and revolts, runaway slaves, fugitives beyond borders, related claims or requests, and demands for restitution and reparations.

- All treaties or agreements, bilateral or multilateral, or diplomatic communications, correspondence, discussions between the United States Government and its Officials (all levels, branches and agencies) and the British, Canadian, French, Spanish, Mexican or any other government with respect to the above or related subjects.

- All efforts by African People (People of African descent) in the United States, the African Diaspora, or Africa to lodge complaints against the U.S. with the League of Nations, the United Nations, and all other international or regional bodies.

- All governments, agencies (federal, state, county or local), corporations, non-governmental organizations, institutions, churches, families, individuals, or entities, domestic or foreign who participated or invested in, or made profits from the above referenced crimes against humanity; and who owns or benefits from these historical and continuing crimes today, including but not limited to those listed in Appendix A.

We request that you give us access to or copies of the following and all other records that are listed in *"American Slavery and the International Slave Trade,"*[97] and all other records responsive to our request, including but not limited to Records of the Supreme Court of the United States (Record Group 267),

---

[97] United States National Archives & Records Administration. *Records that pertain to American Slavery and the International Slave Trade: III. Judicial Records.*

Records of the District Courts of the United States (Record Group 21), Records of the Circuit Courts of the United States and Records of the United States Marshals Service (Record Group 527).

We request that you provide us access to or copies of all records relevant to our FOIA Request in the following and other related record groups: General Records of the Department of Justice (Record Group 60), Records of U.S. Attorneys (Record Group 118), Records of the Office of the Pardon Attorney (Record Group 204), Records of the Solicitor of the Treasury (Record Group 206), Records of the U.S. Courts of Appeals (Record Group 276), and Record copies of publications of the U.S. Supreme Court, U.S. District Courts and U.S. Circuit Courts in Publications of the U.S. Government (Record Group 287).

We further request, as referenced above, that you provide us access to or copies of all records that are relevant or related to our Request from all Congresses and all Sessions of the Senate and House from 1865 to the present, especially those that reference slave-like conditions and practices, including peonage, share-cropping, convict-lease, prison labor, chain-gang labor, colonialism, segregation (Jim Crow), apartheid, etc. We request that you order all agencies under your authority to comply in full and in an expedited manner with this historic and precedent setting FOIA Request, and that you waive all applicable fees.

In order to help you determine our status and make your decision on our fee waiver request, you should know that Bob Brown is an organizer and researcher, who has worked, studied and struggled for 41 years, within and for the Student, Civil and Human Rights, Black Power, National Liberation, Pan-African, and Peace Movements. See Attachment B.

Disclosure of the requested information is in the public interest because it will be meaningfully informative in relation to the subject matter of this FOIA Request; because most of the requested records are not in the public domain, and those that are in the public domain are not accessible to the public that we serve; because their release will likely to contribute to greater public understanding of the United States Government's role, operations and activities, positive and negative, historically and currently, in the struggle to criminalize, prohibit and abolish these crimes; because this FOIA Request is not primarily in our commercial interest; and because we are highly qualified to understand, extract, convey and disseminate the information to the public at large.

Please provide an expedited review of this FOIA Request, which concerns a matter of urgency. As scholars, organizers and activists, we have been primarily engaged in disseminating information and education for more than 40-years. The public has an urgent need for the requested information because:

- The need involves an ongoing discussion about slavery and the slave trade, crimes against humanity and reparations to which informed members of the public might contribute through further research and publication, mass education, organization and mobilization, lobbying or other contacts with public officials, and any delay would further rob the public of detailed information about the role, activities and operations of the United States Government, positive and negative, historically and currently, in the struggle to facilitate, prohibit, or abolish these crimes against humanity. Further delay would also rob the public of its ability to discuss and debate these concerns, make known its views, and contribute to the resolution of issues involved in a timely manner.

- The public, especially the African community, wants and needs to address serious allegations of governmental wrongdoing and cover-up, historically and currently, with respect to these issues in a timely manner.

- Moreover, these crimes against African and world humanity have been committed for over 569-years, and continue to be committed through denial, cover-up, lies, and fraud, governmental and non-governmental; and over 100 million African People have suffered, and their descendants continue to suffer, as a result of these crimes and the continuing denial and cover-up. It is time to redress these issues and resolve them, one way, or the other.

We expect your positive response to this historic and precedent setting FOIA Request within 20 working days as the statute provides. If our request is denied in whole or part, we ask that you justify the denial or all deletions by reference to specific exemptions of the act. We also expect you to release all segregable portions of otherwise exempt material.

Please be assured that we will exhaust all administrative, legal and political remedies to successfully conclude this FOIA Request. Thank you for your consideration.

Sincerely,
Bob Brown, co-director
Pan-African Roots

PART III: PUBLIC COMMITMENT AND OPEN RECORDS REQUESTS

It [is] forbidden to sell men like cattle, which ha[s] been too generally practised in England.

> *Saint Anselm, the Archbishop of Canterbury*
> *National Ecclesiastical Council at Westminster*
> *1102*

Slavery is the most vile and contemptible thing that can exist among men, because man, who is the most noble and free among all the creatures God made, is brought by means of it under the power of another, so that the other can make of him whatever he wishes, like any of the rest of his property, living or dead. And slavery is such a contemptible thing that whoever is subjected to it loses not only the power to make of himself what he wants, but he has not even the power over his own person, except by order of his master.

> *Las Siete Partidas del rey Don*
> *Alfonso el Sabio ...,*
> *Part IV, Title V. C1263*

As all men are by nature free born, and as this kingdom is called the Kingdom of the Franks [freemen], it shall be so in reality.

> *Louis X*
> *King of France*
> *Royal Edict of 1315*

England is too pure an air for slaves to breathe in.

> *Cartwright Decision*
> *1569*

[The Kingdom of Spain gives] liberty to ... all men as well as all women ... so that by their example and by [his] liberality others will do the same.

> *Royal Edicts of November 7, 1695*
> *Issued by Charles II*
> *King of Spain*

Pan-African Roots

1247 E Street SE
Washington, DC 20003
Tel: (202) 544-9355 - Fax: (202) 544-9359
Email: paroots02@yahoo.com

25 October 2004

His Holiness Pope John Paul II
c/o The Apostolic Nunciature
3339 Massachusetts Ave NW
Washington, D.C. 20008

Amended Request for Public Commitment and Information
Fee Waiver and Expedited Review Request.
cc: FOIA Officer and FOIA Appeals Officer.

Your Holiness:

We formally and publicly request that you, the Vatican, the Roman Catholic Church, the Society of Jesus, the Order of the Preachers (Dominicans), the United States Conference of Catholic Bishops, and all of the Church institutions, organizations and agencies formally and publicly commit, once and for all, that "God makes no slaves in the womb,"[98] that the prohibition of man-stealing is well-settled in the Bible in Timothy 1:10, Exodus 21:16, Deuteronomy 24:7, 1 Corinthians 5:11, 1 Corinthians 6:10 and Timothy 1:10-1; that the Vatican was in the forefront of the struggle from at least 441 CE to prohibit and abolish the enslavement of and trafficking in Christians, Europeans, the Indigenous Peoples of the Western Hemisphere and Africans; and that slavery and the slave trade were and are crimes against God, and were and are crimes against humanity.

We also formally and publicly request that Your Holiness give us access to or copies of all records created or obtained by the Vatican, the Roman Catholic Church, the Jesuits, and all other Church structures, organizations and institutions, that pertain to, or reference:

- Their role, operations and activities, historically and currently, in facilitating, prohibiting or combating piracy and privateering, slavery and the slave trade, especially the Trans-Atlantic Slave Trade (also known as the Atlantic Trade, the Triangle Trade, the Colonial Trade, the West Indies Trade, the Coastal Trade, the Intra-state Slave Trade, etc.); and their role in the struggle to declare them crimes against humanity, and repair the damages and injuries that they inflicted upon untold generations of African People.

- Their role, operations and activities, historically and currently, in facilitating, prohibiting or combating slave-like conditions and practices, including but not limited to servitude; forced and compulsory labor; peonage; sharecropping; debt-bondage; convict-lease; chain-gang or prison labor; sweatshop labor; the sale of children; child prostitution; child pornography; the exploitation of child labour; the sexual mutilation of female children; the use of children in armed conflicts; the traffic in persons and in the sale of human organs; the exploitation of prostitution; certain practices under colonialism, segregation and apartheid; racism and racial discrimination, xenophobia and related intolerance.

- Slave, urban and racial disturbances, riots, rebellions, and revolts; runaway slaves, fugitives beyond borders, and related claims or extradition requests; and all demands and proposals for compensation, restitution, reparations or repatriation.

---

[98] Rev. John G. Fee. *An Anti-Slavery Manual, or, The Wrongs of American Slavery Exposed By the Light of the Bible and of Facts, with A Remedy for the Evil (1851)*. Available from http://members.tripod.com/medicolegal/feeasm1851.htm.

- All treaties or agreements, bilateral or multilateral, or diplomatic communications, correspondence, discussions, public and secret, between the United States Government and its Officials (all levels, branches and agencies) and the Vatican, or all other governments with respect to the above or related subjects.

- The world Conference Against Racism, Racial Discrimination, Xenophobia and Related Intolerance, including its preparatory, regional, and expert meetings and seminars; the White House Interagency Task Force on the U.N. World Conference Against Racism; the UN Intergovernmental Working Group on the effective implementation of the Durban Declaration and Programme of Action, and the UNESCO Slave Route Project.

- All efforts by African People in the United States, the African Diaspora, or Africa to lodge complaints against the Vatican, Catholic Church, And Jesuits or other church structures, organizations or institutions with the League of Nations, the United Nations, and all other international or regional bodies.

- All governments, agencies (federal, state, county or local), corporations, non-governmental organizations, institutions, churches, families, individuals, or entities, domestic or foreign who participated or invested in, or made profits from the above referenced crimes against humanity; and who owns or benefits from these historical and continuing crimes today, including but not limited to those listed in Appendix A.

Permit us to offer several reasons why we believe that you should grant this historic and precedent setting Request.

As you are aware, the world Conference Against Racism, Racial Discrimination, Xenophobia and Related Intolerance (WCAR) met from 31 August to 3 September 2001, in Durban, South Africa. Reports reveal that 18,810 delegates from 170 countries participated in WCAR, including 16 heads of state, 58 foreign ministers, 44 ministers, 7,000 non-governmental representatives, and 1,300 journalists. The WCAR Final Declaration and Programme of Action:

Acknowledge[s] that slavery and the slave trade, including the Trans-Atlantic Slave Trade, were appalling tragedies in the history of humanity not only because of their abhorrent barbarism but also in terms of their magnitude, organized nature, and especially their negation of the essence of the victims, … acknowledge[s] that slavery and the slave trade are a crime against humanity and should have always been so, especially the Trans-Atlantic Slave Trade and are among the major sources and manifestations of racism, racial discrimination, xenophobia and related intolerance,… and invite[s] the international community members to honour the memory of the victims of these tragedies. [**Emphasis added.**]

Further note[s] that some [countries} have taken the initiative of regretting or expressing remorse or presenting apologies, and call on all those who have yet contributed to restoring the dignity of all the victims to find appropriate ways to do so…[99]

You are perhaps not aware, that on May 17, 1860, the second National Republican Convention adopted its 1860 National Republican Platform, which declared it resolved:

7. That the new dogma that the Constitution of its own force carries slavery into any or all of the territories of the United States, is a dangerous political heresy, at variance with the explicit provisions of that instrument itself, with contemporaneous exposition, and with legislative and judicial precedent, is revolutionary in its tendency and subversive of the peace and harmony of the country.

---

[99] World Conference Secretariat. Office of the United Nations High Commissioner for Human Rights. Available from http://www.unhchr.ch/html/racism/02-documents-cnt.html.

8. That the formal condition of all the territory of the United States is that of freedom; that as our republican fathers, when they had abolished slavery in all our national territory, ordained that no "person should be deprived of life, liberty or property, without due process of law," it becomes our duty, by legislation, whenever such legislation is necessary, to maintain this provision of the constitution against all attempts to violate it; and we deny the authority of Congress, of a territorial legislature, or of any individuals, to give legal existence to slavery in any territory of the United States.

9. That we brand the recent re-opening of the African Slave trade, under the cover of our national flag, aided by perversions of judicial power, as a crime against humanity, and a burning shame to our country and age, and we call upon congress to take prompt and efficient measures for the total and final suppression of the execrable traffic.[100] [**Emphasis added.**]

In 1808, the United States Government prohibited its citizens from participating in the international slave trade, declaring it piracy in 1820, and participation in it punishable by death. Despite this prohibition, a minimum of 250,000 and perhaps as many as 1,000,000 Africans were kidnapped, enslaved, and illegally imported into the United States via Cuba between 1809 and 1861. In 1839, a prime male slave could be purchased in Cuba for $400 and then sold into slavery for life in Richmond for $1,000, or Charleston for Charleston for $1,150, or Savannah for $1,200 or New Orleans for $1,250. The average daily wage was $1. President James Madison reported to Congress in 1810 that:

It appears that American citizens are instrumental in carrying on a traffic in enslaved Africans, equally in violation of the laws of humanity, and in defiance of those of their own country. The same just and benevolent motives, which produced the interdiction in force against this criminal conduct, will doubtless be felt in Congress, in devising further means of suppressing the evil.

You are perhaps also not aware that William Lloyd Garrison was the first person to declare slavery a crime against humanity in the inaugural edition (1831) of his Liberator newspaper; or that on November 12, 1849, the Vermont Legislature passed "*Joint Resolution No. 42.--Resolutions Relating To The Subject of Slavery*," declaring it:

Resolved by the Senate and House of Representatives, that Slavery is a crime against humanity, and a sore evil in the body politic that was excused by the framers of the Federal Constitution as a crime entailed upon the country by their predecessors, and tolerated solely as a thing of inexorable necessity.[101] [**Emphasis added.**]

The 1860 Republican National Convention selected Abraham Lincoln as its presidential nominee. He campaigned on this platform, and "won the presidency with almost half a million votes more than [Stephen] Douglas, his closest rival. [Lincoln] won the election garnering 39.8 percent of the popular vote. This election firmly established the Republican hold on the presidency for 60 of the next 100 years." Within five years of the 1860 Convention, slavery had been abolished, 4 million slaves were liberated, and the 13th Amendment was passed banning slavery and the slave trade forever from U.S. soil.

It is well-settled, as the WCAR Final Declaration confirms, that prohibitions against piracy and privateering, slavery and the slave trade, including the Trans-Atlantic Slave Trade, and against slave-like conditions and practices, including colonialism, segregation and apartheid, forced and compulsory labor, racism and racial discrimination, xenophobia and related intolerance have achieved the level of customary international law, have attained the status of jus cogens, and are obligato erga omnes. Unfortunately, the

---

[100] Central Pacific Railroad Photographic History Museum. *Republican Party National Platform, 1860.* Available from http://cprr.org/Museum/Ephemera/Republican_Platform_1860.html.

[101] *The Acts and Resolves Passed By The Legislature Of The State of Vermont At The October Session, 1849.* Published By authority. Montpelier: E. P. Walton & Son. 1849.

overwhelming majority of the WCAR Delegates and the public, especially African People worldwide, wrongly believe that this status has only recently been acquired.[102]

Permit us to suggest, as Ethan A. Nadelman suggests, that "most global prohibition regimes, including those targeted against piracy, slavery, and drug trafficking, evidence a common evolutionary pattern consisting of four or five stages."[103] At different stages in their development: (1) the activity is legal and some states participate in it; (2) national and international forces, non-governmental and governmental, attempt to redefine the activity as evil and illegal; (3) these forces agitate for its suppression and criminalization; (4) the activity becomes the subject of national and international criminal laws, conventions and treaties, police and military action; and (5) finally, the activity is prohibited globally.[104] It is axiomatic that this development is extremely uneven, unequal, and costly in time, space and human lives, in justice and equity.

Permit us also to suggest that Judge Fouad Ammoun of the International Court of Justice (ICJ) "has [accurately] described the development of Africa ... [and] eloquently remarked on the evolution of mankind's struggle with the issues of slavery and colonization."[105] He informs us that "before there fell upon it the two greatest plagues in the recorded history of mankind: the slave trade, which ravaged Africa for centuries on an unprecedented scale; and colonialism, which exploited humanity and natural wealth to a relentless extreme," ... Africa boasted thriving states and empires dating back to Roman times."[106]

Judge Ammoun also informs us that "historians have outlined the upward march of mankind from the time when homo sapiens appeared on the face of the globe, first of all in the Near East in what was the land of Canaan[107], up to the age of the greatest thinkers and more particularly, throughout the whole of history of social progress, from the slavery of Antiquity to man's [and woman's] inevitable, irreversible drive towards equality and freedom. This march is like time itself. It never stops. Nothing can stand in its way for long. The texts, whether they be laws, constitutions, declarations, covenants or charters, do but define it and mark its successive phases. They are a mere record of it. In other words, the progressive rights which men, [women] and peoples enjoy are the result much less of those texts than of human progress to which they bear witness."[108]

We are confident that the records requested by and through these historic and precedent setting Request will:

- Bear witness to and prove, once and for all, that piracy and privateering, slavery and the slave trade, including the Trans-Atlantic Slave Trade, and slave-like conditions and practices, including colonialism, segregation, and apartheid, were and are illegal and prohibited, and were and are recognized as crimes against humanity when and where they were committed.

- Help define and mark the successive stages in the development of the 569-year historical and continuing Maafa,[109] and of the unyielding and continuing struggle against it.

---

[102] People incorrectly believe that "the term was first used in the preamble of the Hague Convention of 1907." Wikipedia. Available from http://en.wikipedia.org/wiki/Crime_against_humanity.

[103] Ethan A. Nadelman. Global prohibition regimes: the evolution of norms in international society. Printed in Transnational Crime / edited by Nikos Passas.

[104] Ibid.

[105] *Legal Consequences For States of the Continued Presence of South Africa in Namibia (South West Africa) Notwithstanding Security Council Resolution 276, 1971 I.C.J. 16, 86 (1971) (separate opinion of Judge Ammoun).*

[106] Recent evidence documents that African civilizations predate Roman times.

[107] Recent evidence documents that homo sapiens first emerged in East Africa.

[108] Ethan A. Nadelman. *Global prohibition regimes.*

[109] Maafa, from *Let The Circle Be Unbroken*, by Dr. Marimba Ani is a Kiswahili word for the 563-year historical and continuing enslavement and colonization of Africa and African People.

- Document who the victims were, and who their descendants are today; who committed these crimes, which were and are the greatest theft of land, lives and labor in human history; how this unjust and illegal wealth was converted, consolidated, preserved and transferred across generations and centuries; and who owns and benefits from this unjust enrichment today.

We request that you give us access to or copies of all records that document the role, operations, and activities of the following Popes, and other church officials and structures in the struggle to facilitate, prohibit or abolish the enslavement of and trafficking in Christians, Europeans, the Indigenous Peoples of the Western Hemisphere or Africans:

- Pope Sixtus III (432); Pope Leo I (440); Pope Hilarus (461); Pope Simplicius (468); Pope Felix III II) (483); Pope Gelasius I (492); Pope Anastasius II (496); Anti-Pope Lawrence (498); Pope Symmachus (498); Pope Hormisdas (514); Pope John I (523); Pope Felix IV III) (526); Anti-Pope Dioscorus (530); Pope Boniface II (530); Pope John II (532); Pope Agapitus I (535); Pope Silverius (536); Pope Vigilius (537); Pope Pelagius I (556); Pope John III (561); Pope Benedict I (575); Pope Pelagius II (579); Pope Sabinian (604); Pope Boniface III (606); Pope Boniface IV (607); Pope Deusdedit (615); Pope Boniface V (619); Pope Honorius I (625); Pope John IV (640); Pope Severinus (640); Pope Theodore I (642); Pope Martin I (649); Pope Eugene I (654); Pope Vitalian (657); Pope Adeodatus II (673); Pope Donus (676); Pope Agatho (678); Pope Leo II (682); Pope Benedict II (684); Pope John V (685); Pope Conon (686); Anti-Pope Paschal (687); Anti-Pope Theodore (687) and Pope Sergius I (687).

- Pope John VI (701); Pope John VII (705); Pope Constantine (708); Pope Sisinnius (708); Pope Gregory II (715); Pope Gregory III (731); Pope Zachary (741); Pope Stephen II III) (752); Pope Paul I (757); Anti-Pope Constantine (767); Anti-Pope Philip (768); Pope Stephen III IV) (768); Pope Adrian I (772); Pope Leo III (795); Pope Stephen IV V) (816); Pope Paschal I (817); Pope Eugene II (824); Pope Gregory IV (827); Pope Valentine (827); Anti-Pope John (844); Pope Sergius II (844); Pope Leo IV (847); Anti-Pope Anastasius (855); Pope Benedict III (855); Pope Nicholas I (858); Pope Adrian II (867); Pope John VII (872); Pope Marinus I (882); Pope Adrian III (884); Pope Stephen V VI) (885); Pope Formosus (891); Pope Boniface VI (896); Pope Stephen VI VII) (896); Pope Romanus (897); Pope Theodore II (897); Pope John IX (898); Pope Benedict IV (900); Anti-Pope Christopher (903); Pope Leo V (903); Pope Sergius III (904); Pope Anastasius III (911); Pope Landus (913); Pope John X (914); Pope Leo VI (928); Pope Stephen VII VIII) (928); Pope John XI (931); Pope Leo VII (936); Pope Stephen VIII IX) (939); Pope Marinus II (942); Pope Agapitus II (946); Pope John XII (955); Pope Leo VIII (963); Pope Benedict V (964); Pope John XIII (965); Pope Benedict VI (973); Anti-Pope Boniface VII (974); Pope Benedict VII (974); Pope John XIV (983); Pope John XV (985); Pope Gregory V (996); Anti-Pope John XVI (997) and Pope Sylvester II (999).

- Pope John XVII (1003); Pope John XVIII (1004); Pope Sergius IV (1009); Anti-Pope Gregory (1012); Pope Benedict VIII (1012); Pope John XIX (1024); Pope Benedict IX (1032); Pope Benedict IX (1045); Pope Gregory VI (1045); Pope Sylvester III (1045); Pope Clement II (1046); Pope Benedict IX (1047); Pope Damasus II (1048); Pope Leo IX (1049); Pope Victor II (1055); Pope Stephen IX X) (1057); Anti-Pope Benedict X (1058); Pope Nicholas II (1059); Anti-Pope Honorius II (1061); Pope Alexander II (1061); Anti-Pope Clement III (1080); Pope Victor III (1086); Pope Urban II (1088); Pope Paschal II (1099); Anti-Pope Theodoric (1100); Anti-Pope Albert (1102); Anti-Pope Sylvester IV (1105); Anti-Pope Gregory VIII (1118); Pope Gelasius II (1118); Pope Callistus II (1119); Anti-Pope Celestine II (1124); Pope Honorius II (1124); Anti-Pope Anacletus II (1130); Pope Innocent II (1130); Anti-Pope Victor IV (1138); Pope Celestine II (1143); Pope Lucius II (1144); Pope Eugene III (1145); Pope Anastasius IV (1153); Pope Adrian IV (1154) and Anti-Pope Victor IV (1159).

- Pope Alexander III (1159); Anti-Pope Paschal III (1164); Anti-Pope Callistus III (1168); Anti-Pope Innocent III (1179); Pope Lucius III (1181); Pope Urban III (1185); Pope Clement III (1187); Pope Gregory VIII (1187); Pope Celestine III (1191); Pope Innocent III (1198); Pope Honorius III (1216); Pope Gregory IX (1227); Pope Celestine IV (1241); Pope Innocent IV (1243); Pope Alexander IV (1254); Pope Urban IV (1261); Pope Clement IV (1265); Pope Gregory X (1271); Pope Adrian V (1276); Pope Innocent V (1276); Pope John XXI (1276); Pope Nicholas IV (1277); Pope Boniface VIII (1294); Pope Celestine V (1294); Pope Benedict XI (1303); Pope Clement V (1305); Pope John XXII (1316); Pope John XXII (1323); Anti-Pope Nicholas V (1328); Pope Benedict XII (1334); Pope Clement VI (1342); Pope Clement VI (1349); Pope Innocent VI (1352); Pope Urban V (1362); Pope Gregory XI (1370); Anti-Pope Clement VII (1378); Pope Urban VI (1378); Pope Boniface IX (1389); Anti-Pope Benedict XIII (1394); Pope Innocent VII (1404); Pope Gregory XII (1406); Anti-Pope Alexander V (1409); Anti-Pope John XXIII (1410) and Alexander V (1410) and Pope Martin V (1417)

- Pope Eugene IV (1431); Anti-Pope Felix V (1439); Pope Nicholas V (1447); Pope Nicholas V (1454); Pope Callistus III (1455); Pope Pius II (1458); Pope Paul II (1464); Pope Sixtus IV (1471); Pope Innocent VIII (1484); Pope Alexander VI (1492); Pope Julius II (1503); Pope Pius III (1503); Pope Julius II (1506); Pope Leo X (1513); Pope Adrian VI (1522); Pope Clement VII (1523); Pope Paul III (1534); Pope Julius III (1537); Pope Paul II (1537); Pope Paul III (1537); Pope Paul IV (1548); Pope Pius IV (1550); Pope Gregory XIII (1555); Pope Pius V (1555); Pope Sixtus V (1559); Pope Urban VII (1566); Pope Innocent IX (1572); Pope Clement VIII (1585); Pope Leo XI (1590); Pope Paul V (1591); Pope Gregory XV (1592); Pope Urban VIII (1605); Pope Innocent X (1624); Pope Alexander VII (1639); Pope Clement IX (1639); Pope Clement X (1644); Pope Innocent XI (1655); Pope Alexander VIII (1667); Pope Innocent XII (1670); Pope Clement XI (1676); Pope Innocent XI (1676); Pope Innocent XIII (1689); Pope Clement XII (1700); Pope Benedict XIV (1721); Pope Clement XIII (1730); Pope Clement XIV (1740); Pope Pius VI (1741); Pope Leo XII (1775); Pope Pius VII (1800); Pope Pius VIII (1800); Pope Gregory XVI (1815); Pope Pius IX (1831); Pope Leo XIII (1839); Pope John XXIII (1841); Pope Paul VI (1846) and Pope John Paul I (1878).

We also request that you give us access to or copies of all records that document the following and other related activities and events:

- 400, St. Augustine's call for granting freedom to slaves as a great religious virtue.

- 432, St Patrick's mission in Ireland.

- 441, Church decree censuring slavers.

- 451, decrees of the Councils of the Church, especially the Council of Chalcedon, which were confirmed as laws of the empire to secure their being put in force by the civil power; which were the foundation of international law; and which decreed that imperial laws that were contrary to canon law were and are null and void.

- 452, decree that slaves could be manumitted in ecclesiis, and also freed by any other process (Council of Arles, 452; of Agde, 506; of Orléans, 549; of Mâcon, 585; of Toledo, 589, 633; of Paris, 615.

- 511, decrees declaring the protection of the maltreated slave who has taken refuge in a church (Councils of Orléans, 511, 538, 549, Council of Epone, 517).

- 539, edict that masters had no power to separate families in the sale of slaves, and that it was a crime.

- 541, prohibition of Jews to possess Christian slaves (Council of Orléans, 541; of Mâcon, 581; of Clichy, 625; of Toledo, 589, 633, 656.

- 549, decree mandating the use of church buildings as refuges for escaping slaves.

- 566, decree ordering the excommunication-of-slavers proviso.

- 578, decree calling for rest for slaves on Sundays and Feast days (Council of Auxerrre, 578 and 585; of Chalon-sur-Saône, middle of the seventh century; of Rouen, 650; of Wessex, 691; of Berghamsted, 697).

- 583, decree empowering the church to issue of freedom papers.

- 595, decree freeing slave entrants to monastic life.

- 7th century, Saint Bathilde's (wife of King Clovis II) campaign to stop slave trading and free all slaves.

- 604, decree pronouncing slavery a cruel evil and a great crime, and declaring a severe punishment upon the bishops who authorized it in their bishoprics.

- 616, decree mandating liberty restoration proviso.

- 625, decree banning the acquisition of new slaves, mandating the use of church property to free current slaves, and declaring a prohibition against reducing a free man to slavery (Council of Clichy, 625).

- 644, decree calling for the suppression of the traffic in slaves by forbidding their sale outside the kingdom (Council of Châlon-sur-Saône, between 644 and 650).

- 666, decree banning the shaving of slaves.

- 752, decree guaranteeing the validity of marriage contracted with full knowledge of the circumstances between free persons and slaves ((Councils of Verberie, 752, of Compiègne, 759).

- 844, decree mandating the use of church property to free slaves.

- 851, Saint Anskar's efforts to halt the Viking slave trade.

- 873, order by the rulers of Sardinia to restore freedom to slaves bought from the Greeks.

- 922, decree defining slave trade as homicide.

- 1009, Saint Wulfstan's order forbidding the enslavement of Christians.

- 1027, William the Conqueror's order forbidding the enslavement of Christians.

- 1033, Saint Anselm's order forbidding the enslavement of Christians.

- King Charlemagne's decree against slavery.

- Constantine's order giving authority to the bishops to manumit slaves and [as Emperor) granting Roman citizenship to many of those set free.

- Emperors Constantine's and Constantinus' orders making the subjection of females to slavery a capital crime.

- 1066, William the Conqueror's support for English Bishops who denounced the enslavement of (English) Christians, which led to the elimination of slavery in England by 1200.

- 1102, decree calling for a ban on the slave trade.

- 1435, Pope Eugene IV in his Bull, Sicut Dudum, and a letter written to Bishop Ferdinand of Lanzarote, saying that:

    They have deprived the natives of their property or turned it to their own use, and have subjected some of the inhabitants of said islands to perpetual slavery, sold them to other persons and committed other various illicit and evil deeds against them. We order and command all and each of the faithful of each sex that, within the space of fifteen days of the publication of these letters in the place where they live, that they restore to their earlier liberty all and each person of either sex who were once residents of said Canary Islands. who have been made subject to slavery. These people are to be totally and perpetually free and are to be let go without the exaction or reception of any money.

- 1456, 13-Mar, Papal Bull (Inter Caetera) issued by Pope Nicholas V denouncing the Spanish treatment of Indians:

    This voice says that you are living in deadly sin for the atrocities you tyrannically impose on these innocent people. Tell me what right have you to enslave them? What authority did you use to make war against them who lived at peace on their territories killing them cruelly with methods never before heard of? How can you oppress them and not care to feed or cure them and work them to death to satisfy your greed?

    And why don't you look after their spiritual health so that they should come to know God that they should be baptized and that they should hear Mass and keep the holy days? Aren't they human beings? Have they no rational soul? Aren't you obliged to love them as you love yourselves? Don't you understand? How can you live in such a lethargical dream?

    You must rest assured that you are in no better state of salvation than the Moors or Turks who reject the Christian faith.

- 1462-76, the Vatican opposed the efforts of Spanish slave traders at the Port of Seville to begin the trade in large numbers of slaves.

- 1503, October 30, Queen Isabella's ban on violence against Indians.

- 1514, Pope Leo X's bull denouncing slavery and the slave trade.

- 1515, Bishop Bartolome de Las Casas, the first Spanish priest to be ordained the Western Hemisphere, returned to Spain from Hispaniola to plead to King Carlos I on behalf of enslaved Indians. Las Casas requested that each Spanish resident of Santo Domingo (now known ad Haiti) be granted a license to import twelve African slaves order to release the natives from slavery. Las Casas argued that:

    There can be neither slaves by nature, nor people without freedom and power, nor people without sovereignty.

- 1517, formalization of slave-trading between Africa and America at the suggestion of Bishop Bartolome de Las Casas, and the resultant approval of King Charles of Spain for the importation of 4000 Africans into the Americas.

- 1519, Bartholomew De Las Casas' argument against slavery that no one may be deprived of his liberty nor may any person be enslaved.

- 1534-1549, Pope Paul III wrote a bull against New World slavery, saying that:

    [Satan,] the enemy of the human race, who always opposes all good men so that the race may perish, has thought up a way, unheard of before now, by which he might impede the saving word of God from being preached to the nations. He has stirred up some of his allies who, desiring to satisfy their own avarice, are presuming to assert far and wide that the Indians of the West and the South who have come to our notice in these times be reduced to our service like brute animals, under the pretext that they are lacking in the Catholic faith. And they reduce them to slavery, treating them with afflictions they would scarcely use with brute animals.

Therefore, We ... noting that the Indians themselves indeed are true men., by our Apostolic Authority decree and declare by these present letters that the same Indians and all other peoples—even though they are outside the faith ... should not be deprived of their liberty or their other possessions ... and are not to be reduced to slavery, and that whatever happens to the contrary is to be considered null and void.

- In a second bull on slavery, Paul imposed the penalty of excommunication on anyone, regardless of their "dignity, state, condition, or grade, who in any way may presume to reduce said Indians to slavery or despoil them of their goods."

- 1537, 29-May, Pope Paul III's Letter Apostolic, under the seal of the Fisherman, to the Cardinal Archbishop of Toledo, Spain, denouncing slavery and forbidding the enslavement of the Indigenous Peoples of the Western Hemisphere, calling it "an evil unheard of before now to the enemy of the human race Satan," and ordering the excommunication of the slavers. Pope Paul also supported a Royal edict issued by Charles V of Spain that endeavored to halt mistreatment of Indians:

    Therefore, attending to the fact that the Indians themselves, although they are outside the bosom of the Church, have not been and should not be deprived of their liberty or of ownership of what is their own, and that, since they are men and therefore capable of faith and salvation, they are not to be given into servitude, but rather by preaching, good examples and the like should be invited to eternal life. We.. command that anyone of whatever dignity, state, condition, or grade who works against what is done through you or others to help the Indians in the aforementioned matters incurs the penalty of excommunication.

- 1539, Repetition of Papal condemnations of slavery.

- 1540, Bartolome de Las Casas's debated Juan Gines de Sepulveda before the King of Spain and other members of the clergy:

    Sepulveda's justification of Indian enslavement on the grounds of the gravity of sins of the Indians, especially idolatry; the rudeness of the natives which made it necessary for more refined people like the Spanish to educate them; the goal of spreading the faith; protection of weaker Indians who were subject to human sacrifice and cannibalism.

    Las Casas' response that God did not command war against idolaters; the Indians had rich, vibrant civilizations and sophisticated cultures; peaceful conversion was the most effective means of spreading Catholicism; although human sacrifice was evil, indiscriminate warfare was more evil.

    Las Casas also presented abundant evidence during the debate that Spaniards in the New World were not seeking to enlighten Indians, but to work them to death through enslavement.

- 1542, Papal influence and lobbying by Bishop Bartolome Las Casas, which led to the royal proclamation of the New Laws of the Indies which forbade all future enslavement of Indians; and the violent opposition (riots, petitions, and open rebellion) which these New Laws met from settlers, which caused the monarchy to back away from enforcement of the laws.

- 1542, Bishop Las Casas helped to draft the "New Laws of the Indies" which banned slavery.

- 1548, Pope Paul III allegedly confirmed that any individual may freely buy, sell and own slaves. Runaway slaves were to be returned to their owners for punishment.

- 1566, on his deathbed, Las Casas addressed a memorandum to the King which declared that:

  > All wars called conquests are unjust. The system of encomiendas is tyrannical. The King can not justify wars in the Americas against peaceful peoples. All gold and silver taken from the New World is stolen. Indians have a right to fight against invasion of their land by Spanish conquerors.

- In the closing pages of his history of Spain's conquests in the New World, Las Casas warned his fellow countrymen:

  > I say and hold it certain that all the crimes committed by the Spaniards against these people with such perverse cruelties, have been against the pure and most righteous law of Jesus Christ, and against all natural reason, and to the greatest infamy of His name, and the Christian religion, and the total destruction of the faith. ... And I believe for these impious and ignominious works, so unjustly and tyrannically barbarously committed. ... God will pour His fury and anger upon Spain if she does not perform a great penance.

- 1591, Pope Gregory XIV's condemnation of slavery and the slave trade (*Cum Sicuti*), promising excommunication of clergy who participated in the slavery trade and slavery.

- 1618 to 1632, St. Remolasco redemption of 490,736 slaves.

- 1639, April 22, Pope Urban VIII's condemnation of slavery and the slave trade (*Commissum Nobis*), at the request of the Jesuits of Paraguay, reaffirming the ruling by "our predecessor Paul III that those who reduced others to slavery were subject to excommunication," and forbidding the enslavement of Indians. In his letter to the Collector Jurium of the Apostolic Chamber of Portugal condemning those who should dare:

  > To reduce to slavery the Indians of the Eastern and Southern Indies, to sell them, buy them, exchange them or give them, separate them from their wives and children, despoil them of their goods and properties, conduct or transport them into other regions, or deprive them of liberty in any way whatsoever, retain them in servitude, or lend counsel, succour, favour and co-operation to those so acting, under no matter what pretext or excuse, or who proclaim and teach that this way of acting is allowable and co-operate in any manner whatever in the practices indicated.

- 1642, St. Vincent of Paul's work from 1642 to 1660 to redeem 1,200 slaves [in Algiers and Tunis] at an expense of 1,200,000 livres.

- 1686, 20-Mar, the Congregation of the Holy Office's (the Roman Inquisition) ruling on the matter of slavery. It is asked, they ruled:

  > Whether it is permitted to capture by force and deceit Blacks and other natives who have harmed no one? Answer: no!

  > Whether it is permitted to buy, sell or make contracts in their respect, Blacks or other natives who have harmed no one and been made captives by force of deceit? Answer: no!

  > Whether the possessors of Blacks and other natives who have harmed no one and been captured by force or deceit, are not held to set them free? Answer: yes!

Whether the captors, buyers and possessors of Blacks and other natives who have harmed no one and who have been captured by force or deceit are not held to make compensation to them? Answer: yes!

- 17th century, Bull of Canonization of the Jesuit Peter Claver, and Pope Pius IX's declaration branding the supreme villainy (summum nefas) of the slave traders.

- 1741, 20-December, Pope Benedict XIV's Apostolic Letter (Immensa Pastorum) which was addressed to the Bishops of Brazil, condemning slavery and the slave trade, forbidding the enslavement of Indians, and promising excommunication of clergy who participated in them

- 1794, degree by the French National Assembly during the French Revolution, at the instigation of a Catholic priest, the Abbé H. Grégoire, abolishing slavery and the slave trade in all French colonies, and making all former slaves citizens of France with full and equal rights.

- 1815, the Vatican's efforts at the Congress of Vienna to convince the nations of Europe to prohibit slavery and the slave trade.

- 1829, the Papal request for Mexico to abolish slavery, which Mexico did, throughout its dominions, including Texas and the Southwestern region of the United States.

- 1838, decree condemning all forms of colonial slavery and the slave trade, calling it inhumanum illud commercium, and forbidding all Catholics to propound views contrary to this.

- 1887, the Papal letter which claimed that the Catholic Church struggled from the beginning to see slavery eased and abolished which was oppressing so many people.

- 1888, Cardinal Lavigerie efforts to found the Société Antiesclavagiste, and to abolish slavery and the slave trade in Africa and Brazil.

- 1888, Leo XIII's letter to the Brazilian bishops exhorting them to banish from their country the remnants of slavery, recalling the Church's unceasing efforts over centuries to get rid of colonial slavery and the slave trade, and expressing satisfaction that Brazil had at last abolished it.

- 1890, the Papal encyclical which condemned slavery, slave traders and servitude; called for its abolition in all Catholic Missions; and ordered an annual collection to be made in all Catholic churches for the benefit of the anti-slavery work on an international basis.

We request, formally and publicly, that Your Holiness order all Church structures, organizations and institutions under your authority and control worldwide, to provide us access to or copies of all records that document all governments, agencies, corporations, non-governmental organizations, institutions, churches, families or individuals, domestic or foreign, who were enriched by and through their participation in these crimes; and on who owns, controls or benefits from this wealth today.

Permit us to offer here, several examples of how the Catholic Church in the United States participated in, and was enriched by and through their participation in slavery, the slave trade and racism:

- The Society of Jesus of Maryland was the largest slaveholder on the eastern seaboard of the United States with four [tobacco] plantations in Maryland. According to John Carroll, the first bishop of the new United States, "the Catholic population in Maryland in the [19th century], was about 15,800, about 3,000 children, and the same number are slaves of all ages, who come from Africa."

- The twin purposes of the Jesuit plantations in Maryland were to support the Jesuit mission, of building the Catholic Church in Baltimore, the Mother Church, and in the United States, as well as support Georgetown College, now known as Georgetown University.

- According to the Jesuit Plantation Website, "Slaves were sold to maintain the solvency of the University. In the late 1830s, the Jesuits sold all of their slaves, [272 slaves to Louisiana slaveholders], and in the process, many families were broken up. The money from the sale was used to pay the university's debt and to create an endowment. Students were allowed to bring slaves with them to the university to aid in housekeeping. The university is believed to have held slaves for campus beautification projects. Rev. Thomas F. Mulledy, S.J., a slaveholder and alumnus of Georgetown University," believed that slavery was the best thing for African."

- In the 1860s, 925 of the 1,141 Georgetown University's alumni and students who fought in the Civil War joined the Confederate ranks.

- According to the documentary film," Black Georgetown Remembered," Georgetown University, the District of Columbia, and area realtors, forced many Africans in DC to relocate by means of mass condemnations in order to turn Georgetown into a profitable real estate investment, and provide additional land to the University.

- In 1969, only 30 Black students were enrolled at Georgetown, and racism, racial discrimination and harassment was prominent.

- In 1995, the DC Department of Human Rights and Minority Business Development ruled that there was probable cause to believe that Georgetown University discriminated against its highest-ranking minority employee in its Financial Affairs Division.

We hope that Your Holiness will comply with this Request for a Public Commitment and Information in an expedited manner, and that you will waive all associated costs. Please be advised that we have sent a copy of this Request to the public and the media.

In order to help you determine our status and make your decision on our fee waiver request, you should know that Bob Brown is an organizer and researcher, who has worked, studied and struggled for 41 years, within and for the Student, Civil and Human Rights, Black Power, National Liberation, Pan-African, and Peace Movements. See Attachment B.

We expect your positive response to this historic and precedent setting Request within 20 working days. Thank you for your consideration.

Sincerely,
Bob Brown, co-director
Pan-African Roots

cc: Reverend Monsignor William P. Fay, General Secretary
        United States Conference of Catholic Bishops
        3211 4th Street NE
        Washington, DC 20017-1194

        Father General Peter-Hans Kolvenbach SJ, Superior General of the Society of Jesus
        c/o U.S. Jesuit Conference
        1616 P Street NW Suite 300
        Washington, DC 20036-1420

        FR. Bradley M. Schaeffer
        Chair and President of the U.S. Assistancy of the Society of Jesus
        c/o U.S. Jesuit Conference
        1616 P Street NW Suite 300
        Washington, DC 20036-1420

FR. Michael McCormack, O.P., Director of Communications
Dominican Province of St. Joseph
141 East 65th Street
New York, NY 10021-6607

The Society of Jesus of Maryland
5704 Roland Avenue
Baltimore, Maryland 21210

President's Office
Georgetown University
37th and O Streets NW
Washington, DC 20057

Pan-African Roots

1247 E Street SE
Washington, DC 20003
Tel: (202) 544-9355 - Fax: (202) 544-9359
Email: **paroots02@yahoo.com**

25 October 2004

President José Luis Rodríguez Zapatero
c/o Embassy of the Kingdom of Spain
2375 Pennsylvania Avenue NW
Washington, DC 20037

Amended Request for Public Commitment and Information.
Fee Waiver and Expedited Review Request.
cc: FOIA Officer and FOIA Appeals Officer.

Dear President Rodriquez:

We request, pursuant to Article 105 of the 1978 Constitution of Spain and the Ley 30/1992, de 26 de Noviembre, de Regimen Juridico de las Administraciones Publicas y del Procedimiento Administrativo Comun., that you, King Juan Carlos I de Borbón y Borbón and the Government of Spain publicly and immediately commit to give us access to or copies of all records created or obtained by, or under your authority and control, that pertain to, or reference:

- Spain's role, operations and activities, historically and currently, in facilitating, prohibiting or combating piracy and privateering, slavery and the slave trade, especially the Trans-Atlantic Slave Trade ((also known as the Atlantic Trade, the Triangle Trade, the Colonial Trade, the West Indies Trade, etc.) in Spain and its colonies, especially Florida, Cuba, Mexico and Texas; and their role in the struggle to declare them crimes against humanity, and to repair the damages and injuries that they inflicted upon untold generations of African People.

- Spain's role, operations and activities, historically and currently, in facilitating, prohibiting or combating slave-like conditions and practices, including but not limited to servitude, forced and compulsory labor, peonage, sharecropping, debt-bondage, sweatshop labor, convict-lease, chain-gang or prison labor, the sale of children, child prostitution, child pornography, the exploitation of child labour, the sexual mutilation of female children, the use of children in armed conflicts, the traffic in persons and in the sale of human organs, the exploitation of prostitution, and certain practices under apartheid and colonial regimes, segregation, racism and racial discrimination, xenophobia and related intolerance.

- Spain's knowledge of and response to the Catholic Church's prohibition of slavery and the slave trade; call for emancipation of all slaves and granting them citizenship, and related diplomatic discussions, agreement and treaties.

- The Ports of Cadiz, Seville, and all other Ports in or controlled by the Kingdom of Spain, historically and currently, who participated in, and were and continue to be unjustly enriched by and through the above listed crimes.

- Slave, urban and racial disturbances, riots, rebellions, and revolts, runaway slaves, fugitives beyond borders, related claims or requests, and demands for restitution and reparations.

- All treaties or agreements, bilateral or multilateral, or diplomatic communications, correspondence, discussions, public and secret, between the United States Government and its

Officials (all levels, branches and agencies) and the Spanish, Mexican, or all other governments with respect to the above or related subjects.

- The United Nations World Conference Against Racism, Racial Discrimination, Xenophobia and Related Intolerance (WCAR), including its preparatory, regional and expert meetings and seminars, the White House Interagency Task Force on the U.N. World Conference Against Racism, the U.S. Governmental Delegation, the U.S. Non-Governmental Delegation, the UN Intergovernmental Working Group on the effective implementation of the Durban Declaration and Programme of Action, and the UNESCO Slave Route Project.

- All efforts by African People in the United States, the African Diaspora, or Africa to lodge complaints against the Vatican, Catholic Church, And Jesuits or other church structures, organizations or institutions with the League of Nations, the United Nations, and all other international or regional bodies.

- All governments, agencies (federal, state, county or local), corporations, non-governmental organizations, institutions, churches, families, individuals, or entities, domestic or foreign who participated or invested in, or made profits from the above referenced crimes against humanity; and who owns or benefits from these historical and continuing crimes today, including but not limited to those listed in Appendix A.

As you are aware, the world Conference Against Racism, Racial Discrimination, Xenophobia and Related Intolerance (WCAR) met from 31 August to 3 September 2001, in Durban, South Africa. Reports reveal that 18,810 delegates from 170 countries participated in WCAR, including 16 heads of state, 58 foreign ministers, 44 ministers, 7,000 non-governmental representatives, and 1,300 journalists. The WCAR Final Declaration and Programme of Action:

> Acknowledge[s] that slavery and the slave trade, including the Trans-Atlantic Slave Trade, were appalling tragedies in the history of humanity not only because of their abhorrent barbarism but also in terms of their magnitude, organized nature especially their negation of the essence of the victims, ... acknowledge[s] **that slavery and the slave trade are a crime against humanity and should have always been so**, especially the Trans-Atlantic Slave Trade and are among the major sources and manifestations of racism, racial discrimination, xenophobia and related intolerance,... and invite[s] the international community members to honour the memory of the victims of these tragedies. [**Emphasis added.**]

> Further note[s] that some [countries} have taken the initiative of regretting or expressing remorse or presenting apologies, and call on all those who have yet contributed to restoring the dignity of all the victims to find appropriate ways to do so... [110]

You are perhaps not aware, that on May 17, 1860, the second National Republican Convention adopted its 1860 National Republican Platform, which declared it resolved:

> 7. That the new dogma that the Constitution of its own force carries slavery into any or all of the territories of the United States, is a dangerous political heresy, at variance with the explicit provisions of that instrument itself, with contemporaneous exposition, and with legislative and judicial precedent, is revolutionary in its tendency and subversive of the peace and harmony of the country.

> 8. That the formal condition of all the territory of the United States is that of freedom; that as our republican fathers, when they had abolished slavery in all our national territory, ordained that no "person should be deprived of life, liberty or property, without due process of law," it becomes

---

[110] World Conference Secretariat. Office of the United Nations High Commissioner for Human Rights. Available from http://www.unhchr.ch/html/racism/02-documents-cnt.html.

our duty, by legislation, whenever such legislation is necessary, to maintain this provision of the constitution against all attempts to violate it; and we deny the authority of congress, of a territorial legislature, or of any individuals, to give legal existence to slavery in any territory of the United States.

9. That we brand the recent re-opening of the African Slave Trade, under the cover of our national flag, aided by perversions of judicial power, as a **crime against humanity, and a burning shame to our country and age,** and we call upon congress to take prompt and efficient measures for the total and final suppression of the execrable traffic.[111] [**Emphasis added.**]

In 1808, the United States Government prohibited its citizens from participating in the international slave trade, declaring it piracy in 1820, and participation in it punishable by death. Despite this prohibition, a minimum of 250,000 and perhaps as many as 1,000,000 Africans were kidnapped, enslaved, and illegally imported into the United States via Cuba between 1809 and 1861. In 1839, a prime male slave could be purchased in Cuba for $400 and then sold into slavery for life in Richmond for $1,000 or Charleston for $1,150 or Savannah for $1,200 or New Orleans for $1,250. The average daily wage was one dollar. President James Madison reported to Congress in 1810 that:

> It appears that American citizens are instrumental in carrying on a traffic in enslaved Africans, equally in violation of the laws of humanity, and in defiance of those of their own country. The same just and benevolent motives which produced the interdiction in force against this criminal conduct, will doubtless be felt in Congress, in devising further means of suppressing the evil.

The 1860 Republican National Convention selected Abraham Lincoln as its Presidential nominee. He campaigned on this platform, and "won the presidency with almost half a million votes more than [Stephen] Douglas, his closest rival. [Lincoln] won the election garnering 39.8 percent of the popular vote. This election firmly established the Republican hold on the presidency for 60 of the next 100 years." Within five years of the 1860 Convention, slavery had been abolished, 4 million slaves were liberated, and the 13th Amendment was passed banning slavery and the slave trade forever from U.S. soil.

You are perhaps also not aware that William Lloyd Garrison was the first person to declare slavery a crime against humanity in the inaugural edition (1831) of his Liberator newspaper; or that on November 12, 1849, the Vermont Legislature passed "*Joint Resolution No. 42.--Resolutions Relating To The Subject of Slavery,*" declaring it:

> Resolved by the Senate and House of Representatives, that Slavery is a **crime against humanity, and a sore evil** in the body politic that was excused by the framers of the Federal Constitution as a crime entailed upon the country by their predecessors, and tolerated solely as a thing of inexorable necessity.[112] [**Emphasis added.**]

It is well-settled, as the WCAR Final Declaration confirms, that prohibitions against piracy and privateering, slavery and the slave trade, including the Trans-Atlantic Slave Trade, and against slave-like conditions and practices, including colonialism, segregation and apartheid, forced and compulsory labor, racism and racial discrimination, xenophobia and related intolerance have achieved the level of customary international law, have attained the status of jus cogens, and are obligato erga omnes. Unfortunately, the overwhelming majority of the WCAR Delegates and the public, especially African People world-wide, wrongly believe that this status has only recently been acquired.[113]

---

[111] Central Pacific Railroad Photographic History Museum. Republican Party National Platform, 1860. Available from http://cprr.org/Museum/Ephemera/Republican_Platform_1860.html.

[112] The Acts and Resolves Passed By The Legislature Of The State of Vermont At The October Session, 1849. Published By authority. Montpelier: E. P. Walton & Son. 1849.

[113] People incorrectly believe that "the term was first used in the preamble of the Hague Convention of 1907." Wikipedia. Available from http://en.wikipedia.org/wiki/Crime_against_humanity.

Permit us to suggest, as Ethan A. Nadelman suggests, that "most global prohibition regimes, including those targeted against piracy, slavery, and drug trafficking, evidence a common evolutionary pattern consisting of four or five stages."[114] At different stages in their development: (1) the activity is legal and some states participate in it; (2) national and international forces, non-governmental and governmental, attempt to redefine the activity as evil and illegal; (3) these forces agitate for its suppression and criminalization; (4) the activity becomes the subject of national and international criminal laws, conventions and treaties, police and military action; and (5) finally, the activity is prohibited globally.[115] It is axiomatic that this development is extremely uneven, unequal, and costly in time, space and human lives, in justice and equity.

Permit us also to suggest that Judge Fouad Ammoun of the International Court of Justice (ICJ) "has [accurately] described the development of Africa ... [and] eloquently remarked on the evolution of mankind's struggle with the issues of slavery and colonization."[116] He informs us that "before there fell upon it the two greatest plagues in the recorded history of mankind: the slave trade, which ravaged Africa for centuries on an unprecedented scale; and colonialism, which exploited humanity and natural wealth to a relentless extreme," ... Africa boasted thriving states and empires dating back to Roman times."[117]

Judge Ammoun also informs us that "historians have outlined the upward march of mankind from the time when homo sapiens appeared on the face of the globe, first of all in the Near East in what was the land of Canaan,[118] up to the age of the greatest thinkers and more particularly, throughout the whole of history of social progress, from the slavery of Antiquity to man's [and woman's] inevitable, irreversible drive towards equality and freedom. This march is like time itself. It never stops. Nothing can stand in its way for long. The texts, whether they be laws, constitutions, declarations, covenants or charters, do but define it and mark its successive phases. They are a mere record of it. In other words, the progressive rights which men, [women] and peoples enjoy are the result much less of those texts than of human progress to which they bear witness."[119]

We are confident that the records requested by and through this historic and precedent setting Federal Transparency and Access to Public Government Information Act Request will:

- Bear witness to and prove, once and for all, that piracy and privateering, slavery and the slave trade, including the Trans-Atlantic Slave Trade, and slave-like conditions and practices, including colonialism, segregation and apartheid, were and are illegal and prohibited, and were and are recognized as crimes against humanity when and where they were committed.

- Help define and mark the successive stages in the development of the 569-year historical and continuing Maafa,[120] and of the unyielding and continuing struggle against it.

- Document who the victims were, and who their descendants are today; who committed these crimes, which were and are the greatest theft of land, lives and labor in human history; how this unjust and illegal wealth was converted, consolidated, preserved and transferred across generations and centuries; and who owns and benefits from this unjust enrichment today.

---

[114] Ethan A. Nadelman. *Global prohibition regimes: the evolution of norms in international society.* Printed in Transnational Crime / edited by Nikos Passas.

[115] Ibid.

[116] *Legal Consequences For States of the Continued Presence of South Africa in Namibia (South West Africa) Notwithstanding Security Council Resolution 276, 1971 I.C.J. 16, 86 (1971) (separate opinion of Judge Ammoun).*

[117] Recent evidence documents that African civilizations predate Roman times.

[118] Recent evidence documents that homo sapiens first emerged in East Africa.

[119] Ethan A. Nadelman. *Global prohibition regimes.*

[120] Dr. Marimba Ani. *Let The Circle Be Unbroken.* Maafa is a Kiswahili word for the 563-year historical and continuing enslavement and colonization of Africa and African People.

We request that that you, King Juan Carlos I de Borbón y Borbón, and the Government of the Kingdom of Spain, formally and publicly reaffirm, once and for all, that slavery and the slave trade were and are illegal according to the edicts and municipal laws of Spain and its colonies, and according to canon law and international law; and that slavery and the slave trade were crimes against humanity:

- "Because God makes no slaves in the womb;"[121] because the prohibition of the slave trade is well-settled in the Bible in Timothy 1:10, Exodus 21:16, Deuteronomy 24:7, 1 Corinthians 5:11, 1 Corinthians 6:10 and Timothy 1:10-1; and because the Catholic Church was in the forefront of the struggle from 441 AD to 1890 to prohibit and abolish the trafficking in and enslavement of Christians, Europeans, the Indigenous Peoples of the Western Hemisphere, and African People.

- Because King Charles V of Spain prohibited slavery in 1530; because Emperor Charles II ordered all slaves, including African slaves, be set free in 1540; because King Charles II issued Royal Edicts in 1693 and on November 7, 1695 giving sanctuary to all runaway slaves in Florida and "liberty to … all men as well as all women … so that by their example and by [his] liberality others will do the same;"[122] because slavery and the slave trade was again declared illegal and prohibited in Spain and all of its colonies, including Florida, Mexico and Texas in 1811; because they refused to return runaway slaves; and because the liberty and property of all Spanish citizens, including former slaves, was and is protected by treaties with the United States.

We further request that you,, King Juan Carlos I de Borbón y Borbón, and the Government of the Kingdom of Spain, formally and publicly reaffirm, once and for all, that slavery and the slave trade were and are crimes under Spanish law, and that they were and are crimes against humanity because:

- 1300, the Las Siete Partidas [the Seven Parties] of Alphonse X the Wise, which posed in law 34, rules 1 and 2, the principle of freedom; Las Leys de Toro [The Bull Laws - 1501]; the Las Leys de las Indias [The Indies Laws]; La Novisima Recopilación [The Latest Compilation]; Ley de Enjuiciamento Criminal [The Law of Criminal Proceedings]; Ley de Enjuiciamento Civil [The Law of Civil Proceedings]; The Commercial Code Spanish Penal Code of 1870; and the Codigo Negro Espanol, which we believe was and is inferior and repugnant to canon law, international law, and the municipal laws of Spain then and now, and therefore was and is null and void.

- 1435, Spain invades the Canary Islands and kidnaps slaves. The Vatican orders the Spaniards to put the slave back in the condition that they were found in, upon pain of excommunication.

- 1445, Lançarote de Freitas, a tax-collector from the Portuguese town of Lagos, and the company which he formed, and the 235 Africans he kidnapped and enslaved in Lagos, brought to Seville, and sold into slavery to work the sugar cane fields. Was this sale legal?

- 1452, the New Laws of the Indies which abolished the encomiendas, ended the enslavement of the Indigenous Peoples of the Western Hemisphere, and allegedly gave permission for the importation of African slaves to Spanish colonies in the Western Hemisphere.

- 1454, 8-January, Pope Nicholas V's bull (Romanus Pontifex) granting the Portuguese a perpetual monopoly in trade with Africa, and the Spanish traders who brought slaves from Africa to Spain.

- 1456, 13-March, Papal Bull, Inter Caetera issued on 13 March 1456, Pope Nicholas V granted to Prince Henry as Grand Master of the Order of Christ in Portugal all lands (and peoples) discovered or conquered form Cape Bojafor in Africa to and including the Indies.

---

[121] Rev. John G. Fee. *An Anti-Slavery Manual, or, The Wrongs of American Slavery Exposed By the Light of the Bible and of Facts, with A Remedy for the Evil (1851).* Available from http://members.tripod.com/medicolegal/feeasm1851.htm.

[122] Quoted at *Fort Mose's People.* Available from http://www.millennium.scps.k12.fl.us/fortmose3.html.

- 1462, Pius II declaration of slavery to be a great crime (magnum scelus); Pope Leo X's bull which denounced slavery and the slave trade; and the Portuguese slave traders and merchants who operated in Seville despite Papal opposition.

- 1470, Papal opposition to the Spanish merchants who traded in large numbers of slaves.

- 1474, Dominican Bartolome de Las Casas' campaign against the enslavement of and trafficking in Indians; his proposal that slaves be brought from Africa instead; his later regret for offering this proposal; and his doubt as to whether God would pardon him for this terrible sin.

- 1476, Carlos de Valera of Castille who brings back 400 slaves from Africa.

- 1493, 30-October, Queen Isabella's ban of violence against Indians.

- 1493, 3-November, Columbus' initiation of the first Trans-Atlantic slave voyage with the shipment of several hundred Taino people from Hispaniola to Spain, and the doubts about the legality of their enslavement in Spain.

- 1493, Papal Bull issued by Pope Alexander VI on May 4th, establishing a line of demarcation between Spanish discoveries and Portuguese. The Spanish are to have dominion over any lands they discover west of the line, the Portuguese over lands east of the line.

- 1494 or 1504, the five hundred Carib Indians that Columbus shipped to Seville; his suggestion that they be sold at auction; Queen Isabella's suspension of the Royal order for their sale; her suggestion in a letter to Bishop Fonseca that any sale await an inquiry into the causes for the imprisonment and the lawfulness of their sale; the differing opinions of Theologians on the lawfulness of the sale; Queen Isabella's rejection of Columbus' proposal that Indians be enslaved; and her shipment of the 500 Indians home at her expense.

- 1494, the Treaty of Tordesillas divides the globe between Spain and Portugal along lines similar to those established in 1493 by Pope Alexander VI.

- 1496, 8-June, Columbus returns from his second voyage with 30 Native American slaves, amid continuing doubts about the legality of their enslavement

- 1498, the six hundred Indian slaves that Columbus shipped to Spain after his third voyage; the lawfulness of this sale; and why Columbus was sent back to Spain in chains.

- 1499, Bishop Bartolome de Las Casas' petition to the King of Spain requesting that the enslavement of the Indigenous Peoples of the Western Hemisphere be banned, and the importation of 12 African slaves per settler be allowed instead.

- 1499, the more than 200 slaves who were kidnapped from the northern coast of South America by Amerigo Vespucci and Alonso de Hojeda and sold in Cadiz, allegedly without legal problems.

- 1500, the condition and legal status of the 200,000 Africans who had been imported to the mainland and island regions of Spain.

- 1501-2, the Royal authorization that allowed Nicolas de Ovando, the Spanish governor of Hispaniola, and Juan de Córdoba of Seville to become the first slave trader to introduce African slaves into Hispaniola.

- 1503, 30-October, Queen Isabella's prohibition of violence against Indians.

- 1503, Nicolas de Ovando's, the Spanish governor of Hispaniola, petition to King Ferdinand the Catholic requesting that no more African slaves to be sent to Hispaniola.

- 1503, Pedro Menendez de Avilés, and his expedition to Florida with a thousand men and 500 slaves.

- 1504, 26-November, Queen Isabella's death-bed instructions to the Government regarding the Treatment of Indians: "Whereas, when the islands and mainland of the ocean Sea were conceded to us by the Holy Apostolic See, our principal intention. was to procure, induce, bring, and convert their peoples to our Holy Catholic Faith and to send to the said islands and maintain bishops, religious clerics and other learned and God fearing persons, to instruct the inhabitants and dwellers therein in the Catholic Faith, and to instruct them in, and to bestow upon them, good customs, exercising all proper diligence in this therefore, I beg the King my Lord very affectionately, and I charge and command my said daughter (Juana) and the said prince her husband (Philip I) to carry this out, and that it be their principal purpose, and that they put into it much diligence: and they are not to consent, or give permission, that the Indian inhabitants and dwellers in the said islands and mainland. receive any damage in their persons or goods, but are to order that they be well and justly treated, and if they have received any damage it is to be remedied: and it is to be provided that everything enjoined and commanded us in the said concession be strictly observed."

- 1504, the Royal order which allowed Spaniards to compel natives to work but for wages, but not as slaves.

- 1508, the first official cargo of African slaves to New World.

- 1510, 22-January, the start of the systematic transportation of African slaves to the New World by King Ferdinand's authorization of a shipment of 50 Africans to Santo Domingo, with money lent by the Florentine banker Bartolome di Marchionni; and his order to "Get gold, humanely if possible, but at all hazards - get gold." 3,000 pounds of gold were shipped each year.

- 1511, Antonio de Montesinos' denunciation of the treatment of Indians: "This voice says that you are living in deadly sin for the atrocities you tyrannically impose on these innocent people. Tell me what right have you to enslave them? What authority did you use to make war against them who lived at peace on their territories killing them cruelly with methods never before heard of? How can you oppress them and not care to feed or cure them and work them to death to satisfy your greed? And why don't you look after their spiritual health so that they should come to know God that they should be baptized and that they should hear Mass and keep the holy days? Aren't they human beings? Have they no rational soul? Aren't you obliged to love them as you love yourselves? Don't you understand? How can you live in such a lethargical dream? You must rest assured that you are in no better state of salvation than the Moors or Turks who reject the Christian faith."

- 1512, the Laws of Burgos, the first code regulating Spanish treatment of Indians.

- 1513, the permission given to landowner Amador de Lares allowing him to import into Cuba four African slaves from Hispaniola, the first record of slavery in Cuba.

- 1515, Las Casas's return to Spain in 1515 with Antonio Montesinos to report to King Fernando on the evils he witnessed; and his presentation of his Memorial de remedios to Cardinal Cisneros on how Spaniards and Indians could live together.

- 1516, Archduke Charles' grants to the Florentine merchants a monopoly in the African slave trade.

- 1516, Cardinal De Cisneros' ban on the importation of enslaved Africans into Spain's colonies in the Americas.

- 1516, Carlos I's grant of licenses to his courtiers licenses permitting the importation of 4,000 African slaves annually into the Spanish colonial islands.

- 1517, the formalization of slave trading between Africa and America at the suggestion of Bishop Bartolome de Las Casas, and the resultant approval of King Charles of Spain for the importation of 4000 Africans into the Americas.

- 1518, 8-August, Charles V's escalation of the slave trade with a grant to Lorenzo de Gorrevod to import 4,000 African slaves into New Spain; and the 28 Spanish sugar plantations on Santo Domingo.

- 1519, Bartholomew De Las Casas's argument against slavery: "There isn't, there can be neither slaves by nature, nor people without 'freedom and power ', nor people without sovereignty. No one may be deprived of his liberty nor may any person be enslaved."

- 1522-53, the twelve recorded African slaves revolt in the Dominican Republic, Hispaniola, and the Caribbean.

- 1524, the foundation of the Council of the Indies to help administer the new colonies.

- 1526, the cedula (Royal proclamation) of 1526 provided that any slave could purchase his or her freedom.

- 1527, Bishop Las Casas' History of Indies.

- 1530, Charles V's prohibition of Indian slavery.

- 1530, Juan de la Barrera, the Seville merchant, who began the transportation of slaves directly from Africa to the Western Hemisphere.

- 1530, the Royal cedula which forbade the taking of slaves, even in war, and mandated the liberation of the children of slaves were liberated

- 1532, the two lectures at the University of Salamanca, De Indis Noviter Inventis (On the Indians Lately Discovered) and De Jure Bellis Hispanorum in Barbaros (On the Law of War the Spaniards on the Barbarians), Vitoria laid out principles for governing Christian encounters with Indigenous peoples of the Western Hemisphere. These documents greatly influenced Hugo Grotius, the most prominent of the founders of international law.

- 1533, Cartagena de Indias, Spain's port for the trade of slaves, gold and cargo.

- 1534, Pope Paul III's bull against slavery, which said that Satan was the cause of slavery: [Satan,] the enemy of the human race, who always opposes all good men so that the race may perish, has thought up a way, unheard of before now, by which he might impede the saving word of God from being preached to the nations. He has stirred up some of his allies who, desiring to satisfy their own avarice, are presuming to assert far and wide that the Indians of the West and the South who have come to our notice in these times be reduced to our service like brute animals, under the pretext that they are lacking in the Catholic faith. And they reduce them to slavery, treating them with afflictions they would scarcely use with brute animals. Therefore, We ... noting that the Indians themselves indeed are true men. by our Apostolic Authority decree and declare by these present letters that the same Indians and all other peoples-even though they are outside the faith should not be deprived of their liberty or their other possessions. and are not to be reduced to slavery, and that whatever happens to the contrary is to be considered null and void.

- 1534, Pope Paul III's second bull on slavery, which imposed the penalty of "excommunication on anyone, regardless of their dignity, state, condition, or grade. who in any way may presume to reduce said Indians to slavery or despoil them of their goods."

- 1537, 29-May, Paul III's Letter Apostolic, under the seal of the Fisherman, to the Cardinal Archbishop of Toledo, Spain, denouncing slavery and forbidding the enslavement of the

Indigenous Peoples of the Western Hemisphere, calling it "an evil unheard of before now to the enemy of the human race Satan and excommunicating of the slavers."

- 1537, Pope Paul III's Bull (Sublimis Deus) against slavery, which he issued to the Universal Church, declaring that:

    The exalted God loved the human race so much that He created man in such a condition that he was not only a sharer in good as are other creatures, but also that he would be able to reach and see face to face the inaccessible and invisible Supreme Good. Seeing this and envying it, the enemy of the human race, who always opposes all good men so that the race may perish, has thought up a way, unheard of before now, by which he might impede the saving word of God from being preached to the nations. He (Satan) has stirred up some of his allies who, desiring to satisfy their own avarice, are presuming to assert far and wide that the Indians. be reduced to our service like brute animals, under the pretext that they are lacking the Catholic faith. And they reduce them to slavery, treating them with afflictions they would scarcely use with brute animals. by our Apostolic Authority decree and declare by these present letters that the same Indians and all other peoples - even though they are outside the faith - should not be deprived of their liberty. Rather they are to be able to use and enjoy this liberty and this ownership of property freely and licitly, and are not to be reduced to slavery.

- 1537, Pope Paul III's support of a Royal edict issued by Charles V of Spain that endeavored to halt mistreatment of Indians. Pope Paul III stated:

    Therefore attending to the fact that the Indians themselves although they are outside the bosom of the Church have not been and should not be deprived of their liberty or of ownership of what is their own and that since they are men and therefore capable of faith and salvation they are not to be given into servitude but rather by preaching good examples and the like should be invited to eternal life. We command that anyone of whatever dignity state condition or grade who works against what is done through you or others to help the Indians in the aforementioned matters incurs the penalty of excommunication.

- 1537, the slave traders use of Spanish Florida as a base of operations.

- 1539, Las Casas two year lobbying effort to convince the Council of the Indies to abolish encomiendas. He condemned this system in his Remedies for the Existing Evils, with Twenty Reasons Therefore. The ninth reason was the most simple and obvious, namely that all people in the new world are free.

- 1539, Repetition of Papal condemnations of slavery.

- 1539, the petition sent to the King by the Spanish Cortes (Council) in Valladolid asking him to remedy the cruelties perpetrated against the Indians.

- 1540, King Charles V's grant of an exclusive patent to the Flemish Nobility to import 4,000 Africans annually into Hispaniola, Cuba, Jamaica, and Puerto Rico; and the belief that:

    This great prince was not in all probability aware of the dreadful evils attending this horrible traffic nor of the crying injustice of permitting it; for in 1542 when he made a code of laws for his Indian subjects he liberated all Negroes and by a word put an end to slavery. When however he resigned his crown and retired into a monastery and his minister of mercy Pedro de la Gasca returned to Spain the imperious tyrants of these new dominions returned to their former practices and fastened the yoke on the suffering and unresisting Negroes.

- 1540, Bartolome de Las Casas's debate with Juan Gines de Sepulveda before the King of Spain and other members of the clergy, in which:

    Sepulveda justified: Indian enslavement on the following grounds: the gravity of sins of the Indians, especially idolatry; the rudeness of the natives which made it necessary for more refined people like the Spanish to educate them; the goal of spreading the faith; protection of weaker Indians who were subject to human sacrifice and cannibalism. Las Casas responded: God did not command war against idolaters; Indians had rich, vibrant civilizations and sophisticated cultures; peaceful conversion was the most effective means of spreading Catholicism; although human sacrifice was evil, indiscriminate warfare was more evil. Las Casas also presented abundant evidence during the debate that Spaniards in the New World were not seeking to enlighten Indians, but to work them to death through enslavement.

- 1540, Emperor Charles V's order that all the slaves in the American Isles to be set free; la Gasca's, the governor of the country, unsuccessful attempt to implement this order; and the Emperor's alleged re-imposition of this crime, at the recommendation of la Gasca.

- 1541, June, the Royal cedula which ordered Spanish settlers not to use Indians as pack animals unless they are paid, but this is generally ignored.

- 1542, Papal influence and lobbying by Bishop Bartolome Las Casas, which led to the royal proclamation of the New Laws of the Indies which forbade all future enslavement of Indians; and the violent opposition (riots, petitions, and open rebellion) which these New Laws met from settlers, which caused the monarchy to back away from enforcement of the laws.

- 1548, Bishop Las Casas' last will and testament in which he described his call:

- To act here at home on behalf of all those people out in what we call the Indies, the true possessors of those kingdoms, those territories. To act against the unimaginable, unspeakable violence and evil and harm they have suffered from our people, contrary to all reason, all justice, so as to restore them to the original liberty they were lawlessly deprived of, and get them free of death by violence, death they still suffer."

- 1549, Pope Paul III's bull against New World slavery, declaring Satan the cause of slavery:

    [Satan,] "the enemy of the human race who always opposes all good men so that the race may perish has thought up a way unheard of before now by which he might impede the saving word of God from being preached to the nations. He has stirred up some of his allies who desiring to satisfy their own avarice are presuming to assert far and wide that the Indians of the West and the South who have come to our notice in these times be reduced to our service like brute animals under the pretext that they are lacking in the Catholic faith. And they reduce them to slavery treating them with afflictions they would scarcely use with brute animals. Therefore We, noting that the Indians themselves indeed are true men. by our Apostolic Authority decree and declare by these present letters that the same Indians and all other peoples-even though they are outside the faith. should not be deprived of their liberty or their other possessions. and are not to be reduced to slavery and that whatever happens to the contrary is to be considered null and void."

- 1549, the Royal ban on servicio personal by Indians (i.e. the use of Indians in encomiendas for labor).

- 1550, 1-July, Emperor Charles' order to stop all conquests until theologians and counselors decide the issue. It is said that:

Sepulveda wrote *A Defense for the Book on the Just Causes of the War*, which was printed at Rome in May 1550, and he wrote three other defenses in Spanish, describing the Indians as brutish and cowardly. Fourteen officials and ecclesiastics met for a month during the summer at Valladolid. Sepulveda spoke for three hours and then Las Casas read from his book for five days before the judges began their discussion. Domingo de Soto made a summary, and then Sepulveda wrote a reply to the twelve objections of Las Casas. Sepulveda argued that because of their idolatry and sins against nature, the Indians should be subjugated and protected by the superior Spaniards. He noted that the natives do not have any written laws or even private property. Las Casas responded that the Indians were quite rational and in some respects superior to the Greeks and Romans. He wrote, "No nation exists no matter how rude, uncultivated, barbarous, gross or almost brutal its people may be which may not be persuaded and brought to a good order and way of life and made domestic, mild and tractable provided the method that is proper and natural to men is used; that is love and gentleness and kindness.

- 1550, King Charles V's emancipation of all West Indies slaves.

- 1550, mid-August, King Charles V's decree, as a direct consequence of Bishop Las Casas' work, summoning a Council of Fourteen to determine the enslavement of Indigenous People. Charles V ordered all conquests to cease until it was decided if they were being conducted in a just manner.

- 1552, Bartolome de Las Casas's publication of the *Brief Relations of the Destruction of the Indies*, his account of the oppression of the South American Indians.

- 1555, the order by Queen Mary of England, under pressure from the Spanish, forbidding English involvement in Guinea, and the Spanish slave trade there.

- 1556, Domingo de Soto's argument in *De justicia et de jure libri X (Ten Books on Justice and Law)*, that it is wrong to keep in slavery any person who was born free.

- 1565. the establishment by the Spanish governor of Florida of a settlement for 100 runaway slaves at Gracia Real de Santa Teresa de Mose, the first free African settlement in North America.

- 1566, Bishop Las Casas' deathbed memorandum to the King which declared that:

  All wars called conquests are unjust. The system of encomiendas is tyrannical. The King can not justify wars in the Americas against peaceful peoples. All gold and silver taken from the New World is stolen. Indians have a right to fight against invasion of their land by Spanish conquerors.

- Las Casas' warning in the closing pages of his history of Spain's conquests in the New World that:

  I say and hold it certain that all the crimes committed by the Spaniards against these people with such perverse cruelties have been against the pure and most righteous law of Jesus Christ and against all natural reason and to the greatest infamy of His name and the Christian religion and the total destruction of the faith. And I believe for these impious and ignominious works so unjustly and tyrannically barbarously committed. God will pour His fury and anger upon Spain if she does not perform a great penance.

- 1569, Sevillian Dominican, Tomás de Mercado, publishes *Tratos y contratos de mercaderes (Practices and Contracts of Merchants)*, which attacks the way the slave trade is conducted.

- 1570, the condition and legal status of the 20,569 Africans and 2,435 Mulattos in the Spanish colonies in the Americas in 1570; the 35,089 Africans and 116,529 Mulattos who were there in 1646; the 20,131 Africans and 266,196 Mulattos who were there in 1742; and the 6,100 Africans and 369,790 Mulattos who were there in 1793.

- 1573, Ba*rtolemé Frías de Albornoz's, publication of Arte de Los Contratos (*The Art of Contracts), which cast doubt on the legality of the slave trade condemns it.

- 1583, King Philip II's decision to send some of his enslaved Africans to St. Augustine, Florida.

- 1591, Pope Gregory XIV's condemnation of slavery and the slave trade (Cum Sicuti), promising excommunication of clergy who participated in the slavery trade and slavery.

- 1595, King Philip II's grant to Pedro Gomes Reinal, a Portuguese merchant, a near monopoly the slave trade, authorizing him to provide Spanish America with 4,250 African slaves annually for nine years, with a further 1,000 slaves being provided by other merchants. Gomez allegedly paid the crown 900,000 ducats for this concession.

- 1600, King Philip III's order outlawing the use of Native American slaves in Spanish colonies

- 1600, the death of Pedro Gomes Reinal, and the passage of the Spanish slave-trading monopoly is passed to Jaão Rodrigues Coutinho, Governor of Angola.

- 1602, the Spanish law, which declared that mulattos, convicts, and idle Africans may be shipped to Latin America and forced to work in the mines.

- 1627, Alonso de Sandoval's, a Spanish Peruvian Jesuit, Naturaleza, Policia,. Costumbres i Ritos, Disciplina, i Catechismo Evangelico de todos Etíopes (The Nature, Policy,. Customs and Rituals, Disciplines, and Gospel Catechism of all Ethiopians), which argues that slavery combines all the world's evils.

- 1639, Pope Urban VIII's condemnation of slavery and the slave trade (Commissum Nobis), promising excommunication of clergy who participated in the slavery trade and slavery.

- 1642, St. Vincent of Paul's work from 1642 to 1660 to redeem 1,200 slaves [in Algiers and Tunis] at an expense of 1,200,000 livres.

- 1662-64, the Asiento which was granted to two Genoese merchants, Grillo and Lomelin, giving them permission to import 3,500 slaves annually, and subcontract with any friendly nation.

- 1686, 20-March, the Congregation of the Holy Office's (the Roman Inquisition) ruling on the matter of slavery. It is asked, they ruled:

  > Whether it is permitted to capture by force and deceit Blacks and other natives who have harmed no one? Answer: no! Whether it is permitted to buy, sell or make contracts in their respect, Blacks or other natives who have harmed no one and been made captives by force of deceit? Answer: no! Whether the possessors of Blacks and other natives who have harmed no one and been captured by force or deceit, are not held to set them free? Answer: yes! Whether the captors, buyers and possessors of Blacks and other natives who have harmed no one and who have been captured by force or deceit are not held to make compensation to them? Answer: yes!

- 1693, King Charles I's decree ending the enslavement of the Indigenous Peoples of the Western Hemisphere, and giving permission for the importation of African slaves.

- 1713, 11-April, the Treaty of Utrecht and Asiento which granted to Britain and the South Sea Company a monopoly to import 4,800 African slaves per year into Spain's colonies for 30 years

- 1714, the Ministry of the Indies which was created by Philip V, and its role in slavery, the slave - trade and colonialism.

- 1717, the Casa de Contratación which moved from Seville to Cadiz, and its role in slavery, the slave trade and colonialism.

- 1739, England's contract to import slaves into Spanish colonies canceled, and War of Jenkins Ear.

- 1741, 20-December, Pope Benedict XIV's Apostolic Letter (Immensa Pastorum) which was addressed to the Bishops of Brazil, condemning slavery and the slave trade, forbidding the enslavement of Indians, and promising excommunication of clergy who participated in the slavery trade and slavery.

- 1750-52, Treaty of Madrid, which shifted the Spanish-Portuguese, border in South America; and the Treaty of El Pardo (1761) which annulled the Treaty of Madrid.

- 1783, the English and U.S. ban on the African slave trade in their territories.

- 1789, the Spanish Crown's decree that 150,000 male slaves and all enslaved women and boys under 14 years of age should be freed.

- 1794, the decree by the French National Assembly during the French Revolution, at the instigation of a Catholic priest, the Abbé H. Grégoire, abolishing slavery and the slave trade in all French colonies, and making all former slaves citizens of France with full and equal rights.

- 1797, the Treaty of San Lorenzo.

- 17th century, Bull of Canonization of the Jesuit Peter Claver, and Pope Pius IX's declaration branding the supreme villainy (summum nefas) of the slave traders.

- 1802, 11-August, the Convention for Indemnification With Spain

- 1803, Spanish cessation of the colony of Louisiana back to France on the eve of the Louisiana Purchase; the legal status of the Codigo Espanol Negro and Code Noir; and the condition and legal status of the slaves who had been freed by the 1791 decision of the French Parliament and declared French citizens.

- 1808, the illegal importation of 250 thousand to one million slaves into the United States via the Spanish colony of Cuba from 1808-61.

- 1811, the decision by the Spanish Parliament that declared slave trading a felony; the abolition of slavery in Spain and its colonies; the United States invasion of Florida and war against the Seminoles in order to recapture the runaway slaves.

- 1815, Pope Pius VII's demand that the Congress of Vienna prohibit and suppress of the slave trade; and Spain's position.

- 1815, the Vatican's efforts at the Congress of Vienna to convince the nations of Europe to prohibit slavery and the slave trade.

- 1816, the Seminole who left Florida, took refuge in Guanabacoa, a small town outside of Havana.

- 1817, Spain's formal acceptance of the principle to abolish slavery; its agreement to end the slave trade in 1820; England's payment of £400,000 in indemnity to Spain

- 1821-24, Spain's declaration of the slave trade as illegal; Chile's emancipation of slaves; and the Abolition of slavery in Central America.

- 1825-50, the dozen treaties negotiated by Britain to continue its slave trade in America.

- 1829, the Papal request for Mexico to abolish slavery, which Mexico did, throughout its dominions, including Texas and the Southwestern region of the United States.

- 1838, the decree condemning all forms of colonial slavery and the slave trade, calling it inhumanum illud commercium, and forbidding all Catholics to propound views contrary to this.

- 1887, the Papal letter which claimed that the Catholic Church struggled from the beginning to see a slavery eased and abolished which was oppressing so many people.

- 1888, Cardinal Lavigerie efforts to found the Société Antiesclavagiste, and to abolish slavery and the slave trade in Africa and Brazil.

- 1888, Leo XIII's letter to the Brazilian bishops exhorting them to banish from their country the remnants of slavery, recalling the Church's unceasing efforts over centuries to get rid of colonial slavery and the slave trade, and expressing satisfaction that Brazil had at last abolished it.

- 1890, the Papal encyclical which condemned once slavery again, slave traders and servitude; called for its abolition in all Catholic Missions, ordering an annual collection to be made in all Catholic churches for the benefit of the anti-slavery work, and for combating slavery and the slave trade on an international basis.

Upon information and belief, the Government of the Kingdom of Spain and its Royal Family were and are responsible for:

- 1.1 million Africans, not counting the victims of the Spanish Asiento, who were kidnapped from Africa and sold into slavery in the Americas, and for the destruction of countless villages, nation-states and civilizations in Africa.

- 15,000 Africans slaves were illegally held in slavery in Florida on the eve of its sale in 1819, and 61,000 of their descendants were illegally held in slavery in Florida until 1865.

- 3,000 Africans were illegally held in slavery in Texas on the eve its Independence in 1835, and 200,000 of their descendants were still being illegally held in slavery in Texas and the Southwestern portion of the United States in 1865.

- 250,000 to 1,000 Africans were illegally trafficked into the United States via Cuba from 1808 to 1861.

- The misery of more than 50 million of their descendants who are scattered, suffering and struggling in more than 21 countries today, under slave-like conditions and practices, segregation, racism and racial discrimination, xenophobia and related intolerance until today.

We hope that you will comply with this Request for a Public Commitment and Information in an expedited manner, and that you will waive all associated costs. Please be advised that we have sent a copy of this Request to the public and the media.

We expect your positive response to this historic and precedent setting Information Request within 20 working days. Thank you for your consideration.

Sincerely,
Bob Brown, co-director
Pan-African Roots

Pan-African Roots

1247 E Street SE
Washington, DC 20003
Tel: (202) 544-9355 - Fax: (202) 544-9359
Email: paroots02@yahoo.com

25 October 2004

Mr. Jeb Bush, Governor
Office of the Governor
The Capitol
Tallahassee, FL 32399-0001

Open Records Request.
Fee Waiver and Expedited Review Request.
cc: Open Records Officer and Open Records Appeals Officer.

Dear Governor Bush:

As you are aware, King Charles V of Spain prohibited slavery in 1530; Emperor Charles II ordered all slaves, including African slaves, be set free in 1540; King Charles II of Spain issued Royal Edicts in 1693 and on November 7, 1695 giving sanctuary to all runaway slaves in Florida and "liberty to ... all men as well as all women ... so that by their example and by [his] liberality others will do the same;"[123] slavery and the slave trade was again declared illegal and prohibited in Spain and all of its colonies, including Florida, Mexico and Texas in 1811; they refused to return runaway slaves; and the liberty and property of all Spanish citizens, including former slaves, was and is protected by treaties between Spain, Mexico and the United States.

As you are also aware, 15,000 Africans slaves were illegally held in slavery in Florida on the eve of its Purchase in 1819; 61,000 Africans were illegally held in slavery in Florida until 1865; and their descendants were and are forced to suffer slave-like conditions and practices, segregation, racism and racial discrimination, xenophobia and related intolerance until today. Additionally, 10,000 Africans were illegally removed from Florida to Indian Territory during the "Trail of Tears "in the 1820s and 1830s; 14,000 Africans were still being illegally held in slavery in Oklahoma in 1866; and their descendants were and are forced to suffer slave-like conditions and practices, segregation, racism and racial discrimination, xenophobia and related intolerance until today.

You are perhaps not aware, that on May 17, 1860, the second National Republican Convention adopted its 1860 National Republican Platform, which declared it resolved:

> 7. That the new dogma that the Constitution of its own force carries slavery into any or all of the territories of the United States, is a dangerous political heresy, at variance with the explicit provisions of that instrument itself, with contemporaneous exposition, and with legislative and judicial precedent, is revolutionary in its tendency and subversive of the peace and harmony of the country.

> 8. That the formal condition of all the territory of the United States is that of freedom; that as our republican fathers, when they had abolished slavery in all our national territory, ordained that no "person should be deprived of life, liberty or property, without due process of law," it becomes our duty, by legislation, whenever such legislation is necessary, to maintain this provision of the constitution against all attempts to violate it; and we deny the authority of congress, of a territorial legislature, or of any individuals, to give legal existence to slavery in any territory of the United States.

---

[123] Quoted at *Fort Mose's People*. Available from http://www.millennium.scps.k12.fl.us/fortmose3.html.

135

9. That we brand the recent re-opening of the African Slave Trade, under the cover of our national flag, aided by perversions of judicial power, as a **crime against humanity, and a burning shame to our country and age,** and we call upon congress to take prompt and efficient measures for the total and final suppression of the execrable traffic. [124] [**Emphasis added.**]

In 1808, the United States Government prohibited its citizens from participating in the international slave trade, declaring it piracy in 1820, and participation in it punishable by death. Despite this prohibition, a minimum of 250,000 and perhaps as many as 1,000,000 Africans were kidnapped, enslaved, and illegally imported into the United States via Cuba between 1809 and 1861. In 1839, a prime male slave could be purchased in Cuba for $400 and then sold into slavery for life in Richmond for $1,000 or Charleston for $1,150 or Savannah for $1,200 or New Orleans for $1,250. The average daily wage was one dollar. President James Madison reported to Congress in 1810 that:

> It appears that American citizens are instrumental in carrying on a traffic in enslaved Africans, equally in violation of the laws of humanity, and in defiance of those of their own country. The same just and benevolent motives which produced the interdiction in force against this criminal conduct, will doubtless be felt in Congress, in devising further means of suppressing the evil.

The 1860 Republican National Convention selected Abraham Lincoln as its Presidential nominee. He campaigned on this platform, and "won the presidency with almost half a million votes more than [Stephen] Douglas, his closest rival. [Lincoln] won the election garnering 39.8 percent of the popular vote. This election firmly established the Republican hold on the presidency for 60 of the next 100 years.

You are perhaps also not aware that William Lloyd Garrison was the first person to declare slavery a crime against humanity in the inaugural edition (1831) of his Liberator newspaper; or that on November 12, 1849, the Vermont Legislature passed "*Joint Resolution No. 42.--Resolutions Relating To The Subject of Slavery*," declaring it:

> Resolved by the Senate and House of Representatives, that Slavery is a **crime against humanity, and a sore evil** in the body politic that was excused by the framers of the Federal Constitution as a crime entailed upon the country by their predecessors, and tolerated solely as a thing of inexorable necessity.[125] [**Emphasis added.**]

We therefore ask, pursuant to Fla. Stat. Ann. sections 119.01 to 119.15, access to or copies of all records pertaining to or referencing:

- Florida's operations and activities, historically and currently, in facilitating, prohibiting or combating piracy and privateering, slavery and the slave trade, especially the Trans-Atlantic Slave Trade (also known as the Atlantic Trade, the Triangle Trade, the Colonial Trade, the West Indies Trade, the Coastal Trade, the Intra-state Slave Trade, etc.); and in the struggle to declare them crimes against humanity.

- Florida's role, operations and activities, historically and currently, in facilitating, prohibiting or combating slave-like conditions and practices, including but not limited to servitude, forced and compulsory labor, peonage, sharecropping, debt-bondage, sweatshop labor, convict-lease, chain-gang or prison labor, the sale of children, child prostitution, child pornography, the exploitation of child labour, the sexual mutilation of female children, the use of children in armed conflicts, the traffic in persons and in the sale of human organs, the exploitation of prostitution, and certain practices under apartheid and colonial regimes, segregation, racism and racial discrimination, xenophobia and related intolerance.

---

[124] Central Pacific Railroad Photographic History Museum. *Republican Party National Platform, 1860.* Available from http://cprr.org/Museum/Ephemera/Republican_Platform_1860.html.

[125] *The Acts and Resolves Passed By The Legislature Of The State of Vermont At The October Session, 1849.* Published By authority. Montpelier: E. P. Walton & Son. 1849.

- Florida's knowledge of and response to Spain's and Mexico's abolition of slavery and the slave trade; emancipation of slaves and granting them citizenship; refusal to return runaway slaves; and related claims, diplomatic discussions, agreement and treaties.

- The role of the Port of St. Augustine, all other Florida ports, and all entities headquartered at the Ports, historically and currently, in slavery and the slave trade, and in the trade in slave-produced products such as sugar, molasses, rum, cotton, tobacco, etc.

- All governments, agencies (federal, state, county or local), corporations, non-governmental organizations, institutions, churches, families, individuals, or entities, domestic or foreign who participated or invested in, or made profits from the above referenced crimes against humanity; and who owns or benefits from these historical and continuing crimes today, including but not limited to those listed in Appendix A.

We request access to or copies of all records that pertain to, or reference the subjects listed in the above paragraphs, for the following counties:

1860 United States Census	Slave-Holding Families	Number of Slaves	Value of Slaves ($1,000 @)	Value of Plantations
Alachua	300	4,457	$4,457,000	$1,874,994
Bradford/New Rive	121	744	$744,000	$655,495
Brevard/St Lucie	4	21	$21,000	$41,460
Calhoun	27	524	$524,000	$321,170
Clay	49	519	$519,000	$241,041
Columbia	205	2,063	$2,063,000	$923,715
Dade	2	2	$2,000	$165
Duval	240	1,987	$1,987,000	$297,131
Escambia	237	1,961	$1,961,000	$72,361
Franklin	60	520	$520,000	$7,600
Gadsden	355	5,409	$5,409,000	$2,057,145
Hamilton	156	1,397	$1,397,000	$693,913
Hernando/Benton		200	$200,000	
Hillsborough	120	564	$564,000	$483,899
Holmes	29	112	$112,000	$146,397
Jackson	357	4,903	$4,903,000	$1,922,869
Jefferson	397	6,374	$6,374,000	$2,237,097
Lafayette	42	577	$577,000	$248,481
Leon	515	9,089	$9,089,000	$3,213,130
Levy	46	450	$450,000	$191,418
Liberty	46	521	$521,000	$483,613
Madison	264	4,249	$4,249,000	$2,002,904
Manatee	19	253	$253,000	$303,587
Marion	345	5,314	$5,314,000	$2,491,890
Monroe	91	451	$451,000	$15,020
Nassau	189	1,612	$1,612,000	$305,016
Orange/Mosquito	31	163	$163,000	$167,034

Putnam	103	1,047	$1,047,000	$359,989
Santa Rosa	166	1,371	$1,371,000	$57,728
St Johns	157	1,003	$1,003,000	$151,343
Sumter	67	549	$549,000	$393,136
Suwannee	72	835	$835,000	$446,855
Taylor	23	125	$125,000	$163,141
Volusia	38	297	$297,000	$230,076
Wakulla	116	1,167	$1,167,000	$435,384
Walton	107	441	$441,000	$336,240
Washington	56	474	$474,000	$214,803
TOTAL	5,152	61,745	$61,745,000	$24,187,240

We are especially interested in knowing who owned and controlled the plantations and firms; from whom did they acquire their raw materials and at what price; to whom did they sell their products and at what price; what if any taxes or revenue did the Governments of Florida (state, county and local) and the United States receive; and who owns or controls these farms, companies and related industries today.

We request information about the following and similar corporations, or their predecessor entities, who invested in, or made profits from slavery and the slave trade, or from slave-like practices and conditions:

- Flo-Sun Inc., a Florida corporation, which is owned by Alfonso, Jose, Andres and Alexander Fanjul, the Sultans of Sugar. The Fanjuls control 40% sugar production in Florida, (180,000 acres of land), and in many parts of the Caribbean, including the Dominican Republic, which ships about 100,000 tons of raw, duty-free sugar each year to the U.S. The Fanjuls also own Domino Sugar, Florida Crystals Corporation, and Refined Sugars. Their father and grandfather, Alfonso Fanjul Sr. and Jose Gomez-Mena, presided over one of the largest sugar and slave plantations in Cuba, and they continued to exploit and oppress Africans in the sugar fields through segregation until the victory of the Cuban Revolution.

  In 1989, 20,000 sugarcane harvesters, most of them Jamaican, who used to work for Florida's largest sugar companies, including Florida Crystals, sued "Big Sugar "for years of massive wage cheating and for what has been called 50-years of "modern-day slavery." In May 1992, a Florida court awarded the migrant workers $51 million dollars in a summary judgment. One year later, Flo-Sun mechanized its fields and replaced most, if not all, of its migrant workers. The Fanjul companies are also accused of exploiting Haitian workers in the Dominican Republic.

- Bacardi Limited, which was organized in Cuba in 1862 by Facundo Bacardi Y Maso, and is the largest rum distiller in the world today. Cuba was and is the sugar and rum producing capital of the world. Slavery was not abolished in Cuba until the 1870s; and segregation ended with the Cuban Revolution of 1959. The $2.8 billion Bacardi Empire was built and maintained on slave-produced and segregation produced sugar, molasses and rum. It is currently owned and controlled by 500 of Facundo's descendants, the sixth generation. The Bacardi Family is one of the biggest financiers of right-wing movements and causes in the world today; and is directly responsible for numerous human rights violations, and for crimes against humanity in every corner of the world.

- The leadership of the Cuban community in Miami, many of whom are the grand-sons and grand-daughters, great grandsons and great grand-daughters, of the Cuban slave-trading and slave-holding class; and whose current wealth is dripping in the sweat and blood of African slaves.

We also request access to or copies of all records that pertain to or reference the subjects listed above for the following activities and events:

- 1519, Florida became a refuge for runaway slaves.

- 1600, the Spanish governor of Florida offered freedom to British colonial slaves who escaped to St. Augustine.

- 1687, first eleven fugitive slaves from Charleston, South Carolina arrived by boat and were granted refuge by Governor Cendoya.

- 1695, May 13 and November 7, Spanish King Charles II issued a cedula (proclamation) promising that any English slave (maroon) who came to Spanish territory would be free. He said he was: "Giving liberty to all ... the men as well as the women ... so that by their example and by my liberality others will do the same."

- 1733, James Moore of South Carolina leads attack against St. Augustine in order to recapture runaway slaves.

- 1738, 100 Africans who had escaped from slavery, formed a militia and build Fort Mose in St. Augustine, Florida to protect themselves from the slave catchers of Georgia and the Carolinas.

- 1738, Governor Antonio de Benavides (1734-1737) ignored the royal cedula and sold fugitive slaves back to the English to profit himself. The King replaced him with Benevides and issued new rules prohibiting such sales while also requiring runaways to perform four years of military service to obtain their freedom.

- 1738-39, the Spanish governor of Florida offered freedom to British colonial slaves who escaped to St. Augustine. Three slave revolts occur including the Stono Rebellion, resulting in known deaths to 51 whites and many more slaves.

- 1739, James Oglethorpe, the founder of the British colony of Georgia, invaded Florida, attacked and seized control of Fort Mose.

- 1740, May, Governor Oglethorpe of Georgia invaded Florida again.

- 1763, Florida ceded to Britain under terms of the Treaty of Paris, which ended the French and Indian War (Seven Years War).

- 1764, eight transport ships took Spanish Floridian refugees to Cuba in March 1764. Spanish officials noted that 420 (13.5%) were of African origin. Within the group, 350 were slaves, but 80 (almost one-fifth) were free.

- 1775-76, Florida officially transferred to the United States. The slave population jumps to 3,000. The American Revolution ends and loyalists in the former British colonies flee to East Florida illegally bringing more than 13,000 slaves.

- 1790, Spain allegedly rescinded its policy of religious sanctuary in Florida for Africans who had escaped from slavery. But runaway African slaves kept coming, and the Seminoles and Spanish, continued to harbor them, and refused to send them back. The United States Government sent numerous delegations to Spain and Florida to request that the Seminoles and Spain stop encouraging and harboring runaway slaves, give them back, or pay compensation. Again, the Seminoles and Spain refused, which led to the Seminole Wars.

- 1793, U.S. Army attacks and destroys the African Fort in Florida

- 26-Oct, 1795, Pinckney's Treaty between Spain and US signed, and Spanish agree to stop arming Native Americans and runaway slaves.

- 1809, Slavery abolished in Spain and all of its colonies, including Florida.

- 1810, 27-October, upon their return to Florida, the Spanish reinstated their 1693 fugitive slave policy and declared 250 slaves to be free because they had accepted baptism into the Catholic Church.

- 1813-14, United States troops invade Florida again, led by General Andrew Jackson.

- 1817, First and Second Seminole Wars (1817 -1818 and 1835 1842) some escaped to the Bahamas and others were removed with their Native American allies to the Indian Territory (present day Oklahoma).

- 1817, Spain outlaws the slave trade in all of its provinces to the north of the equator.

- 1819, Spain sells Florida to the United States through the Adams-Onis Treaty. Article VI of the Treaty guaranteed that:

  > The inhabitants, [including Indians and Africans] of the territories which his Catholic Majesty cedes to the United States shall be admitted to the enjoyment of all privileges, rights, and immunities of the citizens of the United States.

- 3-Mar, 1819, Florida became a territory of the United States, William P. Duval being appointed first governor. The following year Tallahassee was selected as the new capital. The refusal of the warlike Seminoles to repair to reservations resulted in the long, costly, and discreditable Indian War (1835-42), which came to an end in the capture by treachery of Osceola.

- 1821, the Adams-Onis Treaty with Article VI intact was ratified by Congress and Florida was transferred to the United States. The first public act by Florida's new governor Andrew Jackson decreed that Article VI was no longer in effect, that Floridians had to apply for naturalization, and that neither Seminoles nor Hispanics with visible African ancestry could become citizens.

- 1820, Spain declares slave trade illegal.

- 1821, the U.S. Army forcibly removed more than 15,000 Cherokees and 3,000 Seminoles to Indian Territory in the Trail of Tears. As many as a quarter of the Indians died during the forced march and the $6 million cost of the removal was deducted from the $9 million offered them for their land in the treaty they were forced to sign.

- 1825-42, the Second Seminole War was fought by 3,000 to 5,000 African and Indian warriors, pitted against four U.S. generals and more than 200,000 troops, at a cost of more than $20 million, and more than 1,500 soldiers and uncounted American civilians dead.

- 1823, the United States outlaws the importation of slaves, but Florida slaveholders continue importing and smuggling slaves into the Southern states.

- 1835, just a few months after the issue of the Farmers Register featuring San José came out, President Jackson ordered the U.S. Army to take the dark Seminoles into custody, return them to slavery, and deport all the light-skinned ones to Oklahoma. Jackson's order triggered what historian Larry Rivers calls the largest slave rebellion in U.S. history.

- 1855-58, the Third Seminole War reduced the Seminole population to about 200.

We formally and publicly request that you comply in an expedited manner with this Request, and that you waive all associated costs. Please be advised that we have disclosed this Request to the public and media.

In order to help you determine our status and make your decision on our fee waiver request, you should know that Bob Brown is an organizer and researcher, who has worked, studied and struggled for 41 years, within and for the Student, Civil and Human Rights, Black Power, National Liberation, Pan-African, and Peace Movements. See Attachment #B.

We expect your positive response to this historic and precedent setting Request within 20 working days. Please be assured that we will exhaust administrative and political remedies. Thank you for your consideration.

Sincerely,
Bob Brown, co-director
Pan-African Roots

Pan-African Roots

1247 E Street SE
Washington, DC 20003
Tel: (202) 544-9355 - Fax: (202) 544-9359
Email: paroots02@yahoo.com

25 October 2004

President Vicente Fox Quesada
Embassy of the Republic of Mexico
1911 Pennsylvania Ave NW
Washington, DC 20006

Federal Transparency and Access to Public Government Information Act Request.
Request for Waiver of Costs and Expedited Review.

Dear President Fox:

We formally and publicly request, pursuant to Article 6 of the 1997 Mexican Constitution and the Federal Transparency and Access to Public Government Information Law, that you, and all agencies and structures in Mexico (federal, state and local), give us access to or copies of all records pertaining to or referencing:

- Mexico's and Spain's role, operations and activities, historically and currently, in facilitating, prohibiting or combating piracy and privateering, slavery and the slave trade, especially the Trans-Atlantic Slave Trade ((also known as the Atlantic Trade, the Triangle Trade, the Colonial Trade, the West Indies Trade, etc.) in Spain and its colonies, especially Florida, Cuba, Mexico and Texas; and their role in the struggle to declare them crimes against humanity, and to repair the damages and injuries that they inflicted upon untold generations of African People.

- Mexico's and Spain's role, operations and activities, historically and currently, in facilitating, prohibiting or combating slave-like conditions and practices, including but not limited to servitude, forced and compulsory labor, peonage, sharecropping, debt-bondage, sweatshop labor, convict-lease, chain-gang or prison labor, the sale of children, child prostitution, child pornography, the exploitation of child labour, the sexual mutilation of female children, the use of children in armed conflicts, the traffic in persons and in the sale of human organs, the exploitation of prostitution, and certain practices under apartheid and colonial regimes, segregation, racism and racial discrimination, xenophobia and related intolerance.

- Mexico's knowledge of and response to the Catholic Church's and Spain's abolition of slavery and the slave trade; emancipation of their slaves and granting them citizenship, and related diplomatic discussions, agreement and treaties.

- Slave, urban and racial disturbances, riots, rebellions, and revolts, runaway slaves, fugitives beyond borders, related claims or requests, and demands for restitution and reparations.

- All treaties or agreements, bilateral or multilateral, or diplomatic communications, correspondence, discussions, public and secret, between the United States Government and its Officials (all levels, branches and agencies) and the Spanish, Mexican, or all other governments with respect to the above or related subjects.

- The United Nations World Conference Against Racism, Racial Discrimination, Xenophobia and Related Intolerance (WCAR), including its preparatory, regional and expert meetings and seminars, the White House Interagency Task Force on the U.N. World Conference Against Racism, the U.S. Governmental Delegation, the U.S. Non-Governmental Delegation, the UN

Intergovernmental Working Group on the effective implementation of the Durban Declaration and Programme of Action, and the UNESCO Slave Route Project.

- All governments, agencies (federal, state, county or local), corporations, non-governmental organizations, institutions, churches, families, individuals, or entities, domestic or foreign who participated or invested in, or made profits from the above referenced crimes against humanity; and who owns or benefits from these historical and continuing crimes today, including but not limited to those listed in Appendix A.

As you are aware, the world Conference Against Racism, Racial Discrimination, Xenophobia and Related Intolerance (WCAR) met from 31 August to 3 September 2001, in Durban, South Africa. Reports reveal that 18,810 delegates from 170 countries participated in WCAR, including 16 heads of state, 58 foreign ministers, 44 ministers, 7,000 non-governmental representatives, and 1,300 journalists. The WCAR Final Declaration and Programme of Action:

Acknowledge[s] that slavery and the slave trade, including the Trans-Atlantic Slave Trade, were appalling tragedies in the history of humanity not only because of their abhorrent barbarism but also in terms of their magnitude, organized nature especially their negation of the essence of the victims, ... acknowledge[s] that slavery and the slave trade are a crime against humanity **and should have always been so**, especially the Trans-Atlantic slave trade and are among the major sources and manifestations of racism, racial discrimination, xenophobia and related intolerance,... and invite[s] the international community members to honour the memory of the victims of these tragedies ...[**Emphasis added.**]

Further note[s] that some [countries} have taken the initiative of regretting or expressing remorse or presenting apologies, and call on all those who have yet contributed to restoring the dignity of all the victims to find appropriate ways to do so... [126]

You are perhaps not aware, that on May 17, 1860, the second National Republican Convention adopted its 1860 National Republican Platform, which declared it resolved:

7. That the new dogma that the Constitution of its own force carries slavery into any or all of the territories of the United States, is a dangerous political heresy, at variance with the explicit provisions of that instrument itself, with contemporaneous exposition, and with legislative and judicial precedent, is revolutionary in its tendency and subversive of the peace and harmony of the country.

8. That the formal condition of all the territory of the United States is that of freedom; that as our republican fathers, when they had abolished slavery in all our national territory, ordained that no "person should be deprived of life, liberty or property, without due process of law," it becomes our duty, by legislation, whenever such legislation is necessary, to maintain this provision of the constitution against all attempts to violate it; and we deny the authority of congress, of a territorial legislature, or of any individuals, to give legal existence to slavery in any territory of the United States.

9. That we brand the recent re-opening of the African Slave Trade, under the cover of our national flag, aided by perversions of judicial power, as a **crime against humanity, and a burning shame to our country and age,** and we call upon congress to take prompt and efficient measures for the total and final suppression of the execrable traffic. [127] [**Emphasis added.**]

---

[126] World Conference Secretariat. Office of the United Nations High Commissioner for Human Rights. Available from http://www.unhchr.ch/html/racism/02-documents-cnt.html.

[127] Central Pacific Railroad Photographic History Museum. *Republican Party National Platform, 1860.* Available from http://cprr.org/Museum/Ephemera/Republican_Platform_1860.html.

In 1808, the United States Government prohibited its citizens from participating in the international slave trade, declaring it piracy in 1820, and participation in it punishable by death. Despite this prohibition, a minimum of 250,000 and perhaps as many as 1,000,000 Africans were kidnapped, enslaved, and illegally imported into the United States via Cuba between 1809 and 1861. In 1839, a prime male slave could be purchased in Cuba for $400 and then sold into slavery for life in Richmond for $1,000 or Charleston for $1,150 or Savannah for $1,200 or New Orleans for $1,250. The average daily wage was one dollar. President James Madison reported to Congress in 1810 that:

> It appears that American citizens are instrumental in carrying on a traffic in enslaved Africans, equally in violation of the laws of humanity, and in defiance of those of their own country. The same just and benevolent motives which produced the interdiction in force against this criminal conduct, will doubtless be felt in Congress, in devising further means of suppressing the evil.

The 1860 Republican National Convention selected Abraham Lincoln as its Presidential nominee. He campaigned on this platform, and "won the presidency with almost half a million votes more than [Stephen] Douglas, his closest rival. [Lincoln] won the election garnering 39.8 percent of the popular vote. This election firmly established the Republican hold on the presidency for 60 of the next 100 years. Within five years of the 1860 Convention, slavery had been abolished, 4 million slaves were liberated, and the 13th Amendment was passed banning slavery and the slave trade forever from U.S. soil.

You are perhaps also not aware that William Lloyd Garrison was the first person to declare slavery a crime against humanity in the inaugural edition (1831) of his Liberator newspaper; or that on November 12, 1849, the Vermont Legislature passed "*Joint Resolution No. 42.--Resolutions Relating To The Subject of Slavery,*" declaring it:

> Resolved by the Senate and House of Representatives, that Slavery is a **crime against humanity, and a sore evil** in the body politic that was excused by the framers of the Federal Constitution as a crime entailed upon the country by their predecessors, and tolerated solely as a thing of inexorable necessity.[128] [**Emphasis added.**]

It is well-settled, as the WCAR Final Declaration confirms, that prohibitions against piracy and privateering, slavery and the slave trade, including the Trans-Atlantic Slave Trade, and against slave-like conditions and practices, including colonialism, segregation and apartheid, forced and compulsory labor, racism and racial discrimination, xenophobia and related intolerance have achieved the level of customary international law, have attained the status of jus cogens, and are obligato erga omnes. Unfortunately, the overwhelming majority of the WCAR Delegates and the public, especially African People world-wide, wrongly believe that this status has only recently been acquired.[129]

Permit us to suggest, as Ethan A. Nadelman suggests, that "most global prohibition regimes, including those targeted against piracy, slavery, and drug trafficking, evidence a common evolutionary pattern consisting of four or five stages."[130] At different stages in their development: (1) the activity is legal and some states participate in it; (2) national and international forces, non-governmental and governmental, attempt to redefine the activity as evil and illegal; (3) these forces agitate for its suppression and criminalization; (4) the activity becomes the subject of national and international criminal laws, conventions and treaties, police and military action; and (5) finally, the activity is

---

[128] *The Acts and Resolves Passed By The Legislature Of The State of Vermont At The October Session, 1849.* Published By authority. Montpelier: E. P. Walton & Son. 1849.

[129] People incorrectly believe that "the term was first used in the preamble of the Hague Convention of 1907." Wikipedia. Available from http://en.wikipedia.org/wiki/Crime_against_humanity.

[130] Ethan A. Nadelman. *Global prohibition regimes: the evolution of norms in international society.* Printed in Transnational Crime / edited by Nikos Passas.

prohibited globally.[131] It is axiomatic that this development is extremely uneven, unequal, and costly in time, space and human lives, in justice and equity.

Permit us also to suggest that Judge Fouad Ammoun of the International Court of Justice (ICJ) "has [accurately] described the development of Africa … [and] eloquently remarked on the evolution of mankind's struggle with the issues of slavery and colonization."[132] He informs us that "before there fell upon it the two greatest plagues in the recorded history of mankind: the slave trade, which ravaged Africa for centuries on an unprecedented scale; and colonialism, which exploited humanity and natural wealth to a relentless extreme," … Africa boasted thriving states and empires dating back to Roman times"[133]

Judge Ammoun also informs us that "historians have outlined the upward march of mankind from the time when homo sapiens appeared on the face of the globe, first of all in the Near East in what was the land of Canaan[134], up to the age of the greatest thinkers and more particularly, throughout the whole of history of social progress, from the slavery of Antiquity to man's [and woman's] inevitable, irreversible drive towards equality and freedom. This march is like time itself. It never stops. Nothing can stand in its way for long. The texts, whether they be laws, constitutions, declarations, covenants or charters, do but define it and mark its successive phases. They are a mere record of it. In other words, the progressive rights which men, [women] and peoples enjoy are the result much less of those texts than of human progress to which they bear witness."[135]

We are confident that the records requested by and through this historic and precedent setting Federal Transparency and Access to Public Government Information Act Request will:

- Bear witness to and prove, once and for all, that piracy and privateering, slavery and the slave trade, including the Trans-Atlantic Slave Trade, and slave-like conditions and practices, including colonialism, segregation and apartheid, were and are illegal and prohibited, and were and are recognized as crimes against humanity when and where they were committed.

- Help define and mark the successive stages in the development of the 569-year historical and continuing Maafa,[136] and of the unyielding and continuing struggle against it.

- Document who the victims were, and who their descendants are today; who committed these crimes, which were and are the greatest theft of land, lives and labor in human history; how this unjust and illegal wealth was converted, consolidated, preserved and transferred across generations and centuries; and who owns and benefits from this unjust enrichment today.

We request that you and the Government of Mexico, formally and publicly reaffirm, once and for all, that slavery and the slave trade were and are illegal according to the edicts and municipal laws of Spain and its colonies, and according to canon law and international law; and that slavery and the slave trade were crimes against humanity:

- "Because God makes no slaves in the womb;"[137] because the prohibition of the slave trade is well-settled in the Bible in Timothy 1:10, Exodus 21:16, Deuteronomy 24:7, 1 Corinthians 5:11, 1 Corinthians 6:10 and Timothy 1:10-1; and because the Catholic Church was in the forefront of

---

[131] Ibid.

[132] *Legal Consequences For States of the Continued Presence of South Africa in Namibia (South West Africa) Notwithstanding Security Council Resolution 276, 1971 I.C.J. 16, 86 (1971) (separate opinion of Judge Ammoun).*

[133] Recent evidence documents that African civilizations predate Roman times.

[134] Recent evidence documents that homo sapiens first emerged in East Africa.

[135] Ethan A. Nadelman. *Global prohibition regimes.*

[136] Dr. Marimba Ani. *Let The Circle Be Unbroken.* Maafa is a Kiswahili word for the 563-year historical and continuing enslavement and colonization of Africa and African People.

[137] Rev. John G. Fee. *An Anti-Slavery Manual, or, The Wrongs of American Slavery Exposed By the Light of the Bible and of Facts, with A Remedy for the Evil (1851).* http://members.tripod.com/medicolegal/feeasm1851.htm

the struggle from 441 AD to 1890 to prohibit and abolish the trafficking in and enslavement of Christians, Europeans, the Indigenous Peoples of the Western Hemisphere, and African People.

- Because King Charles V of Spain prohibited slavery in 1530; because Emperor Charles II ordered all slaves, including African slaves, be set free in 1540; because King Charles II issued Royal Edicts in 1693 and on November 7, 1695 giving sanctuary to all runaway slaves in Florida and "liberty to ... all men as well as all women ... so that by their example and by [his] liberality others will do the same;"[138] because slavery and the slave trade was again declared illegal and prohibited in Spain and all of its colonies, including Florida, Mexico and Texas in 1811; because they refused to return runaway slaves; and because the liberty and property of all Spanish citizens, including former slaves, was and is protected by treaties with the United States.

We further request that you and the Government of Mexico, formally and publicly reaffirm, once and for all, that slavery and the slave trade were and are crimes under Mexican law, and that they were and are crimes against humanity because:

- 1809, all sides in the struggle for the independence waged by Spain's colonies in the Americas promised to emancipate slaves who took part in their military campaigns.

- 1817, 30-Sept, Spain promised to abolish the slave trade by October 31, 1820, in all Spanish territory, and England paid Spain an indemnity of £400,000.

- 1817, slavery was outlawed in the newly independent Latin American republics, and slavery declined through free womb laws and manumissions with apprenticeship.

- 1821, January, the petition of Moses Austin for permission to settle an Anglo-American colony in Texas was officially granted, without giving permission to introduce slaves.

- 1821, United States Government attempts to negotiate a treaty with the Mexican government for the return of fugitive slaves, but, the Mexican Congress refuses to ratify it.

- 1822, 14-Nov, the Congreso Constituyente Mexicano passed an article in its Texas Colonization Bill which said that:

  > There shall not be permitted, after the promulgation of this law, either purchase or sale of slaves that may be introduced into the empire. The children of such slaves, who are born with the empire, shall be free at fourteen years of age.

- 1824, 13-July, the sovereign general Constituent Congress of the United Mexican States issued a decree which included the following:

  > Commerce and traffic in slaves, proceeding from any country and under any flag whatsoever is forever prohibited in the territory of the United Mexican States. Slaves that are introduced contrary to the tenor of the above article are free by virtue of the mere act of treading Mexican territory. Every ship, whether domestic or foreign, in which slaves are transported to or introduced into Mexican territory, shall be irremissibly confiscated, with the remainder of its cargo; and the owner, the purchaser, the captain, the master, and the pilot shall suffer the penalty of a year's imprisonment.

  > This law shall take effect from the day of its publication, but the penalties prescribed in the above article shall be suspended for six months with reference to those colonists who, by virtue of the law of the fourteenth of October last upon the colonization of the isthmus

---

[138] Quoted at *Fort Mose's People*. Available from http://www.millennium.scps.k12.fl.us/fortmose3.html.

of Guazacoalco, may land slaves with the intention of introducing them into Mexican territory.[139]

[Upon information and belief, this law conferred Mexican citizenship on the newly freed slaves; and obligated Mexico to afford them equal recognition and equal protection. The decree was not obeyed in the Mexican province of Texas.]

- 1825, 24-Mar, the colonization law under which all the contracts in Texas were governed, was approved. Article 46 of that law required that new settlers shall subject themselves to the laws that are now, and shall hereafter be established on the subject of the slave trade and slavery.

- 1827, September, the Mexican Congress issued a decree ordering all municipalities to make a list of the slaves within their limits, make a report every three months, emancipate a tenth of the slaves when ownership changes which could only be done through inheritance, and provide the best education that can be given to the emancipated children.

- 1829, the Pope asked Mexico to abolish slavery throughout its dominions, including Texas and the Southwestern region of the United States.

- 1829, 15-Sep, Mr. Vicente Guerrero, the President of the Mexican Republic, signed a decree that declared that slavery was abolished, that all "negroes "were henceforth free, and that owners would receive compensation at some future time.

- 1830, Mexico forbade the further colonization of Texas Territory and prohibited the further importation of slaves into the Territory. The United States Government attempted once again, to negotiate a treaty with the Mexican Government for the return of fugitive slaves, but the Mexican Congress refused to ratify it.

- 1830, President Guerrero ordered an occupation of Texas to enforce the anti-slavery measure.

- 1835, United States Government attempted to negotiate a treaty with the Mexican Government, of behalf of the Texas settlers, for the return of fugitive slaves, but the Mexican Congress refused to ratify it.

- 1835, Dr. John S. Ford, a newspaper editor and former Texas Ranger, suggests that there were more than 4,000 fugitive slaves living in northern Mexico valued at $3,200,000. The Texas Rangers were founded, in part, as slave-catchers.

- 1836, Texas unilaterally declared itself a republic with a constitution permitting the introduction of slavery and forbidding the residence of free Negroes without the consent of its Congress, and began to prepare a war of aggression against Mexico.

- 1836, the state legislature and several Texas cities passed Black Codes to restrict the rights of blacks, to prevent them from having free access to public facilities, and to force them back to the rural areas as agricultural laborers.

- 1837, Congress refused to annex Texas over the issue of slavery.

- 1840, 11,000 Africans were enslaved in Texas; 30,000 in 1845, 58,161in 1850, (27.4 percent of the population), and 182,000 in 1860, (30.2 percent of the population).

- 1840, to 1868 1,500 acts of violence were committed against Africans, and more than 350 Africans were murdered.

---

[139] Professor von Holst. *Constitutional and Political History of the United States. Volume II.* Page 553.

- 1844, Mexican Congressman Lucas Alaman "reconfirmed the fact that all slaves brought to Texas after the July 13, 1824 degree was published should have gained their freedom in virtue of the provision of section 2 of the decree."[140]

- 1844, October, in response to the United States Government's threat to invade Mexico if she continued her refusal to recognize the independence of Texas, and to stop harboring runaway slaves, the Mexican Foreign Minister is reported to have said:

    While one power is seeking more ground to stain by the slavery of an unfortunate branch of the human family, the other is endeavoring, by preserving what belongs to it, to diminish the surface which the former wants for this detestable traffic. Let the world now say which of the two has justice and reason on its side.

- 1848, President Guerrero ordered a military occupation of the State to enforce the anti-slavery measure.

- 1848, Treaty of Guadalupe-Hidalgo ceded California, New Mexico, Arizona, Utah, Nevada, the rest of Texas and other territories for $15 million. Articles VIII and IX of the Treaty pledged that all Mexican citizens, including Africans:

    Who shall prefer to remain in the said territories [of Texas and what is now the Southwestern region of the United States] may either retain the title and rights of Mexican citizens, or acquire those of United States citizens, will be admitted at the proper time.. to the enjoyment of all the rights of citizens of the United States, according to the principles of the Constitution; and in the meantime, shall be maintained and protected in the free enjoyment of their liberty and property, and secured in the free exercise of their religion without restriction.

Despite these prohibitions, edicts and laws, more than 3,000 Africans were illegally held in slavery in Texas on the eve its declaration of independence from Mexico in 1835; 200,000 Africans were still being illegally held in slavery in Texas and the Southwestern portion of the United States in 1865; and their descendants still suffer slave-like conditions and practices, segregation, racism and racial discrimination, xenophobia and related intolerance today.

We request that you comply in an expedited manner with this Request, and that you waive all associated costs. Please be advised that we have disclosed this Request to the public and media.

In order to help you determine our status and make your decision on our fee waiver request, you should know that Bob Brown is an organizer and researcher, who has worked, studied and struggled for 41 years, within and for the Student, Civil and Human Rights, Black Power, National Liberation, Pan-African, and Peace Movements. See Attachment B.

We expect your positive response to this historic and precedent setting Federal Transparency and Access to Public Government Information Act Request within 20 working days as the law provides. Please be assured that we will exhaust all administrative, legal and political remedies to successfully conclude this Request. Thank you for your consideration.

Sincerely,
Bob Brown, co-director
Pan-African Roots

---

[140] *Iniciativa de ley etc. a message to Congress printed in Filisola's Guerra de Tejas.* Volume II. Page 595.

Pan-African Roots
1247 E Street SE
Washington, DC 20003
Tel: (202) 544-9355 - Fax: (202) 544-9359
Email: paroots02@yahoo.com

25 October 2004

Mr. Rick Perry, Governor
Office of the Governor
P.O. Box 12428
Austin, TX 78711

> **Public Information Act Request.**
> **Fee Waiver and Expedited Review Request.**
> **cc: Public Information Officer and Public Information Appeals Officer.**

Dear Governor Perry:

As you are aware, King Charles V of Spain prohibited slavery in 1530; Emperor Charles II ordered all slaves, including African slaves, be set free in 1540; King Charles II of Spain issued Royal Edicts in 1693 and on November 7, 1695 giving sanctuary to all runaway slaves in Florida and "liberty to ... all men as well as all women ... so that by their example and by [his] liberality others will do the same;"[141] slavery and the slave trade were again declared illegal and prohibited in Spain and all of its colonies, including Florida, Mexico and Texas in 1811; Spain, Mexico and Florida refused to return runaway slaves; and the liberty and property of all Spanish citizens, including former slaves, was and is protected by treaties between Spain, Mexico and the United States.

As you are also aware, 3,000 Africans were illegally held in slavery in Texas on the eve its Independence in 1835; 200,000 Africans were still being illegally held in slavery in the Spanish colony of Mexico, and its provinces in Texas and the Southwestern portion of the United States in 1865; and their descendants still suffer slave-like conditions and practices, segregation, racism and racial discrimination, xenophobia and related intolerance in Texas today.

Pursuant to Texas Public Information Act ("the Act ") (Tex. Gov't Code Ann. § 552.001 et seq., formerly Tex. Rev. Civ. Stat. Ann. art. 6252-17a (Vernon 1994 & Supp. 2001), we request access to or copies of all records pertaining to or referencing:

- Texas' role, operations and activities, historically and currently, in facilitating, prohibiting or combating piracy and privateering, slavery and the slave trade, especially the Trans-Atlantic Slave Trade (also known as the Atlantic Trade, the Triangle Trade, the Colonial Trade, the West Indies Trade, the Coastal Trade, the Intra-state Slave Trade, etc.); and in the struggle to declare them crimes against humanity.

- Texas' role, operations and activities, historically and currently, in facilitating, prohibiting or combating slave-like conditions and practices, including but not limited to servitude, forced and compulsory labor, peonage, sharecropping, debt-bondage, sweatshop labor, convict-lease, chain-gang or prison labor, the sale of children, child prostitution, child pornography, the exploitation of child labour, the sexual mutilation of female children, the use of children in armed conflicts, the traffic in persons and in the sale of human organs, the exploitation of prostitution, and certain practices under apartheid and colonial regimes, segregation, racism and racial discrimination, xenophobia and related intolerance.

---

[141] Quoted at *Fort Mose's People*. Available from http://www.millennium.scps.k12.fl.us/fortmose3.html.

- Texas' knowledge of and response to Spain's and Mexico's abolition of slavery and the slave trade; emancipation of slaves and granting them citizenship; refusal to return runaway slaves; and related claims, diplomatic discussions, agreement and treaties.

- All governments, agencies (federal, state, county or local), corporations, non-governmental organizations, institutions, churches, families, individuals, or entities, domestic or foreign who participated or invested in, or made profits from the above referenced crimes against humanity; and who owns or benefits from these historical and continuing crimes today, including but not limited to those listed in Appendix A.

We request access to or copies of all records that pertain to, or reference paragraph number four above, for the following counties:

1860 United States Census	Slave-Holding Families	Percent Total Families	Number of Slaves	Value of Slaves ($1,000 @)	Value of Farms
Anderson	459	6.60%	3,668	$3,668,000	$2,665,801
Angelina	116	33.50%	686	$686,000	$849,609
Atascosa	33	29.30%	107	$107,000	$409,705
Austin	324	19.70%	3,914	$3,914,000	$5,155,960
Bandera	5	11.30%	12	$12,000	$46,721
Bastrop	274	36.60%	2,591	$2,591,000	$1,984,090
Bee	38	48.90%	79	$79,000	$434,214
Bell	179	5.40%	1,005	$1,005,000	$2,216,937
Bexar	294	9.00%	1,395	$1,395,000	$1,095,449
Blanco	M	22.90%	98	$98,000	$955,295
Bosque	51	9.70%	293	$293,000	$405,237
Bowie	201	17.70%	2,651	$2,651,000	$1,724,733
Brazoria	232	26.90%	5,110	$5,110,000	$6,317,905
Brazos	118	16.90%	1,063	$1,063,000	$1,779,188
Burleson	228	57.30%	2,003	$2,003,000	$2,401,548
Burnet	69	41.30%	235	$235,000	$781,304
Caldwell	254		1,610	$1,610,000	$1,348,322
Calhoun	106	24.70%	414	$414,000	$95,189
Cameron	6		7	$7,000	$1,542,587
Cass/Davis	354		3,475	$3,475,000	$1,724,901
Chambers	69	36.90%	513	$513,000	$571,459
Cherokee	456	17.30%	3,246	$3,246,000	$2,118,982
Collin	240	12.50%	1,047	$1,047,000	$3,118,926
Colorado	306	26.60%	3,559	$3,559,000	$3,932,879
Comal	22	6.90%	193	$193,000	$948,951
Comanche	25	32.30%	61	$61,000	$215,503
Cooke	74	23.60%	369	$369,000	$1,033,410
Coryell	81	28.00%	306	$306,000	$895,025
Dallas	228	11.20%	1,074	$1,074,000	$3,553,328
De Witt	201		1,643	$1,643,000	$2,305,993
Denton	87	16.30%	251	$251,000	$973,676
El Paso	3	44.30%	15	$15,000	$437,677

Ellis	196	57.60%	1,104	$1,104,000	$2,258,525
Erath	26	36.10%	118	$118,000	$598,111
Falls	158	37.10%	1,716	$1,716,000	$974,645
Fannin	308	17.60%	1,721	$1,721,000	$2,359,790
Fayette	514	49.20%	3,786	$3,786,000	$3,895,059
Fort Bend	260	22.40%	4,127	$4,127,000	$4,105,908
Freestone	307	0.40%	3,613	$3,613,000	$1,338,670
Frio	2	41.60%	2	$2,000	$16
Galveston	288	41.80%	1,520	$1,520,000	$379,422
Gillespie	7	29.70%	33	$33,000	$523,833
Goliad	119	17.30%	843	$843,000	$1,132,783
Gonzales	384	39.30%	3,168	$3,168,000	$2,638,666
Grayson	236	2.90%	1,292	$1,292,000	$3,105,440
Grimes	505	21.70%	5,468	$5,468,000	$3,997,777
Guadalupe	202	11.90%	1,748	$1,748,000	$2,161,224
Hamilton	12	19.30%	26	$26,000	$13,579
Hardin	35	17.20%	191	$191,000	$164,191
Harris	395	30.00%	2,053	$2,053,000	$663,694
Harrison	713	10.00%	8,784	$8,784,000	$3,693,099
Hays	95	0.30%	797	$797,000	$622,204
Henderson	155	28.40%	1,116	$1,116,000	$848,509
Hidalgo	1	6.50%	1	$1,000	$481,800
Hill	118	51.00%	650	$650,000	$1,360,504
Hopkins	235	24.20%	990	$990,000	$1,820,394
Houston	335	25.60%	2,819	$2,819,000	$1,992,780
Hunt	142	65.30%	577	$577,000	$1,252,620
Jack	19	50.60%	50	$50,000	$108,922
Jackson	155	18.20%	1,194	$1,194,000	$1,775,587
Jasper	170	20.80%	1,611	$1,611,000	$989,363
Jefferson	70	1.20%	309	$309,000	$147,379
Johnson	129	25.20%	513	$513,000	$893,626
Karnes	64	45.60%	327	$327,000	$801,266
Kaufman	128	19.40%	533	$533,000	$1,012,391
Kerr	14	63.20%	49	$49,000	$158,783
Lamar	419	32.10%	2,833	$2,833,000	$2,530,681
Lampasas	32	15.40%	153	$153,000	$316,822
Lavaca	217	18.00%	1,707	$1,707,000	$1,947,907
Leon	320	28.20%	2,620	$2,620,000	$1,471,564
Liberty	136	66.90%	1,079	$1,079,000	$1,279,032
Limestone	182	38.80%	1,072	$1,072,000	$1,411,328
Live Oak	11	26.40%	85	$85,000	$323,110
Llano	21	0.40%	54	$54,000	$434,168
Madison	96	20.50%	675	$675,000	$596,659
Marion	213	19.20%	2,017	$2,017,000	$499,987
Mason	8	37.50%	18	$18,000	$161,217
Matagorda	125	13.70%	2,107	$2,107,000	$1,911,811
Maverick	1	11.70%	1	$1,000	
McLennan	270	60.10%	2,395	$2,395,000	$2,406,295

Medina	22	42.60%	106	$106,000	$394,313
Milam	259	26.00%	1,542	$1,542,000	$1,676,221
Montague	13	19.40%	35	$35,000	$53,764
Montgomery	232	16.90%	2,811	$2,811,000	$969,140
Nacogdoches	383	20.90%	2,359	$2,359,000	$1,812,702
Navarro	251	10.10%	1,890	$1,890,000	$2,432,160
Newton	127	34.30%	1,013	$1,013,000	$769,322
Nueces	52	20.50%	216	$216,000	$1,066,163
Orange	64	29.30%	392	$392,000	$89,102
Palo Pinto	29	43.20%	130	$130,000	$434,492
Panola	445	37.30%	3,058	$3,058,000	$1,946,669
Parker	70	29.70%	222	$222,000	$638,883
Polk	357	12.00%	4,198	$4,198,000	$3,083,773
Presidio	4	9.70%	4	$4,000	$351
Red River	353	35.70%	3,039	$3,039,000	$2,281,725
Refugio	43	58.50%	234	$234,000	$1,711,007
Robertson	188	8.20%	2,258	$2,258,000	$2,235,831
Rusk	734	47.30%	6,132	$6,132,000	$3,628,722
Sabine	135	0.60%	1,150	$1,150,000	$425,810
San Augustine	144	40.70%	1,717	$1,717,000	$770,355
San Patricio	36	6.10%	95	$95,000	$628,266
San Saba	20	41.60%	89	$89,000	$389,812
Shackelford	1	8.60%	9	$9,000	$1,910
Shelby	208	48.90%	1,476	$1,476,000	$769,859
Smith	575	35.90%	4,982	$4,982,000	$2,742,666
Starr	6	38.20%	6	$6,000	$187,631
Stephens/Buchanan	7	36.30%	32	$32,000	$65,680
Tarrant	M	10.60%	850	$850,000	$4,548
Titus	352	25.40%	2,438	$2,438,000	$2,214,859
Travis	425	12.30%	3,136	$3,136,000	$3,586,759
Trinity	145	47.50%	959	$959,000	$537,524
Tyler	197	9.80%	1,148	$1,148,000	$894,753
Upshur	480	47.20%	3,794	$3,794,000	$2,474,065
Uvalde	4	3.70%	27	$27,000	$90,940
Van Zandt	75	39.10%	322	$322,000	$559,603
Victoria	184	14.40%	1,413	$1,413,000	$1,583,026
Walker	376	37.50%	4,135	$4,135,000	$2,070,271
Washington	627	45.30%	7,941	$7,941,000	$5,720,364
Wharton	128	41.80%	2,734	$2,734,000	$2,363,970
Williamson	181	36.80%	891	$891,000	$1,844,450
Wise	53	33.00%	128	$128,000	$388,187
Wood	186	12.70%	1,005	$1,005,000	$801,888
Young	26	20.00%	92	$92,000	$74,270
TOTAL	21,878	38.60%	182,566	$182,566,000	$174,017,451

We are especially interested in knowing who owned and controlled the plantations and firms; from whom did they acquire their raw materials and at what price; to whom did they sell their products and at what price; what if any taxes or revenue did the Governments of Texas (state, county and local) and the United States receive; and who owns or controls these farms, companies and related industries today.

We request access to or copies of all records that pertain to or reference the subjects listed above, for the following:

- 1809, 10-Aug, both sides in the struggle for the independence (1809 to 1826) of Spain's colonies in the Americas promised to emancipate all slaves who took part in military campaigns.

- 1817, 30-Sept., Spain promised to abolish the slave trade by October 31, 1820, in all Spanish territory, and England paid Spain an indemnity of £400,000.

- 1817, slavery was outlawed in the newly independent Latin American republics, and slavery declined through free womb laws and manumissions with apprenticeship.

- 1821, January, the petition of Moses Austin for permission to settle an Anglo-American colony in Texas was officially granted without giving permission to introduce slaves.

- 1821, United States Government attempts to negotiate a treaty with the Mexican government for the return of fugitive slaves, but, the Mexican Congress refused to ratify it.

- 1822, 14-Nov, the Congreso Constituyente Mexicano passed an article in its Texas Colonization Bill which said that:

- There shall not be permitted, after the promulgation of this law, either purchase or sale of slaves that may be introduced into the empire. The children of such slaves, who are born with the empire, shall be free at fourteen years of age.

- 1824, 13-July, the sovereign general Constituent Congress of the United Mexican States issued a decree which included the following:

  > Commerce and traffic in slaves, proceeding from any country and under any flag whatsoever is forever prohibited the territory of the United Mexican States. Slaves that are introduced contrary to the tenor of the above article are free by virtue of the mere act of treading Mexican territory. Every ship, whether domestic or foreign, in which slaves are transported to or introduced into Mexican territory, shall be irremissibly confiscated, with the remainder of its cargo; and the owner, the purchaser, the captain, the master, and the pilot shall suffer the penalty of a year's imprisonment.[142]

  > This law shall take effect from the day of its publication, but the penalties prescribed in the above article shall be suspended for six months with reference to those colonists who, virtue of the law of the fourteenth of October last upon the colonization of the isthmus of Guazacoalco, may land slaves with the intention of introducing them into Mexican territory.[143]

  > This law conferred Mexican citizenship on the newly freed slaves as well; and obligated Mexico to afford them equal recognition and equal protection. The decrees were not obeyed.

- 1825, 24-Mar, the colonization law under which all the contracts in Texas were governed, was approved. Article 46 of that law required that new settlers shall subject themselves to the laws that are now, and shall hereafter be established on the subject of the slave trade and slavery.

---

[142] Professor von Holst. *Constitutional and Political History of the United States. Volume II.* Page 553.
[143] Ibid.

- 1827, September, the Mexican Congress issued a decree ordering all municipalities to make a list of the slaves within their limits, make a report every three months, emancipate a tenth of the slaves when ownership changes which could only be done through inheritance, and provide the best education that can be given to the emancipated children.

- 1829, the Pope asked Mexico to abolish slavery throughout its dominions, including Texas and the Southwestern region of the United States.

- 1829, 15-Sep, Mr. Vicente Guerrero, the President of the Mexican Republic, signed a decree that declared that slavery was abolished, that all negroes were henceforth free, and that owners would receive compensation at some future time.

- 1830, Mexico forbade the further colonization of Texas Territory and prohibited the further importation of slaves into the Territory. The United States Government attempted once again, to negotiate a treaty with the Mexican Government for the return of fugitive slaves, but the Mexican Congress refused to ratify it.

- 1830, President Guerrero ordered a military occupation of Texas to enforce the anti-slavery measure.

- 1835, United States Government attempted to negotiate a treaty with the Mexican Government, of behalf of the Texas settlers, for the return of fugitive slaves, but the Mexican Congress refused to ratify it.

- 1835, Dr. John S. Ford, a newspaper editor and former Texas Ranger, suggests that there were more than 4,000 fugitive slaves living in northern Mexico with and suggests value of $3,200,000.

- 1836, Texas declared itself a republic with a constitution permitting the introduction of slavery and forbidding the residence of free Negroes without the consent of its Congress, and began to prepare a war of aggression, in violation of the laws of war, and international law and treaties, against Mexico.

- 1836, the state legislature and several Texas cities passed Black Codes to restrict the rights of blacks, to prevent them from having free access to public facilities, and to force them back to the rural areas as agricultural laborers.

- 1837, Congress refuses to annex Texas over issue of slavery

- 1840, 11,000 Africans were enslaved in Texas; 30,000 in 1845, 58,161in 1850, 27.4 percent of the population; and 182,000 in 1860, 30.2 percent of the population.

- 1840, to 1868 1,500 acts of violence were committed against Africans, and more than 350 Africans were murdered.

- 1844, Mexican Congressman Lucas Alaman reconfirmed the fact that all slaves brought to Texas after the July 13, 1824 degree was published should have gained their freedom in virtue of the provision of section 2 of the decree.[144]

- 1844, October, in response to the United States Government's threat to invade Mexico if she continued her refusal to recognize the independence of Texas, and to stop harboring runaway slaves, the Mexican Foreign Minister is reported to have said:

  > While one power is seeking more ground to stain by the slavery of an unfortunate branch of the human family, the other is endeavoring, by preserving what belongs to it, to

---

[144] *Iniciativa de ley etc. a message to Congress printed in Filisola's Guerra de Tejas. Volume II.* Page 595.

diminish the surface which the former wants for this detestable traffic. Let the world now say which of the two has justice and reason on its side.

- 1848, President Guerrero ordered a military occupation of the State to enforce the anti-slavery measure.

- 1848, Treaty of Guadalupe-Hidalgo ceded California, New Mexico, Arizona, Utah, Nevada, the rest of Texas and other territories for $15 million. Articles VIII and IX of the Treaty pledged that all Mexican citizens, including Africans:

  Who shall prefer to remain in the said territories [of Texas and what is now the Southwestern region of the United States] may either retain the title and rights of Mexican citizens, or acquire those of United States citizens, will be admitted at the proper time. to the enjoyment of all the rights of citizens of the United States, according to the principles of the Constitution; and the meantime, shall be maintained and protected in the free enjoyment of their liberty and property, and secured in the free exercise of their religion without restriction.

- 1851, several members of the Texas Rangers launch the first organized effort to invade Mexico in order to kidnap runaway slaves.

- 1861, 11-Dec, the United States, excluding the Confederate states, and Mexico concluded an extradition treaty that did not include fugitive slaves, and the U.S. Senate approved it on April 11, 1862.

- 1865, slavery formally ended in Texas after June 19, 1865 (Juneteenth), when Gen. Gordon Granger arrived at Galveston with occupying federal forces and announced emancipation.

- 1865, slavery replaced by slave-like conditions and practices, segregation and Jim Crow, and racism, racial discrimination, xenophobia and related intolerance continues until today.

We also formally and publicly request that you comply in an expedited manner with this Open Records Request, and that you waive all associated costs. Please be advised that we have disclosed this Request to the public and media.

In order to help you determine our status and make your decision on our fee waiver request, you should know that Bob Brown is an organizer and researcher, who has worked, studied and struggled for 41 years, within and for the Student, Civil and Human Rights, Black Power, National Liberation, Pan-African, and Peace Movements. See Attachment B.

We expect your positive response to this historic and precedent setting Public Information Request within 20 working days. Please be assured that we will exhaust administrative and political remedies. Thank you for your consideration.

Sincerely,
Bob Brown, co-director
Pan-African Roots

Pan-African Roots
1247 E Street SE
Washington, DC 20003
Tel: (202) 544-9355 - Fax: (202) 544-9359
Email: **paroots02@yahoo.com**

25 October 2004

President Jacque Chirac
c/o Embassy of the Republic of France
4101 Reservoir Road NW
Washington, DC 20007

Amended Request for Public Commitment and Information.
Request for Waiver of Costs and Expedited Review.

Dear President Chirac:

We request, pursuant to Loi no. 78-753 du 17 juillet 1978 de la liberte d'acces au documents administratifs and Loi no 79-587 du juillet 1979 relative a la motivation des actes administratifs et a l'amelioration des relations entre l'administration et le public, amended by Loi n 2000-321 du 12 avril 2000 relative aux droits des citoyens dans leurs relations avec les administrations (J.O. du 13 avril 2000), that you give us access to or copies of all records created or obtained by the Government of France, or under your authority and control, that pertain to, or reference:

- France's role, operations and activities, historically and currently, in facilitating, prohibiting or combating piracy and privateering, slavery and the slave trade, especially the Trans-Atlantic Slave Trade (also known as the Atlantic Trade, the Triangle Trade, the Colonial Trade, the West Indies Trade, etc.) in France and its colonies, especially Haiti, Martinique and Louisiana; and France's role in the struggle to declare them crimes against humanity, and to repair the damages and injuries that they inflicted upon untold generations of African People.

- France's role, operations and activities, historically and currently, in facilitating, prohibiting or combating slave-like conditions and practices, including but not limited to servitude, forced and compulsory labor, peonage, sharecropping, debt-bondage, sweatshop labor, convict-lease, chain-gang or prison labor, the sale of children, child prostitution, child pornography, the exploitation of child labour, the sexual mutilation of female children, the use of children in armed conflicts, the traffic in persons and in the sale of human organs, the exploitation of prostitution, and certain practices under apartheid and colonial regimes, segregation, racism and racial discrimination, xenophobia and related intolerance.

- The role of the Ports of Nantes, Le Havre, Bordeaux, Marseille, Vannes, Saint Malo, La Rochelle, Bayonne, Rouen, and Brest, the Companie de Indies, the Caisse d'Escompte, the 200 shipping companies, the 166 key families, and all entities headquartered at the Ports, historically and currently, in slavery and the slave trade, and in the trade in slave-produced products such as sugar, molasses, rum, cotton, tobacco, etc.

- Slave, urban and racial disturbances, riots, rebellions, and revolts, runaway slaves, fugitives beyond borders, related claims or requests, and demands for restitution and reparations.

- All treaties or agreements, bilateral or multilateral, or diplomatic communications, correspondence, discussions, public and secret, between the United States Government and its Officials (all levels, branched and agencies) and the French, or all other governments with respect to the above or related subjects.

156

- The United Nations World Conference Against Racism, Racial Discrimination, Xenophobia and Related Intolerance (WCAR), including its preparatory, regional and expert meetings and seminars, the White House Interagency Task Force on the U.N. World Conference Against Racism, the U.S. Governmental Delegation, the U.S. Non-Governmental Delegation, the UN Intergovernmental Working Group on the effective implementation of the Durban Declaration and Programme of Action, and the UNESCO Slave Route Project.

- All governments, agencies (federal, state, county or local), corporations, non-governmental organizations, institutions, churches, families, individuals, or entities, domestic or foreign who participated or invested in, or made profits from the above referenced crimes against humanity; and who owns or benefits from these historical and continuing crimes today, including but not limited to those listed in Appendix A.

As you are aware, the world Conference Against Racism, Racial Discrimination, Xenophobia and Related Intolerance (WCAR) met from 31 August to 3 September 2001, in Durban, South Africa. Reports reveal that 18,810 delegates from 170 countries participated in WCAR, including 16 heads of state, 58 foreign ministers, 44 ministers, 7,000 non-governmental representatives, and 1,300 journalists. The WCAR Final Declaration and Programme of Action:

> Acknowledge[s] that slavery and the slave trade, including the Trans-Atlantic Slave Trade, were appalling tragedies in the history of humanity not only because of their abhorrent barbarism but also in terms of their magnitude, organized nature especially their negation of the essence of the victims, ... acknowledge[s] that slavery and the slave trade are a crime against humanity and should have always been so, especially the Trans-Atlantic slave trade and are among the major sources and manifestations of racism, racial discrimination, xenophobia and related intolerance,... and invite[s] the international community members to honour the memory of the victims of these tragedies. [**Emphasis added.**]

> Further note[s] that some [countries} have taken the initiative of regretting or expressing remorse or presenting apologies, and call on all those who have yet contributed to restoring the dignity of all the victims to find appropriate ways to do so... [145]

You are perhaps not aware, that on May 17, 1860, the second National Republican Convention adopted its 1860 National Republican Platform, which declared it resolved:

> 7. That the new dogma that the Constitution of its own force carries slavery into any or all of the territories of the United States, is a dangerous political heresy, at variance with the explicit provisions of that instrument itself, with contemporaneous exposition, and with legislative and judicial precedent, is revolutionary in its tendency and subversive of the peace and harmony of the country.

> 8. That the formal condition of all the territory of the United States is that of freedom; that as our republican fathers, when they had abolished slavery in all our national territory, ordained that no "person should be deprived of life, liberty or property, without due process of law," it becomes our duty, by legislation, whenever such legislation is necessary, to maintain this provision of the constitution against all attempts to violate it; and we deny the authority of congress, of a territorial legislature, or of any individuals, to give legal existence to slavery in any territory of the United States.

> 9. That we brand the recent re-opening of the African Slave Trade, under the cover of our national flag, aided by perversions of judicial power, as a crime against humanity, and a burning

---

[145] World Conference Secretariat. Office of the United Nations High Commissioner for Human Rights. Available from http://www.unhchr.ch/html/racism/02-documents-cnt.html

shame to our country and age, and we call upon congress to take prompt and efficient measured for the total and final suppression of the execrable traffic.[146] [**Emphasis added.**]

In 1808, the United States Government prohibited its citizens from participating in the international slave trade, declaring it piracy in 1820, and participation in it punishable by death. Despite this prohibition, a minimum of 250,000 and perhaps as many as 1,000,000 Africans were kidnapped, enslaves, and illegally imported into the United States via Cuba between 1809 and 1861. In 1839, a prime male slave could be purchased in Cuba for $400 and then sold into slavery for life in Richmond for $1,000 or Charleston for $1,150 or Savannah for $1,200 or New Orleans for $1,250. The average daily wage was one dollar. President James Madison reported to Congress in 1810 that:

> It appears that American citizens are instrumental in carrying on a traffic in enslaved Africans, equally in violation of the laws of humanity, and in defiance of those of their own country. The same just and benevolent motives which produced the interdiction in force against this criminal conduct, will doubtless be felt in Congress, in devising further means of suppressing the evil.

The 1860 Republican National Convention selected Abraham Lincoln as its Presidential nominee. He campaigned on this platform, and "won the presidency with almost half a million voted more than [Stephen] Douglas, his closest rival. [Lincoln] won the election garnering 39.8 percent of the popular vote. This election firmly established the Republican hold on the presidency for 60 of the next 100 years.

You are perhaps also not aware that William Lloyd Garrison was the first person to declare slavery a crime against humanity in the inaugural edition (1831) of his Liberator newspaper; or that on November 12, 1849, the Vermont Legislature passed "*Joint Resolution No. 42.--Resolutions Relating To The Subject of Slavery*," declaring it:

> Resolved by the Senate and House of Representatives, that Slavery is a crime against humanity, and a sore evil in the body politic that was excused by the framers of the Federal Constitution as a crime entailed upon the country by their predecessors, and tolerated solely as a thing of inexorable necessity.[147] [**Emphasis added.**]

You Sir, are reported to have said that abolition was a founding act of the French Republican history that helped to "reinforce the unity of the nation."

It is well-settled, as the WCAR Final Declaration and your statement confirm, that prohibitions against piracy and privateering, slavery and the slave trade, including the Trans-Atlantic Slave Trade, and against slave-like conditions and practices, including colonialism, segregation and apartheid, forced and compulsory labor, racism and racial discrimination, xenophobia and related intolerance have achieved the level of customary international law, have attained the status of jus cogens, and are obligato erga omnes. Unfortunately, the overwhelming majority of the WCAR Delegated and the public, especially African People world-wide, wrongly believe that this status has only recently been acquired.[148]

Permit us to suggest, as Ethan A. Nadelman suggests, that "most global prohibition regimes, including those targeted against piracy, slavery, and drug trafficking, evidence a common evolutionary pattern consisting of four or five stages."[149] At different stages in their development: (1) the activity is legal and some states participate in it; (2) national and international forces, non-governmental and

---

[146] Central Pacific Railroad Photographic History Museum. *Republican Party National Platform, 1860*. Available from http://cprr.org/Museum/Ephemera/Republican_Platform_1860.html.

[147] The *Acts and Resolves Passed By The Legislature Of The State of Vermont At The October Session, 1849*. Published By authority. Montpelier: E. P. Walton & Son. 1849.

[148] People incorrectly believe that "the term was first used in the preamble of the Hague Convention of 1907. Wikipedia. Crime against humanity. Available from http://en.wikipedia.org/wiki/Crime_against_humanity.

[149] Ethan A. Nadelman. *Global prohibition regimes: the evolution of norms in international society*. Printed in Transnational Crime / edited by Nikos Passas.

governmental, attempt to redefine the activity as evil and illegal; (3) these forces agitate for its suppression and criminalization; (4) the activity becomes the subject of national and international criminal laws, conventions and treaties, police and military action; and (5) finally, the activity is prohibited globally.[150] It is axiomatic that this development is extremely uneven, unequal, and costly in time, space and human lives, in justice and equity.

Permit us also to suggest that Judge Fouad Ammoun of the International Court of Justice (ICJ) "has [accurately] described the development of Africa ... [and] eloquently remarked on the evolution of mankind's struggle with the issue of slavery and colonization."[151] He informs us that "before there fell upon it the two greatest plagues in the recorded history of mankind: the slave trade, which ravaged Africa for centuries on an unprecedented scale; and colonialism, which exploited humanity and natural wealth to a relentless extreme," ... Africa boasted thriving states and empires dating back to Roman times."[152]

Judge Ammoun also informs us that "historians have outlined the upward march of mankind from the time when homo sapiens appeared on the face of the globe, first of all in the Near East in what was the land of Canaan[153], up to the age of the greatest thinkers and more particularly, throughout the whole of history of social progress, from the slavery of Antiquity to man's [and woman's] inevitable, irreversible drive towards equality and freedom. This march is like time itself. It never stops. Nothing can stand in its way for long. The texts, whether they be laws, constitutions, declarations, covenants or charters, do but define it and mark its successive phases. They are a mere record of it. In other words, the progressive rights which men, [women] and peopled enjoy are the result much less of those texts than of human progress to which they bear witness."[154]

We are confident that the records requested by and through this historic and precedent setting Federal Transparency and Access to Public Government Information Act Request will:

- Bear witness to and prove, once and for all, that piracy and privateering, slavery and the slave trade, including the Trans-Atlantic Slave Trade, and slave-like conditions and practices, including colonialism, segregation and apartheid, were and are illegal and prohibited, and were and are recognized as crimes against humanity when and where they were committed.

- Help define and mark the successive staged in the development of the 569-year historical and continuing Maafa,[155] and of the unyielding and continuing struggle against it.

- Document who the victims were, and who their descendants are today; who committed these crimes, which were and are the greatest theft of land, lives and labor in human history; how this unjust and illegal wealth was converted, consolidated, preserved and transferred across generations and centuries; and who owns and benefits from this unjust enrichment today.

We request that that you and the Government of France, formally and publicly reaffirm, once and for all, that slavery and the slave trade were and are illegal according to the edicts and municipal laws of France and its colonies, and according to canon law and international law; and that slavery and the slave trade were crimes against humanity:

- "Because God makes no slaves in the womb;"[156] because the prohibition of the slave trade is well-settled in the Bible in Timothy 1:10, Exodus 21:16, Deuteronomy 24:7, 1 Corinthians 5:11, 1

---

[150] Ibid.

[151] *Legal Consequences For States of the Continued Presence of South Africa in Namibia (South West Africa) Notwithstanding Security Council Resolution 276, 1971 I.C.J. 16, 86 (1971) (separate opinion of Judge Ammoun).*

[152] Recent evidence documents that African civilizations predate Roman times.

[153] Recent evidence documents that homo sapiens first emerged in East Africa.

[154] Ethan A. Nadelman. *Global prohibition regimes.*

[155] Dr. Marimba Ani. *Let The Circle Be Unbroken.* Maafa is a Kiswahili word for the 563-year historical and continuing enslavement and colonization of Africa and African People.

Corinthians 6:10 and Timothy 1:10-1; and because the Catholic Church was in the forefront of the struggle from 441 CE to 1890 to prohibit and abolish the trafficking in and enslavement of Christians, Europeans, the Indigenous Peoples of the Western Hemisphere, and African People.

- Because King Louis X of France issued an edict in 1315 abolishing slavery in France and the French Kingdom, declaring that," as all men are by nature free born, and as this kingdom is called the Kingdom of the Franks [freemen], it shall be so in reality;"[157] because slavery and the slave trade was contrary to the common law of France, and "no slave could touch French soil without instantly becoming a freeman;"[158] because the Code Noir and its offshoots, including the Louisiana Code, were repugnant and inferior to cannon law and customary international law, were never approved by the French Parliament, and were therefore null and void; because Champagne and Bordeaux were the first villages in France to demand, once again, that slavery be abolished in France; because the French National Assembly abolished slavery once again, on February 4, 1794, in France and all French colonies, including Louisiana, and made more than 40,000 enslaves Africans in Louisiana citizens of France; and because the liberty and property of all French citizens, including the former slaves, was and is protected by treaties between France and the United States.

We request that you and the Government of France, formally and publicly reaffirm, once and for all, that slavery and the slave trade were and are crimes under French law, and that they were and are crimes against humanity because:

- 1315, King Louis X issued an edict for the abolition of slavery and the enfranchisement of the people:

    As all men are by nature free born, and as this kingdom is called the Kingdom of Franks [freemen], it shall be so in reality. It is therefore decreed that enfranchisements shall be granted throughout the whole kingdom upon just and reasonable conditions.[159]

- 1318, King Philip V, the Brother of King Louis X, reconfirmed the 1315 Edict.[160]

- 1571, the King issued a royal declaration stipulating that all persons are free in the French Kingdom: "as soon as a slave has reached these frontiers and becomes baptized, he is free."

- 1571, the Parliament of Bordeaux freed all African and Moorish slaves, declaring slavery illegal in France.

- 1628, the Petition of Right was passed.

- 1629, slavery was forbidden in France, once again.

- 1716, prohibition against bringing slaves into France.

- 1718, October, King Louis XV established rules about slaves living in metropolitan France.

- 1738-9, prohibition against bringing slaves into, and on slaves living in France are tightened.

- 1749, Montesquieu writes *The Spirit of Laws*, which condemns slavery as contrary to the fundamental principle of society.

---

[156] Rev. John G. Fee. *An Anti-Slavery Manual, or, The Wrongs of American Slavery Exposed By the Light of the Bible and of Facts, with A Remedy for the Evil (1851)*. Available from http://members.tripod.com/medicolegal/feeasm1851.htm

[157] Edward C. Rogers. *Slavery Illegality in All Ages and Nations*. Available from http://medicolegal.tripod.com/rogersuos.htm

[158] Ibid.

[159] Ibid.

[160] Ibid.

- 1754, 300,000 slaves in the French West Indies.

- 1770, French writer Abbe Raynal published a work calling for a 'Black Spartacus' to arise and avenge slavery which the author calls a crime against nature

- 1786, Louis XVI ordered the improvement of the fate of the slaves fate (break between 12 and 14 p.m. and from sunset to sunrise).

- 1788, 15-May, Constituent Assembly adopted the political rights of colored people born of free parents.

- 1788, February, the Société des Amis des Noirs (Society of the Friends of the Blacks) was founded.

- 1788, in the Le Jeune court case, 14 black slaves brought documented accusations of abuse against a white planter. The case was dismissed out of fear of inciting whites.

- 1789, on the eve of the Revolution, Champagne was the first French village to demand in its List of Grievances, that slavery be abolished.

- 1789, 14-July, French Revolution began.

- 1789, 25-August, the French National Assembly adopted the Declaration of the Rights of Man and of the Citizen, which proclaims the legal equality of all citizens and freedom of speech, press, assembly, and religion, but Napoleon allegedly repudiated this Declaration later.

- 1789, France's new Constitution abolished slavery and freed 700,000 African slaves in the French West Indies and Louisiana; but Napoleon allegedly revoked it later.

- 1789-90, the French Revolution encouraged 91 slave revolts in Martinique and Haiti (St Domingo).

- 1790, 28-March, the French Constituent Assembly, which took the place of the French National Assembly, considered the colonies a part of the French empire, and subject to its laws.

- 1791, 15-May, Africans in the French colonies who are born of free parents are declared equal in civic rights with whites.

- 1791, the French National Assembly granted Africans born of free parents in the French West Indies voting rights and the same privileged as all citizens. The 30,000 white citizens of Saint Domingue prepare to secede.

- 1791, French Constitutional Assembly abolished slavery in France, where there were no slaves, according to the former decision of Louis the XIVth.[161]

- 1791, 22-August, 100,000 slaves revolt in the French colony of St. Domingue, marking the beginning of the Haitian Revolution.[162]

- 1792, 4-April, French National Assembly issued final decree giving all free Africans full citizenship.

- 1792, 19-November, the French Convention declared its willingness to help all subjected peoples achieve their liberty.

---

[161] Pascal Boyries. *Chronology of the abolition of French slavery*. Available from http://perso.wanadoo.fr/yekrik.yekrak/chronoeng.htm.

[162] Lerone Bennett. "*Major Revolts and Escapes*." Before the Mayflower. Johnson Publications.

- 1793, 29-August, Sonthonax arrived in Haiti (Saint-Dominique) as part of a commission to enforce King Louis XVI's edict that both the mulattos and the slaves were to be freed.

- 1794, 4-February, the French National Assembly abolished slavery in France and the French colonies, once again, where there were no slaves, according to the decision of Louis XIV, and confers full citizenship on more than 500,000 Africans in the French West Indies and 40,000 Africans in Louisiana colony.[163]

- 1794, 2-June, Victor Hugo arrived in Guadeloupe and abolished slavery.

- 1795, the French decree of pluviôse 16 year II abolished slavery once again in the French colonies.[164]

- 1796, 18-July, Baco et Burnel landed in Mauritius, and abolished slavery, but is forced to sail away. Slavery illegally remained in effect in Mauritius and Reunion.

- 1799, 13-June, Toussaint L'Ouverture of Haiti signed a treaty with Britain, including secret provisions.

- 1801, 26-July, L'Ouverture published and promulgated a new constitution for San Domingue which abolished slavery.

- 1801, Napoleon illegally decided to establish slavery in France and its colonies.[165]

- 1802, 26-January, Toussaint L'Ouverture invaded Santo Domingo and declared slavery abolished.

- 1803, 20-December, France formally ceded Louisiana Province to the United States. The Louisiana Purchase Treaty stipulated that:

   The inhabitants of the ceded territory shall be incorporated in the Union of the United States, and admitted as soon as possible, according to the principles of the Federal Constitution, to the enjoyment of all the rights, advantages, and immunities of citizens of the United States; and in the meantime, they shall be maintained in the free enjoyment of their liberty, property, and the religion which they profess.[166]

- 1850, 20-March, in a speech to the United States Senate, Senator S.P. Chase said:

   This stipulation, interpreted according to the plain sense of its terms, and carried into effect, would have enfranchised every slave in Louisiana: for no one, I apprehend will venture to affirm that the slaves were not inhabitants. Independently of this stipulation, it was the duty of the Government--even more imperative than in 1787 [the Northwest Ordinance], for since then the whole country south of the Ohio and east of the Mississippi had been formed into slave States and slave Territories--to establish freedom as the fundamental law of the new acquisition. But this duty was not performed. These was some feeble legislation against the introduction of slaves from foreign countries, and of slaves imported since 1798 from other States; but that was all, and that was useless.

- 1815, Napoleon decreed abolition in France during the Hundred Days and the restoration government accepted the decree.

---

[163] Pascal Boyries. *Chronology of the abolition of French slavery.*

[164] Ibid.

[165] Ibid.

[166] The Avalon Project at Yale Law School. *The Louisiana Purchase Treaty, April 30, 1903.*

- 1815, March 29, in the Treaty of Paris, France and Britain declared the slave trade repugnant to principles of natural justice, and France agreed to limit the slave trade to its own colonies and abolish it in 5-years.

- 1815, thanks to the efforts of the Committee on the International Slave Trade Issue, the Vatican and Britain, the Congress of Vienna condemned slave trade.

- 1816, 29-Mar, Napoleon signed a decree abolishing the French slave trade.

- 1818-19, France abolished the slave trade was again, effective in 1826, and it was still illegal for slaves to live in France, "where there were no slaves."

- 1824, France prohibited her ships from transporting slaves across the Mediterranean.

- 1831, all French free people are declared equal and anti-slavery legislation is passed, once again.

- 1831, France and Britain signed a treaty for mutual search of suspected slave ships

- 1836, 26-November, the Parliament of Bordeaux freed all slaves (blacks and moors), declaring, once again, that slavery is illegal in France.

- 1838, 9-June, France recognized Haiti's final and complete independence.

- 1848, 27-April, France abolished slavery, once again, thanks to the work of Victor Schoelder, in all of its colonies, freeing 74,000 people in Martinique, and promising compensation to the slave holders.

- 1850-51, Britain and France entered into a new agreement for a mutual right of search within certain areas.

- 1859-61, France abolished the engage system of forced labor in its colonies.

We further request that you and the Government of France explain why, despite these principled and clear edicts and laws which prohibited slavery and the slave trade, the following activities and events were permitted:

- 1638, France's North American colonies were opened to the trade in enslaved Africans.

- 1642, Louis XIII authorized involvement of France in the triangular trade.

- 1644, a French privateer brought to New Netherlands some Africans who had been taken from a Spanish ship, and sold them as slaves because of their race, despite their claims to be free.

- 1670, a French royal decree brought French shippers into the slave trade, with the rationale that the labor of enslaved Africans helped the growth of France's island colonies.

- 1671, Louis XIV authorized the French slave trade in Saint-Domingue.

- 1676, the Senegal Company transported enslaved Africans to the West Indies and Guiana.

- 1677, England and France sign a maritime agreement permitting English ships to carry Dutch cargoes without fear of French interference.

- 1677-79, French forces in Africa took Dutch ports on the Senegal River and captured Gorée near Cape Verde on October 30

- 1678, there were 27,000 slaves in the French West Indies.

- 1679, the French captured Dutch posts along the Senegalese coast.

- 1685, establishment of the Guinea Company to engage in the slave trade.

- 1685, A Code Noir issued at Paris established humane relations with respect to treatment of slaves on French colonial plantations, but planters generally disregarded the code.

- 1685 May or March, King Louis XIV normalized the triangular trade by imposing the Code Noir (Black Codes) in the French colonies, rejecting the slave from the human category. The Code Noir required religious instruction for slaves, permitted intermarriage, outlawed the working of slaves on Sundays and holidays, but forbade the liberation of mulatto children reaching 21 if their mothers were still enslaved. The progressive elements of the Code Noir were ignored by the French settlers.

- 1688, French Huguenot refugees arrived in South Africa where they strengthened the Dutch settlement founded in 1652.

- 1697, the French established a colonial empire in West Africa under du Brue, in order to secure slaves.

- 1698, the French settle Louisiana, and an Agreement between the St-Domingo and the Guiana company is reached, to boost the slave trade and bring more Africans to St-Domingo. In St-Domingo there are 500 emancipated slaves and 9,000 slaves; in Guadeloupe 239 emancipated slaves and 4,780 slaves; in Martinique 507 emancipated slaves

- 1701, refined sugar, which was produced by slave labor, is the most important export of France.

- 1707, castration was proposed as a legal punishment for slaves in St-Domingo; the crown rejected this proposal.

- 1713, creation of the second Louisiana Company to engage in the slave trade.

- 1716, the first group of African slaves is brought to the Louisiana territory.

- 1724, Mar, A Royal Edict Touching on the State and Discipline of the Black Slaves of Louisiana was proclaimed, establishing the Code Noir in Louisiana.

- 1754, St Domingo 172,000 inhabitants, among them 154,000 slaves.

- 1763, Treaty of Paris ends the Seven Years War: Grenada, Dominica, St Vincent and Tobago given to Britain. Newfoundland [fishing], Guadalupe and Martinique [sugar], Dakar [gum]) given to France.

- 1778, 6-Feb, France recognized the United States as a sovereign nation in Treaty of Amity, also recognizing slavery and the slave trade.

- 1779, St Domingo had 288,800 inhabitants among whom 7,005 free colored people and 248,000 slaves. There were 673,000 slaves in the French West Indies.

- 1783, 3-Sep, the Treaty of Paris is signed by the United States, France, England, Spain, and the Netherlands, ending the American Revolution. Britain liberates and evacuates slaves, despite U.S. protests and claims.

- 1786, 28-June, Treaty of Peace and Friendship With Morocco ends the enslavement of French citizens.

- 1791, in Louisiana, twenty-three slaves are hanged and three white sympathizers deported, following suppression of an African revolt.[167]

---

[167] Roger Davis and Wanda Neal-Davis. *Chronology, A Historical Review, Major Events in Black History 1492 through 1953.*

- 1793, September, British troops, under the leadership of General Whyte, invaded Haiti (St. Domingue) to suppress the Revolution and reinstitute slavery.

- 1794, 8-June, General Whyte issued a Proclamation to the People Haiti ordering the newly freed slaves to lay down their arms and return to the plantations within eight days or be put to death. This British effort to seize control of Haiti was defeated, and thousands of British soldiers lost their lived in the attempt.

- 1796, slave uprisings in Louisiana are suppressed, 50 Africans killed and executed.[168]

- 1800, 1-October, Louisiana Province secretly transferred from Spain back to France in the Treaty of St. Idefonso. Louisiana was "transferred "to Spain, whose King was a cousin of the King of France, in order to keep it out of British hands, and stop the emancipation of its slaves.

- 1802, 20 May, Napoleon sent General Le Clerc, his brother-in-law, with 30,000 French soldiers, to overthrow Toussaint L'Ouverture, and re-impose slavery in Haiti, the French West Indies, and Louisiana.

  > Napoleon asked Le Clerc: Which has been the most prosperous regime for the colonies? Le Clerc responded: The previous one. Well put it back Napoleon decided.[169]

- 1802, 7-June, Toussaint L'Ouverture was betrayed and sent to France in chains.

- 1803, Le Clerc defeated in Haiti, and 24,000 French troops lost to disease and African resistance.

- 1803, March. Pierre Clement de Laussat, whom Napoleon appointed Colonial Prefect, arrived in New Orleans.[170]

- 1803, 7-April, Toussaint L'Ouverture was murdered in captivity in France.

- 1803, 30 April, Napoleon decided to sell Louisiana to the United States for $15,000,000. Robert Livingston (Ambassador to France) and James Madison (Secretary of State) negotiated the sale. Two British banks, Barings and Hopes, lent the money to the US government.[171]

- 1803, 6-June, full powers granted by Napoleon to Colonial Prefect Pierre Clement de Laussat authorizing him to transfer Louisiana to the United States.[172]

- 1803, November, Laussat formally took control of Louisiana when Salcedo, the Spanish Governor, handed him the keys to the City of New Orleans. De Laussat reorganized the city government, and appointed a Mayor and Council of Twelve.[173]

- 1803, 8-November, Mayor De Bore convened the first session of the New Orleans Council.[174]

- 1803, 16 December, Laussat illegally issued a Decree re-instituting and upholding the Louisiana Code of 1724, revoked the French citizenship of, and re-enslaved 40,000 Africans who had been freed by French law in 1794, but not in reality.[175]

---

[168] Ibid.

[169] *Napoleon Restores Slavery.* 2003. Available from http://www.Sakpasse.com.

[170] *A Guide to the Papers of Pierre Clement Laussat: Napoleon's Prefect for the Colony of Louisiana and of General Claude Perrin Victor. Historic New Orleans Collection.* March 1993. Louisiana State University.

[171] *A Comparative Chronology of Money from Ancient Times to the Present Day, 1800 - 1849,* Based on the book: A History of Money from Ancient Times to the Present Day by Glyn Davies, rev. ed. Cardiff: University of Wales Press, 1996. 716p.

[172] *A Guide to the Papers of Pierre Clement Laussat.*

[173] Ruth Asher. *History of the New Orleans Police Department.*

[174] Ibid.

[175] *A Guide to the Papers of Pierre Clement Laussat.*

- 1804, 1-January, Haiti is established as an independent republic. All slaves are freed and all whites that do not flee are allegedly killed. The whites flee to Baltimore and New Orleans.[176]

- 1804, March, Code Napoleon enacted in France.

- 1804, Congress restricted slaves coming into Louisiana Territory to the property of actual settlers, but rejected a motion to limit slavery to one year. The first part of the law was not implemented.

- 1807, President Jefferson imposed a trade embargo on Haiti.

- 1807, 22-December, Embargo Act of 1807 imposed an embargo, which allowed no exports from the US to any country, and restricted imports of certain British and French products.

- 1812, 30-April, Louisiana became a state, with a Constitution allowing slavery.

- 1821, the Missouri Compromise prohibited slavery in the northern half of the Louisiana Purchase.

- 1821, the U.S. Congress declared the transport of slaves to be a form of piracy, yet the slave trade into Louisiana continued, via Cuba.

- 1844, France introduced engagé or forced labour emigration to colonies in order to circumvent the anti-slavery treaties.

Upon information and belief, the Government of France, its Royal Family, and the Bonaparte Family were and are responsible for:

- 1.5 million Africans who were kidnapped from Africa and sold into slavery in the Americas, and for the destruction of countless villages, nation-states and civilizations in Africa.

- 40,000 Africans were illegally held in slavery in Louisiana Province on the eve of its Purchase in 1803; 557,772 Africans were still being illegally held in slavery in Louisiana, Missouri and Arkansas in 1865; and their descendants were and are forced to suffer slave-like conditions and practices, segregation, racism and racial discrimination, xenophobia and related intolerance until today.

- The misery of more than 179 million of their descendants who are scattered, suffering and struggling in more than 24 countries today, under slave-like conditions and practices, segregation, racism and racial discrimination, xenophobia and related intolerance until today.

We hope that you will comply with this Request for a Public Commitment and Information in an expedited manner, and that you will waive all associated costs. Please be advised that we have sent a copy of this Request to the public and the media.

In order to help you determine our status and make your decision on our fee waiver request, you should know that Bob Brown is an organizer and researcher, who has worked, studied and struggled for 41 years, within and for the Student, Civil and Human Rights, Black Power, National Liberation, Pan-African, and Peace Movements. See Attachment B.

We expect your positive response to this historic and precedent setting Information Request within 20 working days. Thank you for your consideration.

Sincerely,
Bob Brown, co-director
Pan-African Roots

---

[176] James Trager. *The People's Chronology*. 1994. MS Bookshelf.

Pan-African Roots
1247 E Street SE
Washington, DC 20003
Tel: (202) 544-9355 - Fax: (202) 544-9359
Email: **paroots02@yahoo.com**

25 October 2004

Mrs. Kathleen Blanco, Governor
Office of the Governor
P. O. Box 94004
Baton Rouge, LA 70804-9004

Open Records Request.
Fee Waiver and Expedited Review Request.
cc: Open Records Officer and Open Records Appeals Officer.

Dear Governor Blanco:

As you are aware, King Louis X of France issued an edict in 1315 abolishing slavery in France and the French Kingdom, declaring that," as all men are by nature free born, and as this kingdom is called the Kingdom of the Franks [freemen], it shall be so in reality;"[177] slavery and the slave trade was contrary to the common law of France, and "no slave could touch French soil without instantly becoming a freeman;"[178] the Code Noir and its offshoots, including the Louisiana Code, were repugnant and inferior to canon law and customary international law, were never approved by the French Parliament, and were therefore null and void; Champagne and Bordeaux were the first villages in France to demand, once again, that slavery be abolished in France; the French National Assembly abolished slavery once again, on February 4, 1794, in France and all French colonies, including Louisiana, and made more than 40,000 enslaved Africans in Louisiana citizens of France; and the liberty and property of all French citizens, including the former slaves, was and is protected by treaties between France and the United States.

As you are also aware, 40,000 Africans were illegally held in slavery in Louisiana Province on the eve of its Purchase in 1803; 311,726 Africans were still being illegally held in slavery by 22,033 slave-holding families in 1860; and their descendants were and are forced to suffer slave-like conditions and practices, segregation, racism and racial discrimination, xenophobia and related intolerance until today.

You are perhaps not aware, that on May 17, 1860, the second National Republican Convention adopted its 1860 National Republican Platform, which declared it resolved:

> 7. That the new dogma that the Constitution of its own force carries slavery into any or all of the territories of the United States, is a dangerous political heresy, at variance with the explicit provisions of that instrument itself, with contemporaneous exposition, and with legislative and judicial precedent, is revolutionary in its tendency and subversive of the peace and harmony of the country.

> 8. That the formal condition of all the territory of the United States is that of freedom; that as our republican fathers, when they had abolished slavery in all our national territory, ordained that no "person should be deprived of life, liberty or property, without due process of law," it becomes our duty, by legislation, whenever such legislation is necessary, to maintain this provision of the constitution against all attempts to violate it; and we deny the authority of congress, of a territorial legislature, or of any individuals, to give legal existence to slavery in any territory of the United States.

---

[177] Edward C. Rogers. *Slavery Illegality in All Ages and Nations.* Available from http://medicolegal.tripod.com/rogersuos.htm
[178] Ibid.

9. That we brand the recent re-opening of the African Slave Trade, under the cover of our national flag, aided by perversions of judicial power, as a **crime against humanity, and a burning shame to our country and age,** and we call upon congress to take prompt and efficient measured for the total and final suppression of the execrable traffic.[179] [**Emphasis added.**]

In 1808, the United States Government prohibited its citizens from participating in the international slave trade, declaring it piracy in 1820, and participation in it punishable by death. Despite this prohibition, a minimum of 250,000 and perhaps as many as 1,000,000 Africans were kidnapped, enslaves, and illegally imported into the United States via Cuba between 1809 and 1861. In 1839, a prime male slave could be purchased in Cuba for $400 and then sold into slavery for life in Richmond for $1,000 or Charleston for $1,150 or Savannah for $1,200 or New Orleans for $1,250. The average daily wage was one dollar. President James Madison reported to Congress in 1810 that:

> It appears that American citizens are instrumental in carrying on a traffic in enslaved Africans, equally in violation of the laws of humanity, and in defiance of those of their own country. The same just and benevolent motives which produced the interdiction in force against this criminal conduct, will doubtless be felt in Congress, in devising further means of suppressing the evil.

The 1860 Republican National Convention selected Abraham Lincoln as its Presidential nominee. He campaigned on this platform, and "won the presidency with almost half a million voted more than [Stephen] Douglas, his closest rival. [Lincoln] won the election garnering 39.8 percent of the popular vote. This election firmly established the Republican hold on the presidency for 60 of the next 100 years.

You are perhaps also not aware that William Lloyd Garrison was the first person to declare slavery a crime against humanity in the inaugural edition (1831) of his Liberator newspaper; or that on November 12, 1849, the Vermont Legislature passed "*Joint Resolution No. 42.--Resolutions Relating To The Subject of Slavery*," declaring it:

> Resolved by the Senate and House of Representatives, that Slavery is a **crime against humanity, and a sore evil** in the body politic that was excused by the framers of the Federal Constitution as a crime entailed upon the country by their predecessors, and tolerated solely as a thing of inexorable necessity.[180] [**Emphasis added.**]

We request, pursuant to La. Rev. Stat. Ann. sections 44:1 to 44:42, that you give us access to or copies of all records created or obtained by the State of Louisiana, or under your authority and control, that pertain to, or reference:

- Louisiana's role, operations and activities, historically and currently, in facilitating, prohibiting or combating piracy and privateering, slavery and the slave trade, especially the Trans-Atlantic Slave Trade ((also known as the Atlantic Trade, the Triangle Trade, the Colonial Trade, the West Indies Trade, etc.), and its role in the struggle to declare them crimes against humanity, and to repair the damages and injuries that they inflicted upon untold generations of Africans.

- Louisiana's role, operations and activities, historically and currently, in facilitating, prohibiting or combating slave-like conditions and practices, including but not limited to servitude, forced and compulsory labor, peonage, sharecropping, debt-bondage, sweatshop labor, convict-lease, chain-gang or prison labor, the sale of children, child prostitution, child pornography, the exploitation of child labour, the sexual mutilation of female children, the use of children in armed conflicts, the traffic in persons and in the sale of human organs, the exploitation of prostitution, and certain

---

[179] Central Pacific Railroad Photographic History Museum. *Republican Party National Platform, 1860.* Available from http://cprr.org/Museum/Ephemera/Republican_Platform_1860.html.

[180] The *Acts and Resolves Passed By The Legislature Of The State of Vermont At The October Session, 1849.* Published By authority. Montpelier: E. P. Walton & Son. 1849.

practices under apartheid and colonial regimes, segregation, racism and racial discrimination, xenophobia and related intolerance.

- Louisiana's knowledge of and response to France's and Haiti's abolition of slavery and the slave trade; emancipation of slaves and granting them citizenship; Napoleon's efforts to reinstitute the Code Noir and Louisiana Code of 1724 and slavery; and related claims, diplomatic discussions, agreement and treaties.

- Slave, urban and racial disturbances, riots, rebellions, and revolts, runaway slaves, fugitives beyond borders, related claims or requests, and demands for restitution and reparations.

- The legal status of slavery, the slave trade, and slave-like practices and conditions, including segregation, convict lease, chain-gang or prison labor in Louisiana's Constitutions, Civil Code and Revised Statues from 1803 to the present; and all state and local court cases by and about the subjects listed above.

- The role of the Port of New Orleans, and all entities headquartered at the Port, historically and currently, in slavery and the slave trade, and in the trade in slave-produced products such as sugar, molasses, rum, cotton, tobacco, etc. Upon information and belief," from 1866 to 1872, the Port of New Orleans received 6,114,000 bales of cotton, one-third of the entire production of the United States. The 1873 New Orleans city directory listed 249 cotton-related businesses, including the Orleans Cotton Press."[181]

- All treaties or agreements, bilateral or multilateral, or diplomatic communications, correspondence, discussions, public and secret, between the United States Government and its Officials (all levels, branched and agencies) and the French, or all other governments with respect to the above or related subjects.

- All governments, agencies (federal, state, county or local), corporations, non-governmental organizations, institutions, churches, families, individuals, or entities, domestic or foreign who participated or invested in, or made profits from the above referenced crimes against humanity; and who owns or benefits from these historical and continuing crimes today, including but not limited to those listed in Appendix A.

We request access to or copies of all records that pertain to, or reference the subjects listed in the above paragraphs, for the following parishes:

1860 United States Census	Number of Slave-Holding Families	Number of Slaves	Value of Slaves ($1,000 @)	Value of Plantations
Ascension	277	7,376	$ 7,376,000	$7,728,141
Assumption	478	8,096	$ 8,096,000	$8,414,383
Avoyelles	554	7,185	$ 7,185,000	$6,088,871
Bienville	M	5,000	$ 5,000,000	
Bossier	427	8,000	$ 8,000,000	$5,700,159
Caddo	490	7,338	$ 7,338,000	$4,434,386
Calcasieu	177	1,171	$ 1,171,000	$542,803

[181] Pamela D. Arceneaux. The Cotton Industry in New Orleans 1835-1885.

Caldwell	188	1,945	$ 1,945,000	$2,053,975
Carroll	598	13,908	$ 13,908,000	$16,907,906
Catahoula	327	6,113	$ 6,113,000	$6,477,579
Claiborne	794	7,848	$ 7,848,000	$3,816,510
Concordia	250	12,542	$ 12,542,000	$14,140,784
De Soto	575	8,507	$ 8,507,000	$3,381,000
East Baton Rouge	651	8,570	$ 8,570,000	$3,699,955
East Feliciana	577	10,593	$ 10,593,000	$3,075,326
Franklin	309	3,402	$ 3,402,000	$2,080,123
Iberville	442	10,680	$ 10,680,000	$14,708,779
Jackson	405	4,098	$ 4,098,000	$2,009,029
Jefferson	309	5,120	$ 5,120,000	$3,089,135
Lafayette	492	4,463	$ 4,463,000	$1,803,316
Lafourche	471	6,395	$ 6,395,000	$5,108,787
Livingston	166	1,311	$ 1,311,000	$549,643
Madison	329	12,477	$ 12,477,000	$12,824,737
Morehouse	466	6,569	$ 6,569,000	$6,189,753
Natchitoches	621	9,434	$ 9,434,000	$5,801,278
Orleans	4,169	14,484	$ 14,484,000	$1,714,290
Ouachita	181	2,840	$ 2,840,000	$2,701,026
Plaquemines	231	5,385	$ 5,385,000	$3,528,896
Pointe Coupee	634	12,903	$ 12,903,000	$11,889,336
Rapides	524	15,358	$ 15,358,000	$11,959,942
Sabine	211	1,713	$ 1,713,000	$757,747
St Bernard	120	2,240	$ 2,240,000	$5,770
St Charles	138	4,182	$ 4,182,000	$4,414,754
St Helena	337	3,711	$ 3,711,000	$1,895,990
St James	469	8,090	$ 8,090,000	$5,378,043
St John The Baptist	355	4,594	$ 4,594,000	$3,322,710
St Landry	963	11,436	$ 11,436,000	$6,281,507
St Martin	605	7,358	$ 7,358,000	$5,688,503
St Mary	432	13,057	$ 13,057,000	$12,326,645
St Tammany	169	1,841	$ 1,841,000	$307,848
Tensas	330	14,592	$ 14,592,000	$17,156,388
Terrebonne	248	6,785	$ 6,785,000	$8,713,709
Union	430	3,745	$ 3,745,000	$1,802,980
Vermillion	184	1,316	$ 1,316,000	$1,013,895
Washington	216	1,690	$ 1,690,000	$550,600
West Baton Rouge	207	5,340	$ 5,340,000	$5,152,785
West Feliciana	298	9,571	$ 9,571,000	$3,163,781
Winn	209	1,354	$ 1,354,000	$756,289
TOTAL	21,824	330,372	$ 330,372,000	$250,353,503

We are especially interested in knowing who owned and controlled the plantations and firms; from whom did they acquire their raw materials and at what price; to whom did they sell their products and at what price; what if any taxes or revenue did the Governments of Louisiana (state, county and local) and the United States receive; and who owns or controls these farms, companies and related industries today.

We also request access to or copies of all records that pertain to or reference the subjects listed above for the following activities and events:

- 1315, King Louis X issued an edict for the abolition of slavery and the enfranchisement of the people:

  > As all men are by nature free born, and as this kingdom is called the Kingdom of Franks [freemen], it shall be so in reality. It is therefore decreed that enfranchisements shall be granted throughout the whole kingdom upon just and reasonable conditions.

- 1318, King Philip V, the Brother of King Louis X, reconfirmed the 1315 Edict.

- 1571, the King issued a royal declaration stipulating that all persons are free in the French Kingdom: "as soon as a slave has reached these frontiers and becomes baptized, he is free."

- 1571, the Parliament of Bordeaux freed all African and Moorish slaves, declaring slavery illegal in France.

- 1628, the Petition of Right was passed.

- 1629, slavery was forbidden in France, once again.

- 1716, prohibition against bringing slaves into France.

- 1718, October, King Louis XV established rules about slaves living in metropolitan France.

- 1738-9, prohibition against bringing slaves into, and on slaves living in France are tightened.

- 1749, Montesquieu writes *The Spirit of Laws*, which condemns slavery as contrary to the fundamental principle of society.

- 1754, 300,000 slaves in the French West Indies.

- 1770, French writer Abbe Raynal published a work calling for a 'Black Spartacus' to arise and avenge slavery which the author calls a crime against nature

- 1786, Louis XVI ordered the improvement of the fate of the slaves (e.g. a break between 12 and 2 p.m. and from sunset to sunrise).

- 1788, 15-May, Constituent Assembly adopted the political rights of colored people born of free parents.

- 1788, February, the Société des Amis des Noirs (Society of the Friends of the Blacks) was founded.

- 1788, in the Le Jeune court case, 14 black slaves brought documented accusations of abuse against a white planter. The case was dismissed out of fear of inciting whites.

- 1789, on the eve of the Revolution, Champagny was the first French village to demand in its List of Grievance, that slavery be abolished.

- 1789, 14-July, French Revolution began.

- 1789, 25-August, the French National Assembly adopted the Declaration of the Rights of Man and of the Citizen, which proclaims the legal equality of all citizens and freedom of speech, press, assembly, and religion, but Napoleon allegedly repudiated this Declaration later.

- 1789, France's new Constitution abolished slavery and freed 700,000 African slaves in the French West Indies and Louisiana; but Napoleon allegedly revoked it later.

- 1789-90, the French Revolution encouraged 91 slave revolts in Martinique and Haiti (St Domingo).

- 1790, 28-March, the French Constituent Assembly, which took the place of the French National Assembly, considered the colonies a part of the French empire, and subject to its laws.

- 1791, 15-May, Africans in the French colonies who were born of free parents were declared equal in civic rights with whites.

- 1791, the French National Assembly granted Africans born of free parents in the French West Indies voting rights and the same privileges as all citizens. The 30,000 white citizens of Saint Domingue prepared to secede.

- 1791, French Constitutional Assembly abolished slavery in France, where there were no slaves, according to the former decision of Louis the XIVth.[182]

- 1791, 22-August, 100,000 slaves revolted in the French colony of St. Domingue, marking the beginning of the Haitian Revolution.[183]

- 1792, 4-April, French National Assembly issued final decree giving all free Africans full citizenship.

- 1792, 19-November, the French Convention declared its willingness to help all subjected peoples achieve their liberty.

- 1793, 29-August, Sonthonax arrived in Haiti (Saint-Dominique) as part of a commission to enforce King Louis XVI's edict that both the mulattos and the slaves were to be freed.

- 1794, 4-February, the French National Assembly abolished slavery in France and the French colonies, once again, where there were no slaves, according to the decision of Louis XIV, and conferred full citizenship on more than 500,000 Africans in the French West Indies and 40,000 Africans in Louisiana colony.[184]

- 1794, 2-June, Victor Hugo arrived in Guadeloupe and abolished slavery.

- 1795, the French decree of pluviôse 16 year II abolished slavery once again in the French colonies.[185]

- 1796, 18-July, Baco et Burnel landed in Mauritius, and abolished slavery, but was forced to sail away. Slavery illegally remained in effect in Mauritius and Reunion.

- 1799, 13-June, Toussaint L'Ouverture of Haiti signed a treaty with Britain, including secret provisions.

- 1801, 26-July, Toussaint L'Ouverture published and promulgated a new constitution for San Domingue which abolished slavery.

- 1801, Napoleon decided to establish slavery in France and its colonies.[186]

- 1802, 26-January, Toussaint L'Ouverture invaded Santo Domingo and declared slavery abolished.

[182] Pascal Boyries. *Chronology of the abolition of French slavery.* Available from http://perso.wanadoo.fr/yekrik.yekrak/chronoeng.htm.

[183] Lerone Bennett. *"Major Revolts and Escapes."* Before the Mayflower. Johnson Publications.

[184] Pascal Boyries.

[185] Ibid.

[186] Ibid.

- 1803, 20-December, France formally ceded Louisiana Province to the United States. The Louisiana Purchase Treaty stipulated that:

  The inhabitants of the ceded territory shall be incorporated in the Union of the United States, and admitted as soon as possible, according to the principled of the Federal Constitution, to the enjoyment of all the rights, advantages, and immunities of citizens of the United States; and in the meantime, they shall be maintained in the free enjoyment of their liberty, property, and the religion which they profess.[187]

- 1850, 20-March, in a speech to the United States Senate, Senator S.P. Chase said:

  This stipulation, interpreted according to the plain sense of its terms, and carries into effect, would have enfranchised every slave in Louisiana: for no one, I apprehend will venture to affirm that the slaves were not inhabitants. Independently of this stipulation, it was the duty of the Government--even more imperative than in 1787 [the Northwest Ordinance], for since then the whole country south of the Ohio and east of the Mississippi had been formed into slave States and slave Territories--to establish freedom as the fundamental law of the new acquisition. But this duty was not performed. These was some feeble legislation against the introduction of slaves from foreign countries, and of slaves imported since 1798 from other States; but that was all, and that was useless.

- 1815, Napoleon decreed abolition in France during the Hundred Days and the restoration government accepted the decree.

- 1815, March 29, in the Treaty of Paris, France and Britain declared the slave trade repugnant to principles of natural justice, and France agreed to limit the slave trade to its own colonies and abolish it in 5-years.

- 1815, thanks to the efforts of the Committee on the International Slave Trade Issue, the Vatican and Britain, the Congress of Vienna condemned slave trade.

- 1816, 29-Mar, Napoleon signed a decree abolishing the French slave trade.

- 1818-19, France abolished the slave trade was again, effective in 1826, and it was still illegal for slaves to live in France, "where there were no slaves."

- 1824, France prohibited her ships from transporting slaves across the Mediterranean.

- 1831, all French free people were declared equal and anti-slavery legislation was passed, once again.

- 1831, France and Britain signed a treaty for mutual search of suspected slave ships

- 1836, 26-November, the Parliament of Bordeaux freed all slaves (blacks and moors), declaring, once again, that slavery was illegal in France.

- 1838, 9-June, France recognized Haiti's final and complete independence.

- 1848, 27-April, France abolished slavery, once again, thanks to the work of Victor Schoelder, in all of its colonies, freeing 74,000 people in Martinique, and promising compensation to the slave holders.

- 1850-51, Britain and France entered into a new agreement for a mutual right of search within certain areas.

- 1859-61, France abolished the engage system of forced labor in its colonies.

---

[187] The Avalon Project at Yale Law School. *The Louisiana Purchase Treaty, April 30, 1903*.

We further request access to or copies of all records that can explain why, despite these principled and clear edicts and laws which prohibited slavery and the slave trade, the following activities and events were permitted:

- 1698, the French settled Louisiana, and an Agreement between the St-Domingo and the Guiana company was reached, to boost the slave trade and bring more Africans to St-Domingo. In St-Domingo there are 500 emancipated slaves and 9,000 slaves; in Guadeloupe 239 emancipated slaves and 4,780 slaves; in Martinique 507 emancipated slaves

- 1713, creation of the second Louisiana Company to engage in the slave trade.

- 1716, the first group of African slaves was brought to the Louisiana territory.

- 1724, Mar, A Royal Edict Touching on the State and Discipline of the Black Slaves of Louisiana was proclaimed, establishing the Code Noir in Louisiana.

- 1791, in Louisiana, twenty-three slaves are hanged and three white sympathizers deported, following suppression of an African revolt.[188]

- 1796, slave uprisings in Louisiana are suppressed, 50 Africans killed and executed.[189]

- 1800, 1 October, Louisiana Province secretly transferred from Spain back to France in the Treaty of St. Idefonso. Louisiana was "transferred "to Spain, whose King was a cousin of the King of France, in order to keep it out of British hands, and stop the emancipation of its slaves.

- 1802, 20 May, Napoleon sent General Le Clerc, his brother-in-law, with 30,000 French soldiers, to overthrow Toussaint L'Ouverture, and illegally re-impose slavery in Haiti, the French West Indies, and Louisiana. It is alleged that:

    > Napoleon asked Le Clerc: "Which has been the most prosperous regime for the colonies?"

    > Le Clerc responded: "The previous one."

    > "Well put it back," Napoleon decided.[190]

- 1803, March. Pierre Clement Laussat, whom Napoleon appointed Colonial Prefect, arrived in New Orleans.[191]

- 1803, 30 April, Napoleon decided to sell Louisiana to the United States for $15,000,000. Robert Livingston (Ambassador to France) and James Madison (Secretary of State) negotiated the sale. Two British banks, Barings and Hopes, lent the money to the US government.[192] The size of the United States was doubled.

- 1803, 6-June, full powers granted by Napoleon to Colonial Prefect Pierre Clement de Laussat authorizing him to transfer Louisiana to the United States.[193]

---

[188] Roger Davis and Wanda Neal-Davis. *Chronology, A Historical Review, Major Events in Black History 1492 through 1953*.

[189] Ibid.

[190] *Napoleon Restores Slavery*. 2003. Available from http://www.Sakpasse.com.

[191] *A Guide to the Papers of Pierre Clement Laussat: Napoleon's Prefect for the Colony of Louisiana and of General Claude Perrin Victor. Historic New Orleans Collection*. March 1993. Louisiana State University.

[192] *A Comparative Chronology of Money from Ancient Times to the Present Day, 1800 – 1849*. Based on the book: A History of Money from Ancient Times to the Present Day by Glyn Davies, rev. ed. Cardiff: University of Wales Press, 1996. 716p.

[193] *A Guide to the Papers of Pierre Clement Laussat*.

- 1803, November, Laussat formally took control of Louisiana when Salcedo, the Spanish Governor, handed him the keys to the City of New Orleans. De Laussat reorganized the city government, and appointed a Mayor and Council of Twelve.[194]

- 1803, 8-November, Mayor Etienne De Bore convened the first session of the New Orleans City Council.[195]

- 1803, 16 December, Laussat illegally issued a Decree re-instituting and upholding the Louisiana Code of 1724, revoked the French citizenship of, and re-enslaved 40,000 Africans who had been freed by French and Louisiana law in 1794, but not in reality.[196]

- 1804, Congress restricted slaves coming into Louisiana Territory to the property of actual settlers, but rejected a motion to limit slavery to one year. The first part of the law was not implemented.

- 1821, the Missouri Compromise prohibited slavery in the northern half of the Louisiana Purchase.

- 1821, the U.S. Congress declared the transport of slaves to be a form of piracy, yet the slave trade into Louisiana continued, via Cuba.

We formally and publicly request that you comply in an expedited manner with this Open Records Request, and that you waive all associated costs. Please be advised that we have disclosed this Request to the public and media.

In order to help you determine our status and make your decision on our fee waiver request, you should know that Bob Brown is an organizer and researcher, who has worked, studied and struggled for 41 years, within and for the Student, Civil and Human Rights, Black Power, National Liberation, Pan-African, and Peace Movements. See Attachment B.

We expect your positive response to this historic and precedent setting Request within 20 working days. Please be assured that we will exhaust administrative and political remedies. Thank you for your consideration.

Sincerely,
Bob Brown, co-director
Pan-African Roots

---

[194] Ruth Asher. *History of the New Orleans Police Department.*

[195] Ibid.

[196] *A Guide to the Papers of Pierre Clement Laussat.*

Pan-African Roots
1247 E Street SE
Washington, DC 20003
Tel: (202-) 544-9355 - Fax: (202) 544-9359
Email: paroots02@yahoo.com

25 October 2004

Queen Elizabeth II
c/o Embassy of the United Kingdom of Great Britain and Ireland
3100 Massachusetts Avenue NW
Washington, DC 20008

AMENDED NATIONAL ARCHIVES AND PUBLIC RECORDS ACT REQUEST.
Fee Waiver and Expedited Review Request.

Dear Queen Elizabeth:

We request, pursuant to the National Archives Act, the Public Records Act, the Freedom of Information (Ireland) Act 1997, the Freedom of Information Act 2000, the Freedom of Information (Scotland) Act 2002, and all other relevant acts, that you give us access to or copies of all records created or obtained by the Government of United Kingdom of Great Britain and Ireland, or under your authority and control, that pertain to or reference:

- The United Kingdom's role, operations and activities, historically and currently, in facilitating, prohibiting or combating slavery and the slave trade, especially the Trans-Atlantic Slave Trade; and in the struggle to declare them crimes against humanity.

- The United Kingdom's role, operations and activities, historically and currently, in facilitating, prohibiting or combating slave-like conditions and practices, including, but not limited to servitude, segregation, apartheid, racism and racial discrimination, xenophobia and related intolerance.

- Slave, urban and racial disturbances, riots, rebellions, and revolts, runaway slaves, fugitives beyond borders, and related claims or demands for compensation, restitution or reparations.

- All treaties or agreements, bilateral or multilateral, or diplomatic communications, correspondence, discussions, public and secret, between the United States Government and its Officials (all levels, branched and agencies) and British, or all other governments with respect to the above or related subjects.

- The United Nations World Conference Against Racism, Racial Discrimination, Xenophobia and Related Intolerance (WCAR), including its preparatory, regional and expert meetings and seminars, the White House Interagency Task Force on the U.N. World Conference Against Racism, the U.S. Governmental Delegation, the U.S. Non-Governmental Delegation, the UN Intergovernmental Working Group on the effective implementation of the Durban Declaration and Programme of Action, and the UNESCO Slave Route Project.

- The role of the Ports of London, Liverpool, Bristol, Manchester, Glasgow and all other British Ports, in the slave trade, slavery, colonialism and apartheid, and in the trade in slave-produced products such as sugar, molasses, rum, tobacco, rice, cotton, textiles, hemp, etc.

- All governments, agencies (federal, state, county or local), corporations, non-governmental organizations, institutions, churches, families, individuals, or entities, domestic or foreign who participated or invested in, or made profits from the above referenced crimes against humanity;

and who owns or benefits from these historical and continuing crimes today, including but not limited to those listed in Appendix A.

As you are aware, the world Conference Against Racism, Racial Discrimination, Xenophobia and Related Intolerance (WCAR) met from 31 Augusts to 3 September 2001, in Durban, South Africa. Reports reveal that 18,810 delegates from 170 countries participated in WCAR, including 16 heads of state, 58 foreign ministers, 44 ministers, 7,000 non-governmental representatives, and 1,300 journalists. The WCAR Final Declaration and Programme of Action:

> Acknowledge[s] that slavery and the slave trade, including the Trans-Atlantic Slave Trade, were appalling tragedies in the history of humanity not only because of their abhorrent barbarism but also in terms of their magnitude, organized nature especially their negation of the essence of the victims, ... acknowledge[s] **that slavery and the slave trade are a crime against humanity and should have always been so**, especially the Trans-Atlantic slave trade and are among the major sources and manifestations of racism, racial discrimination, xenophobia and related intolerance,... and invite[s] the international community members to honour the memory of the victims of these tragedies. [**Emphasis added.**]

> Further note[s] that some [countries} have taken the initiative of regretting or expressing remorse or presenting apologies, and call on all those who have yet contributed to restoring the dignity of all the victims to find appropriate ways to do so... [197]

You are perhaps not aware, that on May 17, 1860, the second National Republican Convention adopted its 1860 National Republican Platform, which declared it resolved:

> 7. That the new dogma that the Constitution of its own force carries slavery into any or all of the territories of the United States, is a dangerous political heresy, at variance with the explicit provisions of that instrument itself, with contemporaneous exposition, and with legislative and judicial precedent, is revolutionary in its tendency and subversive of the peace and harmony of the country.

> 8. That the formal condition of all the territory of the United States is that of freedom; that as our republican fathers, when they had abolished slavery in all our national territory, ordained that no "person should be deprived of life, liberty or property, without due process of law," it becomes our duty, by legislation, whenever such legislation is necessary, to maintain this provision of the constitution against all attempts to violate it; and we deny the authority of congress, of a territorial legislature, or of any individuals, to give legal existence to slavery in any territory of the United States.

> 9. That we brand the recent re-opening of the African Slave Trade, under the cover of our national flag, aided by perversions of judicial power, as a **crime against humanity, and a burning shame to our country and age,** and we call upon congress to take prompt and efficient measured for the total and final suppression of the execrable traffic. [198] [**Emphasis added.**]

In 1808, the United States Government prohibited its citizens from participating in the international slave trade, declaring it piracy in 1820, and participation in it punishable by death. Despite this prohibition, a minimum of 250,000 and perhaps as many as 1,000,000 Africans were kidnapped, enslaves, and illegally imported into the United States via Cuba between 1809 and 1861. In 1839, a prime male slave could be purchased in Cuba for $400 and then sold into slavery for life in Richmond for $1,000 or

---

[197] World Conference Secretariat. Office of the United Nations High Commissioner for Human Rights. Available from http://www.unhchr.ch/html/racism/02-documents-cnt.html

[198] Central Pacific Railroad Photographic History Museum. *Republican Party National Platform, 1860.* Available from http://cprr.org/Museum/Ephemera/Republican_Platform_1860.html.

Charleston for $1,150 or Savannah for $1,200 or New Orleans for $1,250. The average daily wage was one dollar. President James Madison reported to Congress in 1810 that:

> It appears that American citizens are instrumental in carrying on a traffic in enslaved Africans, equally in violation of the laws of humanity, and in defiance of those of their own country. The same just and benevolent motives which produced the interdiction in force against this criminal conduct, will doubtless be felt in Congress, in devising further means of suppressing the evil.

The 1860 Republican National Convention selected Abraham Lincoln as its Presidential nominee. He campaigned on this platform, and "won the presidency with almost half a million voted more than [Stephen] Douglas, his closest rival. [Lincoln] won the election garnering 39.8 percent of the popular vote. This election firmly established the Republican hold on the presidency for 60 of the next 100 years.

You are perhaps also not aware that William Lloyd Garrison was the first person to declare slavery a crime against humanity in the inaugural edition (1831) of his Liberator newspaper; or that on November 12, 1849, the Vermont Legislature passed "*Joint Resolution No. 42.--Resolutions Relating To The Subject of Slavery*," declaring it:

> Resolved by the Senate and House of Representatives, that Slavery is a **crime against humanity, and a sore evil** in the body politic that was excused by the framers of the Federal Constitution as a crime entailed upon the country by their predecessors, and tolerated solely as a thing of inexorable necessity.[199] [**Emphasis added.**]

It is well-settled, as the WCAR Final Declaration confirms, that prohibitions against piracy and privateering, slavery and the slave trade, including the Trans-Atlantic Slave Trade, and against slave-like conditions and practices, including colonialism, segregation and apartheid, forced and compulsory labor, racism and racial discrimination, xenophobia and related intolerance have achieved the level of customary international law, have attained the status of jus cogens, and are obligato erga omnes. Unfortunately, the overwhelming majority of the WCAR Delegated and the public, especially African People world-wide, wrongly believe that this status has only recently been acquired.[200]

Permit us to suggest, as Ethan A. Nadelman suggests, that "most global prohibition regimes, including those targeted against piracy, slavery, and drug trafficking, evidence a common evolutionary pattern consisting of four or five stages."[201] At different stages in their development: (1) the activity is legal and some states participate in it; (2) national and international forces, non-governmental and governmental, attempt to redefine the activity as evil and illegal; (3) these forces agitate for its suppression and criminalization; (4) the activity becomes the subject of national and international criminal laws, conventions and treaties, police and military action; and (5) finally, the activity is prohibited globally.[202] It is axiomatic that this development is extremely uneven, unequal, and costly in time, space and human lives, in justice and equity.

Permit us also to suggest that Judge Fouad Ammoun of the International Court of Justice (ICJ) "has [accurately] described the development of Africa ... [and] eloquently remarked on the evolution of mankind's struggle with the issue of slavery and colonization."[203] He informs us that "before there fell upon it the two greatest plagues in the recorded history of mankind: the slave trade, which ravaged Africa

---

[199] *The Acts and Resolves Passed By The Legislature Of The State of Vermont At The October Session, 1849.* Published By authority. Montpelier: E. P. Walton & Son. 1849.

[200] People incorrectly believe that "the term was first used in the preamble of the Hague Convention of 1907. Wikipedia. Crime against humanity. Available from http://en.wikipedia.org/wiki/Crime_against_humanity.

[201] Ethan A. Nadelman. *Global prohibition regimes: the evolution of norms in international society.* Printed in Transnational Crime / edited by Nikos Passas.

[202] Ibid.

[203] *Legal Consequences For States of the Continued Presence of South Africa in Namibia (South West Africa) Notwithstanding Security Council Resolution 276, 1971 I.C.J. 16, 86 (1971) (separate opinion of Judge Ammoun).*

for centuries on an unprecedented scale; and colonialism, which exploited humanity and natural wealth to a relentless extreme," ... Africa boasted thriving states and empires dating back to Roman times[204]

Judge Ammoun also informs us that "historians have outlined the upward march of mankind from the time when homo sapiens appeared on the face of the globe, first of all in the Near East in what was the land of Canaan[205], up to the age of the greatest thinkers and more particularly, throughout the whole of history of social progress, from the slavery of Antiquity to man's [and woman's] inevitable, irreversible drive towards equality and freedom. This march is like time itself. It never stops. Nothing can stand in its way for long. The texts, whether they be laws, constitutions, declarations, covenants or charters, do but define it and mark its successive phases. They are a mere record of it. In other words, the progressive rights which men, [women] and peopled enjoy are the result much less of those texts than of human progress to which they bear witness."[206]

We are confident that the records requested by this historic and precedent setting Request will:

- Bear witness to and prove, once and for all, that piracy and privateering, slavery and the slave trade, including the Trans-Atlantic Slave Trade, and slave-like conditions and practices, including colonialism, segregation and apartheid, were and are illegal and prohibited, and were and are recognized as crimes against humanity when and where they were committed.

- Help define and mark the successive staged in the development of the 569-year historical and continuing Maafa, and of the unyielding and continuing struggle against it.

- Document who the victims were, and who their descendants are today; who committed these crimes, which were and are the greatest theft of land, lives and labor in human history; how this unjust and illegal wealth was converted, consolidated, preserved and transferred across generations and centuries; and who owns and benefits from this unjust enrichment today.

We request that that you and the Government of the United Kingdom of Great Britain and Ireland, formally and publicly reaffirm, once and for all, that slavery and the slave trade were and are illegal according to the edicts and municipal laws of the United Kingdom and its colonies, and according to canon law and international law; and that slavery and the slave trade were crimes against humanity:

- Because in 1066, the Doomsday Books documented that 7% of the inhabitants of England were villeins (slaves), but villainy (slavery) as a custom and practice disappeared by 1350.

- Because in 1086, William the Conqueror forbade the enslavement of Christians and as a result, all English women and men.

- Because in 1102,"in a national ecclesiastical council, held at Westminster, under the Archbishop of Canterbury, Saint Anselm declared that "it was forbidden to sell men like cattle, which had been too generally practised in England."[207]

- Because the Charter of English liberties, which was the law of the land, guaranteed justice and rights to every man and woman, and prepared the way for the total abolition of slavery.

- Because Ireland had "the honor of the first general emancipation act known in history, when the great Synod of Ireland, under the leadership of St. Lawrence O'Toole, denounced the slave trade in which the Irish had made bond slaves of the English, contrary to the right of Christian freedom;" [declared that], they had purchased of robbers and pirates, as well as of merchants—a crime for which God took vengeance upon the nation by delivering them into like bondage; [and

---

[204] Recent evidence documents that African civilizations predate Roman times.

[205] Recent evidence documents that homo sapiens first emerged in East Africa.

[206] Ethan A. Nadelman. *Global prohibition regimes.*

[207] Ibid.

therefore unanimously] decreed and ordained, that all the English throughout Ireland in a state of slavery, should be restored to their natural freedom."[208]

- Because in 1562, when Queen Elizabeth first heard that John Hawkins had committed an act of piracy, and traded in kidnapped slaves, and launched England's involvement in the slave trade, she reportedly detested the slave-trading voyages as "detestable ventures," and "commented that he would have to pay a very high price for dealing in human lives."[209]

- Because in the Cromwell decision of 1569, British Courts declared that "England was too pure an air for slaves to breathe in,"[210] a decision that ended slave trade and slavery in Britain and all British colonies, for all peoples, and for all times.

- Because in 1600, the British Courts declared in Butts v. Penny that, "there could be no property in the person of a Man ... but by compact or conquest."

- Because in the 1600s, Lord Mansfield declared in Rev v. Cowle, that, "the supremacy of English courts extends itself over its Dependencies, [and that] "the British legislature as to the power to make laws, represents the whole British Empire, and has authority to bind every part and every subject without the least distinction, whether such subjects have the right to vote or not, or whether the law binds places within the realm, or without."[211]

- Because from 1619-1732, the status of servitude had allegedly achieved distinct recognition in the colonial statute law as follows: Virginia, 1619; Massachusetts, 1630-1636; Maryland, 1637; Connecticut, 1643; Rhode Island, 1647; North Carolina, 1665; Pennsylvania, 1682; Georgia, 1732. Upon information and belief, these colonial laws were not approved by the British Parliament or assented to by the King, and were and are therefore illegal, null and void.

- Because between 1628-1726, the prohibition of man-stealing, woman-stealing, child-stealing, kidnapping, piracy, privateering, slavery, the slave trade, and slave-like practices and conditions had been recorded in all British common legal sources, including: Coke on Littleton (1628), Blackstone's Commentaries on the Laws of England (1765-69), Powell on contracts (1790) and Hawkins on crime (1724-26). This prohibition applied to all of Britain's colonies.

- Because in 1640, the Virginia General Assembly launched a 132-year effort to legalize and protect African slavery within her limits. From 1662 to 1772, thirty-one acts were passed by the Provincial Legislature of Virginia. These legislative acts were not approved by the British Parliament or assented to by King, and were and are therefore illegal, null and void.

- Because from 1641-1755, statutory recognition of slavery in English-American colonies had occurred as follows: by Massachusetts in 1641; by Connecticut in 1650; by Virginia in 1661; by Maryland in 1663; by New York and New Jersey in 1664; by South Carolina in 1682; by Pennsylvania and Rhode Island in 1700; by North Carolina in 1715; and by Georgia in 1755. These laws however, were not approved by the British Parliament or assented to by the King, and were and are therefore illegal, null and void.

- Because in 1644, Barbados enacted a Slave Code, the first British colony to do so. Virginia and Maryland adopted this legislation. This legislation was not approved by the British Parliament and or assented to by King, and was and is therefore illegal, null and void.

---

[208] Ibid.

[209] *Spain v. England: The Early History of the Slave Trade.* Available from http://beatl.barnard.columbia.edu/students/his3487/lembrich/seminar51.html

[210] William Goodell. *Slavery and Anti-Slavery.* Available from http://members.tripod.com/medicolegal/goodellsaas.htm

[211] Ibid.

- Because in 1645, the English Parliament passed an Ordinance prohibiting kidnapping.

- Because in 1652, by an act of May 18, 1652, passed by the Commissioners of Providence Plantations and Warwick, it was provided that "no black mankind, or white, being forced to covenant, bond or otherwise, serve any man or his assigns longer than ten years, or until they come to be twenty-four years of age, if they be taken under fourteen, from the time of their coming within the limits of this colony, and at the end or term of ten years to set them free, as the matter is with the English servants."

- Because in 1662, it was declared that "any of His Majesty's subjects of England, Ireland and His Plantations are to be accounted English and no other."

- Because by the end of the 17th century, Grotius, a founder of international law, had declared piracy illegal under international law, and beyond the protection of any state.

- Because in 1706, English "common law [took] no notice of the Negroes for being different from others as, by the common law no man can have property in another except in special instances."

- Because in 1729, Sir Philip Yorke, the Attorney-General of the British realm, delivered an opinion, at the insistence of slave-masters, that "a slave, by coming from the West Indies, either with or without his master, to Great Britain or Ireland, doth not become free; and that his master's property or right in his is not thereby determined or varied; and baptism doth not bestow freedom on him, nor make any alteration in his temporal condition." This opinion, which was used to justify slavery in the colonies, was overturned and declared illegal in 1772.

- Because in August of 1759, in an Order of Council, the British Privy Council disallowed the Two-Penny Act of 1758, an emergency measure that permitted ministers to be paid in deflated currency instead of the Crown-approved Act of 1758 which legally required the payment of 16,000 pounds of tobacco per year. "In approving the 1758 Act, Governor Fauquier disregarded his royal instructions, which required him to include a clause suspending execution of any act that act controverted royal authority until it could be approved by the Crown." This Order implicitly reaffirmed that the Virginia Assembly did not have the right to legislate even in a state of emergency, without royal assent, and unless the laws upheld all rights guaranteed under the British Constitution and the laws of Parliament.

- Because in 1767, Granville Sharp published a protest against slavery, in which he declared "every inhabitant of the king's realm, regardless of color, to be the king's subject, and.. that no one, therefore, had a moral or legal right to enslave any such subject." Sharp further argued that "if color were a basis for slavery, then in a short time any Englishman might be enslaved since there was but little difference between the complexion of a northern Indian and a white man."

- Because in 1772, on April 1, the Virginia House of Burgesses, after imposing another tax of five percent, on all slaves imported into the colony, sent a petition to the King declaring that, "the importation of slaves into the colony from the coast of Africa hath long been considered as a trade of great inhumanity; and under its present encouragement we have too much reason to fear will encourage the very existence of your Majesty's American dominions."

- Because in June of 1772, Lord Mansfield reaffirmed, in the landmark decision of Somerset v. Stewart, that the "air of Britain is too pure for a slave to breathe." This landmark decision freed 15,000 Africans who had been illegally held in slavery in England. Lord Mansfield declared that:

    The state of slavery is of such a nature, that it is incapable of being [legally] introduced [established] on [for] any reasons, moral or political, but only by positive [written] law, which preserves its force long after the reasons, occasion, and time itself from whence it was created, is erased from memory. It [slavery] is so odious that nothing can be suffered to support it, but positive law. Whatever inconveniences, therefore, may follow from the decision, I cannot say this case is allowed or approved by the law of England; and therefore the black must be discharged.

- Arnett G. Lindsay, a student of Dr. Carter G. Woodson at Howard University in 1920, suggests that "the humanitarian spirit of Great Britain which, by the celebrated decision of Lord Mansfield in the Somerset case in 1772 guaranteed to everyman his freedom as soon as he set foot on British soil, extended beyond the limits of the empire. Although this decision of the judge evoked some unfavorable comment, for slavery was the "normal condition of the Negro," his ideas were disseminated by the military authorities defending the Crown in America."[212]

- Because between 1775-1983, during the Revolutionary War, many of the British commanders issued proclamations of freedom to the Negro slaves. Lindsay records that, "Lord Dunmore, the dethroned Governor of Virginia, was among the first to issue a proclamation of freedom to all Negroes who would fight for the King. Soon thereafter, Clinton, the Commander-in-chief of the British forces in America, issued a proclamation to the same effect. Still later, Cornwallis issued a proclamation specifying the grant of "freedom and protection "to all Negroes who would seek his command. Whatever motive prompted the issuance of these orders, it is evident that the status of the Negro during this "emergency" as regarded by Great Britain was that of a freeman."[213]

- Because between 1775-1803, during the American Revolution, and again in the War of 1812, British troops freed and evacuated hundreds of thousands of freed slaves;[214] and the British Government refused to return them to slavery or compensate the U.S. government for them.

- Because the Slave Codes, including but not limited to the Barbados Code, Virginia Code, Black Codes and Jim Crow Laws, like the Nazi and Apartheid Laws, were inferior and repugnant to canon law, customary international law, and to the municipal, imperial and colonial laws of European, Christian, and other Nations, then and now, and therefore were and are null and void.

- Because the governments in the 13 British Colonies made several efforts to abolish slavery and the slave trade before their Declaration of Independence in 1776; and because Thomas Jefferson, in the original draft of the Declaration of Independence, declared that:

> [The King of Britain] **has waged cruel war against human nature itself**, violating it's most sacred rights of life and liberty in the persons of a distant people who never offended him, captivating and carrying them into slavery in another hemisphere, or to incur miserable death in their transportation hither. This piratical warfare, the opprobrium of infidel powers, is the warfare of the Christian king of Great Britain. [Determined to keep open a market where MEN should be bought and sold,] **he has prostituted his negative for suppressing every legislative attempt to prohibit or to restrain this execrable commerce** [determining to keep open a market where MEN should be bought and sold]: and that this assemblage of horrors might want no fact of distinguished die, he is now exciting those very people to rise in arms among us, and to purchase that liberty of which he had deprived them, by murdering the people upon whom he also obtruded them: thus paying off former crimes committed against the liberties of one people, with

[212] Arnett G. Lindsay. *"Diplomatic Relations between the United States and Great Britain Bearing on the Return of Negro Slaves, 1783-1828."* Journal of Negro History 5 (October 1920): 391-419. Republished by Dinsmore Documentation presents Classics on American Slavery.

[213] Ibid.

[214] Ibid.

crimes which he urges them to commit against the lives of another. [215] **[Emphasis added.]**

- Because Vermont prohibited the slave trade and slavery in 1777, followed by Massachusetts and Pennsylvania in 1780, and Connecticut in 1784. Britain did not officially recognize their independence until the Treaty of 1783 ended the American Revolution.

- Because Canada prohibited slavery and the slavery trade in 1793 and 1803, and from that date, Canada harbored, gave sanctuary and citizenship to, and refused to return fugitive slaves.

- Because in 1807, on March 25, the British Parliament passed the Abolition of the Slave Trade Act, which included Lord Greenville's declaration that the slave trade was "contrary to the principles of justice, humanity and sound policy," and he admonished his fellow parliamentarians for "not having abolished the trade long ago."

- Because, in the "Treaty between His Britannic Majesty and His Catholic Majesty, for preventing Their Subjects from engaging in any illicit Traffic in Slaves," which was signed at Madrid on the 23d of September 1817, [it] was "stated, in the second Additional Article of the Treaty signed at Madrid on the 5th day of July of the year 1814, between His Majesty the King of the United Kingdom of Great Britain and Ireland, and His Majesty the King of Spain and the Indies, that "His Catholic Majesty concurs, in the fullest Manner, in the Sentiments of His Britannic Majesty, with respect to the **Injustice and Inhumanity of the Traffic in Slaves**,. and engages, moreover, to prohibit his Subjects from carrying on the Slave Trade." [216] **[Emphasis added.]**

- Because, in the "Convention between His Majesty and the King of the French for the more effectual Suppression of the Traffic in Slaves, signed at Paris the Thirtieth Day of November One thousand eight hundred and thirty-one," the Courts of Great Britain and France, being desirous of rendering more effectual the Means of Suppression which have hitherto been in force against the **criminal Traffic known under the Name of the Slave Trade** ... deemed it expedient to negotiate and conclude a Convention for the Attainment of so salutary an Object." [217] **[Emphasis added.]**

- Because, in the "Supplementary Convention between His Majesty and the King of the French for the more effectual Suppression of the Traffic in Slaves, signed at Paris the Twenty second Day of March One thousand eight hundred and thirty three, His Majesty the King of the United Kingdom of Great Britain and Ireland and His Majesty the King of the French having felt the Necessity of developing some of the Clauses contained in the Convention which was signed between Their Majesties on the Thirtieth Day of November One thousand eight hundred and thirty-one, relating to the **Suppression of the Crime of Slave trade**." **[Emphasis added.]**

We request that you and the Government of the United Kingdom, formally and publicly reaffirm, once and for all, that slavery and the slave trade were and are crimes under British and international law, and that they were and are crimes against humanity.

The Government of the United Kingdom, its Royal, Adventurer, Planter, Trading and Settler Families were and are responsible for:

- 3.1 million Africans who were kidnapped from Africa and sold into slavery in the Americas, and for the destruction of countless villages, nation-States and civilizations in Africa.

---

[215] Ibid.

[216] *William Loney RN - Background-West Africa.*

[217] Ibid.

- 428,000 Africans were illegally held in slavery by Britain in the West Indies, 700,00 in the 13 British colonies of North America, and 100,000 in Cape Town.

- 179 million of their descendants who are scattered, suffering and struggling in more than 24 countries today, under slave-like conditions and practices, segregation, racism and racial discrimination, xenophobia and related intolerance until today.

We hope that you will comply with this Request for a Public Commitment and Information in an expedited manner, and that you will waive all associated costs. Please be advised that we have sent a copy of this Request to the public and the media.

In order to help you determine our status and make your decision on our fee waiver request, you should know that Bob Brown is an organizer and researcher, who has worked, studied and struggled for 41 years, within and for the Student, Civil and Human Rights, Black Power, National Liberation, Pan-African, and Peace Movements. See Attachment B.

We expect your positive response to this historic and precedent setting Information Request within 20 working days. Thank you for your consideration.

Sincerely,
Bob Brown, co-director
Pan-African Roots

Pan-African Roots
1247 E Street SE
Washington, DC 20003
Tel: (202-) 544-9355 - Fax: (202) 544-9359
Email: paroots02@yahoo.com

25 October 2004

Mr. Paul Martin, Prime Minister
c/o Embassy of Canada
501 Pennsylvania Ave NW
Washington, DC 20001

REQUEST FOR ACCESS TO INFORMATION.
Fee Waiver and Expedited Review Request.

Dear Governor Martin:

We request, pursuant to the Access To Information Act, that you give us access to or copies of all records created or obtained by the Government of Canada, or under your authority and control, that pertain to, or reference:

- Canada's role, operations and activities, historically and currently, in facilitating, prohibiting or combating slavery and the slave trade, especially the Trans-Atlantic Slave Trade; and in the struggle to declare them crimes against humanity.

- Canada's role, operations and activities, historically and currently, in facilitating, prohibiting or combating slave-like conditions and practices, including, but not limited to servitude, segregation, apartheid, racism and racial discrimination, xenophobia and related intolerance

- Slave, urban and racial disturbances, riots, rebellions, and revolts, runaway slaves, fugitives beyond borders, and related claims or demands for compensation, restitution or reparations.

- All treaties or agreements, bilateral or multilateral, or diplomatic communications, correspondence, discussions, public and secret, between the United States Government and its Officials (all levels, branched and agencies) and Canadian, British, or all other governments with respect to the above or related subjects.

- The United Nations World Conference Against Racism, Racial Discrimination, Xenophobia and Related Intolerance (WCAR), including its preparatory, regional and expert meetings and seminars, the White House Interagency Task Force on the U.N. World Conference Against Racism, the U.S. Governmental Delegation, the U.S. Non-Governmental Delegation, the UN Intergovernmental Working Group on the effective implementation of the Durban Declaration and Programme of Action, and the UNESCO Slave Route Project.

- All governments, agencies (federal, state, county or local), corporations, non-governmental organizations, institutions, churches, families, individuals, or entities, domestic or foreign who participated or invested in, or made profits from the above referenced crimes against humanity; and who owns or benefits from these historical and continuing crimes today, including but not limited to those listed in Appendix A.

As you are aware, the world Conference Against Racism, Racial Discrimination, Xenophobia and Related Intolerance (WCAR) met from 31 August to 3 September 2001, in Durban, South Africa. Reports reveal that 18,810 delegates from 170 countries participated in WCAR, including 16 heads of state, 58 foreign ministers, 44 ministers, 7,000 non-governmental representatives, and 1,300 journalists. The WCAR Final Declaration and Programme of Action:

Acknowledge[s] that slavery and the slave trade, including the Trans-Atlantic Slave Trade, were appalling tragedies in the history of humanity not only because of their abhorrent barbarism but also in terms of their magnitude, organized nature especially their negation of the essence of the victims, ... acknowledge[s] **that slavery and the slave trade are a crime against humanity and should have always been so,** especially the Trans-Atlantic slave trade and are among the major sources and manifestations of racism, racial discrimination, xenophobia and related intolerance,... and invite[s] the international community members to honour the memory of the victims of these tragedies. [**Emphasis added.**]

Further note[s] that some [countries} have taken the initiative of regretting or expressing remorse or presenting apologies, and call on all those who have yet contributed to restoring the dignity of all the victims to find appropriate ways to do so... [218]

You are perhaps not aware, that on May 17, 1860, the second National Republican Convention adopted its 1860 National Republican Platform, which declared it resolved:

7. That the new dogma that the Constitution of its own force carries slavery into any or all of the territories of the United States, is a dangerous political heresy, at variance with the explicit provisions of that instrument itself, with contemporaneous exposition, and with legislative and judicial precedent, is revolutionary in its tendency and subversive of the peace and harmony of the country.

8. That the formal condition of all the territory of the United States is that of freedom; that as our republican fathers, when they had abolished slavery in all our national territory, ordained that no "person should be deprived of life, liberty or property, without due process of law," it becomes our duty, by legislation, whenever such legislation is necessary, to maintain this provision of the constitution against all attempts to violate it; and we deny the authority of congress, of a territorial legislature, or of any individuals, to give legal existence to slavery in any territory of the United States.

9. That we brand the recent re-opening of the African Slave Trade, under the cover of our national flag, aided by perversions of judicial power, as a **crime against humanity, and a burning shame to our country and age,** and we call upon congress to take prompt and efficient measured for the total and final suppression of the execrable traffic. [219] [**Emphasis added.**]

In 1808, the United States Government prohibited its citizens from participating in the international slave trade, declaring it piracy in 1820, and participation in it punishable by death. Despite this prohibition, a minimum of 250,000 and perhaps as many as 1,000,000 Africans were kidnapped, enslaves, and illegally imported into the United States via Cuba between 1809 and 1861. In 1839, a prime male slave could be purchased in Cuba for $400 and then sold into slavery for life in Richmond for $1,000 or Charleston for $1,150 or Savannah for $1,200 or New Orleans for $1,250. The average daily wage was one dollar. President James Madison reported to Congress in 1810 that:

It appears that American citizens are instrumental in carrying on a traffic in enslaved Africans, equally in violation of the laws of humanity, and in defiance of those of their own country. The same just and benevolent motives which produced the interdiction in force against this criminal conduct, will doubtless be felt in Congress, in devising further means of suppressing the evil.

The 1860 Republican National Convention selected Abraham Lincoln as its Presidential nominee. He campaigned on this platform, and "won the presidency with almost half a million voted more than

---

[218] World Conference Secretariat. Office of the United Nations High Commissioner for Human Rights. Available from http://www.unhchr.ch/html/racism/02-documents-cnt.html.

[219] Central Pacific Railroad Photographic History Museum. *Republican Party National Platform, 1860.* Available from http://cprr.org/Museum/Ephemera/Republican_Platform_1860.html.

186

[Stephen] Douglas, his closest rival. [Lincoln] won the election garnering 39.8 percent of the popular vote. This election firmly established the Republican hold on the presidency for 60 of the next 100 years.

You are perhaps also not aware that William Lloyd Garrison was the first person to declare slavery a crime against humanity in the inaugural edition (1831) of his Liberator newspaper; or that on November 12, 1849, the Vermont Legislature passed "*Joint Resolution No. 42.--Resolutions Relating To The Subject of Slavery,*" declaring it:

> Resolved by the Senate and House of Representatives, that Slavery is a **crime against humanity, and a sore evil** in the body politic that was excused by the framers of the Federal Constitution as a crime entailed upon the country by their predecessors, and tolerated solely as a thing of inexorable necessity.[220] [**Emphasis added.**]

It is well-settled, as the WCAR Final Declaration confirms, that prohibitions against piracy and privateering, slavery and the slave trade, including the Trans-Atlantic Slave Trade, and against slave-like conditions and practices, including colonialism, segregation and apartheid, forced and compulsory labor, racism and racial discrimination, xenophobia and related intolerance have achieved the level of customary international law, have attained the status of jus cogens, and are obligato erga omnes. Unfortunately, the overwhelming majority of the WCAR Delegated and the public, especially African People world-wide, wrongly believe that this status has only recently been acquired.[221]

Permit us to suggest, as Ethan A. Nadelman suggests, that "most global prohibition regimes, including those targeted against piracy, slavery, and drug trafficking, evidence a common evolutionary pattern consisting of four or five stages."[222] At different stages in their development: (1) the activity is legal and some states participate in it; (2) national and international forces, non-governmental and governmental, attempt to redefine the activity as evil and illegal; (3) these forces agitate for its suppression and criminalization; (4) the activity becomes the subject of national and international criminal laws, conventions and treaties, police and military action; and (5) finally, the activity is prohibited globally.[223] It is axiomatic that this development is extremely uneven, unequal, and costly in time, space and human lives, in justice and equity.

Permit us also to suggest that Judge Fouad Ammoun of the International Court of Justice (ICJ) "has [accurately] described the development of Africa ... [and] eloquently remarked on the evolution of mankind's struggle with the issue of slavery and colonization."[224] He informs us that "before there fell upon it the two greatest plagues in the recorded history of mankind: the slave trade, which ravaged Africa for centuries on an unprecedented scale; and colonialism, which exploited humanity and natural wealth to a relentless extreme," ... Africa boasted thriving states and empires dating back to Roman times."[225]

Judge Ammoun also informs us that "historians have outlined the upward march of mankind from the time when homo sapiens appeared on the face of the globe, first of all in the Near East in what was the land of Canaan[226], up to the age of the greatest thinkers and more particularly, throughout the whole of history of social progress, from the slavery of Antiquity to man's [and woman's] inevitable, irreversible

---

[220] *The Acts and Resolves Passed By The Legislature Of The State of Vermont At The October Session, 1849.* Published By authority. Montpelier: E. P. Walton & Son. 1849.

[221] People incorrectly believe that "the term was first used in the preamble of the Hague Convention of 1907." Wikipedia. Available from http://en.wikipedia.org/wiki/Crime_against_humanity.

[222] Ethan A. Nadelman. *Global prohibition regimes: the evolution of norms in international society.* Printed in Transnational Crime / edited by Nikos Passas.

[223] Ibid.

[224] *Legal Consequences For States of the Continued Presence of South Africa in Namibia (South West Africa) Notwithstanding Security Council Resolution 276, 1971 I.C.J. 16, 86 (1971) (separate opinion of Judge Ammoun).*

[225] Recent evidence documents that African civilizations predate Roman times.

[226] Recent evidence documents that homo sapiens first emerged in East Africa.

187

drive towards equality and freedom. This march is like time itself. It never stops. Nothing can stand in its way for long. The texts, whether they be laws, constitutions, declarations, covenants or charters, do but define it and mark its successive phases. They are a mere record of it. In other words, the progressive rights which men, [women] and peopled enjoy are the result much less of those texts than of human progress to which they bear witness."[227]

We are confident that the records requested by this historic and precedent setting Request will:

- Bear witness to and prove, once and for all, that piracy and privateering, slavery and the slave trade, including the Trans-Atlantic Slave Trade, and slave-like conditions and practices, including colonialism, segregation and apartheid, were and are illegal and prohibited, and were and are recognized as crimes against humanity when and where they were committed.

- Help define and mark the successive staged in the development of the 569-year historical and continuing Maafa,[228] and of the unyielding and continuing struggle against it.

- Document who the victims were, and who their descendants are today; who committed these crimes, which were and are the greatest theft of land, lives and labor in human history; how this unjust and illegal wealth was converted, consolidated, preserved and transferred across generations and centuries; and who owns and benefits from this unjust enrichment today.

We request that that you and the Government of Canada, formally and publicly reaffirm that slavery and the slave trade were and are illegal according to the laws of the Britain and Canada, and according to canon law and international law; and that slavery and the slave trade were crimes against humanity:

- Because in 1783, Africans who had been freed by Britain during the American Revolution came to the Maritimes and Upper Canada, and lived as free women and men.

- Because in 1790, the Imperial Statute mandated that any child born of slaves in Upper Canada became free at age 25.

- Because in 1791-94, the French National Assembly abolished slavery in France, and all of France's colonies, including New France, and made all of the former slaves citizens.

- Because in 1793, Canada prohibited slavery and the slave trade.

- Because in 1796, 543 Maroons were exiled from Jamaica and sent to Halifax, Nova Scotia to live, as free women and men.

- Because in 1803-04, William Osgoode, Chief Justice of Lower Canada, ruled that slavery was inconsistent with British Law, and that slaves who left their owners could not be returned.

- Because in 1819, John Beverley Robinson, Attorney General of Upper Canada, ruled that people of African origin who lived in Canada were free with their rights protected by law.

- Because Canada harbored, gave sanctuary and citizenship to, and refused, despite countless claims from and diplomatic negotiations with the United States, to return more than 30,000 fugitive slaves.

We ask that you give us all records that pertain to or reference the above subjects, and that can help us understand why, legally, politically and morally, Canada freed, harbored, protected and respected Africans who were unjustly and illegally enslaved.

---

[227] Ethan A. Nadelman. *Global prohibition regimes.*

[228] Dr. Marimba Ani. *Let The Circle Be Unbroken.* Maafa is a Kiswahili word for the 563-year historical and continuing enslavement and colonization of Africa and African People.

We ask that you comply in an expedited manner with this Request, and waive all associated costs. Please be advised that we have disclosed this Request to the public and media.

In order to help you determine our status and make your decision on our fee waiver request, you should know that Bob Brown is an organizer and researcher, who has worked, studied and struggled for 41 years, within and for the Student, Civil and Human Rights, Black Power, National Liberation, Pan-African, and Peace Movements. See Attachment B.

We expect your positive response to this historic and precedent setting Information Request within 20 working days. Thank you for your consideration.

Sincerely,
Bob Brown, co-director
Pan-African Roots

Pan-African Roots
1247 E Street SE
Washington, DC 20003
Tel: (202) 544-9355 - Fax: (202) 544-9359
Email: paroots02@yahoo.com

25 October 2004

Mr. James H. Douglas, Governor
Office of the Governor
109 State Street
Montpelier, VT 05609

REQUEST FOR PUBLIC COMMITMENT AND INFORMATION.
Public Records Request.
Request for Waiver of Costs and Expedited Review.

Dear Governor Douglas:

As you are aware, Vermont was the first state to prohibit slavery in its Constitution of 1777, and one of the first states to abolish it. Vermont's Congressmen voted in 1820 against the pro-slavery amendments in the United States Congress, and its Legislature's passed a resolution declaring that:

> Slavery **is incompatible with the vital principles of all free governments** and tends to their ruin. It paralyzes industry, the greatest source of national wealth, stifles the love of freedom, and endangers the safety of the nation. It **is prohibited by the laws of nature,** which are equally binding on governments and individuals. **The right to introduce and establish slavery in a free government does not exist**. [**Emphasis added.**]

As you are also perhaps aware, on Nov 12, 1849 the Vermont Legislature passed "*Joint Resolution No. 42.--Resolutions Relating To The Subject of Slavery*" declaring it:

> Resolved by the Senate and House of Representatives, That **Slavery is a crime against humanity**, and a sore evil in the body politic that was **excused** by the framers of the Federal Constitution as a crime entailed upon the country by their predecessors, and **tolerated** solely as a thing of inexorable necessity.[229] [**Emphasis added.**]

We ask that you, the Vermont Legislature, and Vermont's Senators and Congressman publicly reconfirm your commitment to the above resolutions, and especially to the principle that slavery and the slave trade were crimes against humanity in 1820 and 1849, and are crimes against humanity today.

Pursuant to Vermont's Public Records Act, 1 V.S.A. 315-320, we request access to and or copies of any and all records pertaining to and or referencing the legislative history of, discussion and debate on Vermont's Constitution and amendments, the 1820 Congressional vote, and the 1820 and 1849 Legislative Resolutions referred above. We especially seek any and all records that can document and explain the legal, moral, philosophical or religious doctrines upon which Vermont's prohibition of slavery in its Constitution and laws, and these resolutions were based; about who introduced and voted for them, and why; about whether the requests for action which they included were implemented; and whether any responses were received.

We also request that you provide us access to and or copies of any and all records pertaining to and or referencing:

---

[229] *The Acts and Resolves Passed By The Legislature Of The State of Vermont At The October Session, 1849.* Published By authority. Montpelier: E.P. Walton & Son. 1849.

- Vermont's role, operations and activities, historically and currently, in facilitating, prohibiting and or combating piracy and privateering, slavery and the slave trade, especially the Trans-Atlantic Slave trade (also known as the Atlantic Trade, the Triangle Trade, the Colonial Trade, the West Indies Trade, the Coastal Trade, the Intra-State Slave trade, etc.); and in the struggle to declare them crimes against humanity.

- Vermont's role, operations and activities, historically and currently, in facilitating, prohibiting and or combating slave-like conditions and practices, including but not limited to servitude, forced and compulsory labor, peonage, sharecropping, debt-bondage, sweatshop labor, convict-lease, chain-gang and prison labor, the sale of children, child prostitution, child pornography, the exploitation of child labour, the sexual mutilation of female children, the use of children in armed conflicts, the traffic in persons and in the sale of human organs, the exploitation of prostitution, and certain practices under apartheid and colonial regimes, segregation, racism and racial discrimination, xenophobia and related intolerance.

- Vermont's knowledge and understanding of the legal status, from at least the Doomsday Book of 1066 to the American Revolution of 1776, under canon law, international law, and the municipal laws of France, Britain, and their colonies, of man-stealing and kidnapping, piracy and privateering, torture and murder, slavery and the slave trade (also known as the Trans-Atlantic Slave trade, the Atlantic Trade, the Coastal Trade, the West Indies Trade, the Coastal Trade), and especially their status, official and unofficial, as crimes against humanity.

- Vermont's relationship to and correspondence with Britain, its Kings and Queens, Board of Trade and Plantations, Privy Council, the Royal Africa Company, and any and all other governmental and parastatal structures, especially with respect to piracy and privateering, slavery and the slave trade, colonialism, and related commercial activities.

- The legal status of man-stealing and kidnapping, of piracy and privateering, torture and murder, slavery and the slave trade, slave-like practices and conditions, including but not limited to segregation, racism and racial discrimination, xenophobia and related intolerance, and of crimes against humanity in Vermont during its years as a colony of France and England (1609-1777), fourteen years of its independence (1777-91), from 1776 to 1865, from 1865 to 1965, and from 1965 to today.

- The role, operations, activities and efforts of the Officials and Government of Vermont, all levels (federal, state, local and county) and all branches (legislative, executive and judicial), to prohibit and abolish piracy and privateering, slavery and the slave trade and colonialism, and have them publicly and legally declared crimes against humanity; and their role, activities, operations and efforts to abolish there current manifestations and practices today.

- Vermont's knowledge and legal understanding of, and response to Lord Mansfield's 1772 decision in Somerset v. Stewart.

- Vermont's Constitution and amendments, especially Article 1 that prohibits slavery. We are especially interested in discovering when the Constitution was written, who authored it, what legal doctrines did they base it on, in cannon law, international law, and municipal law; and what contact that they with the authors of the Constitutions of the 13 other British Colonies?

- Vermont's role, operations, and activities during the battles at Ticonderoga from May 10, 1775 to July 7, 1777, especially its liberation of slaves.

- The "Act to Prevent the Sale and Transportation of Negroes and Malattoes Out of This State" which was passed by the Vermont Legislature in 1786.

- The Embargo Act of 1807, its impact on the slave trade and slavery, and on the international commerce in slave-produced products and services, especially with Britain, Canada and other countries.

- The War of 1812 and the dispute between the United States and Britain over the evacuation of and compensation for slaves.

- The Vermont Colonization Society (1819); the Ferrisburg Anti-Slavery Society (1833); the Vermont Anti-Slavery Society (1834) and the 89 local anti-slavery societies with over 5,000 members that had been formed by 1837; the first anti-slavery party movement which was founded in 1835; the Anti-Slavery Party (1839) and the Liberty Party (1840) and the Republican Party of Vermont, and their struggle to prohibit and abolish piracy and privateering, slavery and the slave trade and colonialism, and have them publicly and legally declared crimes against humanity.

- The anti-slavery resolutions that were introduced into the Vermont Legislature in 1833 by Jonathan P. Miller, and his role in the world's Anti-Slavery Convention in London in 1840.

- The tours of Samuel May (1835) and Frederick Douglas' (1845), and the Government of Vermont's efforts to facilitate, and or hinder, to protect or harass them.

- Vermont's 1837 resolution to the U.S. Congress protesting against slavery in the District of Columbia, the admission of Texas as a slave state, and Senator Calhoun's response to Vermont's resolutions which was recorded in The Congressional Globe:

   > Calhoun deemed the present moment one of deepest importance. A great step has been take in the progress of events.. He had long foreseen the present state of things and now the time had actually come when it was to be determined whether we are to remain as one united and happy people or whether this union is to be dissolved by the hand of violence. Vermont has struck a deep and dangerous blow into the vitals of our confederacy.

- Vermont's Senators continued denunciation in 1837 of the practice of slavery, asking for its abolition in Washington, DC.

- Passage of a law in 1843 by the Vermont Legislature forbidding sheriffs, bailiffs, jailers, constables, and citizens from detaining fugitives and forbid state officials from imprisoning or assigning federal authorities in the recapture of escaped slaves.

- The vote by Vermont's Congressman for the Compromise of 1850, the Vermont Legislature's passage of an act to impede the carrying out of the Fugitive Slave Act, the Vermont Legislature's protests to other state legislatures, and Virginia's response:

   > The legislature of Virginia declines to consider the resolutions of the state of Vermont, relative to the peace of the world until that body shall show itself careful of the peace of the Union by conforming to the enactments of the Constitution of the United States and laws passed.

- The 1st and 2nd Confiscation Acts and the refusal of Vermont to return captured slaves to their masters in any state.

- Vermont's understanding of the legal and social status and condition of slaves, especially fugitive slaves in Canada, and Vermont's role in the Underground Railroad.

- The Emancipation Proclamation; and any and all discussions about Compensated Emancipation, Emigration or Repatriation, and Reparations; and Vermont' understanding of, position on, and role in these discussions over these issues, historically and currently.

- Vermont's ratification of the 13th and 14th and 15th Amendments to the United States Constitution which abolished the practice of slavery and gave former slaves US citizenship and all its privileges.

- Vermont's role, operations and activities, historical and current, in struggling to prohibit, abolish and combat the establishment of slave-like conditions and practices, and segregation in the wake of the aborted and failed efforts at Reconstruction; and prohibiting, abolishing and combating segregation, apartheid, racism and racial discrimination, xenophobia, and related intolerance.

- All governments, agencies (federal, state, county or local), corporations, non-governmental organizations, institutions, churches, families, individuals, or entities, domestic or foreign who participated or invested in, or made profits from the above referenced crimes against humanity; and who owns or benefits from these historical and continuing crimes today, including but not limited to those listed in Appendix A.

We are especially interested in knowing if slave-produced products, including but not limited to cotton, sugar, molasses and rum were used or produced; who owned and controlled these firms; from whom did they acquire their raw materials and at what price; whom did they sell their products to and at what price; what if any taxes or revenue did the Governments of Virginia (state, county and local) and the United States receive; and who owns and or controls these companies, their successor entities, and related industries in Vermont today.

Please provide any and all records that pertain to, or reference the cotton mill which was built at Montpelier in 1810, one of the first 50 mills erected in the United States, that produced 121,326 yards of cotton cloth valued at $39,937 in 1810; the 125 distilleries that produced 173,285 gallons of liquor valued at $129,964 in 1810; the 27 cotton and woolen factories and 150 distilleries in 1823; the nine cotton mills employing 241 people and with an output valued at $280,300 in 1850; and the eight cotton mills that employed 451 persons in 1870.

Please provide also any and all records that pertain to, or reference the manufacturing industry in the following counties, especially whether any slave labor or products produced by slave labor were used or produced; and any and all companies, governmental agencies, not-for-profit institutions, families or individuals who invested in or received profits from any and all aspects of slavery and the slave trade, or its related activities and industries, in Vermont, the United States or any where in the world:

	Employees	Capital Investment	Annual Product
Addison County	597	$289,375	$659,838
Bennington County	769	$468,050	$880,216
Caledonia County	816	$444,180	$799,053
Chittenden County	1,216	$771,610	$1,320,730
Essex County	55	$31,250	$48,794
Franklin County	394	$147,710	$285,697
Grand Isle County	47	$13,100	$15,600
Lamoille County	146	$110,300	$175,861
Orange County	253	$171,045	$219,165
Orleans County	125	$64,450	$119,036
Rutland County	1,379	$828,975	$1,284,760
Washington County	449	$231,337	$525,236

Windham County	922	$476,720	$831,209
Windsor County	1,277	$953,275	$1,405,730
TOTAL	8,445	$5,001,377	$8,570,925

We also formally and publicly request that you comply in an expedited manner with this Open Records Request, and that you waive all costs associated with it. Please be advised that we have disclosed this Request to the general public and media.

We expect your positive response to this historic and precedent setting Open Records Request within 20 working days. Please be assured that we will exhaust any and all administrative and political remedies. Thank you for your consideration.

Sincerely,
Bob Brown, co-director
Pan-African Roots

Pan-African Roots

1247 E Street SE
Washington, DC 20003
Tel: (202-) 544-9355 - Fax: (202) 544-9359
Email: paroots02@yahoo.com

25 October 2004

Mr. Mark Warner, Governor
Office of the Governor
State Capitol
Richmond, VA 23219

Open Records Request.
Fee Waiver and Expedited Review Request.
cc: Open Records Officer and Open Records Appeals Officer.

Dear Governor Warner:

As you are perhaps aware, 694,000 Africans were illegally held in slavery in the 13 original British Colonies from 1619 to 1776, over one half of them in Virginia and Maryland; 3,208,393 Africans were still being illegally held in slavery in these states in 1865; and their descendants were and are forced to suffer slave-like conditions and practices, segregation, racism and racial discrimination today.

You are perhaps not aware, that on May 17, 1860, the second National Republican Convention adopted its 1860 National Republican Platform, which declared it resolved:

> 7. That the new dogma that the Constitution of its own force carries slavery into any or all of the territories of the United States, is a dangerous political heresy, at variance with the explicit provisions of that instrument itself, with contemporaneous exposition, and with legislative and judicial precedent, is revolutionary in its tendency and subversive of the peace and harmony of the country.

> 8. That the formal condition of all the territory of the United States is that of freedom; that as our republican fathers, when they had abolished slavery in all our national territory, ordained that no "person should be deprived of life, liberty or property, without due process of law," it becomes our duty, by legislation, whenever such legislation is necessary, to maintain this provision of the constitution against all attempts to violate it; and we deny the authority of congress, of a territorial legislature, or of any individuals, to give legal existence to slavery in any territory of the United States.

> 9. That we brand the recent re-opening of the African Slave Trade, under the cover of our national flag, aided by perversions of judicial power, as a **crime against humanity, and a burning shame to our country and age,** and we call upon congress to take prompt and efficient measured for the total and final suppression of the execrable traffic. [230] [**Emphasis added.**]

The 1860 Republican National Convention selected Abraham Lincoln as its Presidential nominee. He campaigned on this platform, and "won the presidency with almost half a million voted more than [Stephen] Douglas, his closest rival. [Lincoln] won the election garnering 39.8 percent of the popular vote. This election firmly established the Republican hold on the presidency for 60 of the next 100 years.

You are perhaps also not aware that William Lloyd Garrison was the first person to declare slavery a crime against humanity in the inaugural edition (1831) of his Liberator newspaper; or that on November

---

[230] Central Pacific Railroad Photographic History Museum. *Republican Party National Platform, 1860.* Available from http://cprr.org/Museum/Ephemera/Republican_Platform_1860.html.

12, 1849, the Vermont Legislature passed "*Joint Resolution No. 42.--Resolutions Relating To The Subject of Slavery*," declaring it:

> Resolved by the Senate and House of Representatives, that Slavery is a **crime against humanity, and a sore evil** in the body politic that was excused by the framers of the Federal Constitution as a crime entailed upon the country by their predecessors, and tolerated solely as a thing of inexorable necessity.[231] [**Emphasis added.**]

We ask that you, as the Governor of Virginia, publicly reconfirm your commitment to the principle that slavery and the slave trade were and are crimes against humanity.

We request, pursuant to Open Records Law: Va. Code Ann. sections 2.1-340 to 2.1-346.1, that you give us access to or copies of all records created or obtained by the State of Virginia, or under your authority and control, that pertain to, or reference:

- Virginia's role, operations and activities, historically and currently, in facilitating, prohibiting or combating slavery and the slave trade, especially the Trans-Atlantic Slave Trade; and in the struggle to declare them crimes against humanity.

- Virginia's role, operations and activities, historically and currently, in facilitating, prohibiting or combating slave-like conditions and practices, including, but not limited to servitude, segregation, apartheid, racism and racial discrimination, xenophobia and related intolerance

- Slave, urban and racial disturbances, riots, rebellions, and revolts, runaway slaves, fugitives beyond borders, and related claims or demands for compensation, restitution or reparations.

- All governments, agencies (federal, state, county or local), corporations, non-governmental organizations, institutions, churches, families, individuals, or entities, domestic or foreign who participated or invested in, or made profits from the above referenced crimes against humanity; and who owns or benefits from these historical and continuing crimes today, including but not limited to those listed in Appendix A.

We are interested in knowing who owned and controlled these entities; from whom did they acquire their raw materials and at what price; to whom did they sell their products and at what price; what if any taxes or revenue did the Governments of Virginia (state, county and local) and the United States receive; and who owns or controls these entities today. We request access to or copies of all records that pertain to, or reference the subjects listed in the above paragraphs, for the following counties:

	Number of Slave-Holding Families	Number of Slaves	Value of Slaves ($1,000 @)	Value of Plantations
Accomack	773	$4,507	$4,507,000	$4,567,821
Albemarle	1,306	$13,916	$13,916,000	$10,536,129
Alleghany	134	$990	$990,000	$1,442,832
Amelia	536	$7,655	$7,655,000	$2,896,612
Amherst	685	$6,278	$6,278,000	$3,459,429
Appomattox	520	$4,600	$4,600,000	$2,348,225
Arlington/Alexandria	251	$1,386	$1,386,000	$966,929

---

[231] *The Acts and Resolves Passed By The Legislature Of The State of Vermont At The October Session, 1849.* Published By authority. Montpelier: E. P. Walton & Son. 1849.

Augusta		811	$5,616	$5,616,000	$12,856,818
Barbour		41	95	$95,000	$2,986,256
Bath		115	946	$946,000	$1,743,081
Bedford		1,129	10,176	$10,176,000	$7,653,371
Berkeley		333	1,650	$1,650,000	$4,061,985
Boone		36	158	$158,000	$758,698
Botetourt		332	2,769	$2,769,000	$3,989,244
Braxton		26	104	$104,000	$806,271
Brooke		12	18	$18,000	$2,821,601
Brunswick		772	9,146	$9,146,000	$2,973,966
Buchanan		3	30	$30,000	$323,427
Buckingham		718	8,811	$8,811,000	$4,188,460
Cabell		84	305	$305,000	$1,894,197
Calhoun		3	9	$9,000	$469,003
Campbell		1,705	11,580	$11,580,000	$4,316,942
Caroline		725	10,672	$10,672,000	$5,094,730
Carroll		82	262	$262,000	$1,128,437
Charles City		191	2,947	$2,947,000	$1,488,517
Charlotte		609	9,238	$9,238,000	$5,078,990
Chesterfield		806	8,354	$8,354,000	$3,830,034
Clarke		344	3,375	$3,375,000	$4,132,270
Clay		3	21	$21,000	$234,579
Craig		130	420	$420,000	$1,139,804
Culpeper		611	6,675	$6,675,000	$5,756,534
Cumberland		452	6,705	$6,705,000	$2,869,661
Dinwiddie		1,826	12,774	$12,774,000	$3,355,637
Doddridge		17	34	$34,000	$1,199,381
Elizabeth City		277	2,417	$2,417,000	$1,469,343
Essex		398	6,696	$6,696,000	$2,852,405
Fairfax		529	3,116	$3,116,000	$4,432,832
Fauquier		933	10,455	$10,455,000	$12,044,359
Fayette		63	271	$271,000	$1,490,171
Floyd		125	475	$475,000	$1,363,701
Fluvanna		521	4,994	$4,994,000	$2,829,079
Franklin		996	6,351	$6,351,000	$4,489,129
Frederick		406	2,259	$2,259,000	$4,761,249
Giles		145	778	$778,000	$2,136,889
Gilmer		20	52	$52,000	$784,611
Gloucester		487	5,736	$5,736,000	$2,363,694
Goochland		537	6,139	$6,139,000	$3,051,119
Grayson		124	547	$547,000	$1,937,163
Greenbrier		267	1,525	$1,525,000	$6,616,684
Greene		225	1,984	$1,984,000	$1,462,144
Greensville		268	4,167	$4,167,000	$1,288,957
Halifax		1,051	14,897	$14,897,000	$8,087,969
Hampshire		244	1,213	$1,213,000	$5,019,671
Hancock	M		2	$2,000	$1,925,501
Hanover		903	9,483	$9,483,000	$5,047,547

197

Hardy	157	1,073	$1,073,000	$3,179,923
Harrison	159	582	$582,000	$5,438,104
Henrico	2,339	20,041	$20,041,000	$5,900,216
Henry	422	5,018	$5,018,000	$2,785,211
Highland	116	402	$402,000	$1,859,730
Highland	470			
Jackson	25	55	$55,000	$1,611,975
James City	230	2,586	$2,586,000	$1,198,957
Jefferson	634	3,960	$3,960,000	$6,357,760
Kanawha	265	2,184	$2,184,000	$2,186,075
King And Queen	449	6,139	$6,139,000	$2,848,510
King George	314	3,673	$3,673,000	$2,237,000
King William	366	5,525	$5,525,000	$2,963,860
Lancaster	259	2,869	$2,869,000	$1,561,053
Lee	151	824	$824,000	$3,375,472
Lewis	60	230	$230,000	$1,619,666
Logan	40	148	$148,000	$780,967
Loudoun	670	5,501	$5,501,000	$12,137,829
Louisa	765	10,194	$10,194,000	$5,267,955
Lunenburg	545	7,305	$7,305,000	$2,770,615
Madison	455	4,397	$4,397,000	$3,367,562
Marion	32	63	$63,000	$3,724,137
Marshall	14	29	$29,000	$2,892,156
Mason	70	376	$376,000	$2,305,056
Mathews	386	3,008	$3,008,000	$1,684,404
Mecklenburg	760	12,420	$12,420,000	$4,356,609
Mercer	66	362	$362,000	$1,908,575
Middlesex	204	2,375	$2,375,000	$1,341,812
Monongalia	37	101	$101,000	$3,462,217
Monroe	196	1,114	$1,114,000	$4,446,711
Montgomery	283	2,219	$2,219,000	$3,617,688
Morgan	30	94	$94,000	$653,346
Nansemond	619	5,481	$5,481,000	$2,128,668
Nelson	554	6,238	$6,238,000	$4,577,308
New Kent	291	3,374	$3,374,000	$1,597,719
Nicholas	46	154	$154,000	$4,099,741
Norfolk	1,464	9,004	$9,004,000	$2,824,790
Northampton	400	3,872	$3,872,000	$2,530,112
Northumberland	401	3,439	$3,439,000	$2,034,440
Nottoway	375	6,468	$6,468,000	$2,058,008
Ohio	43	100	$100,000	$2,768,600
Orange	480	6,111	$6,111,000	$4,445,521
Page	177	850	$850,000	$2,658,456
Patrick	318	2,070	$2,070,000	$1,590,483
Pendleton	52	244	$244,000	$2,090,605
Pittsylvania	1,413	14,340	$14,340,000	$6,854,937
Pleasants	5	15	$15,000	$764,285
Pocahontas	64	252	$252,000	$2,477,470

Powhatan	375	5,403	$5,403,000	$2,521,528
Preston	20	67	$67,000	$2,921,454
Prince Edward	582	7,341	$7,341,000	$3,398,846
Prince George	344	4,997	$4,997,000	$2,316,127
Prince William	273	2,356	$2,356,000	$2,825,116
Princess Anne	506	3,186	$3,186,000	$2,309,332
Pulaski	157	1,589	$1,589,000	$2,772,946
Putnam	93	580	$580,000	$1,581,201
Raleigh	21	57	$57,000	$513,944
Randolph	56	183	$183,000	$1,935,895
Rappahannock	398	3,520	$3,520,000	$3,427,886
Richmond	259	2,466	$2,466,000	$1,506,937
Ritchie	12	38	$38,000	$1,792,549
Roane	23	72	$72,000	$657,595
Roanoke	259	2,643	$2,643,000	$2,715,248
Rockbridge	569	3,985	$3,985,000	$6,785,558
Rockingham	420	2,387	$2,387,000	$11,412,117
Russell	171	1,099	$1,099,000	$2,998,609
Scott	127	490	$490,000	$2,692,021
Shenandoah	117	753	$753,000	$4,598,898
Smyth	218	1,037	$1,037,000	$3,116,485
Southampton	494	5,408	$5,408,000	$2,333,479
Spotsylvania	1,031	7,786	$7,786,000	$2,859,754
Stafford	621	3,314	$3,314,000	$1,856,028
Surry	188	2,515	$2,515,000	$1,334,803
Sussex	428	6,384	$6,384,000	$2,184,596
Taylor	47	112	$112,000	$1,302,688
Tazewell	223	1,202	$1,202,000	$3,521,333
Tucker	5	20	$20,000	$366,828
Tyler	8	18	$18,000	$1,792,615
Upshur	51	212	$212,000	$2,024,130
Warren	229	1,575	$1,575,000	$2,603,781
Warwick	91	1,019	$1,019,000	$508,137
Washington	386	2,547	$2,547,000	$4,965,205
Wayne	37	143	$143,000	$1,139,490
Webster	1	3	$3,000	$260,536
Westmoreland	380	3,704	$3,704,000	$2,249,227
Wetzel	6	10	$10,000	$1,405,030
Wirt	11	23	$23,000	$732,265
Wise	13	66	$66,000	$689,182
Wood	64	176	$176,000	$1,986,437
Wyoming	6	64	$64,000	$354,263
Wythe	271	2,162	$2,162,000	$4,442,888
York	226	1,925	$1,925,000	$1,357,187
TOTAL	52,128	487,295	$487,295,000	$441,236,556

We ask that you comply in an expedited manner with this Request, and waive all associated costs. Please be advised that we have disclosed this Request to the public and media.

In order to help you determine our status and make your decision on our fee waiver request, you should know that Bob Brown is an organizer and researcher, who has worked, studied and struggled for 41 years, within and for the Student, Civil and Human Rights, Black Power, National Liberation, Pan-African, and Peace Movements. See Attachment B.

We expect your positive response to this historic and precedent setting Request within 20 working days. Please be assured that we will exhaust administrative and political remedies. Thank you for your consideration.

Sincerely,
Bob Brown, co-director
Pan-African Roots

Pan-African Roots

1247 E Street SE
Washington, DC 20003
Tel: (202) 544-9355 - Fax: (202) 544-9359
Email: paroots02@yahoo.com

25 October 2004

Mr. Rod Blagojevich, Governor
State Capitol
207 Statehouse
Springfield, IL 62706

AMENDED OPEN RECORDS REQUEST.
Fee Waiver and Expedited Review Request.

Dear Governor Blagojevich:

As you are perhaps aware, in 1720, Philip Francis Renault landed 500 Africans at St. Philip, and sold them to the French settlers. They had been kidnapped from Africa, transported and enslaved in Santo Domingo, known as Haiti today.

As you are also perhaps aware, Article VI of the Northwest Ordinance of 1787 provided: "there shall be neither slavery nor involuntary servitude in the said territory, otherwise than in the punishment of crimes, whereof the party shall have been duly convicted."

Governors St. Clair, Ninian, Harrison, and others, claimed that the Northwest Ordinance of 1787 did not affect the prior status of these slaves. The legislature, executive branch and courts of Illinois held this view until at least 1845. According to the website of the Office of the Secretary of State, African People were illegally held in slavery in the following counties. Thousands were also held in a legal fiction called voluntary servitude.

County	Number of Slaves		
	1820	1830	1840
Alexander		6	
Bond	27	1	5
Brown	1		3
Clay		2	
Clinton	7	5	10
Fayette		24	
Franklin	7	9	5
Gallatin	267	184	24
Greene		9	
Hamilton		2	
Hardin			13
Jackson	39	21	
Jackson	1		
Jersey			2
Jo Daviess		31	6
Johnson	13	11	15

Madison	110	24	10
Marion		1	
Monroe	13	38	11
Montgomery		4	
Perry		4	
Pope		25	
Randolph	233	211	133
Sangamon		13	6
Schuyler			9
Shelby		2	
St Clair	98	96	59
Tazewell		4	
Union	24	4	4
Washington	26	13	
Wayne	3	3	
White	48		15
Winnebago			1
TOTAL	848	627	330

From at least 1835, Abraham Lincoln, Lyman Trumbull, Gustav Koerner, John M. Palmer and other lawyers advised Africans illegally held in bondage that they were entitled to their freedom. Cases, however, involving the rights of Africans progressed through the courts, very slowly.

In 1845, the case of Jarrot v. Jarrot was decided by the Supreme Court of Illinois. According to the complaint, Joseph Jarrot, Pelaque, his mother, and Angelique, his grandmother were held in slavery by the Lebrun and Jarrot families from at least 1784. Lyman Trumbull, Joseph's attorney and the "father "of the 13th Amendment to the United States Constitution, brought an action of assumpsit on Joseph's behalf for work and labor in the St. Clair County Circuit Court. Joseph claimed that his labor for the past five years was worth five dollars above his clothing and his board. The County Court decided the case in Joseph's favor. The Illinois Supreme Court upheld that decision in the following language:

> If words are not mere empty sounds, if they mean anything, then the plaintiff is free by virtue of the express declaration of the Northwest Ordinance and the Constitution of Illinois.[232]

According to Judge P. Hand," the effect of this decision was to liberate all the French negro slaves and their children in Illinois from the bondage which for fifty-eight years had illegally deprived them and their ancestors of their freedom."[233] The Illinois Supreme Court ordered Julia Jarrot to pay Joseph the $5 owed him, a precedent for the payment of compensation for illegally extorted slave labor.

Upon information and belief, a number of entities invested in or profited from slavery, the slave trade, and slave-like practices and conditions in Illinois. On March 29, 1837, the Illinois and St. Louis Railroad, one of the Illinois Central Railroad's earliest predecessor lines, was chartered by a five-man syndicate that included John Reynolds and Vital Jarrot, in order to haul over 300,000 bushels of coal, food and other raw materials yearly to Illinoistown, (now known as East St. Louis), and then by the Wiggins Ferry across the Mississippi River to St. Louis. By 1873, though "a succession of changes of ownership and names,

---

[232] Honorable Judge P. Hand. *Negro Slavery in Illinois. Illinois Trails and History Genealogy*. Available from http://www.iltrails.org.
[233] Ibid.

this line had become a part of the Illinois Central System known as the Cairo Short Line, ... the richest dollar-per-mile railroad in America."[234]

John Reynolds was a former Governor of Illinois, a Justice of the Illinois Supreme Court, member of the Illinois State Legislature, and one of its Congressional Representatives. Like many of the initial governors and officials of the State of Illinois, Reynolds owned slaves, and proudly said so in his autobiography, *My Own Times*. His wife, Julien Dubuque and her family, also owned slaves. In a letter dated May 14, 1815, Governor Reynolds asked a St. Louis newspaper to run the following advertisement:

> Fifty dollars reward will be given to any person who will deliver to me in Cahokia a negro boy named 'Moses,' who ran away from me in Cahokia about two months since. He is about 16 years old, well made and did belong to McKnight and Brady, in St. Louis, where he has been seen frequently, and is supposed to be harbored there or about there. He had on a hunting shirt when he left me.[235]

Vital Jarrot was also a descendant of the original French settlers in Illinois. His father and mother, Nicolas and Julia Jarrot, were members of the richest slave-holding family in St. Clair County, Cahokia and East St. Louis. Julia's family, the Beauvais, "owned eighty slaves, and furnished to the royal magazine eighty-thousand weight of flour, which was only part of one's year's harvest."[236]

William Lloyd Garrison was the first person to declare slavery a crime against humanity in the inaugural edition (1831) of his <u>Liberator</u> newspaper. On November 12, 1849, the Vermont Legislature passed "*Joint Resolution No. 42.-- --Resolutions Relating To The Subject of Slavery*," declaring it:

> Resolved by the Senate and House of Representatives, That Slavery is a **crime against humanity**, and a sore evil in the body politic that was **excused** by the framers of the Federal Constitution as **a crime entailed** upon the country by their predecessors, and **tolerated** solely as a thing of inexorable necessity.[237] [**Emphasis added.**]

In 1860, the Illinois Central Railroad and the Central Pacific Railroad helped organize and finance the 1860 Republican National Convention, which was held in Chicago. They participated in the decision to include paragraphs 7 through 9 in the 1860 Republican National Platform, declaring:

> 7. That the new dogma that the Constitution of its own force carries slavery into any or all of the territories of the United States, is a dangerous political heresy, at variance with the explicit provisions of that instrument itself, with contemporaneous exposition, and with legislative and judicial precedent, is revolutionary in its tendency and subversive of the peace and harmony of the country.

> 8. That the normal condition of all the territory of the United States is that of freedom. That as our Republican fathers, **when they had abolished slavery in all our national territory,** ordained that "no person should be deprived of life, liberty or property, without due process of law," it becomes our duty by legislation, whenever such legislation is necessary, to maintain this provision of the Constitution against all attempts to violate it; and **we deny the authority** of Congress, of a territorial legislature, or of any individuals, **to give legal existence to slave**ry in any territory of the United States. [**Emphasis added.**]

> 9. That we [the Republican Party] brand the recent re-opening of the African Slave Trade [from Cuba], under the cover of our national flag, aided by perversions of judicial power, as **a crime**

---

[234] East St. Louis Action Project. *The New Era of Transportation.* University of Illinois at Urbana-Champaign.

[235] Ibid.

[236] Formerly available from the Cahokia website.

[237] *The Acts and Resolves Passed By The Legislature Of The State of Vermont At The October Session, 1849.* Published By authority. Montpelier: E. P. Walton & Son. 1849.

against humanity, and a burning shame to our country and age, and we call upon congress to take prompt and efficient measures for the total and final suppression of that execrable traffic.[238] **[Emphasis added.]**

The 1860 Republican National Convention selected Abraham Lincoln as its Presidential nominee. He campaigned on this platform, and "won the presidency with almost half a million votes more than [Stephen] Douglas, his closest rival. [Lincoln] won the election garnering 39.8 percent of the popular vote. This election firmly established the Republican hold on the presidency for 60 of the next 100 years.

With these considerations in mind, we formally and publicly request, pursuant to, Ill. Comp. Stat. tit. 5 sections 140/1 to140/11, access to or copies of all records pertaining to or referencing:

- Illinois' role, operations and activities, historically and currently, in facilitating, prohibiting or combating slavery and the slave trade, especially the Trans-Atlantic Slave Trade; and in the struggle to declare them crimes against humanity.

- Illinois' role, operations and activities, historically and currently, in facilitating, prohibiting or combating slave-like conditions and practices, including, but not limited to servitude, segregation, apartheid, racism and racial discrimination, xenophobia and related intolerance

- Slave, urban and racial disturbances, riots, rebellions, and revolts, runaway slaves, fugitives beyond borders, and related claims or demands for compensation, restitution or reparations.

- The Trail of Tears as it passed through Illinois, especially the condition and legal status of the Africans--freedmen and slaves, who were among its victims.

- All court and govermental records documenting or referencing Jarrot v. Jarrot, or documenting and referencing slavery, servitude, or slave-like practices and conditions in Illinois.

- All governments, agencies (federal, state, county or local), corporations, non-governmental organizations, institutions, churches, families, individuals, or entities, domestic or foreign who participated or invested in, or made profits from the above referenced crimes against humanity; and who owns or benefits from these historical and continuing crimes today, including but not limited to those listed in Appendix A.

We request all records that document or reference slavery or servitude in the above counties, especially the names of the slave-holding families, and their descendants today, and the names of the slaves, and their descendants today. We want to know what type of work these slaves performed, whether all slaves, especially Joseph, and their descendants were freed as ordered by the Court, and whether Joseph and they were paid for their 58-years of illegal enslavement.

We further request that you, as the Governor of the State of Illinois, immediately and publicly reaffirm that slavery and the slave trade were and are illegal in the State of Illinois, that they were and are crimes against humanity, and that these Africans, and their descendants today, were and are entitled to assumpsit, as ordered by the Court. We further ask that you convene a series of meetings to investigate and discuss ways and means to resolve this sordid affair.

We ask that you comply in an expedited manner with this Request, and waive all associated costs. Please be advised that we have disclosed this Request to the public and media.

In order to help you determine our status and make your decision on our fee waiver request, you should know that Bob Brown is an organizer and researcher, who has worked, studied and struggled for 41 years, within and for the Student, Civil and Human Rights, Black Power, National Liberation, Pan-African, and Peace Movements. See Attachment B.

---

[238] Central Pacific Railroad Photographic History Museum. *Republican Party National Platform, 1860.* Available from http://cprr.org/Museum/Ephemera/Republican_Platform_1860.html.

204

Disclosure of the requested information is in the public interest and a matter of urgency. It will be meaningfully informative in relation to the subject matter of this FOIA Request, and because its release will likely contribute significantly to greater public understanding of the government's role, operations, and activities in the struggle to facilitate, prohibit and abolish these crimes. Most of the requested records are not in the public domain, and those that are in the public domain are not accessible to the public that we serve. This Request is not primarily in our commercial interest. We are qualified and able to extract, convey and disseminate the information to the public at large.

We expect your positive response to this historic and precedent setting Request within 20 working days. Please be assured that we will exhaust all administrative, political, legal remedies. Thank you for your consideration.

Sincerely,
Bob Brown, co-director
Pan-African Roots

Pan-African Roots

1247 E Street SE
Washington, DC 20003
Tel: (202) 544-9355 - Fax: (202) 544-9359
Email: paroots02@yahoo.com

25 October 2004

Mr. Richard M. Daley, Mayor
City Hall, 5th Floor
121 North LaSalle Street
Chicago, IL 60602-1284

FREEDOM OF INFORMATION ACT REQUEST
CHICAGO SLAVERY ERA DISCLOSURE REQUEST
Fee Waiver and Expedited Review Request.

Dear Mayor Daley:

This is to inform you that, pursuant to Ill. Comp. Stat. tit. 5 sections 140/1 to140/11, we have sent the enclosed Freedom of Information Request to Mr. Rod Blagojevich, Governor of Illinois.

As you are perhaps aware, on 13 November 2003, we filed Freedom of Information Act Request No: 03/6/24 with the City of Chicago "requesting all Vendor Affidavits and/or related records, that have been filed with the Department of Procurement Services pursuant to the requirements of the Chicago Slavery Era Disclosure Ordinance."

On 19 November 2003, we received a reply from Mr. Steve Geocaris, Managing Deputy Procurement Officer, suggesting that if we needed additional information that is not available on their website, we "should submit a revised written request identifying that information." Please consider this letter and the enclosed letter to Governor Blagojevich, our revised written Freedom of Information Act and Chicago Slavery Era Disclosure Act Request.

We formally and publicly request that the City of Chicago, you, and all departments or agencies under your authority and control, provide us with (1) all of the records requested in our letter to the Governor, including information on the entities listed in Appendix A; (2) a list of all entities that are currently doing business with the City of Chicago, with the date and amount of award, and completion or renewal date; (3) a list of all contracts that have been awarded by the City of Chicago since February 2002, with the date and amount of award, completion or renewal date, and the required Certification Regarding Slavery Era Information; and (4) a list of all bids or proposals for pending or future awards. We also ask that you waive all costs associated with this Request.

We request that you, as the Mayor of the City of Chicago, publicly and immediately reaffirm that African People were illegally held in slavery in Illinois from at least 1787 to 1845, that slavery was and is a crime against humanity, and that these enslaved Africans, and their descendants, were and are owed compensation for their labor. We further ask that you convene a series of meetings to investigate and discuss ways and means to resolve this sordid affair.

We expect your positive response to this historic and precedent setting Request within 20 working days. Please be assured that we will exhaust administrative, legal and political remedies. Thank you for your consideration.

Sincerely,
Bob Brown, co-director
Pan-African Roots

PART IV: CALL FOR MORE STUDY AND WORK

In the new African renaissance, we place great emphasis on the presentation of history. Our history needs to be written as the history of our society, not as the story of European adventures. African society must be treated as enjoying its own integrity; its history must be a mirror of that society, and the European contact must find its place in this history only as an African experience, even if as a crucial one. That is to say, the European contact needs to be assessed and judged from the point of view of the principles animating African society, and from the point of view of the harmony and progress of this society. When history is presented in this way, ... it can become a map of the growing tragedy and the final triumph of our society.

Osagefyo Kwame Nkrumah
Consciencism: Philosophy and the Ideology for De-colonization. Page 64.

On 24 August 2004, Pan-African Roots convened a Press Conference at the Nation Press Club in Washington, DC to announce that we had filed the first round in a series of historic and precedent setting Freedom of Information Act, Open and Public Records Act, and Information Requests. We have spent the past sixty days amending and re-filing these Requests, preparing them for publication as a model FOI Request and an educational tool. We will spend the next sixty days exhausting administrative remedies in preparation for the filing of a massive and landmark FOIA lawsuit in January of 2005.

We are firmly and irrevocably convinced, as the timeline of events, edicts, laws, decisions and pronouncements in our Requests reveal, that the requested records, in the hands of the People, especially the Reparations Movement, once properly interpreted will:

- Bear witness to and prove, once and for all, that piracy, slavery and the slave trade, including the Trans-Atlantic Slave Trade, and slave-like conditions and practices, including colonialism, segregation and apartheid, were illegal and prohibited, and were recognized as crimes against humanity when and where they were committed.

- Help define and mark the successive stages in the development of the 569-year historical and continuing Maafa, and of the unyielding and continuing struggle against it.

- Document who the victims of the Maafa were, and who their descendants are today; who committed these crimes, which were and are the greatest theft of land, lives and labor in human history; how this unjust and illegal wealth was converted, consolidated, preserved and transferred across generations and centuries; and who owns and benefits from this unjust enrichment today.

We issue an open appeal and call to the Reparations Movement, throughout Africa, the African Diaspora, and the world, for more study (research), more work (mass education and organization), and more struggle (administrative, political and legal). We are confident that the Reparations Movement will grow and develop in its intensity, scope and scale, world-wide, and become increasingly more Pan-African and more radical.

We hope that this initial and incomplete research effort contributes, in some small way, to its inevitable victory. We are honored to be afforded the privilege of making this humble contribution!

Appendix A: List of U.S. Entities To Be Researched

The United States Government
- 400,000+ slave-holding families
- 30+ slave-holding states
- 1,200+slave-holding counties
- thousands of slave-holding municipalities
- thousands of quasi-governmental organizations

Slave-Holding States, Counties and Families
State of Alabama
- Autauga County, 576 families holding 9,607 slaves in 1860.
- Baldwin County, 289 families holding 3,714 slaves in 1860.
- Barbour County, 1,143 families holding 16,150 slaves in 1860.
- Bibb County, 447 families holding 3,842 slaves in 1860.
- Blount County, 125 families holding 666 slaves in 1860.
- Butler County, 748 families holding 6,818 slaves in 1860.
- Calhoun/Benton County, 567 families holding 4,342 slaves in 1860.
- Chambers County, 1,298 families holding 11,849 slaves in 1860.
- Cherokee County, 498 families holding 3,002 slaves in 1860.
- Choctaw County, 640 families holding 7,094 slaves in 1860.
- Clarke County, 645 families holding 7,436 slaves in 1860.
- Coffee County, 239 families holding 1,417 slaves in 1860.
- Conecuh County, 398 families holding 4,882 slaves in 1860.
- Coosa County, 641 families holding 5,212 slaves in 1860.
- Covington County, 144 families holding 821 slaves in 1860.
- Dale County, 314 families holding 1,809 slaves in 1860.
- Dallas County, 1,280 families holding 25,760 slaves in 1860.
- De Kalb County, 165 families holding 848 slaves in 1860.

- Fayette County, 330 families holding 1,703 slaves in 1860.
- Franklin County, 519 families holding 8,495 slaves in 1860.
- Greene County, 1,115 families holding 23,598 slaves in 1860.
- Henry County, 489 families holding 4,433 slaves in 1860.
- Jackson County, 482 families holding 3,405 slaves in 1860.
- Jefferson County, 284 families holding 2,649 slaves in 1860.
- Lauderdale County, 522 families holding 6,737 slaves in 1860.
- Lawrence County, 391 families holding 6,788 slaves in 1860.
- Limestone County, 661 families holding 8,085 slaves in 1860.
- Lowndes County, 1,098 families holding 19,340 slaves in 1860.
- Macon County, 1,020 families holding 18,176 slaves in 1860.
- Madison County, 1,117 families holding 14,573 slaves in 1860.
- Marengo County, 944 families holding 24,409 slaves in 1860.
- Marion County, 204 families holding 1,283 slaves in 1860.
- Marshall County, 224 families holding 1,821 slaves in 1860.
- Mobile County, 1,785 families holding 11,376 slaves in 1860.
- Monroe County, 676 families holding 8,705 slaves in 1860.
- Montgomery County, 1,385 families holding 23,710 slaves in 1860.
- Morgan/Cotaco County, 391 families holding 3,706 slaves in 1860.
- Perry County, 1,045 families holding 18,206 slaves in 1860.
- Pickens County, 1,071 families holding 12,191 slaves in 1860.
- Pike County, 999 families holding 8,785 slaves in 1860.
- Randolph County, 406 families holding 1,904 slaves in 1860.

- Russell County, 1,044 families holding 15,638 slaves in 1860.
- Shelby County, 428 families holding 3,622 slaves in 1860.
- St Clair County, 257 families holding 1,768 slaves in 1860.
- Sumter County, 889 families holding 18,091 slaves in 1860.
- Talladega County, 796 families holding 8,865 slaves in 1860.
- Tallapoosa County, 776 families holding 6,672 slaves in 1860.
- Tuscaloosa County, 886 families holding 10,145 slaves in 1860.
- Walker County, 102 families holding 519 slaves in 1860.
- Washington County, 179 families holding 2,494 slaves in 1860.
- Wilcox County, 1,044 families holding 17,797 slaves in 1860.
- Winston/Hancock County, 14 families holding 122 slaves in 1860.

State of Arkansas
- Arkansas County, 260 families holding 4,921 slaves in 1860.
- Ashley County, 417 families holding 3,761 slaves in 1860.
- Benton County, 107 families holding 384 slaves in 1860.
- Bradley County, 311 families holding 2,690 slaves in 1860.
- Calhoun County, 133 families holding 981 slaves in 1860.
- Carroll County, 84 families holding 330 slaves in 1860.
- Chicot County, 225 families holding 7,512 slaves in 1860.
- Clark County, 335 families holding 2,214 slaves in 1860.
- Columbia County, 429 families holding 3,599 slaves in 1860.
- Conway County, 110 families holding 802 slaves in 1860.
- Craighead County, 25 families holding 87 slaves in 1860.
- Crawford County, 153 families holding 858 slaves in 1860.
- Crittenden County, 153 families holding 2,347 slaves in 1860.
- Dallas County, 316 families holding 3,494 slaves in 1860.
- Desha County, 204 families holding 3,784 slaves in 1860.
- Drew County, 393 families holding 3,497 slaves in 1860.
- Franklin County, 129 families holding 962 slaves in 1860.
- Fulton County, 26 families holding 88 slaves in 1860.
- Greene County, 56 families holding 189 slaves in 1860.
- Hempstead County, 447 families holding 5,398 slaves in 1860.
- Hot Spring County, 124 families holding 613 slaves in 1860.
- Independence County, 246 families holding 1,337 slaves in 1860.
- Izard County, 65 families holding 382 slaves in 1860.
- Jackson County, 298 families holding 2,535 slaves in 1860.
- Jefferson County, 563 families holding 7,146 slaves in 1860.
- Johnson County, 170 families holding 973 slaves in 1860.
- Lafayette County, 271 families holding 4,311 slaves in 1860.
- Lawrence County, 139 families holding 494 slaves in 1860.
- Madison County, 82 families holding 296 slaves in 1860.
- Marion County, 70 families holding 261 slaves in 1860.
- Mississippi County, 76 families holding 1,461 slaves in 1860.
- Monroe County, 178 families holding 2,226 slaves in 1860.
- Montgomery County, 24 families holding 92 slaves in 1860.
- Newton County, 11 families holding 24 slaves in 1860.
- Ouachita County, 587 families holding 4,478 slaves in 1860.
- Perry County, 30 families holding 303 slaves in 1860.
- Phillips County, 549 families holding 8,941 slaves in 1860.
- Pike County, 63 families holding 227 slaves in 1860.
- Poinsett County, 133 families holding 1,086 slaves in 1860.

- Polk County, 59 families holding 172 slaves in 1860.
- Pope County, 209 families holding 978 slaves in 1860.
- Prairie County, 371 families holding 2,839 slaves in 1860.
- Pulaski County, 377 families holding 3,505 slaves in 1860.
- Randolph County, 85 families holding 359 slaves in 1860.
- Saline County, 169 families holding 749 slaves in 1860.
- Scott County, 50 families holding 215 slaves in 1860.
- Searcy County, 20 families holding 93 slaves in 1860.
- Sebastian County, 121 families holding 680 slaves in 1860.
- Sevier County, 357 families holding 3,366 slaves in 1860.
- St Francis County, 311 families holding 2,621 slaves in 1860.
- Union County, 607 families holding 6,331 slaves in 1860.
- Van Buren County, 53 families holding 200 slaves in 1860.
- Washington County, 301 families holding 1,493 slaves in 1860.
- White County, 250 families holding 1,432 slaves in 1860.
- Yell County, 149 families holding 998 slaves in 1860.

State of Connecticut
- Fairfield County, 470 families holding 799 slaves in 1790.
- Hartford County, 157 families holding 256 slaves in 1790.
- Litchfield County, 119 families holding 203 slaves in 1790.
- Middlesex County, 114 families holding 192 slaves in 1790.
- New Haven County, 241 families holding 387 slaves in 1790.
- New London County, 329 families holding 581 slaves in 1790.
- Tolland County, 35 families holding 46 slaves in 1790.
- Windha County, 98 families holding 184 slaves in 1790.

State of Delaware
- Kent County, unknown number of families holding 2,300 slaves in 1790; and 66 families holding 203 slaves in 1860.
- New Castle County, unknown number of families holding 2,562 slaves in 1790.
- Sussex County, unknown number of families holding 4,025 slaves in 1790.

State of Florida
- Alachua County, 300 families holding 4,457 slaves in 1860.
- Bradford/New River County, 121 families holding 744 slaves in 1860.
- Brevard/St Lucie County, 4 families holding 21 slaves in 1860.
- Calhoun County, 27 families holding 524 slaves in 1860.
- Clay County, 49 families holding 519 slaves in 1860.
- Columbia County, 205 families holding 2,063 slaves in 1860.
- Dade County, 2 families holding 2 slaves in 1860.
- Duval County, 240 families holding 1,987 slaves in 1860.
- Escambia County, 237 families holding 1,961 slaves in 1860.
- Franklin County, 60 families holding 520 slaves in 1860.
- Gadsden County, 355 families holding 5,409 slaves in 1860.
- Hamilton County, 156 families holding 1,397 slaves in 1860.
- Hernando/Benton County, unknown number of families holding 200 slaves in 1860.
- Hillsborough County, 120 families holding 564 slaves in 1860.
- Holmes County, 29 families holding 112 slaves in 1860.
- Jackson County, 357 families holding 4,903 slaves in 1860.
- Jefferson County, 397 families holding 6,374 slaves in 1860.
- Lafayette County, 42 families holding 577 slaves in 1860.
- Leon County, 515 families holding 9,089 slaves in 1860.
- Levy County, 46 families holding 450 slaves in 1860.
- Liberty County, 46 families holding 521 slaves in 1860.

- Madison County, 264 families holding 4,249 slaves in 1860.
- Manatee County, 19 families holding 253 slaves in 1860.
- Marion County, 345 families holding 5,314 slaves in 1860.
- Monroe County, 91 families holding 451 slaves in 1860.
- Nassau County, 189 families holding 1,612 slaves in 1860.
- Orange/Mosquito County, 31 families holding 163 slaves in 1860.
- Putna County, 103 families holding 1,047 slaves in 1860.
- Santa Rosa County, 166 families holding 1,371 slaves in 1860.
- St Johns County, 157 families holding 1,003 slaves in 1860.
- Sumter County, 67 families holding 549 slaves in 1860.
- Suwannee County, 72 families holding 835 slaves in 1860.
- Taylor County, 23 families holding 125 slaves in 1860.
- Volusia County, 38 families holding 297 slaves in 1860.
- Wakulla County, 116 families holding 1,167 slaves in 1860.
- Walton County, 107 families holding 441 slaves in 1860.
- Washington County, 56 families holding 474 slaves in 1860.

State of Georgia

- Appling County, 122 families holding 745 slaves in 1860.
- Baker County, 183 families holding 3,492 slaves in 1860.
- Baldwin County, 486 families holding 4,929 slaves in 1860.
- Banks County, 162 families holding 1,086 slaves in 1860.
- Bartow/Cass County, 425 families holding 4,282 slaves in 1860.
- Berrien County, 109 families holding 432 slaves in 1860.
- Bibb County, 793 families holding 6,790 slaves in 1860.
- Brooks County, 262 families holding 3,282 slaves in 1860.
- Bryan County, 111 families holding 2,379 slaves in 1860.
- Bulloch County, 255 families holding 2,162 slaves in 1860.
- Burke County, unknown number of families holding 2,392 slaves in 1790; and 720 families holding 12,052 slaves in 1860.
- Butts County, 317 families holding 3,067 slaves in 1860.
- Calhoun County, 210 families holding 2,731 slaves in 1860.
- Camden County, unknown number of families holding 70 slaves in 1790.
- Campbell County, 278 families holding 2,004 slaves in 1860.
- Carroll County, 360 families holding 1,862 slaves in 1860.
- Catoosa County, 119 families holding 710 slaves in 1860.
- Charlton County, 55 families holding 557 slaves in 1860.
- Chatha County, unknown number of families holding 8,201 slaves in 1790.
- Chatha County, 1,205 families holding 14,807 slaves in 1860.
- Chattahoochee County, 234 families holding 2,758 slaves in 1860.
- Chattooga County, 276 families holding 2,054 slaves in 1860.
- Cherokee County, 207 families holding 1,199 slaves in 1860.
- Clarke County, 544 families holding 5,660 slaves in 1860.
- Clay County, 193 families holding 2,253 slaves in 1860.
- Clayton County, 170 families holding 1,226 slaves in 1860.
- Clinch County, 74 families holding 449 slaves in 1860.
- Cobb County, 529 families holding 3,819 slaves in 1860.
- Coffee County, 75 families holding 663 slaves in 1860.
- Colquitt County, 27 families holding 110 slaves in 1860.
- Columbia County, 487 families holding 8,293 slaves in 1860.
- Coweta County, 691 families holding 7,248 slaves in 1860.
- Crawford County, 369 families holding 4,270 slaves in 1860.
- Dade County, 46 families holding 300 slaves in 1860.

- Dawson County, 62 families holding 326 slaves in 1860.
- De Kalb County, 303 families holding 2,000 slaves in 1860.
- Decatur County, 465 families holding 5,924 slaves in 1860.
- Dooly County, 347 families holding 4,070 slaves in 1860.
- Dougherty County, 322 families holding 6,079 slaves in 1860.
- Early County, 237 families holding 4,057 slaves in 1860.
- Echols County, 49 families holding 314 slaves in 1860.
- Effingha County, unknown number of families holding 750 slaves in 1790; and 242 families holding 2,165 slaves in 1860.
- Elbert County, 470 families holding 5,711 slaves in 1860.
- Emanuel County, 174 families holding 1,294 slaves in 1860.
- Fannin County, 40 families holding 143 slaves in 1860.
- Fayette County, 288 families holding 2,019 slaves in 1860.
- Floyd County, 529 families holding 5,913 slaves in 1860.
- Forsyth County, 187 families holding 890 slaves in 1860.
- Franklin County, unknown number of families holding 156 slaves in 1790; and 217 families holding 1,313 slaves in 1860.
- Fulton County, 478 families holding 2,955 slaves in 1860.
- Gilmer County, 35 families holding 167 slaves in 1860.
- Glascock County, 94 families holding 758 slaves in 1860.
- Glynn County, unknown number of families holding 215 slaves in 1790; and 140 families holding 2,839 slaves in 1860.
- Gordon County, 297 families holding 2,106 slaves in 1860.
- Greene County, unknown number of families holding 1,377 slaves in 1790; and 577 families holding 8,398 slaves in 1860.
- Gwinnett County, 368 families holding 2,551 slaves in 1860.
- Habersha County, 109 families holding 787 slaves in 1860.

- Hall County, 246 families holding 1,261 slaves in 1860.
- Hancock County, 430 families holding 8,137 slaves in 1860.
- Haralson County, 63 families holding 229 slaves in 1860.
- Harris County, 575 families holding 7,736 slaves in 1860.
- Hart County, 217 families holding 1,528 slaves in 1860.
- Heard County, 350 families holding 2,811 slaves in 1860.
- Henry County, 564 families holding 4,515 slaves in 1860.
- Houston County, 560 families holding 10,755 slaves in 1860.
- Irwin County, 44 families holding 246 slaves in 1860.
- Jackson County, 492 families holding 3,329 slaves in 1860.
- Jasper County, 496 families holding 6,954 slaves in 1860.
- Jefferson County, 431 families holding 6,045 slaves in 1860.
- Johnson County, 84 families holding 849 slaves in 1860.
- Jones County, 328 families holding 5,989 slaves in 1860.
- Laurens County, 227 families holding 3,269 slaves in 1860.
- Lee County, 322 families holding 4,947 slaves in 1860.
- Liberty County, unknown number of families holding 4,025 slaves in 1790; and 281 families holding 6,083 slaves in 1860.
- Lincoln County, 248 families holding 3,768 slaves in 1860.
- Lowndes County, 251 families holding 2,399 slaves in 1860.
- Lumpkin County, 58 families holding 432 slaves in 1860.
- Macon County, 442 families holding 4,865 slaves in 1860.
- Madison County, 275 families holding 1,992 slaves in 1860.
- Marion County, 432 families holding 3,529 slaves in 1860.
- McIntosh County, 156 families holding 4,063 slaves in 1860.
- Meriwether County, 689 families holding 8,748 slaves in 1860.

- Miller County, 65 families holding 640 slaves in 1860.
- Milton County, 102 families holding 617 slaves in 1860.
- Mitchell County, 141 families holding 1,589 slaves in 1860.
- Monroe County, 790 families holding 10,177 slaves in 1860.
- Montgomery County, 119 families holding 977 slaves in 1860.
- Morgan County, 424 families holding 7,006 slaves in 1860.
- Murray County, 151 families holding 1,442 slaves in 1860.
- Muscogee County, 762 families holding 7,445 slaves in 1860.
- Newton County, 679 families holding 6,458 slaves in 1860.
- Oglethorpe County, 526 families holding 7,514 slaves in 1860.
- Paulding County, 136 families holding 572 slaves in 1860.
- Pickens County, 37 families holding 246 slaves in 1860.
- Pierce County, 55 families holding 233 slaves in 1860.
- Pike County, 553 families holding 4,722 slaves in 1860.
- Polk County, 226 families holding 2,440 slaves in 1860.
- Pulaski County, 345 families holding 4,106 slaves in 1860.
- Putna County, 402 families holding 7,138 slaves in 1860.
- Quitman County, 167 families holding 1,625 slaves in 1860.
- Rabun County, 49 families holding 206 slaves in 1860.
- Randolph County, 434 families holding 4,467 slaves in 1860.
- Richmond County, unknown number of families holding 4,116 slaves in 1790; and 901 families holding 8,389 slaves in 1860.
- Schley County, 188 families holding 2,348 slaves in 1860.
- Screven County, 378 families holding 4,530 slaves in 1860.
- Spalding County, 488 families holding 3,819 slaves in 1860.
- Stewart County, 608 families holding 7,884 slaves in 1860.
- Sumter County, 393 families holding 4,890 slaves in 1860.
- Talbot County, 648 families holding 8,603 slaves in 1860.
- Taliaferro County, 271 families holding 2,849 slaves in 1860.
- Tattnall County, 177 families holding 1,157 slaves in 1860.
- Taylor County, 228 families holding 2,397 slaves in 1860.
- Telfair County, 98 families holding 836 slaves in 1860.
- Terrell County, 350 families holding 2,888 slaves in 1860.
- Thomas County, 405 families holding 6,244 slaves in 1860.
- Towns County, 23 families holding 108 slaves in 1860.
- Troup County, 769 families holding 10,002 slaves in 1860.
- Twiggs County, 297 families holding 5,318 slaves in 1860.
- Union County, 33 families holding 116 slaves in 1860.
- Upson County, 496 families holding 4,888 slaves in 1860.
- Walker County, 234 families holding 1,535 slaves in 1860.
- Walton County, 584 families holding 4,621 slaves in 1860.
- Ware County, 57 families holding 377 slaves in 1860.
- Warren County, 452 families holding 5,379 slaves in 1860.
- Washington County, unknown number of families holding 694 slaves in 1790; and 560 families holding 6,532 slaves in 1860.
- Wayne County, 63 families holding 621 slaves in 1860.
- Webster County, 257 families holding 2,287 slaves in 1860.
- White County, 47 families holding 263 slaves in 1860.
- Whitfield County, 318 families holding 1,732 slaves in 1860.
- Wilcox County, 57 families holding 421 slaves in 1860.
- Wilkes County, unknown number of families holding 7,268 slaves in 1790; and 518 families holding 7,953 slaves in 1860.

- Wilkinson County, 387 families holding 3,887 slaves in 1860.
- Worth County, 81 families holding 632 slaves in 1860.

State of Kentucky

- Adair County, 331 families holding 1,602 slaves in 1860.
- Allen County, 272 families holding 1,522 slaves in 1860.
- Anderson County, 267 families holding 1,357 slaves in 1860.
- Ballard County, 320 families holding 1,718 slaves in 1860.
- Barren County, 689 families holding 4,078 slaves in 1860.
- Bath County, 425 families holding 2,500 slaves in 1860.
- Boone County, 450 families holding 1,745 slaves in 1860.
- Bourbon County, unknown number of families holding 908 slaves in 1790.
- Bourbon County, 858 families holding 6,767 slaves in 1860.
- Boyd County, 49 families holding 156 slaves in 1860.
- Boyle County, 503 families holding 3,279 slaves in 1860.
- Bracken County, 176 families holding 750 slaves in 1860.
- Breathitt County, 46 families holding 190 slaves in 1860.
- Breckinridge County, 424 families holding 2,340 slaves in 1860.
- Bullitt County, 277 families holding 1,458 slaves in 1860.
- Butler County, 196 families holding 770 slaves in 1860.
- Caldwell County, 374 families holding 2,406 slaves in 1860.
- Calloway County, 320 families holding 1,492 slaves in 1860.
- Campbell County, 49 families holding 116 slaves in 1860.
- Carroll County, 238 families holding 1,045 slaves in 1860.
- Carter County, 56 families holding 309 slaves in 1860.
- Casey County, 109 families holding 666 slaves in 1860.
- Christian County, 979 families holding 9,951 slaves in 1860.
- Clark County, 757 families holding 4,762 slaves in 1860.
- Clay County, 71 families holding 349 slaves in 1860.
- Clinton County, 77 families holding 258 slaves in 1860.
- Crittenden County, 211 families holding 939 slaves in 1860.
- Cumberland County, 251 families holding 1,413 slaves in 1860.
- Daviess County, 637 families holding 3,515 slaves in 1860.
- Edmonson County, 63 families holding 273 slaves in 1860.
- Estill County, 107 families holding 507 slaves in 1860.
- Fayette County, unknown number of families holding 3,752 slaves in 1790.
- Fayette County, 1,200 families holding 10,015 slaves in 1860.
- Fleming County, 513 families holding 2,018 slaves in 1860.
- Floyd County, 39 families holding 147 slaves in 1860.
- Franklin County, 556 families holding 3,384 slaves in 1860.
- Fulton County, 242 families holding 1,078 slaves in 1860.
- Gallatin County, 162 families holding 708 slaves in 1860.
- Garrard County, 591 families holding 3,578 slaves in 1860.
- Grant County, 187 families holding 696 slaves in 1860.
- Graves County, 566 families holding 2,845 slaves in 1860.
- Grayson County, 93 families holding 351 slaves in 1860.
- Green County, 339 families holding 2,372 slaves in 1860.
- Greenup County, 88 families holding 363 slaves in 1860.
- Hancock County, 148 families holding 818 slaves in 1860.
- Hardin County, 507 families holding 2,530 slaves in 1860.
- Harlan County, 19 families holding 127 slaves in 1860.
- Harrison County, 586 families holding 3,289 slaves in 1860.

- Hart County, 322 families holding 1,395 slaves in 1860.
- Henderson County, 712 families holding 5,767 slaves in 1860.
- Henry County, 676 families holding 3,311 slaves in 1860.
- Hickman County, 283 families holding 1,249 slaves in 1860.
- Hopkins County, 433 families holding 2,009 slaves in 1860.
- Jackson County, 4 families holding 7 slaves in 1860.
- Jefferson County, unknown number of families holding 903 slaves in 1790.
- Jefferson County, 2,258 families holding 10,304 slaves in 1860.
- Jessamine County, 492 families holding 3,698 slaves in 1860.
- Johnson County, 11 families holding 27 slaves in 1860.
- Kenton County, 214 families holding 567 slaves in 1860.
- Knox County, 106 families holding 489 slaves in 1860.
- Larue County, 205 families holding 900 slaves in 1860.
- Laurel County, 35 families holding 186 slaves in 1860.
- Lawrence County, 38 families holding 146 slaves in 1860.
- Letcher County, 29 families holding 108 slaves in 1860.
- Lewis County, 71 families holding 230 slaves in 1860.
- Lincoln County, unknown number of families holding 1,094 slaves in 1790; and 496 families holding 3,430 slaves in 1860.
- Livingston County, 251 families holding 1,222 slaves in 1860.
- Logan County, 1,056 families holding 6,356 slaves in 1860.
- Lyon County, 178 families holding 1,094 slaves in 1860.
- Madison County, unknown number of families holding 737 slaves in 1790; and 877 families holding 6,034 slaves in 1860.
- Magoffin County, 13 families holding 71 slaves in 1860.
- Marion County, 605 families holding 3,479 slaves in 1860.

- Marshall County, 123 families holding 351 slaves in 1860.
- Mason County, unknown number of families holding 229 slaves in 1790; and 727 families holding 3,772 slaves in 1860.
- McCracken County, 368 families holding 1,738 slaves in 1860.
- McLean County, 263 families holding 888 slaves in 1860.
- Meade County, 371 families holding 1,932 slaves in 1860.
- Mercer County, unknown number of families holding 1,339 slaves in 1790; and 574 families holding 3,274 slaves in 1860.
- Metcalfe County, 171 families holding 781 slaves in 1860.
- Monroe County, 191 families holding 922 slaves in 1860.
- Montgomery County, 455 families holding 2,752 slaves in 1860.
- Morgan County, 51 families holding 170 slaves in 1860.
- Muhlenberg County, 327 families holding 1,584 slaves in 1860.
- Nelson County, unknown number of families holding 1,248 slaves in 1790; and 977 families holding 5,530 slaves in 1860.
- Nicholas County, 365 families holding 1,614 slaves in 1860.
- Ohio County, 290 families holding 1,292 slaves in 1860.
- Oldha County, 364 families holding 2,431 slaves in 1860.
- Owen County, 376 families holding 1,660 slaves in 1860.
- Owsley County, 27 families holding 112 slaves in 1860.
- Pendleton County, 121 families holding 424 slaves in 1860.
- Perry County, 28 families holding 73 slaves in 1860.
- Pike County, 28 families holding 97 slaves in 1860.
- Powell County, 31 families holding 125 slaves in 1860.
- Pulaski County, 280 families holding 1,330 slaves in 1860.
- Rockcastle County, 92 families holding 357 slaves in 1860.
- Rowan County, 32 families holding 142 slaves in 1860.

- Russell County, 128 families holding 559 slaves in 1860.
- Scott County, 943 families holding 5,744 slaves in 1860.
- Shelby County, 1,039 families holding 6,634 slaves in 1860.
- Simpson County, 427 families holding 2,307 slaves in 1860.
- Spencer County, 398 families holding 2,205 slaves in 1860.
- Taylor County, 273 families holding 1,597 slaves in 1860.
- Todd County, 525 families holding 4,849 slaves in 1860.
- Trigg County, 478 families holding 3,448 slaves in 1860.
- Trimble County, 182 families holding 831 slaves in 1860.
- Union County, 485 families holding 3,105 slaves in 1860.
- Warren County, 792 families holding 5,318 slaves in 1860.
- Washington County, 420 families holding 2,822 slaves in 1860.
- Wayne County, 205 families holding 987 slaves in 1860.
- Webster County, 244 families holding 1,083 slaves in 1860.
- Whitley County, 54 families holding 183 slaves in 1860.
- Woodford County, unknown number of families holding 2,220 slaves in 1790; and 637 families holding 5,829 slaves in 1860.

State of Louisiana
- Ascension County, 277 families holding 7,376 slaves in 1860.
- Assumption County, 478 families holding 8,096 slaves in 1860.
- Avoyelles County, 554 families holding 7,185 slaves in 1860.
- Bienville County, unknown number of families holding 5,000 slaves in 1860.
- Bossier County, 427 families holding 8,000 slaves in 1860.
- Caddo County, 490 families holding 7,338 slaves in 1860.
- Calcasieu County, 177 families holding 1,171 slaves in 1860.
- Caldwell County, 188 families holding 1,945 slaves in 1860.
- Carroll County, 598 families holding 13,908 slaves in 1860.
- Catahoula County, 327 families holding 6,113 slaves in 1860.
- Claiborne County, 794 families holding 7,848 slaves in 1860.
- Concordia County, 250 families holding 12,542 slaves in 1860.
- De Soto County, 575 families holding 8,507 slaves in 1860.
- East Baton Rouge County, 651 families holding 8,570 slaves in 1860.
- East Feliciana County, 577 families holding 10,593 slaves in 1860.
- Franklin County, 309 families holding 3,402 slaves in 1860.
- Iberville County, 442 families holding 10,680 slaves in 1860.
- Jackson County, 405 families holding 4,098 slaves in 1860.
- Jefferson County, 309 families holding 5,120 slaves in 1860.
- Lafayette County, 492 families holding 4,463 slaves in 1860.
- Lafourche County, 471 families holding 6,395 slaves in 1860.
- Livingston County, 166 families holding 1,311 slaves in 1860.
- Madison County, 329 families holding 12,477 slaves in 1860.
- Morehouse County, 466 families holding 6,569 slaves in 1860.
- Natchitoches County, 621 families holding 9,434 slaves in 1860.
- Orleans County, 4,169 families holding 14,484 slaves in 1860.
- Ouachita County, 181 families holding 2,840 slaves in 1860.
- Plaquemines County, 231 families holding 5,385 slaves in 1860.
- Pointe Coupee County, 634 families holding 12,903 slaves in 1860.
- Rapides County, 524 families holding 15,358 slaves in 1860.
- Sabine County, 211 families holding 1,713 slaves in 1860.
- St Bernard County, 120 families holding 2,240 slaves in 1860.
- St Charles County, 138 families holding 4,182 slaves in 1860.

- St Helena County, 337 families holding 3,711 slaves in 1860.
- St James County, 469 families holding 8,090 slaves in 1860.
- St John The Bapti County, 355 families holding 4,594 slaves in 1860.
- St Landry County, 963 families holding 11,436 slaves in 1860.
- St Martin County, 605 families holding 7,358 slaves in 1860.
- St Mary County, 432 families holding 13,057 slaves in 1860.
- St Tammany County, 169 families holding 1,841 slaves in 1860.
- Tensas County, 330 families holding 14,592 slaves in 1860.
- Terrebonne County, 248 families holding 6,785 slaves in 1860.
- Union County, 430 families holding 3,745 slaves in 1860.
- Vermillion County, 184 families holding 1,316 slaves in 1860.
- Washington County, 216 families holding 1,690 slaves in 1860.
- West Baton Rouge County, 207 families holding 5,340 slaves in 1860.
- West Feliciana County, 298 families holding 9,571 slaves in 1860.
- Winn County, 209 families holding 1,354 slaves in 1860.

State of Massachusetts

- Barnstable County, unknown number of families holding 0 slaves in 1790.
- Berkshire County, unknown number of families holding 0 slaves in 1790.
- Bristol County, unknown number of families holding 0 slaves in 1790.
- Dukes County, unknown number of families holding 0 slaves in 1790.
- Essex County, unknown number of families holding 0 slaves in 1790.
- Hampshire County, unknown number of families holding 0 slaves in 1790.
- Middlesex County, unknown number of families holding 0 slaves in 1790.
- Nantucket County, unknown number of families holding 0 slaves in 1790.
- Plymouth County, unknown number of families holding 0 slaves in 1790.
- Suffolk County, unknown number of families holding 0 slaves in 1790.

- Worcester County, unknown number of families holding 0 slaves in 1790.

State of Maryland

- Allegany County, unknown number of families holding 258 slaves in 1790.
- Allegany County, 187 families holding 666 slaves in 1860.
- Anne Arundel County, 1,096 families holding 10,130 slaves in 1790; and 801 families holding 7,332 slaves in 1860.
- Baltimore City County, 389 families holding 1,255 slaves in 1790; and 1,296 families holding 2,218 slaves in 1860.
- Baltimore County, 1,029 families holding 5,877 slaves in 1790; and 756 families holding 3,182 slaves in 1860.
- Calvert County, unknown number of families holding 4,305 slaves in 1790; and 528 families holding 4,609 slaves in 1860.
- Caroline County, 418 families holding 2,057 slaves in 1790; and 190 families holding 739 slaves in 1860.
- Carroll County, 208 families holding 783 slaves in 1860.
- Cecil County, 539 families holding 3,407 slaves in 1790; and 172 families holding 950 slaves in 1860.
- Charles County, 1,221 families holding 10,085 slaves in 1790; and 817 families holding 9,653 slaves in 1860.
- Dorchester County, 296 families holding 5,337 slaves in 1790; and 754 families holding 4,123 slaves in 1860.
- Frederick County, 678 families holding 3,641 slaves in 1790; and 794 families holding 3,243 slaves in 1860.
- Harford County, 586 families holding 3,417 slaves in 1790; and 657 families holding 1,800 slaves in 1860.
- Howard County, 476 families holding 2,862 slaves in 1860.
- Kent County, 781 families holding 5,433 slaves in 1790.
- Montgomery County, 933 families holding 6,030 slaves in 1790; and 770 families holding 5,421 slaves in 1860.
- Prince Georges County, 978 families holding 11,176 slaves in 1790; and 847 families holding 12,479 slaves in 1860.

- Queen Annes County, 828 families holding 6,674 slaves in 1790; and 573 families holding 4,174 slaves in 1860.
- Somerset County, unknown number of families holding 7,070 slaves in 1790; and 747 families holding 5,089 slaves in 1860.
- St Marys County, 892 families holding 6,985 slaves in 1790; and 761 families holding 6,549 slaves in 1860.
- Talbot County, 651 families holding 4,777 slaves in 1790; and 506 families holding 3,725 slaves in 1860.
- Washington County, 269 families holding 1,286 slaves in 1790; and 398 families holding 1,435 slaves in 1860.
- Worcester County, 642 families holding 3,836 slaves in 1790; and 934 families holding 3,648 slaves in 1860.

State of Maine
- Cumberland County, unknown number of families holding 0 slaves in 1790.
- Hancock County, unknown number of families holding 0 slaves in 1790.
- Lincoln County, unknown number of families holding 0 slaves in 1790.
- Washington County, unknown number of families holding 0 slaves in 1790.
- York County, unknown number of families holding 0 slaves in 1790.

State of Missouri
- Adair County, 33 families holding 86 slaves in 1860.
- Andrew County, 240 families holding 880 slaves in 1860.
- Atchison County, 29 families holding 59 slaves in 1860.
- Audrain County, 327 families holding 1,166 slaves in 1860.
- Barry County, 54 families holding 247 slaves in 1860.
- Barton County, 11 families holding 21 slaves in 1860.
- Bates County, 112 families holding 442 slaves in 1860.
- Benton County, 123 families holding 599 slaves in 1860.
- Bollinger County, 55 families holding 245 slaves in 1860.
- Boone County, 885 families holding 5,034 slaves in 1860.

- Buchanan County, 468 families holding 2,011 slaves in 1860.
- Butler County, 15 families holding 52 slaves in 1860.
- Caldwell County, 72 families holding 222 slaves in 1860.
- Callaway County, 855 families holding 4,523 slaves in 1860.
- Camden County, 66 families holding 206 slaves in 1860.
- Cape Girardeau County, 302 families holding 1,533 slaves in 1860.
- Carroll County, 262 families holding 1,068 slaves in 1860.
- Carter County, 8 families holding 20 slaves in 1860.
- Cass/Van Buren County, 307 families holding 1,010 slaves in 1860.
- Cedar County, 72 families holding 211 slaves in 1860.
- Chariton County, 410 families holding 2,839 slaves in 1860.
- Christian County, 66 families holding 229 slaves in 1860.
- Clark County, 122 families holding 455 slaves in 1860.
- Clay County, 652 families holding 3,455 slaves in 1860.
- Clinton County, 283 families holding 1,144 slaves in 1860.
- Cole County, 169 families holding 987 slaves in 1860.
- Cooper County, 732 families holding 3,800 slaves in 1860.
- Crawford County, 52 families holding 182 slaves in 1860.
- Dade County, 107 families holding 346 slaves in 1860.
- Dallas County, 40 families holding 114 slaves in 1860.
- Daviess County, 116 families holding 358 slaves in 1860.
- De Kalb County, 52 families holding 137 slaves in 1860.
- Dent County, 45 families holding 156 slaves in 1860.
- Dunklin County, 44 families holding 171 slaves in 1860.
- Franklin County, 293 families holding 1,601 slaves in 1860.

- Gasconade County, 28 families holding 76 slaves in 1860.
- Gentry County, 44 families holding 118 slaves in 1860.
- Greene County, 338 families holding 1,668 slaves in 1860.
- Grundy County, 97 families holding 285 slaves in 1860.
- Harrison County, 13 families holding 25 slaves in 1860.
- Henry/Rives County, 298 families holding 1,245 slaves in 1860.
- Hickory County, 60 families holding 195 slaves in 1860.
- Holt County, 88 families holding 309 slaves in 1860.
- Howard County, 801 families holding 5,886 slaves in 1860.
- Howell County, 15 families holding 36 slaves in 1860.
- Iron County, 67 families holding 313 slaves in 1860.
- Jackson County, 898 families holding 3,944 slaves in 1860.
- Jasper County, 107 families holding 335 slaves in 1860.
- Jefferson County, 137 families holding 564 slaves in 1860.
- Johnson County, 465 families holding 1,896 slaves in 1860.
- Knox County, 94 families holding 284 slaves in 1860.
- Laclede County, 67 families holding 305 slaves in 1860.
- Lafayette County, 909 families holding 6,374 slaves in 1860.
- Lawrence County, 76 families holding 284 slaves in 1860.
- Lewis County, 350 families holding 1,279 slaves in 1860.
- Lincoln County, 573 families holding 2,840 slaves in 1860.
- Linn County, 143 families holding 577 slaves in 1860.
- Livingston County, 139 families holding 605 slaves in 1860.
- Macon County, 200 families holding 660 slaves in 1860.
- Madison County, 107 families holding 467 slaves in 1860.
- Maries County, 26 families holding 64 slaves in 1860.
- Marion County, 817 families holding 3,017 slaves in 1860.
- McDonald County, 23 families holding 72 slaves in 1860.
- Mercer County, 12 families holding 24 slaves in 1860.
- Miller County, 71 families holding 238 slaves in 1860.
- Mississippi County, 160 families holding 1,010 slaves in 1860.
- Moniteau County, 187 families holding 745 slaves in 1860.
- Monroe County, 733 families holding 3,021 slaves in 1860.
- Montgomery County, 373 families holding 1,647 slaves in 1860.
- Morgan County, 138 families holding 649 slaves in 1860.
- New Madrid County, 236 families holding 1,777 slaves in 1860.
- Newton County, 141 families holding 426 slaves in 1860.
- Nodaway County, 35 families holding 127 slaves in 1860.
- Oregon County, 13 families holding 26 slaves in 1860.
- Osage County, 71 families holding 256 slaves in 1860.
- Ozark County, 11 families holding 43 slaves in 1860.
- Pemiscot County, 74 families holding 268 slaves in 1860.
- Perry County, 187 families holding 739 slaves in 1860.
- Pettis County, 393 families holding 1,882 slaves in 1860.
- Phelps County, 24 families holding 84 slaves in 1860.
- Pike County, 871 families holding 4,055 slaves in 1860.
- Platte County, 674 families holding 3,313 slaves in 1860.
- Polk County, 146 families holding 512 slaves in 1860.
- Pulaski County, 20 families holding 56 slaves in 1860.
- Putna County, 12 families holding 31 slaves in 1860.

- Ralls County, 378 families holding 1,791 slaves in 1860.
- Randolph County, 504 families holding 2,619 slaves in 1860.
- Ray County, 475 families holding 2,047 slaves in 1860.
- Reynolds County, 14 families holding 38 slaves in 1860.
- Ripley County, 30 families holding 78 slaves in 1860.
- Saline County, 693 families holding 4,876 slaves in 1860.
- Schuyler County, 16 families holding 39 slaves in 1860.
- Scotland County, 51 families holding 131 slaves in 1860.
- Scott County, 91 families holding 503 slaves in 1860.
- Shannon County, 3 families holding 13 slaves in 1860.
- Shelby County, 234 families holding 724 slaves in 1860.
- St Charles County, 379 families holding 2,181 slaves in 1860.
- St Clair County, 133 families holding 574 slaves in 1860.
- St Francois County, 195 families holding 877 slaves in 1860.
- St Louis County, 1,156 families holding 4,346 slaves in 1860.
- Ste Genevieve County, 119 families holding 617 slaves in 1860.
- Stoddard County, 83 families holding 215 slaves in 1860.
- Stone County, 8 families holding 16 slaves in 1860.
- Sullivan County, 28 families holding 102 slaves in 1860.
- Taney County, 24 families holding 82 slaves in 1860.
- Texas County, 21 families holding 56 slaves in 1860.
- Vernon County, 54 families holding 136 slaves in 1860.
- Warren County, 229 families holding 1,034 slaves in 1860.
- Washington County, 188 families holding 1,028 slaves in 1860.
- Wayne County, 71 families holding 261 slaves in 1860.
- Webster County, 73 families holding 220 slaves in 1860.
- Wright County, 29 families holding 66 slaves in 1860.

State of Mississippi

- Adams County, 688 families holding 14,292 slaves in 1860.
- Amite County, 628 families holding 7,900 slaves in 1860.
- Attala County, 637 families holding 5,015 slaves in 1860.
- Bolivar County, 297 families holding 9,078 slaves in 1860.
- Calhoun County, 371 families holding 1,823 slaves in 1860.
- Carroll County, 963 families holding 13,808 slaves in 1860.
- Chickasaw County, 702 families holding 9,087 slaves in 1860.
- Choctaw County, 616 families holding 4,197 slaves in 1860.
- Claiborne County, 424 families holding 12,296 slaves in 1860.
- Clarke County, 430 families holding 5,076 slaves in 1860.
- Coahoma County, 230 families holding 5,085 slaves in 1860.
- Copiah County, 737 families holding 7,965 slaves in 1860.
- Covington County, 204 families holding 1,563 slaves in 1860.
- De Soto County, 1,089 families holding 13,987 slaves in 1860.
- Franklin County, 354 families holding 4,752 slaves in 1860.
- Greene County, 93 families holding 705 slaves in 1860.
- Hancock County, unknown number of families holding 857 slaves in 1860.
- Harrison County, 161 families holding 1,015 slaves in 1860.
- Hinds County, 1,421 families holding 22,363 slaves in 1860.
- Holmes County, 806 families holding 11,975 slaves in 1860.
- Issaquena County, 115 families holding 7,244 slaves in 1860.
- Itawamba County, 518 families holding 3,528 slaves in 1860.
- Jackson County, 146 families holding 1,087 slaves in 1860.

- Jasper County, 503 families holding 4,549 slaves in 1860.
- Jefferson County, 425 families holding 12,396 slaves in 1860.
- Jones County, 116 families holding 407 slaves in 1860.
- Kemper County, 552 families holding 5,741 slaves in 1860.
- Lafayette County, 714 families holding 7,129 slaves in 1860.
- Lauderdale County, 577 families holding 5,088 slaves in 1860.
- Lawrence County, 450 families holding 3,696 slaves in 1860.
- Leake County, 470 families holding 3,056 slaves in 1860.
- Lowndes County, 1,006 families holding 16,730 slaves in 1860.
- Madison County, 965 families holding 18,118 slaves in 1860.
- Marion County, 210 families holding 2,185 slaves in 1860.
- Marshall County, 1,295 families holding 17,439 slaves in 1860.
- Monroe County, 810 families holding 12,729 slaves in 1860.
- Neshoba County, 374 families holding 2,212 slaves in 1860.
- Newton County, 413 families holding 3,379 slaves in 1860.
- Noxubee County, 748 families holding 15,496 slaves in 1860.
- Oktibbeha County, 549 families holding 7,631 slaves in 1860.
- Panola County, 629 families holding 8,557 slaves in 1860.
- Perry County, 95 families holding 738 slaves in 1860.
- Pike County, 587 families holding 4,935 slaves in 1860.
- Pontotoc County, 851 families holding 7,596 slaves in 1860.
- Rankin County, 684 families holding 7,103 slaves in 1860.
- Scott County, 368 families holding 2,959 slaves in 1860.
- Simpson County, 274 families holding 2,324 slaves in 1860.
- Smith County, 331 families holding 2,195 slaves in 1860.
- Sunflower County, unknown number of families holding 3,917 slaves in 1860.
- Tallahatchie County, 360 families holding 5,054 slaves in 1860.
- Tippah County, 826 families holding 6,331 slaves in 1860.
- Tishomingo County, 707 families holding 4,981 slaves in 1860.
- Tunica County, 132 families holding 3,483 slaves in 1860.
- Warren County, 821 families holding 13,763 slaves in 1860.
- Washington County, unknown number of families holding 14,467 slaves in 1860.
- Wayne County, 92 families holding 1,947 slaves in 1860.
- Wilkinson County, 499 families holding 13,132 slaves in 1860.
- Winston County, 460 families holding 4,223 slaves in 1860.
- Yalobusha County, 721 families holding 9,531 slaves in 1860.
- Yazoo County, 699 families holding 16,716 slaves in 1860.

State of North Carolina
- Alamance County, 520 families holding 3,445 slaves in 1860.
- Alexander County, 136 families holding 611 slaves in 1860.
- Alleghany County, 55 families holding 206 slaves in 1860.
- Anson County, 174 families holding 829 slaves in 1790; and 616 families holding 6,951 slaves in 1860.
- Ashe County, 82 families holding 391 slaves in 1860.
- Beaufort County, 290 families holding 1,622 slaves in 1790; and 558 families holding 5,878 slaves in 1860.
- Bertie County, 607 families holding 5,121 slaves in 1790; and 468 families holding 8,185 slaves in 1860.
- Bladen County, 237 families holding 1,686 slaves in 1790; and 384 families holding 5,327 slaves in 1860.
- Brunswick County, 116 families holding 1,511 slaves in 1790; and 258 families holding 3,631 slaves in 1860.
- Buncombe County, 284 families holding 1,933 slaves in 1860.

- Burke County, 173 families holding 600 slaves in 1790; and 210 families holding 2,371 slaves in 1860.
- Cabarrus County, 425 families holding 3,040 slaves in 1860.
- Caldwell County, 175 families holding 1,088 slaves in 1860.
- Camden County, 201 families holding 1,038 slaves in 1790; and 277 families holding 2,127 slaves in 1860.
- Carteret County, 155 families holding 709 slaves in 1790; and 217 families holding 1,969 slaves in 1860.
- Caswell County, unknown number of families holding 2,736 slaves in 1790; and 748 families holding 9,355 slaves in 1860.
- Catawba County, 300 families holding 1,664 slaves in 1860.
- Chatha County, 314 families holding 1,558 slaves in 1790; and 769 families holding 6,246 slaves in 1860.
- Cherokee County, 96 families holding 519 slaves in 1860.
- Chowan County, 313 families holding 2,587 slaves in 1790; and 278 families holding 3,713 slaves in 1860.
- Cleveland County, 383 families holding 2,131 slaves in 1860.
- Columbus County, 283 families holding 2,463 slaves in 1860.
- Craven County, 576 families holding 3,663 slaves in 1790; and 674 families holding 6,189 slaves in 1860.
- Cumberland County, 423 families holding 2,180 slaves in 1790; and 809 families holding 5,830 slaves in 1860.
- Currituck County, 257 families holding 1,103 slaves in 1790; and 340 families holding 2,523 slaves in 1860.
- Davidson County, 482 families holding 3,076 slaves in 1860.
- Davie County, 281 families holding 2,392 slaves in 1860.
- Dobbs County, 336 families holding 2,012 slaves in 1790.
- Duplin County, 255 families holding 1,386 slaves in 1790; and 676 families holding 7,124 slaves in 1860.
- Edgecombe County, 491 families holding 3,167 slaves in 1790; and 672 families holding 10,108 slaves in 1860.

- Forsyth County, 304 families holding 1,764 slaves in 1860.
- Franklin County, 388 families holding 2,701 slaves in 1790; and 605 families holding 7,076 slaves in 1860.
- Gaston County, 360 families holding 2,199 slaves in 1860.
- Gates County, 344 families holding 2,217 slaves in 1790; and 365 families holding 3,901 slaves in 1860.
- Granville County, unknown number of families holding 4,163 slaves in 1790; and 1,006 families holding 11,086 slaves in 1860.
- Greene County, 404 families holding 3,947 slaves in 1860.
- Guilford County, 179 families holding 616 slaves in 1790; and 493 families holding 3,625 slaves in 1860.
- Halifax County, 734 families holding 6,697 slaves in 1790; and 695 families holding 10,349 slaves in 1860.
- Harnett County, 244 families holding 2,584 slaves in 1860.
- Haywood County, 63 families holding 313 slaves in 1860.
- Henderson County, 209 families holding 1,382 slaves in 1860.
- Hertford County, 359 families holding 2,448 slaves in 1790; and 432 families holding 4,445 slaves in 1860.
- Hyde County, 247 families holding 1,143 slaves in 1790; and 248 families holding 2,791 slaves in 1860.
- Iredell County, 232 families holding 868 slaves in 1790; and 587 families holding 4,177 slaves in 1860.
- Jackson County, 43 families holding 268 slaves in 1860.
- Johnston County, 249 families holding 1,328 slaves in 1790; and 486 families holding 4,916 slaves in 1860.
- Jones County, 217 families holding 1,655 slaves in 1790; and 261 families holding 3,413 slaves in 1860.
- Lenoir County, 525 families holding 5,140 slaves in 1860.
- Lincoln County, 283 families holding 855 slaves in 1790; and 283 families holding 2,115 slaves in 1860.

- Macon County, 82 families holding 519 slaves in 1860.
- Madison County, 46 families holding 213 slaves in 1860.
- Martin County, 277 families holding 1,829 slaves in 1790; and 368 families holding 4,309 slaves in 1860.
- McDowell County, 213 families holding 1,305 slaves in 1860.
- Mecklenburg County, 423 families holding 1,608 slaves in 1790; and 846 families holding 6,541 slaves in 1860.
- Montgomery County, 180 families holding 837 slaves in 1790; and 236 families holding 1,823 slaves in 1860.
- Moore County, 88 families holding 371 slaves in 1790; and 469 families holding 2,518 slaves in 1860.
- Nash County, 328 families holding 2,008 slaves in 1790; and 482 families holding 4,680 slaves in 1860.
- New Hanover County, 341 families holding 3,737 slaves in 1790; and 938 families holding 10,331 slaves in 1860.
- Northampton County, 583 families holding 4,414 slaves in 1790; and 542 families holding 6,804 slaves in 1860.
- Onslow County, 278 families holding 1,747 slaves in 1790; and 313 families holding 3,499 slaves in 1860.
- Orange County, unknown number of families holding 2,060 slaves in 1790; and 665 families holding 5,108 slaves in 1860.
- Pasquotank County, 299 families holding 1,600 slaves in 1790; and 348 families holding 2,983 slaves in 1860.
- Perquimans County, 322 families holding 1,883 slaves in 1790; and 259 families holding 3,558 slaves in 1860.
- Person County, 488 families holding 5,195 slaves in 1860.
- Pitt County, 401 families holding 2,364 slaves in 1790; and 817 families holding 8,473 slaves in 1860.
- Polk County, 88 families holding 620 slaves in 1860.
- Randolph County, 137 families holding 460 slaves in 1790; and 343 families holding 1,645 slaves in 1860.
- Richmond County, 142 families holding 583 slaves in 1790; and 498 families holding 5,453 slaves in 1860.
- Robeson County, 163 families holding 533 slaves in 1790; and 671 families holding 5,455 slaves in 1860.
- Rockingha County, 212 families holding 1,113 slaves in 1790; and 630 families holding 6,318 slaves in 1860.
- Rowan County, 432 families holding 1,741 slaves in 1790; and 520 families holding 3,930 slaves in 1860.
- Rutherford County, 164 families holding 609 slaves in 1790; and 351 families holding 2,391 slaves in 1860.
- Sampson County, 239 families holding 1,177 slaves in 1790; and 679 families holding 7,028 slaves in 1860.
- Stanly County, 202 families holding 1,169 slaves in 1860.
- Stokes County, 202 families holding 778 slaves in 1790; and 246 families holding 2,469 slaves in 1860.
- Surry County, 163 families holding 692 slaves in 1790; and 210 families holding 1,246 slaves in 1860.
- Tyrrell County, 210 families holding 1,597 slaves in 1860.
- Union County, 387 families holding 2,246 slaves in 1860.
- Wake County, 390 families holding 2,472 slaves in 1790; and 1,195 families holding 10,733 slaves in 1860.
- Warren County, 459 families holding 4,713 slaves in 1790; and 564 families holding 10,401 slaves in 1860.
- Washington County, 222 families holding 2,465 slaves in 1860.
- Watauga County, 31 families holding 104 slaves in 1860.
- Wayne County, 254 families holding 1,546 slaves in 1790; and 532 families holding 5,451 slaves in 1860.
- Wilkes County, 131 families holding 553 slaves in 1790; and 228 families holding 1,208 slaves in 1860.
- Wilson County, 446 families holding 3,496 slaves in 1860.
- Yadkin County, 162 families holding 1,436 slaves in 1860.

- Yancey County, 62 families holding 362 slaves in 1860.

State of New Hampshire

- Cheshire County, 16 families holding 18 slaves in 1790.
- Grafton County, 13 families holding 21 slaves in 1790.
- Hillsborough County, 0 families holding 0 slaves in 1790.
- Rockingha County, 76 families holding 97 slaves in 1790.
- Strafford County, 18 families holding 21 slaves in 1790.

State of New Jersey

- Bergen County, unknown number of families holding 2,301 slaves in 1790.
- Burlington County, unknown number of families holding 227 slaves in 1790.
- Cape May County, unknown number of families holding 141 slaves in 1790.
- Cumberland County, unknown number of families holding 120 slaves in 1790.
- Essex County, unknown number of families holding 1,171 slaves in 1790.
- Gloucester County, unknown number of families holding 191 slaves in 1790.
- Hunterdon County, unknown number of families holding 1,301 slaves in 1790.
- Middlesex County, unknown number of families holding 1,318 slaves in 1790.
- Monmouth County, unknown number of families holding 1,596 slaves in 1790.
- Morris County, unknown number of families holding 636 slaves in 1790.
- Sale County, unknown number of families holding 172 slaves in 1790.
- Somerset County, unknown number of families holding 1,810 slaves in 1790.
- Sussex County, unknown number of families holding 439 slaves in 1790.

State of New York

- Albany County, 1,474 families holding 3,722 slaves in 1790.
- Clinton County, 6 families holding 16 slaves in 1790.
- Columbia County, 528 families holding 1,633 slaves in 1790.
- Dutchess County, 670 families holding 1,864 slaves in 1790.
- Kings County, 333 families holding 1,482 slaves in 1790.

- Montgomery County, 300 families holding 588 slaves in 1790.
- New York County, 1,115 families holding 2,373 slaves in 1790.
- Ontario County, 4 families holding 10 slaves in 1790.
- Orange County, 415 families holding 961 slaves in 1790.
- Queens County, 775 families holding 2,308 slaves in 1790.
- Richmond County, 238 families holding 755 slaves in 1790.
- Suffolk County, 496 families holding 1,105 slaves in 1790.
- Ulster County, 878 families holding 2,914 slaves in 1790.
- Washington County, 24 families holding 46 slaves in 1790.
- Westchester County, 540 families holding 1,416 slaves in 1790.

State of Pennsylvania

- Allegheny County, 66 families holding 159 slaves in 1790.
- Bedford County, 24 families holding 46 slaves in 1790.
- Berks County, 31 families holding 60 slaves in 1790.
- Bucks County, 134 families holding 261 slaves in 1790.
- Chester County, 88 families holding 144 slaves in 1790.
- Cumberland County, 117 families holding 223 slaves in 1790.
- Dauphin County, 92 families holding 210 slaves in 1790.
- Delaware County, 24 families holding 49 slaves in 1790.
- Fayette County, 100 families holding 282 slaves in 1790.
- Franklin County, 163 families holding 326 slaves in 1790.
- Huntingdon County, 24 families holding 43 slaves in 1790.
- Lancaster County, 193 families holding 347 slaves in 1790.
- Luzerne County, 7 families holding 11 slaves in 1790.
- Mifflin County, 39 families holding 59 slaves in 1790.
- Montgomery County, 72 families holding 113 slaves in 1790.

- Northampton County, 16 families holding 20 slaves in 1790.
- Northumberland County, 48 families holding 87 slaves in 1790.
- Philadelphia County, 220 families holding 373 slaves in 1790.
- Washington County, 123 families holding 263 slaves in 1790.
- Westmoreland County, 53 families holding 128 slaves in 1790.
- York County, 224 families holding 503 slaves in 1790.

State of rhode Island
- Bristol County, 53 families holding 98 slaves in 1790.
- Kent County, 32 families holding 63 slaves in 1790.
- Newport County, 180 families holding 372 slaves in 1790.
- Providence County, 54 families holding 81 slaves in 1790.
- Washington County, 142 families holding 344 slaves in 1790.

State of South Carolina
- Abbeville County, 331 families holding 1,665 slaves in 1790; and 1,467 families holding 20,502 slaves in 1860.
- Anderson County, 1,103 families holding 8,425 slaves in 1860.
- Barnwell County, 1,198 families holding 17,401 slaves in 1860.
- Beaufort County, 578 families holding 14,236 slaves in 1790; and 1,070 families holding 32,530 slaves in 1860.
- Charleston County, 2,538 families holding 50,633 slaves in 1790; and 2,880 families holding 37,290 slaves in 1860.
- Chester County, 230 families holding 938 slaves in 1790; and 909 families holding 10,868 slaves in 1860.
- Chesterfield County, 411 families holding 4,348 slaves in 1860.
- Claremont County, 170 families holding 2,110 slaves in 1790.
- Clarendon County, 79 families holding 602 slaves in 1790; and 537 families holding 8,566 slaves in 1860.
- Colleton County, 968 families holding 32,307 slaves in 1860.
- Darlington County, 939 families holding 11,877 slaves in 1860.
- Edgefield County, 599 families holding 3,619 slaves in 1790; and 1,681 families holding 24,060 slaves in 1860.
- Fairfield County, 254 families holding 1,485 slaves in 1790; and 822 families holding 15,534 slaves in 1860.
- Georgetown County, 842 families holding 13,131 slaves in 1790; and 481 families holding 18,109 slaves in 1860.
- Greenville County, 819 families holding 7,049 slaves in 1860.
- Horry County, 247 families holding 2,359 slaves in 1860.
- Kershaw County, 373 families holding 7,841 slaves in 1860.
- Lancaster County, 222 families holding 1,370 slaves in 1790; and 528 families holding 5,650 slaves in 1860.
- Laurens County, 300 families holding 1,120 slaves in 1790; and 1,093 families holding 13,200 slaves in 1860.
- Lexington County, 609 families holding 6,202 slaves in 1860.
- Marion County, 846 families holding 9,951 slaves in 1860.
- Marlboro County, 489 families holding 6,893 slaves in 1860.
- Newberry County, 302 families holding 1,144 slaves in 1790; and 937 families holding 13,695 slaves in 1860.
- Orangeburg County, 1,069 families holding 16,583 slaves in 1860.
- Pendleton County, 251 families holding 834 slaves in 1790.
- Pickens County, 529 families holding 4,195 slaves in 1860.
- Richland County, 187 families holding 1,437 slaves in 1790; and 604 families holding 11,005 slaves in 1860.
- Spartanburg County, 242 families holding 866 slaves in 1790; and 1,007 families holding 8,240 slaves in 1860.
- Sumter County, 822 families holding 16,682 slaves in 1860.
- Union County, 231 families holding 1,215 slaves in 1790; and 676 families holding 10,801 slaves in 1860.
- Williamsburg County, 491 families holding 10,259 slaves in 1860.

- York County, 227 families holding 923 slaves in 1790; and 1,096 families holding 9,984 slaves in 1860.

State of Tennessee

- Anderson County, 110 families holding 583 slaves in 1860.
- Bedford County, 980 families holding 6,744 slaves in 1860.
- Benton County, 113 families holding 534 slaves in 1860.
- Bledsoe County, 115 families holding 689 slaves in 1860.
- Blount County, 241 families holding 1,363 slaves in 1860.
- Bradley County, 250 families holding 1,173 slaves in 1860.
- Campbell County, 62 families holding 366 slaves in 1860.
- Cannon County, 203 families holding 974 slaves in 1860.
- Carroll County, 704 families holding 4,064 slaves in 1860.
- Carter County, 82 families holding 374 slaves in 1860.
- Cheatha County, 278 families holding 1,882 slaves in 1860.
- Claiborne County, 139 families holding 743 slaves in 1860.
- Cocke County, 172 families holding 849 slaves in 1860.
- Coffee County, 308 families holding 1,529 slaves in 1860.
- Cumberland County, 33 families holding 121 slaves in 1860.
- Davidson County, 2,153 families holding 14,790 slaves in 1860.
- De Kalb County, 236 families holding 1,025 slaves in 1860.
- Decatur County, 136 families holding 784 slaves in 1860.
- Dickson County, 310 families holding 2,201 slaves in 1860.
- Dyer County, 415 families holding 2,641 slaves in 1860.
- Fayette County, 1,124 families holding 15,473 slaves in 1860.
- Fentress County, 55 families holding 187 slaves in 1860.
- Franklin County, 561 families holding 3,551 slaves in 1860.
- Gibson County, 1,011 families holding 6,141 slaves in 1860.
- Giles County, 1,243 families holding 10,848 slaves in 1860.
- Grainger County, 199 families holding 1,065 slaves in 1860.
- Greene County, 307 families holding 1,297 slaves in 1860.
- Grundy County, 63 families holding 266 slaves in 1860.
- Hamilton County, 287 families holding 1,419 slaves in 1860.
- Hancock County, 67 families holding 246 slaves in 1860.
- Hardeman County, 672 families holding 7,236 slaves in 1860.
- Hardin County, 280 families holding 1,623 slaves in 1860.
- Hawkins County, 311 families holding 1,925 slaves in 1860.
- Haywood County, 894 families holding 11,026 slaves in 1860.
- Henderson County, 476 families holding 3,283 slaves in 1860.
- Henry County, 716 families holding 5,530 slaves in 1860.
- Hickman County, 306 families holding 1,753 slaves in 1860.
- Humphreys County, 279 families holding 1,463 slaves in 1860.
- Jackson County, 230 families holding 1,212 slaves in 1860.
- Jefferson County, 349 families holding 2,096 slaves in 1860.
- Johnson County, 60 families holding 233 slaves in 1860.
- Knox County, 447 families holding 2,370 slaves in 1860.
- Lauderdale County, 313 families holding 2,854 slaves in 1860.
- Lawrence County, 234 families holding 1,160 slaves in 1860.
- Lewis County, 42 families holding 247 slaves in 1860.
- Lincoln County, 905 families holding 6,847 slaves in 1860.
- Macon County, 199 families holding 929 slaves in 1860.
- Madison County, 988 families holding 10,012 slaves in 1860.

- Marion County, 124 families holding 678 slaves in 1860.
- Marshall County, 706 families holding 4,480 slaves in 1860.
- Maury County, 1,501 families holding 14,654 slaves in 1860.
- McMinn County, 414 families holding 1,909 slaves in 1860.
- McNairy County, 356 families holding 1,900 slaves in 1860.
- Meigs County, 116 families holding 638 slaves in 1860.
- Monroe County, 255 families holding 1,600 slaves in 1860.
- Montgomery County, 956 families holding 9,554 slaves in 1860.
- Morgan County, 25 families holding 120 slaves in 1860.
- Obion County, 516 families holding 2,399 slaves in 1860.
- Overton County, 248 families holding 1,087 slaves in 1860.
- Perry County, 118 families holding 548 slaves in 1860.
- Polk County, 74 families holding 434 slaves in 1860.
- Putna County, 146 families holding 682 slaves in 1860.
- Rhea County, 103 families holding 615 slaves in 1860.
- Roane County, 273 families holding 1,748 slaves in 1860.
- Robertson County, 729 families holding 4,861 slaves in 1860.
- Rutherford County, 1,316 families holding 12,984 slaves in 1860.
- Scott County, 10 families holding 59 slaves in 1860.
- Sequatchie County, 34 families holding 201 slaves in 1860.
- Sevier County, 96 families holding 538 slaves in 1860.
- Shelby County, 2,056 families holding 16,953 slaves in 1860.
- Smith County, 654 families holding 4,228 slaves in 1860.
- Stewart County, 277 families holding 2,415 slaves in 1860.
- Sullivan County, 246 families holding 1,074 slaves in 1860.
- Sumner County, 951 families holding 7,700 slaves in 1860.
- Tipton County, 489 families holding 5,288 slaves in 1860.
- Union County, 57 families holding 182 slaves in 1860.
- Van Buren County, 36 families holding 239 slaves in 1860.
- Warren County, 367 families holding 2,320 slaves in 1860.
- Washington County, 236 families holding 952 slaves in 1860.
- Wayne County, 240 families holding 1,269 slaves in 1860.
- Weakley County, 686 families holding 4,213 slaves in 1860.
- White County, 243 families holding 1,145 slaves in 1860.
- Williamson County, 1,207 families holding 12,367 slaves in 1860.
- Wilson County, 1,325 families holding 7,964 slaves in 1860.

State of Texas
- Anderson County, 459 families holding 3,668 slaves in 1860.
- Angelina County, 116 families holding 686 slaves in 1860.
- Atascosa County, 33 families holding 107 slaves in 1860.
- Austin County, 324 families holding 3,914 slaves in 1860.
- Bandera County, 5 families holding 12 slaves in 1860.
- Bastrop County, 274 families holding 2,591 slaves in 1860.
- Bee County, 38 families holding 79 slaves in 1860.
- Bell County, 179 families holding 1,005 slaves in 1860.
- Bexar County, 294 families holding 1,395 slaves in 1860.
- Blanco County, unknown number of families holding 98 slaves in 1860.
- Bosque County, 51 families holding 293 slaves in 1860.
- Bowie County, 201 families holding 2,651 slaves in 1860.
- Brazoria County, 232 families holding 5,110 slaves in 1860.
- Brazos County, 118 families holding 1,063 slaves in 1860.

- Burleson County, 228 families holding 2,003 slaves in 1860.
- Burnet County, 69 families holding 235 slaves in 1860.
- Caldwell County, 254 families holding 1,610 slaves in 1860.
- Calhoun County, 106 families holding 414 slaves in 1860.
- Cameron County, 6 families holding 7 slaves in 1860.
- Cass/Davis County, 354 families holding 3,475 slaves in 1860.
- Chambers County, 69 families holding 513 slaves in 1860.
- Cherokee County, 456 families holding 3,246 slaves in 1860.
- Collin County, 240 families holding 1,047 slaves in 1860.
- Colorado County, 306 families holding 3,559 slaves in 1860.
- Comal County, 22 families holding 193 slaves in 1860.
- Comanche County, 25 families holding 61 slaves in 1860.
- Cooke County, 74 families holding 369 slaves in 1860.
- Coryell County, 81 families holding 306 slaves in 1860.
- Dallas County, 228 families holding 1,074 slaves in 1860.
- De Witt County, 201 families holding 1,643 slaves in 1860.
- Denton County, 87 families holding 251 slaves in 1860.
- El Paso County, 3 families holding 15 slaves in 1860.
- Ellis County, 196 families holding 1,104 slaves in 1860.
- Erath County, 26 families holding 118 slaves in 1860.
- Falls County, 158 families holding 1,716 slaves in 1860.
- Fannin County, 308 families holding 1,721 slaves in 1860.
- Fayette County, 514 families holding 3,786 slaves in 1860.
- Fort Bend County, 260 families holding 4,127 slaves in 1860.
- Freestone County, 307 families holding 3,613 slaves in 1860.
- Frio County, 2 families holding 2 slaves in 1860.
- Galveston County, 288 families holding 1,520 slaves in 1860.
- Gillespie County, 7 families holding 33 slaves in 1860.
- Goliad County, 119 families holding 843 slaves in 1860.
- Gonzales County, 384 families holding 3,168 slaves in 1860.
- Grayson County, 236 families holding 1,292 slaves in 1860.
- Grimes County, 505 families holding 5,468 slaves in 1860.
- Guadalupe County, 202 families holding 1,748 slaves in 1860.
- Hamilton County, 12 families holding 26 slaves in 1860.
- Hardin County, 35 families holding 191 slaves in 1860.
- Harris County, 395 families holding 2,053 slaves in 1860.
- Harrison County, 713 families holding 8,784 slaves in 1860.
- Hays County, 95 families holding 797 slaves in 1860.
- Henderson County, 155 families holding 1,116 slaves in 1860.
- Hidalgo County, 1 families holding 1 slaves in 1860.
- Hill County, 118 families holding 650 slaves in 1860.
- Hopkins County, 235 families holding 990 slaves in 1860.
- Houston County, 335 families holding 2,819 slaves in 1860.
- Hunt County, 142 families holding 577 slaves in 1860.
- Jack County, 19 families holding 50 slaves in 1860.
- Jackson County, 155 families holding 1,194 slaves in 1860.
- Jasper County, 170 families holding 1,611 slaves in 1860.
- Jefferson County, 70 families holding 309 slaves in 1860.
- Johnson County, 129 families holding 513 slaves in 1860.
- Karnes County, 64 families holding 327 slaves in 1860.

- Kaufman County, 128 families holding 533 slaves in 1860.
- Kerr County, 14 families holding 49 slaves in 1860.
- Lamar County, 419 families holding 2,833 slaves in 1860.
- Lampasas County, 32 families holding 153 slaves in 1860.
- Lavaca County, 217 families holding 1,707 slaves in 1860.
- Leon County, 320 families holding 2,620 slaves in 1860.
- Liberty County, 136 families holding 1,079 slaves in 1860.
- Limestone County, 182 families holding 1,072 slaves in 1860.
- Live Oak County, 11 families holding 85 slaves in 1860.
- Llano County, 21 families holding 54 slaves in 1860.
- Madison County, 96 families holding 675 slaves in 1860.
- Marion County, 213 families holding 2,017 slaves in 1860.
- Mason County, 8 families holding 18 slaves in 1860.
- Matagorda County, 125 families holding 2,107 slaves in 1860.
- Maverick County, 1 families holding 1 slaves in 1860.
- McLennan County, 270 families holding 2,395 slaves in 1860.
- Medina County, 22 families holding 106 slaves in 1860.
- Mila County, 259 families holding 1,542 slaves in 1860.
- Montague County, 13 families holding 35 slaves in 1860.
- Montgomery County, 232 families holding 2,811 slaves in 1860.
- Nacogdoches County, 383 families holding 2,359 slaves in 1860.
- Navarro County, 251 families holding 1,890 slaves in 1860.
- Newton County, 127 families holding 1,013 slaves in 1860.
- Nueces County, 52 families holding 216 slaves in 1860.
- Orange County, 64 families holding 392 slaves in 1860.
- Palo Pinto County, 29 families holding 130 slaves in 1860.
- Panola County, 445 families holding 3,058 slaves in 1860.
- Parker County, 70 families holding 222 slaves in 1860.
- Polk County, 357 families holding 4,198 slaves in 1860.
- Presidio County, 4 families holding 4 slaves in 1860.
- Red River County, 353 families holding 3,039 slaves in 1860.
- Refugio County, 43 families holding 234 slaves in 1860.
- Robertson County, 188 families holding 2,258 slaves in 1860.
- Rusk County, 734 families holding 6,132 slaves in 1860.
- Sabine County, 135 families holding 1,150 slaves in 1860.
- San Augustine County, 144 families holding 1,717 slaves in 1860.
- San Patricio County, 36 families holding 95 slaves in 1860.
- San Saba County, 20 families holding 89 slaves in 1860.
- Shackelford County, 1 families holding 9 slaves in 1860.
- Shelby County, 208 families holding 1,476 slaves in 1860.
- Smith County, 575 families holding 4,982 slaves in 1860.
- Starr County, 6 families holding 6 slaves in 1860.
- Stephens/Buchanan County, 7 families holding 32 slaves in 1860.
- Tarrant County, unknown number of families holding 850 slaves in 1860.
- Titus County, 352 families holding 2,438 slaves in 1860.
- Travis County, 425 families holding 3,136 slaves in 1860.
- Trinity County, 145 families holding 959 slaves in 1860.
- Tyler County, 197 families holding 1,148 slaves in 1860.
- Upshur County, 480 families holding 3,794 slaves in 1860.
- Uvalde County, 4 families holding 27 slaves in 1860.

- Van Zandt County, 75 families holding 322 slaves in 1860.
- Victoria County, 184 families holding 1,413 slaves in 1860.
- Walker County, 376 families holding 4,135 slaves in 1860.
- Washington County, 627 families holding 7,941 slaves in 1860.
- Wharton County, 128 families holding 2,734 slaves in 1860.
- Williamson County, 181 families holding 891 slaves in 1860.
- Wise County, 53 families holding 128 slaves in 1860.
- Wood County, 186 families holding 1,005 slaves in 1860.
- Young County, 26 families holding 92 slaves in 1860.

State of Virginia

- Accomack County, unknown number of families holding 4,262 slaves in 1790; and 773 families holding 4,507 slaves in 1860.
- Albemarle County, unknown number of families holding 5,579 slaves in 1790; and 1,306 families holding 13,916 slaves in 1860.
- Alleghany County, 134 families holding 990 slaves in 1860.
- Amelia County, unknown number of families holding 11,307 slaves in 1790; and 536 families holding 7,655 slaves in 1860.
- Amherst County, unknown number of families holding 5,296 slaves in 1790; and 685 families holding 6,278 slaves in 1860.
- Appomattox County, 520 families holding 4,600 slaves in 1860.
- Arlington/Alexandria County, 251 families holding 1,386 slaves in 1860.
- Augusta County, unknown number of families holding 1,567 slaves in 1790; and 811 families holding 5,616 slaves in 1860.
- Barbour County, 41 families holding 95 slaves in 1860.
- Bath County, 115 families holding 946 slaves in 1860.
- Bedford County, unknown number of families holding 2,754 slaves in 1790; and 1,129 families holding 10,176 slaves in 1860.

- Berkeley County, unknown number of families holding 2,932 slaves in 1790; and 333 families holding 1,650 slaves in 1860.
- Boone County, 36 families holding 158 slaves in 1860.
- Botetourt County, unknown number of families holding 1,259 slaves in 1790; and 332 families holding 2,769 slaves in 1860.
- Braxton County, 26 families holding 104 slaves in 1860.
- Brooke County, 12 families holding 18 slaves in 1860.
- Brunswick County, unknown number of families holding 6,776 slaves in 1790; and 772 families holding 9,146 slaves in 1860.
- Buchanan County, 3 families holding 30 slaves in 1860.
- Buckingha County, unknown number of families holding 4,168 slaves in 1790; and 718 families holding 8,811 slaves in 1860.
- Cabell County, 84 families holding 305 slaves in 1860.
- Calhoun County, 3 families holding 9 slaves in 1860.
- Campbell County, unknown number of families holding 2,488 slaves in 1790; and 1,705 families holding 11,580 slaves in 1860.
- Caroline County, unknown number of families holding 10,292 slaves in 1790; and 725 families holding 10,672 slaves in 1860.
- Carroll County, 82 families holding 262 slaves in 1860.
- Charles City County, unknown number of families holding 3,141 slaves in 1790; and 191 families holding 2,947 slaves in 1860.
- Charlotte County, unknown number of families holding 4,816 slaves in 1790; and 609 families holding 9,238 slaves in 1860.
- Chesterfield County, unknown number of families holding 7,487 slaves in 1790; and 806 families holding 8,354 slaves in 1860.
- Clarke County, 344 families holding 3,375 slaves in 1860.
- Clay County, 3 families holding 21 slaves in 1860.
- Craig County, 130 families holding 420 slaves in 1860.
- Culpeper County, unknown number of families holding 8,226 slaves in 1790; and 611 families holding 6,675 slaves in 1860.

- Cumberland County, unknown number of families holding 4,434 slaves in 1790; and 452 families holding 6,705 slaves in 1860.
- Dinwiddie County, unknown number of families holding 7,334 slaves in 1790; and 1,826 families holding 12,774 slaves in 1860.
- Doddridge County, 17 families holding 34 slaves in 1860.
- Elizabeth City County, unknown number of families holding 1,876 slaves in 1790; and 277 families holding 2,417 slaves in 1860.
- Essex County, unknown number of families holding 5,440 slaves in 1790; and 398 families holding 6,696 slaves in 1860.
- Fairfax County, unknown number of families holding 4,574 slaves in 1790; and 529 families holding 3,116 slaves in 1860.
- Fauquier County, unknown number of families holding 6,642 slaves in 1790; and 933 families holding 10,455 slaves in 1860.
- Fayette County, 63 families holding 271 slaves in 1860.
- Floyd County, 125 families holding 475 slaves in 1860.
- Fluvanna County, unknown number of families holding 1,466 slaves in 1790; and 521 families holding 4,994 slaves in 1860.
- Franklin County, unknown number of families holding 1,073 slaves in 1790; and 996 families holding 6,351 slaves in 1860.
- Frederick County, unknown number of families holding 4,250 slaves in 1790; and 406 families holding 2,259 slaves in 1860.
- Giles County, 145 families holding 778 slaves in 1860.
- Gilmer County, 20 families holding 52 slaves in 1860.
- Gloucester County, unknown number of families holding 7,063 slaves in 1790; and 487 families holding 5,736 slaves in 1860.
- Goochland County, unknown number of families holding 4,656 slaves in 1790; and 537 families holding 6,139 slaves in 1860.
- Grayson County, 124 families holding 547 slaves in 1860.
- Greenbrier County, unknown number of families holding 319 slaves in 1790; and 267 families holding 1,525 slaves in 1860.
- Greene County, 225 families holding 1,984 slaves in 1860.

- Greensville County, unknown number of families holding 3,620 slaves in 1790; and 268 families holding 4,167 slaves in 1860.
- Halifax County, unknown number of families holding 5,565 slaves in 1790; and 1,051 families holding 14,897 slaves in 1860.
- Hampshire County, unknown number of families holding 454 slaves in 1790; and 244 families holding 1,213 slaves in 1860.
- Hancock County, unknown number of families holding 2 slaves in 1860.
- Hanover County, unknown number of families holding 8,223 slaves in 1790; and 903 families holding 9,483 slaves in 1860.
- Hardy County, unknown number of families holding 369 slaves in 1790; and 157 families holding 1,073 slaves in 1860.
- Harrison County, unknown number of families holding 67 slaves in 1790; and 159 families holding 582 slaves in 1860.
- Henrico County, unknown number of families holding 5,819 slaves in 1790; and 2,339 families holding 20,041 slaves in 1860.
- Henry County, unknown number of families holding 1,551 slaves in 1790; and 422 families holding 5,018 slaves in 1860.
- Highland County, 116 families holding 402 slaves in 1860.
- Isle of Wight County, unknown number of families holding 3,867 slaves in 1790; and 470 families holding 3,570 slaves in 1860.
- Jackson County, 25 families holding 55 slaves in 1860.
- James City County, unknown number of families holding 2,405 slaves in 1790; and 230 families holding 2,586 slaves in 1860.
- Jefferson County, 634 families holding 3,960 slaves in 1860.
- Kanawha County, 265 families holding 2,184 slaves in 1860.
- King And Queen County, unknown number of families holding 5,143 slaves in 1790; and 449 families holding 6,139 slaves in 1860.
- King George County, unknown number of families holding 4,157 slaves in 1790; and 314 families holding 3,673 slaves in 1860.

- King Willia County, unknown number of families holding 5,151 slaves in 1790; and 366 families holding 5,525 slaves in 1860.
- Lancaster County, unknown number of families holding 3,236 slaves in 1790; and 259 families holding 2,869 slaves in 1860.
- Lee County, 151 families holding 824 slaves in 1860.
- Lewis County, 60 families holding 230 slaves in 1860.
- Logan County, 40 families holding 148 slaves in 1860.
- Loudoun County, unknown number of families holding 4,030 slaves in 1790; and 670 families holding 5,501 slaves in 1860.
- Louisa County, unknown number of families holding 4,573 slaves in 1790; and 765 families holding 10,194 slaves in 1860.
- Lunenburg County, unknown number of families holding 4,332 slaves in 1790; and 545 families holding 7,305 slaves in 1860.
- Madison County, 455 families holding 4,397 slaves in 1860.
- Marion County, 32 families holding 63 slaves in 1860.
- Marshall County, 14 families holding 29 slaves in 1860.
- Mason County, 70 families holding 376 slaves in 1860.
- Mathews County, 386 families holding 3,008 slaves in 1860.
- Mecklenburg County, unknown number of families holding 6,762 slaves in 1790; and 760 families holding 12,420 slaves in 1860.
- Mercer County, 66 families holding 362 slaves in 1860.
- Middlesex County, unknown number of families holding 2,558 slaves in 1790; and 204 families holding 2,375 slaves in 1860.
- Monongalia County, unknown number of families holding 154 slaves in 1790; and 37 families holding 101 slaves in 1860.
- Monroe County, 196 families holding 1,114 slaves in 1860.
- Montgomery County, unknown number of families holding 828 slaves in 1790; and 283 families holding 2,219 slaves in 1860.
- Morgan County, 30 families holding 94 slaves in 1860.
- Nansemond County, unknown number of families holding 3,817 slaves in 1790; and 619 families holding 5,481 slaves in 1860.
- Nelson County, 554 families holding 6,238 slaves in 1860.
- New Kent County, unknown number of families holding 3,700 slaves in 1790; and 291 families holding 3,374 slaves in 1860.
- Nicholas County, 46 families holding 154 slaves in 1860.
- Norfolk County, unknown number of families holding 5,345 slaves in 1790; and 1,464 families holding 9,004 slaves in 1860.
- Northampton County, unknown number of families holding 3,244 slaves in 1790; and 400 families holding 3,872 slaves in 1860.
- Northumberland County, unknown number of families holding 4,460 slaves in 1790; and 401 families holding 3,439 slaves in 1860.
- Nottoway County, 375 families holding 6,468 slaves in 1860.
- Ohio County, unknown number of families holding 281 slaves in 1790; and 43 families holding 100 slaves in 1860.
- Orange County, unknown number of families holding 4,421 slaves in 1790; and 480 families holding 6,111 slaves in 1860.
- Page County, 177 families holding 850 slaves in 1860.
- Patrick County, 318 families holding 2,070 slaves in 1860.
- Pendleton County, unknown number of families holding 73 slaves in 1790; and 52 families holding 244 slaves in 1860.
- Pittsylvania County, unknown number of families holding 2,979 slaves in 1790; and 1,413 families holding 14,340 slaves in 1860.
- Pleasants County, 5 families holding 15 slaves in 1860.
- Pocahontas County, 64 families holding 252 slaves in 1860.
- Powhatan County, unknown number of families holding 4,325 slaves in 1790; and 375 families holding 5,403 slaves in 1860.
- Preston County, 20 families holding 67 slaves in 1860.
- Prince Edward County, unknown number of families holding 3,986 slaves in 1790;

and 582 families holding 7,341 slaves in 1860.

- Prince George County, unknown number of families holding 4,519 slaves in 1790; and 344 families holding 4,997 slaves in 1860.
- Prince Willia County, unknown number of families holding 4,704 slaves in 1790; and 273 families holding 2,356 slaves in 1860.
- Princess Anne County, unknown number of families holding 3,202 slaves in 1790; and 506 families holding 3,186 slaves in 1860.
- Pulaski County, 157 families holding 1,589 slaves in 1860.
- Putna County, 93 families holding 580 slaves in 1860.
- Raleigh County, 21 families holding 57 slaves in 1860.
- Randolph County, unknown number of families holding 19 slaves in 1790; and 56 families holding 183 slaves in 1860.
- Rappahannock County, 398 families holding 3,520 slaves in 1860.
- Richmond County, unknown number of families holding 3,984 slaves in 1790; and 259 families holding 2,466 slaves in 1860.
- Ritchie County, 12 families holding 38 slaves in 1860.
- Roane County, 23 families holding 72 slaves in 1860.
- Roanoke County, 259 families holding 2,643 slaves in 1860.
- Rockbridge County, unknown number of families holding 682 slaves in 1790; and 569 families holding 3,985 slaves in 1860.
- Rockingha County, unknown number of families holding 772 slaves in 1790; and 420 families holding 2,387 slaves in 1860.
- Russell County, unknown number of families holding 190 slaves in 1790; and 171 families holding 1,099 slaves in 1860.
- Scott County, 127 families holding 490 slaves in 1860.
- Shenandoah County, unknown number of families holding 512 slaves in 1790; and 117 families holding 753 slaves in 1860.
- Smyth County, 218 families holding 1,037 slaves in 1860.
- Southampton County, unknown number of families holding 5,993 slaves in 1790; and 494 families holding 5,408 slaves in 1860.

- Spotsylvania County, unknown number of families holding 5,933 slaves in 1790; and 1,031 families holding 7,786 slaves in 1860.
- Stafford County, unknown number of families holding 4,036 slaves in 1790; and 621 families holding 3,314 slaves in 1860.
- Surry County, unknown number of families holding 3,097 slaves in 1790; and 188 families holding 2,515 slaves in 1860.
- Sussex County, unknown number of families holding 5,387 slaves in 1790; and 428 families holding 6,384 slaves in 1860.
- Taylor County, 47 families holding 112 slaves in 1860.
- Tazewell County, 223 families holding 1,202 slaves in 1860.
- Tucker County, 5 families holding 20 slaves in 1860.
- Tyler County, 8 families holding 18 slaves in 1860.
- Upshur County, 51 families holding 212 slaves in 1860.
- Warren County, 229 families holding 1,575 slaves in 1860.
- Warwick County, unknown number of families holding 990 slaves in 1790; and 91 families holding 1,019 slaves in 1860.
- Washington County, unknown number of families holding 450 slaves in 1790; and 386 families holding 2,547 slaves in 1860.
- Wayne County, 37 families holding 143 slaves in 1860.
- Webster County, 1 families holding 3 slaves in 1860.
- Westmoreland County, unknown number of families holding 4,425 slaves in 1790; and 380 families holding 3,704 slaves in 1860.
- Wetzel County, 6 families holding 10 slaves in 1860.
- Wirt County, 11 families holding 23 slaves in 1860.
- Wise County, 13 families holding 66 slaves in 1860.
- Wood County, 64 families holding 176 slaves in 1860.
- Wyoming County, 6 families holding 64 slaves in 1860.
- Wythe County, 271 families holding 2,162 slaves in 1860.

- York County, unknown number of families holding 2,760 slaves in 1790; and 226 families holding 1,925 slaves in 1860.

Shipping Industry
- 600 Ports in Europe, Africa & Americas
- Port of Alicante
- Port of Amsterdam
- Port of Antwerp
- Port of Autoridad Portuaria de Cartagena
- Port of Autoridad Portuaria de Valencia
- Port of Barcelona
- Port of Bilbao
- Port of Bremen
- Port of Brest
- Port of Brussels
- Port of Cadiz
- Port of Calais
- Port of Cannes
- Port of Cartagena
- Port of Copenhagen
- Port of de Barcelona
- Port of de Marseille
- Port of Dublin
- Port of Gent
- Port of Hamburg
- Port of Havre
- Port of Helsinki
- Port of Le Havre
- Port of Lisbon
- Port of Marseille
- Port of Nice
- Port of Rotterdam
- The Aspinwall Family
- The Cabot Family
- The Coster Family
- The Crowinshield Family
- The Griswold Family
- The Haven Family
- The Howland Family
- The Livingston Family
- The Perkins Family
- The Russell Family
- The Schermerhorn Family
- The Shipley Family
- The Sturgis Family
- American Association of Port Authorities
- Alabama State Port Authority
- Brazos River Harbor Navigation District
- Bridgeport Port Authority
- Chesapeake Port Authority
- Delaware River Port Authority
- Georgia Ports Authority
- Greater Baton Rouge Port Commission
- Greater Lafourche Port Commission
- Illinois International Port Authority
- Jacksonville Port Authority
- Jacksonville Seaport Authority
- Key West Port & Transit Authority
- Lake Charles Harbor & Terminal District
- Manatee County Port Authority
- Maryland Port Administration
- Massachusetts Port Authority
- Mississippi State Port Authority at Gulfport
- Nassau County Port Authority
- New Bedford Harbor Development Commission
- New York City Economic Development Corp.
- New Hampshire Division of Ports & Harbors
- North Carolina State Ports Authority
- Orange County Navigation Port District
- Oregon International Port of Coos Bay
- Panama City Port Authority
- Philadelphia Regional Port Authority
- Plaquemines Port, Harbor & Terminal District
- Port Authority of New York & New Jersey
- Port Everglades
- Port Freeport
- Port Isabel-San Benito Navigation District
- Port Manatee
- Port of Baltimore
- Port of Baton Rouge
- Port of Beaumont
- Port of Brownsville
- Port of Chicago
- Port of Corpus Christi Authority
- Port of Galveston
- Port of Grays Harbor
- Port of Houston Authority
- Port of Hueneme/Oxnard Harbor District
- Port of Iberia
- Port of Kalama
- Port of Lake Charles
- Port of Longview
- Port of Miami
- Port of New Hampshire
- Port of New London
- Port of New Orleans
- Port of Orange, TX

- Port of Palm Beach
- Port of Pascagoula
- Port of Pensacola
- Port of Philadelphia and Camden
- Port of Ponce
- Port of Port Arthur
- Port of Richmond
- Port of Shreveport/Bossier
- Port of South Louisiana
- Port of St. Petersburg
- Port of Wilmington, Delaware
- Puerto Rico Ports Authority
- Rhode Island Economic Development Corp.
- South Carolina State Ports Authority
- South Jersey Port Commission
- St. Bernard Port, Harbor & Terminal
- St. Lucie County Port & Airport Authority
- Tampa Port Authority
- Virgin Islands Port Authority
- Virginia Port Authority

Gun Industry
- The Colt Family
- The Du Pont Family
- The Hartley Family
- The Pardee Family
- The Smith Wesson Family
- The Whitney Family
- The Winchester Family
- Colt Patent Firearms Manufacturing Company
- E. I. Du Pont De Nemours & Company
- Remington Arms Company
- Smith & Wesson Firearms
- Union Metallic Cartridge Company
- Whitney Arms Company
- Winchester Repeating Arms

Tobacco Slave Markets
- Abington
- Alexandria
- Boonville
- Fayetteville
- Washington, DC
- Wheeling

Tobacco Growers
- The Atkinson Family
- The Auborn Family
- The Basham Family (Basham Roanoke Plantation)

- The Belle, Aire Family
- The Black, Walnut Family
- The Brown Family
- The Bruce Family (Tarover Plantation)
- The Burwell Family (Whitemarsh Plantation)
- The Byrd, Bland, Harrison, Coles, Carrington, Bruce Family (Westover & Berry Hill Plantations)
- The Carter, Chinn, Hill, Marders, Weir Family (Aries, Ben Lomond, Blenheim, Cancer Farm, Capricorn, Carter Grove, Charles Carter of Cleve, Corotoman, Edge Hill, Hardin, Leo, Liberia, Libra, Nomini/Nominy Hall, Oatlands, Pittsylvania, Roe, Scorpio, Shirley, Sudley & Virgo Plantations)
- The Cary Family (Ampthill Plantation)
- The Coke Family
- The Corbin Family (Buckingham Middlesex Plantation)
- The Custis Family
- The Drewry, Helm Family (Harris and Phipps Plantation)
- The Elgin Family (Elgin Plantation)
- The Fairfax Family (Northern Neck Plantation)
- The Fitzhugh Family (Chatham Plantation)
- The Garnett Family
- The Greenfield Family
- The Grymes Family (Brandon & Smithfield Plantations)
- The Hairston Family (Beaver Creek, Berkeley, Brandon, Burnt Chimneys Tobacco, Camp Branch, Chatmoss, Hordsville, Kittewan, Leatherwood, Magna Vista, Marrowbone, Maycock, North Bend, Oak Hill, Royal Oak, Saura Town, Shawnee & Windsor Plantations)
- The Harrison, Rowland, Tyler Family (Edgewood & Sherwood Forest Plantations)
- The Hawfeild Family
- The Hendrick Family (Hendrick Plantation)
- The Henry Family
- The Hermitage Family
- The Hill Family
- The Hurst Family (Hurst & River Bend Farm Plantations)
- The Irby Family (Pleasant Hill Plantation)
- The James Family

- The Jefferson Family
- The La Vista Family
- The Lee Family (Bellevue, Ditchley, Lansdowne, Lee Hall, Leesylvania, Stratford Hall & Wilderness (Aka Commons) Plantations)
- The Links Family
- The Little Family
- The Livingston Family
- The Ludlow Family (Green Spring Plantation)
- The Mason Family
- The Mayhurst Family
- The Moore Family (Chelsea Plantation)
- The Nelson Family
- The Overton Family (Prospect Hill Plantation)
- The Page Family (North End Plantation)
- The Palmore Family (Scotts Hill Plantation)
- The Pendolton Family
- The Pocket Family
- The Randolph Family (Chatesworth, Dungeness, Eastern View, Green Creek, Tazewell Estate & Tuckahoe Plantations)
- The Redfeild Family
- The Richmond, Falls Family
- The Roane Family (Spring Garden Plantation)
- The Rogers, Bird Family (Rogers Farm, Bird Rogers Farm & John Rogers Plantations)
- The Rosny Family
- The Ruffin Family (Evelynton Plantation)
- The Ryan Family
- The Scotten Family
- The Skipwith Family (Prestwould Plantation)
- The Southall, Vaiden, Stubblefeild Family (Piney Grove At Southall Plantation)
- The Spotswood Family
- The Stratford Family
- The Sweethall Family
- The Talbutt Family (Rose Hill Plantation)
- The Tayloe Family
- The Terrell Family (Richard Terrell Farm Plantation)
- The Vanderbilt Family (Biltmore Estate Plantation)

- The Waring Family (Edenatta, Glencairn, Greenfield, Port Micon & Thomas Neck Plantations)
- The Washington Family (Belmont & Mt. Vernon Plantations)
- The Whitley Family (John Whitley Farm)
- The Wilkins Family (Belmont Plantation)
- The Woodson Family (Woodson Plantation)
- Airwell Plantation
- Arlington Plantation
- Barn Elms Plantation
- Carysbrook Plantation
- Cecil R. Byrum Plantation
- Cedar Grove Plantation
- Ceelys Plantation
- Chantilly Plantation
- Cloverland Plantation
- Cooleemee Plantation
- Curles Neck Plantation
- Elmwood Plantation
- Endfield Plantation
- Glenmary Plantation
- Gunston Hall Plantation
- Lanesville King Plantation
- Morrisania Plantation
- Mount Pleasant Plantation
- Mt. Airy Plantation
- Mt. Stuart Plantation
- Northumberland Plantation
- Oak Grove Plantation
- Poplar Forest Plantation
- Red Hill Plantation
- Reeds Plantation
- Richmond Hill Plantation
- Richneck Plantation
- Roanoke Plantation
- Sabine Hall Plantation
- Trenton Plantation
- Westmoreland Plantation
- White House Plantation
- Willow Grove Plantation
- Wilton Plantation

Tobacco Warehouses
- Bright Belt Warehouse Association
- Burley Auction Warehouse Association

Tobacco Merchants & Auctioneers
- Austin & Wilmering
- Haggerty & Austen John Hagger
- James & Horner Tobacco

- John Haggerty & Sons Auction
- Leggett Fox & Company Auction
- Leggett Pearsall & Company

Tobacco Dealers
- Association of Dark Leaf Tobacco Dealers
- Dimon Inc.
- Standard Commercial Corporation
- Universal Corporation

Tobacco Manufacturers
- The Duke Family (American Tobacco Company)
- The Ligget, Meyers Family (Ligget & Meyers Tobacco Company, Liggett & Meyers Inc.)
- The Lorrilard Family (Lorillard Brothers, Lorillard Tobacco Company Inc., Lorrilard Tobacco Company, P. Lorrilard & Company, P. Lorrilard & Sons)
- The Phillip Morris Family (Philip Morris Companies Inc.)
- The Reynolds Family (RJ Reynolds Tobacco Company, RJ Reynolds Tobacco Holdings Inc.)
- The Ryan Family
- Altadis Usa Inc.
- American Brands Inc.
- British American Tobacco Inc.
- Brown & Williamson Tobacco Company
- Conwood Sales Company LP
- Gallaher Group PLC
- General Cigar Holdings Inc.
- Imperial Tobacco Group PLC.
- Japan Tobacco
- Luckett Tobaccos Inc.
- Mayflower Tobacco Company
- Mrs George B. Miller & Company
- Reemtsma
- Scottendillon Tobacco Company
- Smokeless Tobacco
- Standard Commerical UK
- Swedish Match
- Swisher International
- United States Tobacco Inc.
- UST Inc.

Tobacco Associations
- Council For Tobacco Research
- Friends of Tobacco
- International Tobacco Growers Association
- Retail Tobacco Dealers of America

- Smokeless Tobacco Council
- South Carolina Warehouse Association
- Tobacco Institute

Sugar Slave Markets
- Fant's Building

Sugar Slave Trading Firms
- Mosley & Spragins

Sugar Growers
- The Atkins Family (E. Atkins & Company and American Sugar)
- The Barrow Family (Eldorado & Highland Plantations)
- The Bell Family (Johnson Bell Saloon Plantation)
- The Besland Family (William Besland Plantation)
- The Blanche Family (Marydale Plantation)
- The Boney Family (Duckport Plantation)
- The Bosley Family (Telegram Plantation)
- The Boucry Family (Bonne Esperance Plantation)
- The Bradford Family (Myrtles Plantation)
- The Braga Family (Braga Brothers)
- The Bragg Family (Bivouac Plantation)
- The Bray Family (Cotile Plantation)
- The Bringier Family (L'hermitage Plantation)
- The Buhler Family (Winter Plantation)
- The Burnside Family (Houmas Plantation)
- The Butler Family (Cedars Plantation)
- The Caroll Family (Ackbar Plantation)
- The Chinn Family (Fair Oaks Plantation)
- The De Ternant Family (Parlange Plantation)
- The Delaney Family (Louisiana Plantation)
- The Delogny, Destrehan, Rost Family (Destrehan Plantation)
- The Derbanne, Hertzog Family (Rosedew Plantation)
- The Dtrepagnier, Butler, McCutchon Family (Ormond Plantation)
- The Duplantier Family (Magnolia Mound Plantation)
- The Fanjul Family
- The Ferrier Family (Joseph Ferrier Farm Plantation)
- The Fox Family (Hygiene Plantation)
- The Gee Family (Gee Plantation)

- The Gillespie Family (Indian Village Plantation)
- The Havemeyer Family (Havemeyer & Company Sugar Refiners, Havemeyer & Elder Sugar)
- The Houbre Family (Valery Houbre Farm)
- The Keary Family (Catalpa Plantation)
- The Kenner Family (Ashland (Aka Belle Helene) Plantation)
- The Ledoux Family (Ledoux and Hall Plantation)
- The Lewis Family (Thomas Lewis Plantation)
- The Liddell Family (Llanada Plantation)
- The Locoul Family (Laura Plantation)
- The Marmillion Family (San Francisco Plantation)
- The Metarie, Ridge Family (Metarie Ridge Plantation)
- The Minor Family (Hollywood Plantation)
- The Minor Family (Lake Plantation)
- The Minor Family (Southdown Plantation)
- The Minor Family (Waterloo Plantation)
- The Moore Family (Moreland Plantation)
- The Mulholland Family (Inglewood Plantation)
- The Mulon Family (Francois Mulon Farm)
- The Pellerin, Sterling, Peebles, Wyche Family (Belmont Plantation)
- The Peytavin Family (Ancient Domain Plantation)
- The Powell Family (Mt. Flat Plantation)
- The Randolph Family (Nottoway Plantation)
- The Richardson Family (Bayside Plantation)
- The Roman Family (Oak Alley Plantation)
- The Roosevelt Family
- The Sharp Family (Bon Ridge Plantation)
- The Spreckels Family (Bay Sugar Refining Company)
- The Stuart Family
- The Thibodeaux Family (St. Bridget/ Brigitte Plantation)
- The Thurston Family (Thurston Place Plantation)
- The Tucker (Robert) Family (Robert Tucker Plantation)
- The Tureaud Family (Tezcuco Plantation)
- The Ventress Family (Caledonia, Lake Home & Longwood Plantations)

- The Wilkins Family (Ashton Plantation)
- Aristide Landry Plantation
- Atahoe Plantation
- Bellewood Plantation
- Bragg Plantation
- Cane River Creole Plantation
- Chappin Plantation
- Cherokee Plantation
- Dugas Plantation
- Elm Hall Plantation
- Foley Plantation
- George Tucker Plantation
- Good Hope Plantation
- Hard Times Plantation
- Hatch Plantation
- Huston Plantation
- Johnson Plantation
- Knight Family Plantation
- L.T. and Trails Plantation
- Laurel Valley Plantation
- Le Blanc Plantation
- Leighton Plantation
- Logan Plantation
- M A Patout & Sons Ltd. Plantation
- Maning Plantation
- Melrose Plantation
- Monot Plantation
- Oakland Plantation
- Old Johnson Plantation
- Pierre Rost Plantation
- Pitre Plantation
- Ranche Plantation
- Ross Plantation
- Starlight Plantation
- Sugar Cane Growers Cooperative of Florida
- Sugar Growers
- Sweet Home Plantation
- Theoda Plantation
- United States Sugar Corporation
- Vick Plantation
- Westfield Plantation
- Whitehead Plantation
- Woodlawn Plantation

Sugar Manufacturers
- Alexander Baldwin Inc.
- Amalgamated Sugar Company LLC
- American Crystal Sugar Company
- American Sugar Refining Company
- British Sugar Plc

- C & H Sugar Company Inc.
- Chicago Sweeteners Incorporated
- Coffee Sugar & Cocoa Exchange
- Connell Company
- Csm Sugar Division
- Domino Sugar
- Elisha Atkins & Company and Trinidad
- Florida Crystals Inc.
- General Mills Inc.
- Gramercy
- Group Sopex
- Hershey Foods Corporation
- Holly Sugar Corporation
- Imperial Savannah Lp
- Imperial Sugar Company
- Indiana Sugars
- Ingenio Y Refineria San Martin Del Ta
- Kellog Company
- Lambre Brothers Cotton Gin
- Lihue Plantation Company Ltd.
- Liquid Sugars Inc.
- Malaco Kbb
- Monitor Sugar Company
- Monsanto
- Napier Brown & Company Limited
- National City Lines Inc.
- Nestle Holdings Inc.
- Nestle Usa Inc.
- Northbrook Corporation
- Oahu Sugar Company Ltd. Inc.
- Okeelanta Corporation
- Olokele Sugar Company Ltd.
- Pioneer Mill Company Ltd. Inc.
- Qa Products Inc. Csm N.V.
- R. L. & A. Stuart Sugar Refiners
- R.B. & J.H. Williams Cotton Gin
- Seabord Corporation
- Simmons Harold C's Trust
- Snake Rive Sugar Company
- Spreckels Sugar Company
- Sterling Sugars Inc.
- Tasr Company
- Tate & Lyle Plc
- Tootsie Roll Company Inc.
- Tootsie Roll Industries Inc.
- Trinidad Sugar Company
- U.S. Sugar Corporation

Sugar Manufacturers-Beverages
- Allied Domecg Plc
- Bacardi Limited

- Brown (Foreman
- Cadbury Schweppes
- Coca Cola
- Conagra Grocery
- Destileria Serrales
- Diego PLC
- Distileria
- Ebenezer Stevens & Sons Liquors
- John B Sanfilippo & Son Inc.
- Mars Inc.
- Pepsi Cola
- Pernard Richard
- Rich Foods

Sugar Associations
- American Sugar Alliance
- Sugar Bureau
- Sugar Cane Growers Association
- Sugar Cane Growers Cooperative of Florida
- World Association of Beet and Cane Growers
- World Sugar Research Organisation

Cotton Slave Markets
- Augusta Trading Post
- Forks of Road
- Lazaretto Landing

Cotton Slave Trading Firms
- A.J. & D.W. Orr
- Clark & Grubb
- Harrison & Pitts
- Hatcher & McGeehee
- J.B. Allgood & Charles F. Stub
- James Dean/ Deane
- John Jossey
- McKee & Lowe
- Nowell
- Rafe Phillips
- S. Ogletree

Cotton Growers
- The Allen Family (Bverly Plantation)
- The Ashley Williams Family (Lebanon Plantation)
- The Blackwell Family (Blackwell Plantation)
- The Bunkley Family (Piney Bluff Plantation)
- The Delaney Family (Louisiana Plantation)
- The Dennis, Grimes Family (Dennis & Grimes Plantations)

- The Dickey Family (Hogback Plantation)
- The Eastland Family
- The Englishs Family (English Plantation)
- The Hurst Family (Hurst Plantation)
- The Inman Jones Family (Magruder/ McGruder Plantation)
- The James Stillwell Family (King Ranch)
- The King Family (King Bay Plantation)
- The Kingsley, Gibbs Family (Kingsley Plantation)
- The Middleton Family
- The Miller Greene Family (Dungeness Plantation)
- The Munroe Family (Springdale Farm Plantation)
- The Nash Family (Nash Plantation)
- The Owens Family (Brantley Plantation)
- The Pruitt Family (Robert Pruitt Plantation)
- The Reed Family (Reed Plantation)
- The Riceboro Family (Bonaventure Riceboro Plantation)
- The Shropshire Family (Shropshire Plantation)
- The Thomass Family (Cottage Plantation)
- The Ventress Family (Longwood Plantation)
- The Vincent Family (Yankee Hall Plantation)
- The Walters Family (Walters Plantation)
- The Ward (Joshua J.) Family
- The Waring Family (Greenfield Plantation)
- The Wise Family (Florida Plantation)
- Alabama Farmer Coop
- Ampthill Plantation
- Antrim Plantation
- Bellvue Plantation
- Benceville Plantation
- Berne Plantation
- Black Hammock Plantation
- Black Point Plantation
- Boggy Swamp Plantation
- Bolingbrook Plantation
- Bourbon Plantation
- Brick Hill Plantation
- Broken Arrown Plantation
- Brownsville Ranch Properties
- Bull Head Plantation
- Cambray Plantation
- Canebrake Plantation
- Canty Creek Plantation
- Carlawater Plantation
- Cason Plantation
- Cedar Hill Plantation
- Cherry Point Plantation
- Clinton Plantation
- Cohen Hill Plantation
- Cunningham Plantation
- Delta & Pine Land Company
- Drysdale Plantation
- Duncan Family Plantation
- Fairfield Plantation
- Five Oaks Plantation
- Gatehouse Plantation
- Goreman Bluff Plantation
- Grey Plantation
- Hairstons Bend Plantation
- Half Moon Plantation
- Hazelhurst Plantation
- Hermitage Plantation
- Hickory Bluff Plantation
- Honey Creek Plantation
- Hopewell Plantation
- Hull Plantation
- Idlewind Plantation
- Incachee Plantation
- Ivanhoe Plantation
- Kilpatrick Plantation
- King & Queen Plantation
- L.A. Cliatt Plantation
- Langsbury Plantation
- Laurel Island Plantation
- Linda Plantation
- Little Huntington Plantation
- London Hill Plantation
- Long Bluff Plantation
- Marianna Plantation
- Maryfield Plantation
- Maybank Plantation
- McGriff Plantation
- Moire Plantation
- Montgomery Hill Plantation
- Monticello Plantation
- Morrison Plantation
- New Canaan Plantation
- New Town Plantation
- Oak Lawn Plantation
- Oakland Plantation
- Oaks Plantation
- Parrish Plantation
- Pine Barrins Plantation
- Pine Dale Plantation

- Plains Cotton Association
- Plum Orchards Plantation
- Pond Spring Plantation
- Reddicks Plantation
- Refuge Plantation
- Richmond Hill Plantation
- Royal Plantation
- Rural Felicity Plantation
- Shugart Plantation
- Spring Bluff Plantation
- Springs Plantation
- Stafford Place Plantation
- Staple Cotton Association
- Stave Landing Plantation
- Sunnyside Plantation
- Thandy Hall Plantation
- Thornhill Plantation
- Vaden Plantation
- Vernon Plantation
- Wambassie Plantation
- Waverly Plantation
- Wayside Plantation
- West End Plantation
- White Oak Plantation
- Woodbine Plantation
- Woodlawn Plantation
- Yellow Bluff Plantation

Cotton Manufacturers
- Alabama Gin Company
- Alba Waldensian Inc.
- Anderson Clayton Calif. Gins
- Avondale Incorporated
- Avondale Mills Inc.
- Bayou Gin Company Inc.
- Beltwide Cotton Cooperative
- Burke Mills Inc.
- Burlington Coat
- Burlington Industries Inc.
- Calcot Ltd.
- Cargill Cotton
- Carolinas Cotton Growers
- Carter Holdings Inc.
- Chickasaw Coop Gin Assn
- Concord Fabrics Inc.
- Concordia Farmers Gin Company Inc.
- Cone Mills Corporation
- Conley's Planters Gin Company
- Delta Gin Company
- Delta Grain & Gin Company
- Delta Woodside Industries Inc.

- Dixie Group Inc.
- Farmers Coop Compress
- Farmers Coop Gin of El Campo
- Farmers Gin Company Inc.
- Farmers Gin of Ashland
- Farmers Gin of Tallulah
- Farmers Union Gin Company
- Fruit of Loom
- Georgia Cotton Commission
- Greenwood Mills
- Griffin Gin Company
- Guilford Mills Inc.
- Hartmarx Corporation
- Hope Agriculture
- Inman Mills
- Jess Smith & Sons Cotton LLC
- Jones Apparel Group Inc.
- Kearney Companies Inc.
- Kilbourn Mills
- Lambre Brothers Cotton Gin
- Levi Strauss & Co.
- Louisiana Delta Plantation Gin
- Massachusets Mills
- Milliken & Company Inc.
- Mohawk Industries Inc.
- Moody Compress & Warehouse Company
- Mount Vernon Mills Inc.
- National L.L.C.
- National Spinning Company Inc.
- New Gin Company
- North Carolina Cotton Press
- Nunn Cotton Company
- Parkdale Mills Inc.
- Paul Reinhart Inc.
- Pepperell Estate In Maine
- Plains Cotton Coop Association
- Planters Cotton Oil Mill
- Planters Gin Company
- Progressive Cotton Gin C
- R.B. & J.H. Williams Cotton Gin
- Sara Lee Branded Apparel
- Shaw Industries Inc.
- Southern Mills Inc.
- Staplcotn Coop Association
- Vf Corporation
- Warnaco Group Inc.
- Washington Mills
- Woolen & Worsted Mills Inc

Cotton Merchants

- The Brown Ives Gammel Family (Brown & Almy, Brown & Ives)
- The Copes Family (Caleb Cope & Company)
- The Davis Brooks Family (Davis Brooks & Company)
- The Morgan Family (E. D. Morgan & Company)
- The Field Family (Field Enterprises, Field Palmer & Leiter)
- The Appleton Family (Lowell Mills)
- The Woolworth Family (Woolworths)
- The Abraham Family
- The Alley Family
- The Bogert Family
- The Carow Family
- The Grosvenor Family
- The Harriman Family
- The Higgins Family (Carpet Factory)
- The Laverty Family
- The Lawrence Family
- The Livingston Family
- The McBride Family
- The Mullanphy Family
- The Palmer Family
- The Slater Family (Samuel Slater & Company, Samuel Slater & Sons)
- The Smith Family
- The Stewart Family
- The Tiffany Family
- The Townsend Family
- The Van Nest Family
- The Wallace Family
- The Young Family
- A.T. Stewart & Company
- Abraham & Straus Company
- American Woolen Company
- Atlantic Cotton Association
- B. Altman & Company Department Stores
- Barnwell & Hays Cotton Company
- Belk Stores
- Boggs Sampson & Thompson Auctioners
- Bruce Allbright Cotton
- Brunson & Company Inc.
- Calcot Ltd.
- Canale Cotton Company
- Cargill Cotton
- Carson Pirie Scott Company
- Caryle Industries Inc.
- Chelsea Jute Mills
- Chesebrough & Van Alen Importers
- Deca International Inc.
- Deltic Timber
- Donaldson Brothers Commission Merchants
- Dunavant Enterprises Inc.
- Eastern Trading Company (Memphis
- F. W. Woolworth & Company
- Federated Department Stores
- Fitch & Company
- Fitch Brothers & Company Marseille and F
- Francis & Company Inc.
- Gap Inc.
- Geo. H. McFadden & Bro.
- George Douglass & Company Commission Gerald C. Marshall
- H & J Cotton Company Inc.
- Hohenberg Brothers Co.
- Howard & Scofield Tailors
- Humphreys & Biddle Liverpool
- James L. Loeb Jr.
- Jess Smith & Sons Cotton LLC
- John S. Schermerhorn & Son
- Johnston Cotton Company Inc.
- Jonathan Goodhue & Company
- Joseph Foulke & Sons
- Kennett C. Jabbour
- Lyons Cotton Inc.
- Mark Dutra
- Marshall Field & Company
- Montgomery Ward
- Neiman Marcus
- New York Board of Trade
- Noble Ellington Cotton Company
- Otis & Swan
- Otto Goedecke Inc.
- Palmer & Leiter
- Paul Reinhart Inc.
- Peabody Riggs & Company Baltimore
- Production Marketing L.L.C.
- Richardson & May
- Roswell Reed & Company
- Saks
- Seam
- Sears Roebusk & Company
- Shawsheen Mills
- Thomas Buchanan & Son
- Tiffany & Company
- Tonnelee & Hall
- Tonnelee & Salles
- W. Woolworth & Company
- W.L. Gore & Associates Inc.

- Wallace L. Darneille
- Wanamakers
- Weil Brothers Cotton Inc.
- Western Cotton Shippers Association

Cotton Mills
- The Appleton Family
- The Pepperell Family
- The Slater Family (Samuel Slater & Sons)
- Archer Daniels Midland Company
- Brooks Cotton Company Inc.
- Caney Valley Cotton Company
- Chickasha Cotton Oil Company
- Cone Mills Corporation
- East Cotton Company
- Farmers Cotton Company Inc.
- Greenwood Mills
- Guilford Mills Inc.
- John Shoaf Cotton Company
- Mid-South Cotton Sales Inc.
- Milliken & Company Inc.
- Mohawk Industries Inc.
- Mount Vernon Mills Inc.
- National & Providence Worsted Mills
- Nunn Cotton Company
- Parkdale Mills Inc.
- Patton Cotton Marketing Inc.
- S. M. Bryles & Company Inc.
- Shaw Industries Inc.
- Spring Industries
- Tom R. Pitts Cotton Inc.
- Walcot Trading Company LLC
- West Point Stevens

Other Slave-Holding Families
- The Acklen (Jos. A. S.) Family
- The Agnew Family
- The Aiken (William) Family
- The Allston (R. F. W.) Family
- The Blake (Arthur and Joseph) Family
- The Blake (Daniel) Family
- The Brown (Jerrett) Family
- The Burneside (J.) Family
- The Butler (Jno.) Family
- The Calhoun (Meredith) Family
- The Duncan (Stephen) Family
- The Forest Family (Columbia Agriculture Plantation)
- The Forest Family (Poplar Agriculture Plantation)
- The Forest Family (Roseburg Agriculture Plantation)
- The Forest Family (Shadwell Plantation)
- The Forest Family (Slocan Agriculture Plantation)
- The Forest Family (Taiga Agriculture Plantation)
- The Forest Family (Universal Agriculture Plantation)
- The Gobain BTI Inc. (Saint Plantation)
- The Helm Family (Helm Plantation)
- The Heyward (Charles) Family
- The Jenkins Family (Green Bottom Plantation)
- The Manning (John L.) Family
- The Read (J. Harleston) Family
- The Robinson (Jno.) Family
- The Sambler Family
- The Scofield Family
- The Williamson Family
- The Worthington (Elisha) Family
- Beau Fort Plantation
- Chericoke Plantation
- Cona Plantation
- Crum Plantation
- Elliot Plantation
- Georgia Plantation
- Hardin Plantation
- Harriett Bluff Plantation
- Homeward Plantation
- Ravensworth Plantation

Agricultural Equipment Industry
- Allaire Family (Allaire-Howell Works)
- Ames Family (Ames Shovel Company)
- Deering Family (Deering Harvester Company)
- McCormick Family (International Harvester Company, McCormick Harvester Company)
- Singer Family (M. Singer Sewing Machines)
- Caterpillar Tractor
- Continental Eagle Corporation
- Oliver Chilled Plow Works
- Oliver Farm Equipment Company

Mining, Energy & Construction Industries
- The Althause Family
- The Atkinson Family
- The Baker Family
- The Benjamin Family
- The Bing Group
- The Bingham Family

- The Bishop Family
- The Bodine Family
- The Boorman Family
- The Bostswick Family
- The Brevoort Family
- The Brewster Family
- The Bryant-Mackay Family
- The Carnegie Family
- The Carvallo Family
- The Clark Family
- The Coleman Family
- The Cooper Family
- The Cornwall Family
- The Coxe Family
- The Crerar Family
- The Daly Family
- The David Family
- The Davis Family
- The Daviselkins Family
- The Dodge Family
- The Edenborn Family
- The Elkins Family
- The Fair Family
- The Fisher Family
- The Flagler Family
- The Flood Family
- The Frick Family
- The Gates Family
- The Giraud Family
- The Goelet Family
- The Guggenheim Family
- The Haggin Family
- The Hale Family
- The Harkness Family
- The Hayward Family
- The Hearst Family
- The Hendricks Family
- The James Family
- The Jay Family
- The Jennings Family
- The Johnston Family
- The Lauder Family
- The Lee Family
- The Lockhart Family
- The Lovett Family
- The Mackay Family
- The Mellon Family
- The Murchison Family
- The Norris Family
- The Obrien Family
- The Oliver Family
- The Pardee Family
- The Payne Family
- The Payne-Whitney Family
- The Peck Family
- The Phelps-Dodge Family
- The Phipps Family
- The Pitcairn Family
- The Pratt Family
- The Rockefeller Family
- The Rogers Family
- The Ross Family
- The Saltus Family
- The Schwab Family
- The Sharon Family
- The Stephens Family
- The Stokes Family
- The Stone Family
- The Thomson Family
- The Thorne Family
- The Vandergrift Family
- The Ward Family
- The Warden Family
- The Wolfe Family
- Alrowa Metal Products Company
- Aluminum Company of America
- American Steel & Wire Company
- Anaconda Copper Company
- Bethlehem Steel Corporation
- Boorman Johnston & Company Iron
- Calloway Furnace
- Canam Manac Group Inc.
- Canton Iron Works
- Carnegie Steel Company
- Charles Machine Works Inc.
- Chevron-Texaco Corporation
- Chicago Rolling Mill Company
- Cleveland Rolling Mill
- Comstock Lode Silver Mines
- Consolidated Virginia Mine
- Cooper Hewitt & Company
- Cornwall Ore Bank Company
- Coxe Brothers & Company
- David Ross Forge & Furnace
- Davis Coal & Coke Company
- Delhi-Taylor Oil Corporation.
- Dodge & Company
- Dodge Brothers Company
- Double Life Corporation Inc.
- Fisher Dynamics Company
- General Safety Company
- Gilbert & Gillespie Hardware

244

- Guggenheim Brothers Company
- Guggenheim Sons Company
- Gulf Oil Company
- Hendricks & Son
- Hendricks Brothers Copper Works
- Isaac Guggenheim Estate
- J. & J. Giraud Coopers
- K Guggenheims Sons Company
- Lexington Mine
- Monarch Cement Company
- New Jersey Steel Company
- Oliver & Snyder Steel Company
- Oliver Ames & Sons Corporation
- Oliver Iron & Steel Company
- Oxford Ironworks
- Peck & Son Iron Foundries
- Pennsylvania Coal Company
- Phelps & Peck
- Phelps & Peck Metal Traders
- Phelps Dodge & Company
- Phelps-Dodge Corporation
- Philadelphia Smelting & Refining
- Pittsburgh Plate Glass Company
- Robinson Consolidated Mining Company
- S. B. Althause Iron Works
- Saltus Brothers Iron Merchants
- Siam Cement Public Company Limited
- Standard Oil Company
- Standard Oil Company of New Jersey
- Stonewall Furnace
- Texaco
- Trenton Iron Works
- U. S. Steel Company
- Union Iron Works
- United Verde Copper Company
- Vermillion Range Iron Ore Deposits
- West Virginia Coal Company

Railroads
- Amercan Shortline Railroad Association
- American Association of Railroads
- Baltimore & Ohio Railroad
- Burlington Northern Santa Fe
- Canadian National
- Conrail
- CSX Transportation
- Kansas Southern
- Metropolitan Street Railways
- National Passenger Railroad Corporation Amtrak
- Norfolk Southern

- Philadelphia Rapid Transit
- Philadelphia Traction Company
- Pullman Palace Car Company
- Union Pacific
- Westinghouse Air Brake Company

Telegraph Industries
- The Cornell Family
- The Johnson Family (Victor Talking Machine Company)
- The Morse Family
- Adams Express Company
- Albany & Buffalo Telegraph Company
- Commercial Cable Company
- Pikes Peak Express Company
- Western Union Telegraph

Banking Industry
- The Baker Family
- The Barclay Family (Barclays Bank PLC)
- The Baring Family (Baring Brothers & Company)
- The Belmont Family (August Belmont & Company)
- The Biddle Family
- The Blumenthal Family
- The Bowdoin Family
- The Brown, Harriman Family (Alexander Brown & Sons, Brown Brothers & Company, Brown Shipley & Company, John A. Brown & Company, Nicholas Brown & Company, Brown Brothers Harriman & Company)
- The Colgate Family
- The Converse Family
- The Crowninshield Family
- The Dodge Family
- The Drexel Family
- The Du Pont Family
- The Garrett Family (Robert Garrett & Sons)
- The Hancock Family
- The Harriman Family (Low Harriman & Company)
- The Hill-Dodge Banking Company
- The Iselin Family
- The Jesup Family
- The Kahn Family
- The Kean Family
- The Keene Family
- The Kuhn, Loeb Family (Kuhn Loeb & Company, Loeb & Company)

- The Lehman Family (Lehman Brothers, Lehman Brothers Holdings Inc)
- The Mellon Family (Mellon National Bank, T. Mellon & Sons)
- The Mills Family
- The Moffatt Family
- The Morgan, Kennedy Family (D. Morgan & Company, J. P. Morgan & Company, J. P. Morgan Chase Bank, J. S. Morgan & Company, J.P. Morgan Chase & Company, J.P. Morgan Chase Bank, J. S. Kennedy & Company, Morgan & Company)
- The Peabody Family (George Peabody & Company, Riggs National Bank)
- The Phelan Family
- The Phelps Stokes Family (Phelps Stokes & Company)
- The Phipps Family
- The Pyne Family
- The Riggs Family (Cocoran & Riggs, Riggs & Company, Riggs National Bank)
- The Rockefeller Family
- The Rothschild Family (N. M. Rothschild & Sons)
- The Sage Family
- The Schermerhorn Family
- The Schiff Family
- The Spencer Family
- The Stillman Family (Stillman Bancorp N.A.)
- The Sturgis Family
- The Taylor Family
- The Van Rensselaer Family
- The Vanderbilt Family
- The Warburg Family
- The Wolf Family
- 2nd Bank of United States
- A & A Lawrence
- A. Iselin & Company
- ABN Amco Bank
- American Express Company
- Bank of America
- Bank of California
- Bank of D. O. Mills & Company
- Bank of England
- Bank of New York
- Bank of New York
- Bank One
- Bankers Trust Company
- Barclay & Livingston
- Beneficial Mutual Savings Bank

- Bessemer Trust Company
- Canal Bank
- Chase National Bank
- Chemical Bank
- Citibank
- Citicorp
- Citizens Bank of Massachusetts
- Citizens Bank of Pennsylvania
- Citizens First National Bank
- Commerce Bank
- Commerce Bank -Pennsylvania
- Corcoran & Riggs
- Corn Exchange National Bank
- Credit Mobilier
- Crocker National Bank
- De Witt Savings Bank
- Delaware Trust Company
- Deutsche Banc AG
- Drexel & Company
- Drexel Morgan & Company
- Dun & Bradstreet Corporation
- Emigrant Savings Bank
- Fargo & Company
- First Data Western Union
- First National Bank
- First National Bank of New York
- First Savanna Savings Bank
- First Union National Bank
- FleetBoston
- Girard Bank
- Goddard Brothers
- Greenpoint Bank
- Guardian Trust Company
- Harriman & Company
- ING-Barings
- Iselin & Company
- J. Giraud
- Jacob Little & Company Brokers
- Lazard Freres
- Manhattan Bank
- Manhattan Company
- Mechanics Bank
- Mercantile Bank
- Merchants Bank
- Merchants Bank of Salem, Mass
- Metropolitan Bank and Trust Company
- Metropolitan Bank of New York
- National Bank of New York City
- National City Bank
- National State Bank
- Philadelphia Trust Company

- State Street Bank and Trust Company
- The Bank of New York
- Thomas Hancock & Company
- Union Bank
- Union Planters National Bank
- United Bank of Philadelphia
- United Savings Bank
- United States Trust Company of New York
- US Bank of Pennsylvania
- Wells Fargo & Company

Insurance Industry
- The Allen Family (New York Life Insurance & Trust Company)
- The Brooks Family (New England Marine Insurance Company)
- The Ludlow Family (New York Life Insurance & Trust Company)
- The Morgan Family
- The Thompson Family (New York Life Insurance Company)
- Aetna Inc.
- Aetna Insurance Company
- AIG
- American Insurance Company
- Equitable Insurance Company
- Lloyd's of London
- Manhattan Fire Insurance Company
- Manhattan Fire Insurance Company
- New England Marine Insurance Company
- New York Life Insurance & Trust Company
- New York Life Insurance Company
- Society of Lloyds
- Southern Mutual Insurance Company

Colleges and Universities
- Allegheny College
- Amherst College
- Boston University
- Bowdoin College
- Brown University
- Cincinnati College
- Citadel
- City College of New York
- Colby College
- Colgate College
- College of Charleston
- College of New Jersey
- College of William & Mary
- Columbia University
- Cornell University

- Dartmouth University
- Davidson College
- Dickinson College
- Duke University
- Emory College
- Emory University
- Fordham University
- Franklin College
- George Washington University
- Georgetown College
- Georgetown University
- Georgia Female College
- Guilford College
- Hamilton College
- Hamden-Sidney College
- Harvard College
- Harvard University
- Haverford College
- Hobart Geneva College
- Holy Cross College
- Illinois College
- Indiana University
- John Hopkins University
- King's College
- Lafayette College
- Manhattan College
- Massachusetts Institute of Technology
- Miami University
- Middlebury College
- Mount Holyoke College
- Mt. Holyoke College
- Naval Academy
- New York University
- Notre Dame
- Oberlin College
- Ohio University
- Princeton University
- Rensselaer Polytechnic Institute
- Rutgers University
- South Carolina College
- St. Johns University
- St. Mary's Seminary
- The Military Academy
- Transylvania University
- Tufts University
- Tulane University
- Union College
- University of North Carolina
- University of Chicago
- University of Georgia
- University of Michigan

- University of Minnesota
- University of Missouri
- University of North Carolina
- University of Notre Dame
- University of Pennsylvania
- University of Pittsburgh
- University of Rochester
- University of the South
- University of Tennessee
- University of Texas
- University of Vermont
- University of Virginia
- University of Wisconsin
- Vanderbilt University
- Vassar College
- Wabash College
- Washington & Jefferson University
- Washington & Lee University
- Washington College
- Washington University
- Wellesley University
- Wesleyan University
- West Point
- Williams College
- Yale University

Appendix B: Biography of Bob Brown

Bob Brown is an organizer, lecturer, research specialist, and writer focusing on revolutionary movements and organizations for global justice. His primary focus is the Pan-African, National Liberation, Black Power, Anti-globalization, Solidarity, Peace, Anti-Globalization, Anti-Repression, Reparations, and Student Movements.

Bob is an organizer and researcher, who has worked, studied and struggled for 41 years, within and for the Student, Civil and Human Rights, Black Power, National Liberation, Pan-African and Peace Movements. He was a member, from 1963 to 1968, of the Chicago Chapter of the Congress of Racial Equality (CORE); a director, from 1967 to 1968, of the Midwest Office of the Student Nonviolent Coordinating Committee (SNCC); a co-founder with Congressman Bob Rush and member, from 1968 to 1969, of the Illinois Chapter of the Black Panther Party (BPP); and an organizer, from 1972 to 2002, for the All-African People's Revolutionary Party (A-APRP). He served as a political secretary and research assistant to Kwame Ture, formerly known as Stokely Carmichael, from 1967 to his transition in 1998.

Among other assignments and responsibilities, Bob has served as an Advisor to the Rev. Willie Wilson for Mayor of Washington, DC Campaign (2002); as advisor to Dr. J. Archie Hargraves, Pastor of the South Shore Community Church and President of the Communiversity (1995-2002); as the National Campaign Manager of the Pan-Africanist Congress of Azania's (South Africa) Presidential Campaign (2004) and Local Government Elections Campaign (2000); as an Advisor to Dr. Conrad Worrill and the National Black United Front's Project on Human Rights and Genocide which submitted a petition to the United Nations in Geneva with 157,000 signatures charging the U.S. Government with genocide (1996); as an Advisor to Rev. Al Sharpton and the National Director of the Campaign to Cash the Check which organized demonstrations at the Democratic and Republican National Conventions (1996); as a Consultant to Minister Louis Farrakhan and the National Coordinator of Logistics and Operations and National Field Director of the Million Man March and Stay-at-Home Campaign (1995); as a Consultant to the Carol Mosley-Braun for Senator of Illinois Campaign (1993); as an Advisor Harold Washington and an Organization Specialist for the Harold Washington for Mayor of Chicago Campaign (1983 and 1987); as a National Staff Member of the Jesse Jackson for President Campaign (1983); as a Co-Coordinator of Third World Outreach for the Mobilization for Survival and the June 12th Disarmament Campaign, which organized a million person demonstration at the United Nations (1983); and as a participant in the 1965 Chicago Freedom Movement which was co-led by Bob Lucas of Chicago CORE, Lawrence Landry of ACT, Monroe Sharpe of SNCC, Al Raby of the Coordinating Council of Community Organizations, and Dr. Martin Luther King of the Southern Christian Leadership Conference (SCLC).

Bob has worked with and supported the Alliance for Global Justice, the American Indian Movement and International Indian Treaty Council, the Azanian Peoples Organization, the Black Conscious Movement of Azania, the Black Consciousness Movement of Brazil, the Committee against Registration and the Draft, the Committee in Solidarity with the People of El Salvador, the DC Hands off Cuba Committee, the DC-Havana Sister City Project, the Democratic Party of Guinea, the Emancipation Support Committee of Trinidad, the Eritrean People's Liberation Front, the Irish Republican Socialist Party, the La Raza Unida Party, the Movement for Justice in Gambia, the National Joint Action Committee of Trinidad, the Nicaragua Network, the Palestine Liberation Organization, the Puerto Rican Socialist Party, the Sandinista Front for National Liberation, Sein Fein, the Young Koreans United, and a host of other organizations worldwide

He was one of 7,000 delegates, from every corner of Africa, the African Diaspora and the world, who participated in the Non-Governmental Forum of the World Conference Against Racism, Racial Discrimination, Xenophobia, and Related Intolerance (WCAR) which met in Durban, South Africa from 27 August to 1 September 2001.

As a lecturer during the past 37 years, Bob has traveled to and/or delivered presentations at hundreds of colleges and universities and scores of public and private schools, books stores, churches, community centers and radio stations, and at thousands of meetings, conferences, and demonstrations in at least 40 states within the United States. He booked and coordinated, worldwide, from 1970 to 1988, the All-African People's Revolutionary Party's recruitment and fund raising drives which featured Kwame Ture (aka Stokely Carmichael). Internationally, Bob has traveled to, made presentations and/or participated in meetings and demonstrations in Austria, Azania (South Africa), Belgium, Brazil, Canada, Cuba, Egypt, England, Ethiopia, France, Gambia, Germany, Ghana, Guinea, Iraq, Northern Ireland, Italy, Jordan, Lebanon, Libya, Netherlands, Nigeria, Scotland, Senegal, St. Marten, Switzerland, Trinidad and Zimbabwe.

As a research specialist and writer, Bob has authored and coordinated the publication and mass distribution of millions of movement leaflets, pamphlets, posters, and other educational materials. His current research projects include: a definitive political biography of and docudrama about Kwame Ture; comprehensive histories of the Black Power, Pan-African, Anti-Repression, Reparations, and Student Movements; and a major study of COINTELPRO, of the right and left, and political repression against Africa and African People.